IDENTITY THEFT BREACHES

IDENTITY THEFT BREACHES

CARY S. LOGWELLER
EDITOR

Nova Science Publishers, Inc.
New York

For permission to use material from this book please contact us:
Telephone 631-231-7269; Fax 631-231-8175
Web Site: http://www.novapublishers.com

LIBRARY OF CONGRESS CATALOGING-IN-PUBLICATION DATA

Identity theft breaches / editor: Cary S. Logweller.
p. cm.
Includes index.
ISBN 978-1-60692-227-9 (hardcover)
1. Identity theft--United States. 2. Identity theft--United States--Prevention. 3. Consumer protection--United States. I. Logweller, Cary S.
HV6679.I34 2009
364.16'330973--dc22 2008052171

Published by Nova Science Publishers, Inc. ✢ New York

CONTENTS

PREFACE

Crime has moved yet another step forward in its unyielding progression through society. Now it is identity theft. Trying to combat both legal and illegal theft continues to occupy a large portion of the average citizen's life. Identity theft or identity fraud generally involves "stealing" another person's personal identifying information—such as Social Security number (SSN), date of birth, and mother's maiden name—and then using the information to fraudulently establish credit, run up debt, or take over existing financial accounts. This new book focuses on current breaches in the wall of privacy.

From Main Street to Wall Street, from the back porch to the front office, from the kitchen table to the conference room, Americans are talking about identity theft. The reason: millions of Americans each year suffer the financial and emotional trauma it causes. This crime takes many forms, but it invariably leaves victims with the task of repairing the damage to their lives. It is a problem with no single cause and no single solution.

Identity theft (ID theft) is an issue that continues to plague consumers, businesses, and law enforcement. To provide greater insight into the prevalence and cost of ID theft, the Federal Trade Commission (FTC) has sponsored its second ID theft survey of adults in the United States.

In the course of a busy day, you may write a check at the grocery store, charge tickets to a ball game, rent a car, mail your tax returns, change service providers for your cell phone, or apply for a credit card. Chances are you don't give these everyday transactions a second thought. But an identity thief does.

Most companies keep sensitive personal information in their files—names, Social Security numbers, credit card, or other account data—that identifies customers or employees.

This information often is necessary to fill orders, meet payroll, or perform other necessary business functions. However, if sensitive data falls into the wrong hands, it can lead to fraud, identity theft, or similar harms. Given the cost of a security breach—losing your customers' trust and perhaps even defending yourself against a lawsuit—safeguarding personal information is just plain good business.

While comprehensive data do not exist, available evidence suggests that breaches of sensitive personal information have occurred frequently and under widely varying circumstances. For example, more than 570 data breaches were reported in the news media from January 2005 through December 2006, according to lists maintained by private groups that track reports of breaches. These incidents varied significantly in size and occurred across a wide range of entities, including federal, state, and local government agencies; retailers; financial institutions; colleges and universities; and medical facilities.

This book provides an overview of state laws on identity theft. It discusses state laws that penalize identity theft, as well as state laws that assist identity theft victims, including those that permit consumers to block unauthorized persons from obtaining their credit information, known as "security freezes." The report also includes a survey of state "credit freeze" statutes. The report concludes with summaries of federal identity theft legislation pending in the 110th Congress.

According to the Federal Trade Commission, identity theft is the most common complaint from consumers in all fifty states, and complaints regarding identity theft have grown for four consecutive years. Victims of identity theft may incur damaged credit records, unauthorized charges on credit cards, and unauthorized withdrawals from bank accounts. Sometimes, victims must change their telephone numbers or even their social security numbers. Victims may also need to change addresses that were falsified by the impostor. With media reports of information security breaches increasing, concerns about new cases of widespread identity theft have received significant attention in Congress.

Recent headlines about data breaches and losses of personal information have prompted many companies to advertise products or services to help consumers prevent or minimize their risk of identity theft.

The Fair Credit Reporting Act (FCRA) requires each of the nationwide consumer reporting companies—Equifax, Experian, and TransUnion—to provide you with a free copy of your credit report, at your request, once every 12 months.

According to the Federal Trade Commission (FTC), the nation's consumer protection agency, phishers send an email or pop-up message that claims to be from a business or organization that you may deal with—for example, an Internet service provider (ISP), bank, online payment service, or even a government agency. The message may ask you to "update," "validate," or "confirm" your account information. Some phishing emails threaten a dire consequence if you don't respond. The messages direct you to a Web site that looks just like a legitimate organization's site. But it isn't. It's a bogus site whose sole purpose is to trick you into divulging your personal information so the operators can steal your identity and run up bills or commit crimes in your name.

In: Identity Theft Breaches
Editor: Cary S. Logweller

ISBN 978-1-60692-227-9

Chapter 1

THE PRESIDENT'S IDENTITY THEFT TASK FORCE: COMBATING IDENTITY THEFT; A STRATEGIC PLAN

GLOSSARY OF ACRONYMS

AAMVA–American Association of Motor Vehicle Administrators
AARP–American Association of Retired Persons
ABA–American Bar Association
APWG–Anti-Phishing Working Group
BBB–Better Business Bureau
BIN–Bank Identification Number
BJA–Bureau of Justice Assistance
BJS–Bureau of Justice Statistics
CCIPS–Computer Crime and Intellectual Property Section (DOJ)
CCMSI–Credit Card Mail Security Initiative
CFAA–Computer Fraud and Abuse Act
CFTC–Commodity Futures Trading Commission
CIO–Chief Information Officer
CIP–Customer Identification Program
CIRFU–Cyber Initiative and Resource Fusion Center
CMRA–Commercial Mail Receiving Agency
CMS–Centers for Medicare and Medicaid Services (HHS)
CRA–Consumer reporting agency
CVV2–Card Verification Value 2
DBFTF–Document and Benefit Fraud Task Force
DHS–Department of Homeland Security
DOJ–Department of Justice
DPPA–Drivers Privacy Protection Act of 1994
FACT Act–Fair and Accurate Credit Transactions Act of 2003
FBI–Federal Bureau of Investigation
FCD–Financial Crimes Database FCRA–Fair Credit Reporting Act
FCU Act–Federal Credit Union Act

FDI Act–Federal Deposit Insurance Act
FDIC–Federal Deposit Insurance Corporation
FEMA–Federal Emergency Management Agency
FERPA–Family and Educational Rights and Privacy Act of 1974
FFIEC–Federal Financial Institutions Examination Council
FIMSI–Financial Industry Mail Security Initiative
FinCEN–Financial Crimes Enforcement Network (Department of Treasury)
FISMA–Federal Information Security Management Act of 2002
FRB–Federal Reserve Board of Governors
FSI–Financial Services, Inc.
FTC–Federal Trade Commission
FTC Act–Federal Trade Commission Act
GAO–Government Accountability Office
GLB Act–Gramm-Leach-Bliley Act
HHS–Department of Health and Human Services
HIPAA–Health Insurance Portability and Accountability Act of 1996
IACP–International Association of Chiefs of Police
IAFCI–International Association of Financial Crimes Investigators
IC3–Internet Crime Complaint Center
ICE–U.S. Immigration and Customs Enforcement
IRS–Internal Revenue Service
IRS CI–IRS Criminal Investigation Division
IRTPA–Intelligence Reform and Terrorism Prevention Act of 2004
ISI–Intelligence Sharing Initiative (U.S. Postal Inspection Service)
ISP–Internet service provider
ISS LOB–Information Systems Security Line of Business
ITAC–Identity Theft Assistance Center
ITCI–Information Technology Compliance Institute
ITRC–Identity Theft Resource Center
MCC–Major Cities Chiefs
NAC–National Advocacy Center
NASD–National Association of Securities Dealers, Inc.
NCFTA–National Cyber Forensic Training Alliance
NCHELP–National Council of Higher Education Loan Programs
NCUA–National Credit Union Administration
NCVS–National Crime Victimization Survey
NDAA–National District Attorneys Association
NIH–National Institutes of Health
NIST–National Institute of Standards and Technology
NYSE–New York Stock Exchange
OCC–Office of the Comptroller of the Currency
OIG–Office of the Inspector General
OJP–Office of Justice Programs (DOJ)
OMB–Office of Management and Budget
OPM–Office of Personnel Management
OTS–Office of Thrift Supervision

OVC–Office for Victims of Crime (DOJ)
PCI–Payment Card Industry
PIN–Personal Identification Number
PMA–President's Management Agenda
PRC–Privacy Rights Clearinghouse
QRP–Questionable Refund Program (IRS CI)
RELEAF–Operation Retailers and Law Enforcement Against Fraud
RISS–Regional Information Sharing Systems
RITNET–Regional Identity Theft Network
RPP–Return Preparer Program (IRS CI)
SAR–Suspicious Activity Report
SBA–Small Business Administration
SEC–Securities and Exchange Commission
SMP–Senior Medicare Patrol
SSA–Social Security Administration
SSL–Security Socket Layer
SSN–Social Security number
TIGTA–Treasury Inspector General for Tax Administration
UNC C–United Nations Crime Commission
USA PATRIOT Act–Uniting and Strengthening America by Providing Appropriate Tools Required to Intercept and Obstruct Terrorism Act of 2001 (Pub. L. No. 107-56)
USB–Universal Serial Bus
US-CERT–United States Computer Emergency Readiness Team
USPIS–United States Postal Inspection Service
USSS–United States Secret Service
VHA–Veterans Health Administration
VOIP–Voice Over Internet Protocol
VPN–Virtual private network
WEDI–Workgroup for Electronic Data Interchange

Identity Theft Task Force Members

Alberto R. Gonzales, Chairman
Attorney General
Deborah Platt Majoras, Co-Chairman
Chairman, Federal Trade Commission
Henry M. Paulson
Department of Treasury
Carlos M. Gutierrez
Department of Commerce
Michael O. Leavitt
Department of Health and Human Services
R. James Nicholson

Department of Veterans Affairs
Michael Chertoff
Department of Homeland Security
Rob Portman
Office of Management and Budget
John E. Potter
United States Postal Service
Ben S. Bernanke
Federal Reserve System
Linda M. Springer
Office of Personnel Management
Sheila C. Bair
Federal Deposit Insurance Corporation
Christopher Cox
Securities and Exchange Commission
JoAnn Johnson
National Credit Union Administration
Michael J. Astrue
Social Security Administration
John C. Dugan
Office of the Comptroller of the Currency
John M. Reich
Office of Thrift Supervision

LETTER TO THE PRESIDENT

April 11, 2007
The Honorable George W. Bush
President of the United States
The White House
Washington, D.C.

Dear Mr. President

By establishing the President's Task Force on Identity Theft by Executive Order 13402 on May 10, 2006, you launched a new era in the fight against identity theft. As you recognized, identity theft exacts a heavy financial and emotional toll from its victims, and it severely burdens our economy. You called for a coordinated approach among government agencies to vigorously combat this crime. Your charge to us was to craft a strategic plan aiming to make the federal government's efforts more effective and efficient in the areas of identity theft awareness, prevention, detection, and prosecution. To meet that charge, we examined the tools law enforcement can use to prevent, investigate, and prosecute identity theft crimes; to recover the proceeds of these crimes; and to ensure just and effective punishment of identity thieves. We also surveyed current education efforts by government agencies and the private sector on how individuals and corporate citizens can protect personal data. And because government must help reduce, rather than exacerbate, incidents of identity theft, we worked with many federal agencies to determine how the government can increase safeguards to better secure the personal data that it and private businesses hold. Like you, we spoke to many citizens whose lives have been uprooted by identity theft, and heard their suggestions on ways to help consumers guard against this crime and lessen the burdens of their recovery. We conducted meetings, spoke with stakeholders, and invited public comment on key issues.

The views you expressed in the Executive Order are widely shared. There is a consensus that identity theft's damage is widespread, that it targets all demographic groups, that it harms both consumers and businesses, and that its effects can range far beyond financial harm. We were pleased to learn that many federal departments and agencies, private businesses, and universities are trying to create a culture of security, although some have been faster than others to construct systems to protect personal information.

There is no quick solution to this problem. But, we believe that a coordinated strategic plan can go a long way toward stemming the injuries caused by identity theft and, we hope, putting identity thieves out of business. Taken as a whole, the recommendations that comprise this strategic plan are designed to strengthen the efforts of federal, state, and local law enforcement officers; to educate consumers and businesses on deterring, detecting, and defending against identity theft; to assist law enforcement officers in apprehending and prosecuting identity thieves; and to increase the safeguards employed by federal agencies and the private sector with respect to the personal data with which they are entrusted.

Thank you for the privilege of serving on this Task Force. Our work is ongoing, but we now have the honor, under the provisions of your Executive Order, of transmitting the report and recommendations of the President's Task Force on Identity Theft.

Very truly yours,

Alberto R. Gonzales, *Chairman*
Deborah Platt Majoras, *Co-Chairman*
Attorney General Chairman, Federal Trade Commission

I. Executive Summary

From Main Street to Wall Street, from the back porch to the front office, from the kitchen table to the conference room, Americans are talking about identity theft. The reason: millions of Americans each year suffer the financial and emotional trauma it causes. This crime takes many forms, but it invariably leaves victims with the task of repairing the damage to their lives. It is a problem with no single cause and no single solution.

A. Introduction

Eight years ago, Congress enacted the Identity Theft and Assumption Deterrence Act,[1] which created the federal crime of identity theft and charged the Federal Trade Commission

(FTC) with taking complaints from identity theft victims, sharing these complaints with federal, state, and local law enforcement, and providing the victims with information to help them restore their good name. Since then, federal, state, and local agencies have taken strong action to combat identity theft. The FTC has developed the Identity Theft Data Clearinghouse into a vital resource for consumers and law enforcement agencies; the Department of Justice (DOJ) has prosecuted vigorously a wide range of identity theft schemes under the identity theft statutes and other laws; the federal financial regulatory agencies[2] have adopted and enforced robust data security standards for entities under their jurisdiction; Congress passed, and the Department of Homeland Security issued draft regulations on, the REAL ID Act of 2005; and numerous other federal agencies, such as the Social Security Administration (SSA), have educated consumers on avoiding and recovering from identity theft. Many private sector entities, too, have taken proactive and significant steps to protect data from identity thieves, educate consumers about how to prevent identity theft, assist law enforcement in apprehending identity thieves, and assist identity theft victims who suffer losses.

Over those same eight years, however, the problem of identity theft has become more complex and challenging for the general public, the government, and the private sector. Consumers, overwhelmed with weekly media reports of data breaches, feel vulnerable and uncertain of how to protect their identities. At the same time, both the private and public sectors have had to grapple with difficult, and costly, decisions about investments in safeguards and what more to do to protect the public. And, at every level of government—from the largest cities with major police departments to the smallest towns with one fraud detective—identity theft has placed increasingly pressing demands on law enforcement.

Public comments helped the Task Force define the issues and challenges posed by identity theft and develop its strategic responses. To ensure that the Task Force heard from all stakeholders, it solicited comments from the public.

In addition to consumer advocacy groups, law enforcement, business, and industry, the Task Force also received comments from identity theft victims themselves.[3] The victims wrote of the burdens and frustrations associated with their recovery from this crime. Their stories reaffirmed the need for the government to act quickly to address this problem.

The overwhelming majority of the comments received by the Task Force strongly affirmed the need for a fully coordinated approach to fighting the problem through prevention, awareness, enforcement, training, and victim assistance. Consumers wrote to the Task Force exhorting the public and private sectors to do a better job of protecting their Social Security numbers (SSNs), and many of those who submitted comments discussed the challenges raised by the overuse of Social Security numbers as identifiers. Others, representing certain business sectors, pointed to the beneficial uses of SSNs in fraud detection. The Task Force was mindful of both considerations, and its recommendations seek to strike the appropriate balance in addressing SSN use. Local law enforcement officers, regardless of where they work, wrote of the challenges of multi-jurisdictional investigations, and called for greater coordination and resources to support the investigation and prosecution of identity thieves. Various business groups described the steps they have taken to minimize the occurrence and impact of the crime, and many expressed support for risk-based, national data security and breach notification requirements.

These communications from the public went a long way toward informing the Task Force's recommendation for a fully coordinated strategy. Only an approach that encompasses effective prevention, public awareness and education, victim assistance, and law enforcement measures, and fully engages federal, state, and local authorities will be successful in protecting citizens and private entities from the crime.

B. The Strategy

Although identity theft is defined in many different ways, it is, fundamentally, the misuse of another individual's personal information to commit fraud. Identity theft has at least three stages in its "life cycle," and it must be attacked at each of those stages:

First, the Identity Thief Attempts to Acquire a Victim's Personal Information

Criminals must first gather personal information, either through low-tech methods—such as stealing mail or workplace records, or "dumpster diving" —or through complex and high-tech frauds, such as hacking and the use of malicious computer codes. The loss or theft of personal information by itself, however, does not immediately lead to identity theft. In some cases, thieves who steal personal items inadvertently steal personal informationthat is stored in or with the stolen personal items, yet never make use of the personal information. It has recently been reported that, during the past year, the personal records of nearly 73 million people have been lost or stolen, but that there is no evidence of a surge in identity theft or financial fraud as a result. Still, because any loss or theft of personal information is troubling and potentially devastating for the persons involved, a strategy to keep consumer data out of the hands of criminals is essential.

Second, the Thief Attempts to Misuse the Information He Has Acquired

In this stage, criminals have acquired the victim's personal information and now attempt to sell the information or use it themselves. The misuse of stolen personal information can be classified in the following broad categories:

Existing account fraud: This occurs when thieves obtain account information involving credit, brokerage, banking, or utility accounts that are already open. Existing account fraud is typically a less costly, but more prevalent, form of identity theft. For example, a stolen credit card may lead to thousands of dollars in fraudulent charges, but the card generally would not provide the thief with enough information to establish a false identity. Moreover, most credit card companies, as a matter of policy, do not hold consumers liable for fraudulent charges, and federal law caps liability of victims of credit card theft at $50.

New account fraud: Thieves use personal information, such as Social Security numbers, birth dates, and home addresses, to open new accounts in the victim's name, make charges indiscriminately, and then disappear. While this type of identity theft is less likely to occur, it imposes much greater costs and hardships on victims.

In addition, identity thieves sometimes use stolen personal information to obtain government, medical, or other benefits to which the criminal is not entitled.

Third, an Identity Thief has Completed His Crime and Is Enjoying the Benefits, While the Victim Is Realizing the Harm

At this point in the life cycle of the theft, victims are first learning of the crime, often after being denied credit or employment, or being contacted by a debt collector seeking payment for a debt the victim did not incur.

In light of the complexity of the problem at each of the stages of this life cycle, the Identity Theft Task Force is recommending a plan that marshals government resources to crack down on the criminals who traffic in stolen identities, strengthens efforts to protect the personal information of our nation's citizens, helps law enforcement officials investigate and prosecute identity thieves, helps educate consumers and businesses about protecting themselves, and increases the safeguards on personal data entrusted to federal agencies and private entities.

The Plan focuses on improvements in four key areas:

- keeping sensitive consumer data out of the hands of identity thieves through better data security and more accessible education;
- making it more difficult for identity thieves who obtain consumer data to use it to steal identities;
- assisting the victims of identity theft in recovering from the crime; and
- deterring identity theft by more aggressive prosecution and punishment of those who commit the crime.

In these four areas, the Task Force makes a number of recommendations summarized in greater detail below. Among those recommendations are the following broad policy changes:

- that federal agencies should reduce the unnecessary use of Social Security numbers (SSNs), the most valuable commodity for an identity thief;
- that national standards should be established to require private sector entities to safeguard the personal data they compile and maintain and to provide notice to consumers when a breach occurs that poses a significant risk of identity theft;
- that federal agencies should implement a broad, sustained awareness campaign to educate consumers, the private sector, and the public sector on deterring, detecting, and defending against identity theft; and
- that a National Identity Theft Law Enforcement Center should be created to allow law enforcement agencies to coordinate their efforts and information more efficiently, and investigate and prosecute identity thieves more effectively.

The Task Force believes that all of the recommendations in this strategic plan—from these broad policy changes to the small steps—are necessary to wage a more effective fight against identity theft and reduce its incidence and damage. Some recommendations can be implemented relatively quickly; others will take time and the sustained cooperation of government entities and the private sector. Following are the recommendations of the President's Task Force on Identity Theft:

PREVENTION: KEEPING CONSUMER DATA OUT OF THE HANDS OF CRIMINALS

Identity theft depends on access to consumer data. Reducing the opportunities for thieves to get the data is critical to fighting the crime. Government, the business community, and consumers have roles to play in protecting data.

Data compromises can expose consumers to the threat of identity theft or related fraud, damage the reputation of the entity that experienced the breach, and carry financial costs for everyone involved. While "perfect security" does not exist, all entities that collect and maintain sensitive consumer information must take reasonable and appropriate steps to protect it.

Data Security in Public Sector

➢ Decrease the Unnecessary Use of Social Security Numbers in the Public Sector by Developing Alternative Strategies for Identity Management

- Survey current use of SSNs by federal government
- Issue guidance on appropriate use of SSNs
- Establish clearinghouse for "best" agency practices that minimize use of SSNs
- Work with state and local governments to review use of SSNs

➢ Educate Federal Agencies on How to Protect Data; Monitor Their Compliance with Existing Guidance

- Develop concrete guidance and best practices
- Monitor agency compliance with data security guidance
- Protect portable storage and communications devices

➢ Ensure Effective, Risk-Based Responses to Data Breaches Suffered by Federal Agencies

- Issue data breach guidance to agencies
- Publish a "routine use" allowing disclosure of information after a breach to those entities that can assist in responding to the breach

Data Security in Private Sector

➢ Establish National Standards for Private Sector Data Protection Requirements and Breach Notice Requirements

➢ Develop Comprehensive Record on Private Sector Use of Social Security Numbers

➢ Better Educate the Private Sector on Safeguarding Data

- Hold regional seminars for businesses on safeguarding information
- Distribute improved guidance for private industry Initiate Investigations of Data Security Violations

➢ Initiate a Multi-Year Public Awareness Campaign

- Develop national awareness campaign
- Enlist outreach partners
- Increase outreach to traditionally underserved communities
- Establish "Protect Your Identity" Days

➢ Develop Online Clearinghouse for Current Educational Resources

PREVENTION: MAKING IT HARDER TO MISUSE CONSUMER DATA

Because security systems are imperfect and thieves are resourceful, it is essential to reduce the opportunities for criminals to misuse the data they steal. An identity thief who wants to open new accounts in a victim's name must be able to (1) provide identifying information to allow the creditor or other grantor of benefits to access information on which to base a decision about eligibility; and (2) convince the creditor that he is the person he purports to be.

Authentication includes determining a person's identity at the beginning of a relationship (sometimes called verification), and later ensuring that he is the same person who was originally authenticated. But the process can fail: Identity documents can be falsified; the accuracy of the initial information and the accuracy or quality of the verifying sources can be questionable; employee training can be insufficient; and people can fail to follow procedures.

Efforts to facilitate the development of better ways to authenticate consumers without burdening consumers or businesses—for example, multi-factor authentication or layered security—would go a long way toward preventing criminals from profiting from identity theft.

➢ Hold Workshops on Authentication

- Engage academics, industry, entrepreneurs, and government experts on developing and promoting better ways to authenticate identity
- Issue report on workshop findings

➢ Develop a Comprehensive Record on Private Sector Use of SSNs

VICTIM RECOVERY: HELPING CONSUMERS REPAIR THEIR LIVES

Identity theft can be committed despite a consumer's best efforts at securing information. Consumers have a number of rights and resources available, but some surveys indicate that they are not as well-informed as they could be. Government agencies must work together to ensure that victims have the knowledge, tools, and assistance necessary to minimize the damage and begin the recovery process.

- ➢ Provide Specialized Training About Victim Recovery to First Responders and Others Offering Direct Assistance to Identity Theft Victims

- Train law enforcement officers
- Provide educational materials for first responders that can be used as a reference guide for identity theft victims
- Create and distribute an ID Theft Victim Statement of Rights
- Design nationwide training for victim assistance counselors

- ➢ Develop Avenues for Individualized Assistance to Identity Theft Victims
- ➢ Amend Criminal Restitution Statutes to Ensure That Victims Recover the Value of Time Spent in Trying to Remediate the Harms Suffered
- ➢ Assess Whether to Implement a National System That Allows Victims to Obtain an Identification Document for Authentication Purposes
- ➢ Assess Efficacy of Tools Available to Victims

- Conduct assessment of FACT Act remedies under FCRA
- Conduct assessment of state credit freeze laws

LAW ENFORCEMENT: PROSECUTING AND PUNISHING IDENTITY THIEVES

Strong criminal law enforcement is necessary to punish and deter identity thieves. The increasing sophistication of identity thieves in recent years has meant that law enforcement agencies at all levels of government have had to increase the resources they devote to investigating related crimes. The investigations are labor-intensive and generally require a staff of detectives, agents, and analysts with multiple skill sets. When a suspected theft involves a large number of potential victims, investigative agencies often need additional personnel to handle victim-witness coordination.

Coordination and Information/Intelligence Sharing

- ➢ Establish a National Identity Theft Law Enforcement Center
- ➢ Develop and Promote the Use of a Universal Identity Theft Report Form
- ➢ Enhance Information Sharing Between Law Enforcement and the Private Sector

- Enhance ability of law enforcement to receive information from financial institutions
- Initiate discussions with financial services industry on countermeasures to identity theft
- Initiate discussions with credit reporting agencies on preventing identity theft.

Coordination with Foreign Law Enforcement

- Encourage Other Countries to Enact Suitable Domestic Legislation Criminalizing Identity Theft
- Facilitate Investigation and Prosecution of International Identity Theft by Encouraging Other Nations to Accede to the Convention on Cybercrime
- Identify the Nations that Provide Safe Havens for Identity Thieves and Use All Measures Available to Encourage Those Countries to Change Their Policies
- Enhance the United States Government's Ability to Respond to Appropriate Foreign Requests for Evidence in Criminal Cases Involving Identity Theft
- Assist, Train, and Support Foreign Law Enforcement.

Prosecution Approaches and Initiatives

- Increase Prosecutions of Identity Theft

- Designate an identity theft coordinator for each United States Attorney's Office to design a specific identity theft program for each district
- Evaluate monetary thresholds for prosecution
- Encourage state prosecution of identity theft
- Create working groups and task forces

- Conduct Targeted Enforcement Initiatives

- Conduct enforcement initiatives focused on using unfair or deceptive means to make SSNs available for sale
- Conduct enforcement initiatives focused on identity theft related to the health care system
- Conduct enforcement initiatives focused on identity theft by illegal aliens

- Review Civil Monetary Penalty Programs.

Gaps in Statutes Criminalizing Identity Theft

- Close the Gaps in Federal Criminal Statutes Used to Prosecute Identity Theft-Related Offenses to Ensure Increased Federal Prosecution of These Crimes

- Amend the identity theft and aggravated identity theft statutes to ensure that identity thieves who misappropriate information belonging to corporations and organizations can be prosecuted
- Add new crimes to the list of predicate offenses for aggravated identity theft offenses

- Amend the statute that criminalizes the theft of electronic data by eliminating the current requirement that the information must have been stolen through interstate communications
- Penalize creators and distributors of malicious spyware and keyloggers
- Amend the cyber-extortion statute to cover additional, alternate types of cyber-extortion

➢ Ensure That an Identity Thief's Sentence Can Be Enhanced When the Criminal Conduct Affects More Than One Victim

Law Enforcement Training

➢ Enhance Training for Law Enforcement Officers and Prosecutors

- Develop course at National Advocacy Center focused on investigation and prosecution of identity theft
- Increase number of regional identity theft seminars
- Increase resources for law enforcement on the Internet
- Review curricula to enhance basic and advanced training on identity theft

Measuring the Success of Law Enforcement

➢ Enhance the Gathering of Statistical Data Impacting the Criminal Justice System's Response to Identity Theft

- Gather and analyze statistically reliable data from identity theft victims
- Expand scope of national crime victimization survey
- Review U.S. Sentencing Commission data
- Track prosecutions of identity theft and resources spent
- Conduct targeted surveys

II. The Contours of the Identity Theft Problem

Every day, too many Americans learn that their identities have been compromised, often in ways and to an extent they could not have imagined. Identity theft victims experience a sense of hopelessness when someone steals their good name and good credit to commit fraud. These victims also speak of their frustration in fighting against an unknown opponent.

Identity theft—the misuse of another individual's personal information to commit fraud—can happen in a variety of ways, but the basic elements are the same. Criminals first gather personal information, either through low-tech methods such as stealing mail or workplace records, or "dumpster diving," or through complex and high-tech frauds such as hacking and the use of malicious computer code.

> "I was absolutely heartsick to realize our bank accounts were frozen, our names were on a bad check list, and my driver's license was suspended. I hold three licenses in the State of Ohio—my driver's license, my real estate license, and my R.N. license. After learning my driver's license was suspended, I was extremely fearful that my professional licenses might also be suspended as a result of the actions of my imposter."
>
> —Maureen Mitchell Testimony before House Committee on Financial Services, Subcommittee on Financial Institutions and Consumer Credit, June 24, 2003.

These data thieves then sell the information or use it themselves to open new credit accounts, take over existing accounts, obtain government benefits and services, or even evade law enforcement by using a new identity. Often, individuals learn that they have become victims of identity theft only after being denied credit or employment, or when a debt collector seeks payment for a debt the victim did not incur.

Individual victim experiences best portray the havoc that identity thieves can wreak. For example, in July 2001, an identity thief gained control of a retired Army Captain's identity when Army officials at Fort Bragg, North Carolina, issued the thief an active duty military identification card in the retired captain's name and with his Social Security number. The military identification, combined with the victim's then-excellent credit history, allowed the identity thief to go on an unhindered spending spree lasting several months. From July to December 2001, the identity thief acquired goods, services, and cash in the victim's name valued at over $260,000. The victim identified more than 60 fraudulent accounts of all types that were opened in his name: credit accounts, personal and auto loans, checking and savings accounts, and utility accounts. The identity thief purchased two trucks valued at over $85,000 and a Harley-Davidson motorcycle for $25,000. The thief also rented a house and purchased a time-share in Hilton Head, South Carolina, in the victim's name.[4]

In another instance, an elderly woman suffering from dementia was victimized by her caregivers, who admitted to stealing as much as $200,000 from her before her death. The thieves not only used the victim's existing credit card accounts, but also opened new credit accounts in her name, obtained financing in her name to purchase new vehicles for themselves, and, using a fraudulent power of attorney, removed $176,000 in U.S. Savings Bonds from the victim's safe-deposit boxes.[5]

In these ways and others, consumers' lives are disrupted and displaced by identity theft. While federal agencies, the private sector, and consumers themselves already have accomplished a great deal to address the causes and impact of identity theft, much work remains to be done. The following strategic plan focuses on a coordinated government response to: strengthen efforts to prevent identity theft; investigate and prosecute identity theft; raise awareness; and ensure that victims receive meaningful assistance.

A. Prevalence and Costs of Identity Theft

There is considerable debate about the prevalence and cost of identity theft in the United States. Numerous studies have attempted to measure the extent of this crime. DOJ, FTC, the Gartner Group, and Javelin Research are just some of the organizations that have published reports of their identity theft surveys.[6] While some of the data from these surveys differ, there is agreement that identity theft exacts a serious toll on the American public.

Although greater empirical research is needed, the data show that annual monetary losses are in the billions of dollars. This includes losses associated with new account fraud, a more costly, but less prevalent form of identity theft, and misuse of existing accounts, a more prevalent but less costly form of identity theft. Businesses suffer most of the direct losses from both forms of identity theft because individual victims generally are not held responsible for fraudulent charges. Individual victims, however, also collectively spend billions of dollars recovering from the effects of the crime.

In addition to the losses that result when identity thieves fraudulently open accounts or misuse existing accounts, monetary costs of identity theft include indirect costs to businesses for fraud prevention and mitigation of the harm once it has occurred (e.g., for mailing notices to consumers and upgrading systems). Similarly, individual victims often suffer indirect financial costs, including the costs incurred in both civil litigation initiated by creditors and in overcoming the many obstacles they face in obtaining or retaining credit. Victims of non-financial identity theft, for example, health-related or criminal record fraud, face other types of harm and frustration.

In addition to out-of-pocket expenses that can reach thousands of dollars for the victims of new account identity theft, and the emotional toll identity theft can take, some victims have to spend what can be a considerable amount of time to repair the damage caused by the identity thieves. Victims of new account identity theft, for example, must correct fraudulent information in their credit reports and monitor their reports for future inaccuracies, close existing bank accounts and open new ones, and dispute charges with individual creditors.

Consumers' fears of becoming identity theft victims also may harm our digital economy. In a 2006 online survey conducted by the Business Software Alliance and Harris Interactive, nearly one in three adults (30 percent) said that security fears compelled them to shop online less or not at all during the 2005/2006 holiday season.[7] Similarly, a Cyber Security Industry Alliance survey in June 2005 found that 48 percent of consumers avoided making purchases on the Internet because they feared that their financial information might be stolen.[8] Although no studies have correlated these attitudes with actual online buying habits, these surveys indicate that security concerns likely inhibit some commercial use of the Internet.

In an article entitled "Waitress Gets Own ID

When "carding" a patron, the Associated Press reported, a bar waitress checking to see whether a patron was old enough to legally drink alcohol was handed her own stolen driver's license, which she had reported missing weeks earlier in Lakewood, Ohio. The patron was later charged with identity theft and receiving stolen property.

B. Identity Thieves: Who They Are

Unlike some groups of criminals, identity thieves cannot be readily classified. No surveys provide comprehensive data on their primary personal or demographic characteristics. For the most part, victims are not in a good position to know who stole their information or who misused it. According to the FTC's 2003 survey of identity theft, about 14 percent of victims claim to know the perpetrator, who may be a family member, friend, or in-home employee.

Identity thieves can act alone or as part of a criminal enterprise. Each poses unique threats to the public.

Individuals

According to law enforcement agencies, identity thieves often have no prior criminal background and sometimes have pre-existing relationships with the victims. Indeed, identity thieves have been known to prey on people they know, including coworkers, senior citizens for whom they are serving as caretakers, and even family members. Some identity thieves rely on techniques of minimal sophistication, such as stealing mail from homeowners' mailboxes or trash containing financial documents. In some jurisdictions, identity theft by illegal immigrants has resulted in passport, employment, and Social Security fraud. Occasionally, small clusters of individuals with no significant criminal records work together in a loosely knit fashion to obtain personal information and even to create false or fraudulent documents.[9]

A number of recent reports have focused on the connection between individual methamphetamine ("meth") users and identity theft.[10] Law enforcement agencies in Albuquerque, Honolulu, Phoenix, Sacramento, Seattle, and other cities have reported that meth addicts are engaging in identity and data theft through burglaries, mail theft, and theft of wallets and purses. In Salt Lake City, meth users reportedly are organized by white-supremacist gangs to commit identity theft.[11] Tellingly, as meth use has risen sharply in recent years, especially in the western United States, some of the same jurisdictions reporting the highest levels of meth use also suffer from the highest incidence of identity theft. Some state law enforcement officials believe that the two increases might be related, and that identity theft may serve as a major funding mechanism for meth labs and purchases.

Significant Criminal Groups and Organizations

Law enforcement agencies around the country have observed a steady increase in the involvement of groups and organizations of repeat offenders or career criminals in identity theft. Some of these groups—including national gangs such as Hell's Angels and MS-13—are formally organized, have a hierarchical structure, and are well-known to law enforcement because of their longstanding involvement in other major crimes such as drug trafficking. Other groups are more loosely-organized and, in some cases, have taken advantage of the Internet to organize, contact each other, and coordinate their identity theft activities more efficiently. Members of these groups often are located in different countries and communicate primarily via the Internet. Other groups have a real-world connection with one another and share a nationality or ethnic group.

Law enforcement agencies also have seen increased involvement of foreign organized criminal groups in computer- or Internet-related identity theft schemes. In Asia and Eastern Europe, for example, organized groups are increasingly sophisticated both in the techniques they use to deceive Internet users into disclosing personal data, and in the complexity of tools they use, such as keyloggers (programs that record every keystroke as an Internet user logs onto his computer or a banking website), spyware (software that covertly gathers user information through the user's Internet connection, without the user's knowledge), and botnets (networks of computers that criminals have compromised and taken control of for some other purpose, ranging from distribution of spam and malicious computer code to attacks on other computers). According to law enforcement agencies, such groups also are demonstrating increasing levels of sophistication and specialization in their online crime, even selling goods and services—such as software templates for making counterfeit identification cards and payment card magnetic strip encoders—that make the stolen data even more valuable to those who have it.

In July 2003, a Russian computer hacker was sentenced in federal court to a prison term of four years for supervising a criminal enterprise in Russia dedicated to computer hacking, fraud, and extortion. The defendant hacked into the computer system of Financial Services, Inc. (FSI), an internet web hosting and electronic banking processing company located in Glen Rock, New Jersey, and stole 11 passwords used by FSI employees to access the FSI computer network as well as a text file containing approximately 3,500 credit card numbers and associated card holder information for FSI customers. One of the defendant's accomplices then threatened FSI that the hacker group would publicly release this stolen credit card information and hack into and further damage the FSI computer system unless FSI paid $6,000. After a period of negotiation, FSI eventually agreed to pay $5,000.

In sentencing the defendant, the federal judge described the scheme as an "unprecedented, wide-ranging, organized criminal enterprise" that "engaged in numerous acts of fraud, extortion, and intentional damage to the property of others, involving the sophisticated manipulation of computer data, financial information, and credit card numbers." The court found that the defendant was responsible for an aggregate loss to his victims of approximately $25 million.

C. How Identity Theft Happens: The Tools of the Trade

Consumer information is the currency of identity theft, and perhaps the most valuable piece of information for the thief is the SSN. The SSN and a name can be used in many cases to open an account and obtain credit or other benefits in the victim's name. Other data, such as personal identification numbers (PINs), account numbers, and passwords, also are valuable because they enable thieves to access existing consumer accounts.

Identity theft is prevalent in part because criminals are able to obtain personal consumer information everywhere such data are located or stored. Homes and businesses, cars and health-club lockers, electronic networks, and even trash baskets and dumpsters have been targets for identity thieves. Somethieves use more technologically-advanced means to extract information from computers, including malicious-code programs that secretly log information or give criminals access to it.

The following are among the techniques most frequently used by identity thieves to steal the personal information of their victims.

> A ramp agent for a major airline participated in a scheme to steal financial documents, including checks and credit cards, from the U.S. mail at Thurgood Marshall Baltimore-Washington International Airport and transfer those financial documents to his coconspirators for processing. The conspirators used the documents to obtain cash advances and withdrawals from lines of credit. In September 2005, a federal judge sentenced the ramp agent to 14 years in prison and ordered him to pay $7 million in restitution.

Common Theft and Dumpster Diving

While often considered a "high tech" crime, data theft often is no more sophisticated than stealing paper documents. Some criminals steal documents containing personal information from mail boxes; indeed, mail theft appears to be a common way that meth users and producers obtain consumer data.[12] Other identity thieves simply take documents thrown into unprotected trash receptacles, a practice known as "dumpster diving."[13] Still others steal information using techniques no more sophisticated than purse snatching.

Progress is being made in reducing the opportunities that identity thieves have to obtain personal information in these ways. The Fair and Accurate Credit Transactions Act of 2003 (FACT Act)[14] requires merchants that acceptcredit or debit cards to truncate the numbers on receipts that are electronically printed—a measure that is intended, among other things, to reduce the ability of a "dumpster diver" to obtain a victim's credit card number simply by looking through that victim's discarded trash. Merchants had a period of time to comply with that requirement, which now is in full effect.[15]

Employee/Insider Theft

Dishonest insiders can steal sensitive consumer data by removing paper documents from a work site or accessing electronic records. Criminals also may bribe insiders, or become employees themselves to access sensitive data at companies. The failure to disable a terminated employee's access to a computer system or confidential databases contained within the system also could lead to the compromise of sensitive consumer data. Many federal agencies have taken enforcement actions to punish and deter such insider compromise.

Source: U.S. Department of Justice

Partial display of credit cards, checks, and identifying documents seized in federal investigation of identity theft ring in Maryland, 2005.

> In December 2003, the Office of the Comptroller of the Currency (OCC) directed a large financial institution to improve its employee screening policies, procedures, systems, and controls after finding that the institution had inadvertently hired a convicted felon who used his new post to engage in identity theft- related crimes. Deficiencies in the institution's screening practices came to light through the OCC's review of the former employee's activities.

Electronic Intrusions or Hacking

Hackers steal information from public and private institutions, including large corporate databases and residential wireless networks. First, they can intercept data during transmission, such as when a retailer sends payment card information to a card processor. Hackers have developed tools to penetrate firewalls, use automated processes to search for account data or other personal information, export the data, and hide their tracks.[16] Several recent government enforcement actions have targeted this type of data theft.

Second, hackers also can gain access to underlying applications—programs used to "communicate" between Internet users and a company's internal databases, such as programs to retrieve product information. One research firm estimates that nearly 75 percent of hacker attacks are targeted at the application, rather than the network.[17] It is often difficult to detect the hacker's application-level activities, because the hacker connects to the website through the same legitimate route any customer would use, and the communication is thus seen as permissible activity.

In December 2004, a federal district judge in North Carolina sentenced a defendant to 108 months in prison after he pleaded guilty to crimes stemming from his unauthorized access to the nationwide computer system used by the Lowe's Corporation to process credit card transactions. To carry out this scheme, the defendant and at least one other person secretly compromised the wireless network at a Lowe's retail store in Michigan and gained access to Lowe's central computer system.

The defendant then installed a computer program designed to capture customer credit card information on the computer system of several Lowe's retail stores. After an FBI investigation of the intrusion, the defendant and a confederate were charged.

According to the Secret Service, many major breaches in the credit card system in 2006 originated in the Russian Federation and the Ukraine, and criminals operating in those two countries have been directly involved in some of the largest breaches of U.S. financial systems for the past five years.

Social Engineering: Phishing, Malware/Spyware, and Pretexting

Identity thieves also use trickery to obtain personal information from unwitting sources, including from the victim himself. This type of deception, known as "social engineering," can take a variety of forms.

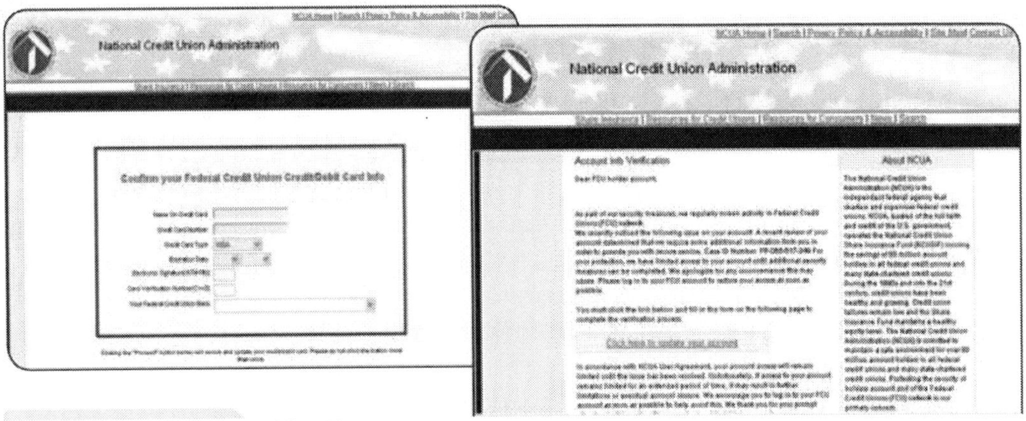

Source: Anti-Phishing Working Group.

"Phishing" Email and Associated Website Impersonating National Credit Union Administration Email and Website.

Phishing: "Phishing" is one of the most prevalent forms of social engineering. Phishers send emails that appear to be coming from legitimate, well-known sources—often, financial institutions or government agencies. In one example, these email messages tell the recipient that he must verify his personal information for an account or other service to remain active. The emails provide a link, which goes to a website that appears legitimate. After following the link, the web user is instructed to enter personal identifying information, such as his name, address, account number, PIN, and SSN. This information is then harvested by the phishers. In a variant of this practice, victims receive emails warning them that to avoid losing something of value (e.g., Internet service or access to a bank account) or to get something of value, they must click on a link in the body of the email to "reenter" or "validate" their personal data. Such phishing schemes often mimic financial institutions' web sites and emails, and a number of them have even mimicked federal government agencies to add credibility to their demands for information. Additionally, phishing recently has taken on a new form, dubbed "vishing," in which the thieves use Voice Over Internet Protocol (VOIP) technology to spoof the telephone call systems of financial institutions and request callers provide their account information.[18]

> At the beginning of the 2006 tax filing season, identity thieves sent emails that purported to originate from the IRS's website to taxpayers, falsely informing them that there was a problem with their tax refunds. The emails requested that the taxpayers provide their SSNs so that the IRS could match their identities to the proper tax accounts. In fact, when the users entered their personal information – such as their SSNs, website usernames and passwords, bank or credit-card account numbers and expiration dates, among other things – the phishers simply harvested the data at another location on the Internet. Many of these schemes originated abroad, particularly in Eastern Europe. Since November 2005, the Treasury Inspector General for Tax Admin istration (TIGTA) and the IRS have received over 17,500 complaints about phishing scams, and TIGTA has identified and shut down over 230 phishing host sites targeting the IRS.

Malware/Spyware/Keystroke Loggers: Criminals also can use spyware to illegally gain access to Internet users' computers and data without the users' permission. One email-based form of social engineering is the use of enticing emails offering free pornographic images to a group of victims; by opening the email, the victim launches the installation of malware, such as spyware or keystroke loggers, onto his computer. The keystroke loggers gather and send information on the user's Internet sessions back to the hacker, including user names and passwords for financial accounts and other personal information. These sophisticated methods of accessing personal information through malware have supplemented other long-established methods by which criminals obtain victims' passwords and other useful data—such as "sniffing" Internet traffic, for example, by listening to network traffic on a shared physical network, or on unencrypted or weakly encrypted wireless networks.

Pretexting: Pretexting [19] is another form of social engineering used to obtain sensitive information. In many cases, pretexters contact a financial institution or telephone company, impersonating a legitimate customer, and request that customer's account information. In other cases, the pretext is accomplished by an insider at the financial institution, or by fraudulently opening an online account in the customer's name.[20]

Stolen Media

In addition to instances of deliberate theft of personal information, data also can be obtained by identity thieves in an "incidental" manner. Criminals frequently steal data storage devices, such as laptops or portable media, that contain personal information.[21] Although the criminal originally targeted the hardware, he may discover the stored personal information and realize its value and possibility for exploitation. Unless adequately safeguarded—such as through the use of technological tools for protecting data—this information can be accessed and used to steal the victim's identity. Identity thieves also may obtain consumer data when it is lost or misplaced.

> In January 2006, the FTC settled a lawsuit against data broker ChoicePoint, Inc., alleging that it violated the FCRA when it failed to perform due diligence in evaluating and approving new customers. The FTC alleged that ChoicePoint approved as customers for its consumer reports identity thieves who lied about their credentials and whose applications should have raised obvious red flags. Under the settlement, ChoicePoint paid $10 million in civil penalties and $5 million in consumer redress and agreed to implement new procedures to ensure that it provides consumer reports only to legitimate businesses for lawful purposes, to establish a comprehensive information security program, and to obtain audits by an independent security professional every other year until 2026.

Failure to "Know Your Customer"

Data brokers compile consumer information from a variety of public and private sources and then offer it for sale to different entities for a range of purposes. For example, government agencies often purchase consumer information from data brokers to locate witnesses or beneficiaries, or for law enforcement purposes. Identity thieves, however, can steal personal information from data brokers who fail to ensure that their customers have a legitimate need for the data.

The Fair Credit Reporting Act (FCRA) and the Gramm-Leach-Bliley Act (GLB Act) impose specific duties on certain types of data brokers that disseminate particular types of information.[22] For example, the FCRA requires data brokers that are consumer reporting agencies to make reasonable efforts to verify the identity of their customers and to ensure that those customers have a permissible purpose for obtaining the information. The GLB Act limits the ability of a financial institution to resell covered financial information.

Existing laws, however, do not reach every kind of personal information collected and sold by data brokers. In addition, when data brokers fail to comply with their statutory duties, they open the door to criminals who can access the personal information held by the data brokers by exploiting poor customer verification practices.

"Skimming"

Because it is possible to use someone's credit account without having physical access to the card, identity theft is easily accomplished when a criminal obtains a receipt with the credit account number, or uses other technology to collect that account information.[23] For example, over the past several years, law enforcement authorities have witnessed a substantial increase in the use of devices known as "skimmers." A skimmer is an inexpensive electronic device with a slot through which a person passes or "skims" a credit or debit card. Similar to the device legitimate businesses use in processing customer card payments, the skimmer reads and records the magnetically encoded data on the magnetic stripe on the back of the card. That data then can be downloaded either to make fraudulent copies of real cards, or to make purchases when the card is not required, such as online.

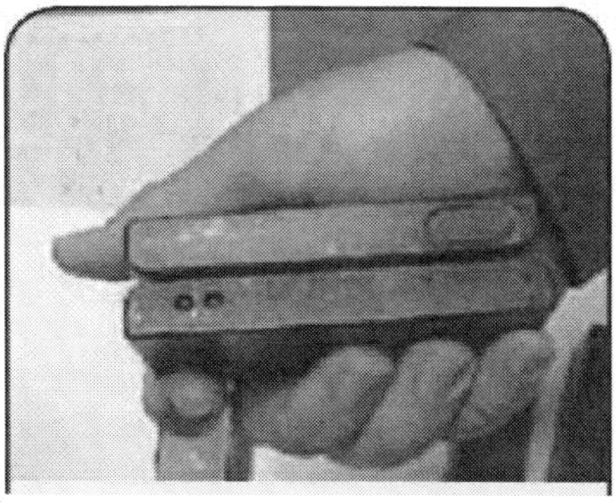

Source: Durham, Ontario Police.

A "skimmer".

A retail employee, such as a waiter, can easily conceal a skimmer until a customer hands him a credit card. Once he is out of the customer's sight, he can skim the card through the device, and then swipe it through the restaurant's own card reader to generate a receipt for the customer to sign. The waiter then can pass the recorded data to an accomplice, who can encode the data on blank cards with magnetic stripes. A variation of skimming involves an ATM-mounted device that is able to capture the magnetic information on the consumer's card, as well as the consumer's password.

D. What Identity Thieves Do with the Information they Steal: The Different Forms of Identity Theft

Once they obtain victims' personal information, criminals misuse it in endless ways, from opening new accounts in the victim's name, to accessing the victim's existing accounts, to using the victim's name when arrested. Recent survey data show that misuse of existing credit accounts, however, represents the single largest category of fraud.

Misuse of Existing Accounts

Misuse of existing accounts can involve credit, brokerage, banking, or utility accounts, among others. The most common form, however, involves credit accounts. This occurs when an identity thief obtains either the actual credit card, the numbers associated with the account, or the information derived from the magnetic strip on the back of the card. Because it is possible to make charges through remote purchases, such as online sales or by telephone, identity thieves are often able to commit fraud even as the card remains in the consumer's wallet.

> In March 2006, a former candidate for the presidency of Peru pleaded guilty in a federal district court to charges relating to a large- scale credit card fraud and money laundering conspiracy. The defendant collected stolen credit card numbers from people in Florida who had used skimmers to obtain the information from customers of retail businesses where they worked, such as restaurants and rental car companies. He used some of the credit card fraud proceeds to finance various trips to Peru during his candidacy.

Recent complaint data suggest an increasing number of incidents involving unauthorized access to funds in victims' bank accounts, including checking accounts—sometimes referred to as "account takeovers."[24] The Postal Inspection Service reports that it has seen an increase in account takeovers originating outside the United States. Criminals also have attempted to access funds in victims' online brokerage accounts.[25] Federal law limits the liability consumers face from existing account misuse, generally shielding victims from direct losses due to fraudulent charges to their accounts. Nevertheless, consumers can spend many hours disputing the charges and making other corrections to their financial records.[26]

> In December 2005, a highly organized ring involved in identity theft, counterfeit credit and debit card fraud, and fencing of stolen products was shut down when Postal Inspectors and detectives from the Hudson County, New Jersey, Prosecutor's Office arrested 13 of its members. The investigation, which began in June 2005, uncovered more than 2,000 stolen identities and at least $1.3 million worth of fraudulent transactions. The investigation revealed an additional $1 million in fraudulent credit card purchases in more than 30 states and fraudulent ATM withdrawals. The account information came from computer hackers outside the United States who were able to penetrate corporate databases. Additionally, the ring used counterfeit bank debit cards encoded with legitimate account numbers belonging to unsuspecting victims to make fraudulent withdrawals of hundreds of thousands of dollars from ATMs in New Jersey, New York, and other states.

New Account Fraud

A more serious, if less prevalent, form of identity theft occurs when thieves are able to open new credit, utility, or other accounts in the victim's name, make charges indiscriminately, and then disappear. Victims often do not learn of the fraud until they are contacted by a debt collector or are turned down for a loan, a job, or other benefit because of a negative credit rating. While this is a less prevalent form of fraud, it causes more financial harm, is less likely to be discovered quickly by its victims, and requires the most time for recovery.

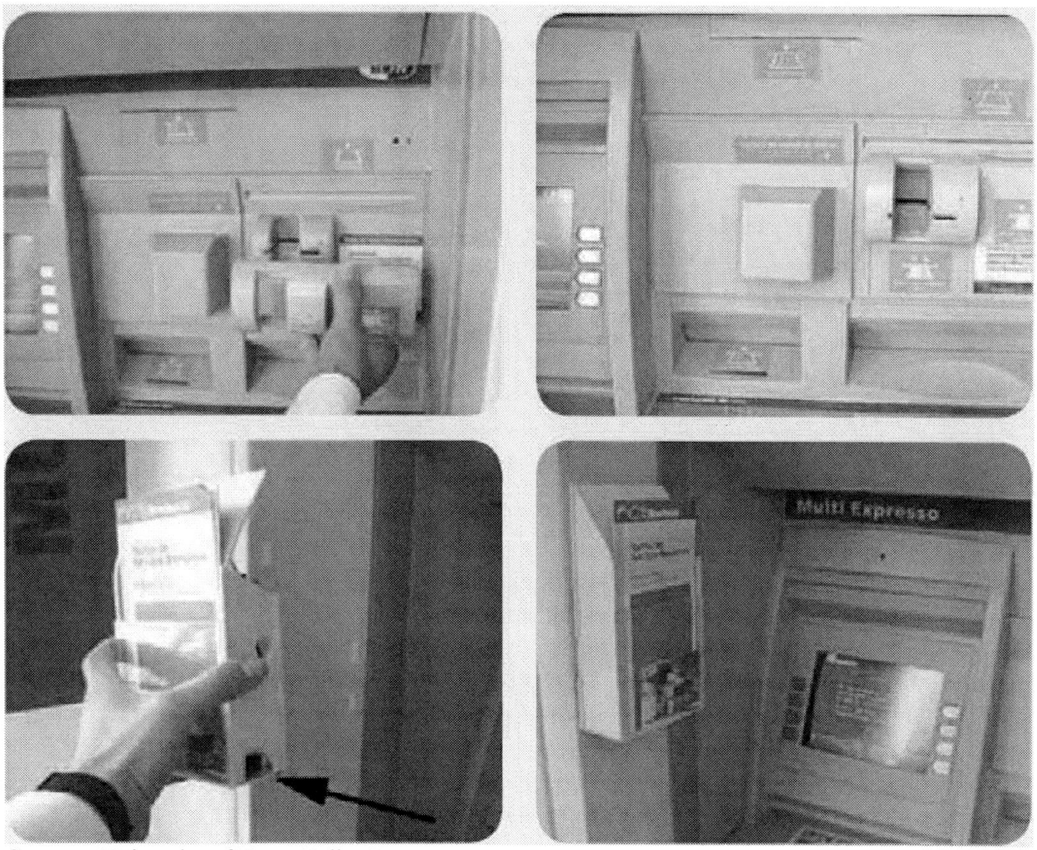

Source: University of Texas Police Department.

Criminal's skimmer, mounted and colored to resemble exterior of real ATM. A pinhole camera is mounted inside a plastic brochure holder to capture customer's keystrokes.

When criminals establish new credit card accounts in others' names, the sole purpose is to make the maximum use of the available credit from those accounts, whether in a short time or over a longer period. By contrast, when criminals establish new bank or loan accounts in others' names, the fraud often is designed to obtain a single disbursement of funds from a financial institution. In some cases, the criminal deposits a check drawn on an account with insufficient funds, or stolen or counterfeit checks, and then withdraws cash.

Immigration Fraud

In various parts of the country, illegal immigrants use fraudulently obtained SSNs or passports to obtain employment and assimilate into society. In extreme cases, an individual SSN may be passed on to and used by many illegal immigrants.[27] Although victims of this type of identity theft may not necessarily suffer financial harm, they still must spend hour upon hour attempting to correct their personal records to ensure that they are not mistaken for an illegal immigrant or cheated out of a government benefit.

> Federal identity theft charges were brought against 148 illegal aliens accused of stealing the identities of lawful U.S. citizens in order to gain employment. The aliens being criminally prosecuted were identified as a result of Operation Wagon Train, an investigation led by agents from U.S. Immigration and Customs Enforcement (ICE), working in conjunction with six U.S. Attorney's Offices. Agents executed civil search warrants at six meat processing plants. Numerous alien workers were arrested, and many were charged with aggravated identity theft, state identity theft, or forgery. Many of the names and Social
>
> Security numbers being used at the meat processing plants were reported stolen by identity theft victims to the FTC. In many cases, victims indicated that they received letters from the Internal Revenue Service demanding back taxes for income they had not reported because it was earned by someone working under their name. Other victims were denied driver's licenses, credit, or even medical services because someone had improperly used their personal information before.

Medical Identity Theft

Recent reports have brought attention to the problem of medical identity theft, a crime in which the victim's identifying information is used to obtain or make false claims for medical care.[28] In addition to the financial harm associated with other types of identity theft, victims of medical identity theft may have their health endangered by inaccurate entries in their medical records. This inaccurate information can potentially cause victims to receive improper medical care, have their insurance depleted, become ineligible for health or life insurance, or become disqualified from some jobs. Victims may not even be aware that a theft has occurred because medical identity theft can be difficult to discover, as few consumers regularly review their medical records, and victims may not realize that they have been victimized until they receive collection notices, or they attempt to seek medical care themselves, only to discover that they have reached their coverage limits.

Other Frauds

Identity theft is inherent in numerous other frauds perpetrated by criminals, including mortgage fraud and fraud schemes directed at obtaining government benefits, including disaster relief funds. The IRS's Criminal Investigation Division, for example, has seen an increase in the use of stolen SSNs to file tax returns. In some cases, the thief files a fraudulent return seeking a refund before the taxpayer files. When the real taxpayer files, the IRS may not accept his return because it is considered a duplicate return. Even if the taxpayer ultimately is made whole, the government suffers the loss from paying multiple refunds.

With the advent of the prescription drug benefit of Medicare Part D, the Department of Health and Human Services' Office of the Inspector General (HHS OIG) has noted a growing incidence of health care frauds involving identity theft. These frauds include telemarketers who fraudulently solicit potential Medicare Part D beneficiaries to disclose information such as their Health Insurance Claim Number (which includes the SSN) and bank account information, as well as marketers who obtain identities from nursing homes and other adult care facilities (including deceased beneficiaries and severely cognitively impaired persons) and use them fraudulently to enroll unwilling beneficiaries in alternate Part D plans in order to increase their sales commissions. The types of fraud that can be perpetrated by an identity thief are limited only by the ingenuity and resources of the criminal.

> In July 2006, DOJ charged a defendant with 66 counts of false claims to the government, mail fraud, wire fraud, and aggravated identity theft, relating to the defendant's allegedly fraudulent applications for disaster assistance from the Federal Emergency Management Agency (FEMA) following Hurricane Katrina. Using fictitious SSNs and variations of her name, the defendant allegedly received $277,377 from FEMA.
>
> Robert C. Ingardia, a registered representative who had been associated with several broker-dealers, assumed the identity of his customers. Without authorization, Mr. Ingardia changed the address information for their accounts, sold stock in the accounts worth more than $800,000, and, in an effort to manipulate the market for two thinly-traded penny stock companies, used the cash proceeds of the sales to buy more than $230,000 worth of stock in the companies. The SEC obtained a temporary restraining order against Mr. Ingardia in 2001, and a civil injunction against him in 2003 after the United States Attorney's Office for the Southern District of New York obtained a criminal conviction against him in 2002.

III. A Strategy to Combat Identity Theft

Identity theft is a multi-faceted problem for which there is no simple solution. Because identity theft has several stages in its "life cycle," it must be attacked at each of those stages, including:

- when the identity thief attempts to acquire a victim's personal information;
- when the thief attempts to misuse the information he has acquired; and
- after an identity thief has completed his crime and is enjoying the benefits, while the victim is realizing the harm.

The federal government's strategy to combat identity theft must address each of these stages by:

- keeping sensitive consumer data out of the hands of identity thieves in the first place through better data security and by educating consumers on how to protect it;
- making it more difficult for identity thieves, when they are able to obtain consumer data, to use the information to steal identities;

- assisting victims in recovering from the crime; and
- deterring identity theft by aggressively prosecuting and punishing those who commit the crime.

A great deal already is being done to combat identity theft, but there are several areas in which we can improve. The Task Force's recommendations, as described below, are focused on those areas.

A. Prevention: Keeping Consumer Data out of the Hands of Criminals

Identity thieves can ply their trade only if they get access to consumer data. Reducing the opportunities for identity thieves to obtain the data in the first place is the first step to reducing identity theft. Government, the business community, and consumers all play a role in protecting data.

Data compromises can expose consumers to the threat of identity theft or related fraud, damage the reputation of the entity that experienced the breach, and impose the risk of substantial costs for all parties involved. Although there is no such thing as "perfect security," some entities fail to adopt even basic security measures, including many that are inexpensive and readily available.

The link between a data breach and identity theft often is unclear. Depending on the nature of the breach, the kinds of information breached, and other factors, a particular breach may or may not pose a significant risk of identity theft. Little empirical evidence exists on the extent to which, and under what circumstances, data breaches lead to identity theft, and some studies indicate that data breaches and identity theft may not be strongly linked.[29] Nonetheless, because data thieves search for rich targets of consumer data, it is critical that organizations that collect and maintain sensitive consumer information take reasonable steps to protect it and explore new technologies to prevent data compromises.

1. Decreasing the Unnecessary Use of Social Security Numbers

The SSN is especially valuable to identity thieves, because often it is the key piece of information used in authenticating the identities of consumers. An identity thief with a victim's SSN and certain other information generally can open accounts or obtain other benefits in the victim's name. As long as SSNs continue to be used for authentication purposes, it is important to prevent thieves from obtaining them.

SSNs are readily available to criminals because they are widely used as consumer identifiers throughout the private and public sectors. Although originally created in 1936 to track workers' earnings for social benefits purposes, use of SSNs has proliferated over ensuing decades. In 1961, the Federal Civil Service Commission established a numerical identification system for all federal employees using the SSN as the identification number.

The next year, the IRS decided to begin using the SSN as its taxpayer identification number (TIN) for individuals. Indeed, the use by federal agencies of SSNs for the purposes of employment and taxation, employment verification, and sharing of data for law enforcement purposes, is expressly authorized by statute.

The simplicity and efficiency of using a seemingly unique number that most people already possessed encouraged widespread use of the SSN as an identifier by both government agencies and private enterprises, especially as they adapted their record-keeping and business systems to automated data processing. The use of SSNs is now common in our society.

Employers must collect SSNs for tax reporting purposes. Doctors or hospitals may need them to facilitate Medicare reimbursement. SSNs also are used in internal systems to sort and track information about individuals, and in some cases are displayed on identification cards. In 2004, an estimated 42 million Medicare cards displayed the entire SSN, as did approximately 8 million Department of Defense insurance cards. In addition, although the Veterans Health Administration (VHA) discontinued the issuance of Veterans Identification Cards that display SSNs in March 2004, and has issued new cards that do not display SSNs, the VHA estimates that between 3 million and 4 million previously issued cards containing SSNs remain in circulation with veterans receiving VA health care services. Some universities still use the SSN as the students' identification number for a range of purposes, from administering loans to tracking grades, and may place it on students' identification cards, although usage for these purposes is declining.

In September 2006, a defendant was sentenced by a federal judge in Pennsylvania to six months in prison after pleading guilty to Social Security card misuse and possession of a false immigration document. The defendant provided a fraudulent Permanent Resident Alien card and a fraudulent Social Security card to a state trooper as evidence of authorized stay and employment in the United States. The case was investigated by the SSA's Office of Inspector General (OIG), ICE, and the Pennsylvania State Police.

SSNs also are widely available in public records held by federal agencies, states, local jurisdictions, and courts. As of 2004, 41 states and the District of Columbia, as well as 75 percent of U.S. counties, displayed SSNs in public records.[30] Although the number and type of records in which SSNs are displayed vary greatly across states and counties, SSNs are most often found in court and property records.

No single federal law regulates comprehensively the private sector or government use, display, or disclosure of SSNs; instead, there are a variety of laws governing SSN use in certain sectors or in specific situations.

> In June 2006, a federal judge in Massachusetts sentenced a defendant to five years in prison after a jury convicted him of passport fraud, SSN fraud, aggravated identity theft, identification document fraud, and furnishing false information to the SSA. The defendant had assumed the identity of a deceased individual and then used fraudulent documents to have the name of the deceased legally changed to a third name. He then used this new name and SSN to obtain a new SSN card, driver's licenses, and United States passport. The case was initiated based on information from the Joint Terrorism Task Force in Springfield, Massachusetts. The agencies involved in the investigation included SSA OIG, Department of State, Massachusetts State Police, and the Springfield and Boston police departments.

With respect to the private sector, for example, the GLB Act restricts the redisclosure to third parties of non-public personal information, such as SSNs, that was originally obtained from customers of a financial institution; the Health Insurance Portability and Accountability Act (HIPAA) limits covered health care organizations' disclosure of SSNs without patient authorization; and the Driver's Privacy Protection Act prohibits state motor vehicle departments from disclosing SSNs, subject to 14 "permissible uses."[31] In the public sector, the Privacy Act of 1974 requires federal agencies to provide notice to, and obtain consent from, individuals before disclosing their SSNs to third parties, except for an established routine use or pursuant to another Privacy Act exception.[32] A number of state statutes restrict the use and display of SSNs in certain contexts.[33] Even so, a report by the Government Accountability Office (GAO) concluded that, despite these laws, there were gaps in how the use and transfer of SSNs are regulated, and that these gaps create a risk that SSNs will be misused.[34]

There are many necessary or beneficial uses of the SSN. SSNs often are used to match consumers with their records and databases, including their credit files, to provide benefits and detect fraud. Federal, state, and local governments rely extensively on SSNs when administering programs that deliver services and benefits to the public.

Although SSNs sometimes are necessary for legal compliance or to enable disparate organizations to communicate about individuals, other uses are more a matter of convenience or habit. In many cases, for example, it may be unnecessary to use an SSN as an organization's internal identifier or to display it on an identification card. In these cases, a different unique identifier generated by the organization could be equally suitable, but without the risk inherent in the SSN's use as an authenticator.

Some private sector entities and federal agencies have taken steps to reduce unnecessary use of the SSN. For example, with guidance from the SSA OIG, the International Association of Chiefs of Police (IACP) adopted a resolution in September 2005 to end the practice of displaying SSNs in posters and other written materials relating to missing persons. Some health insurance providers also have stopped using SSNs as the subscriber's identification number.[35] Additionally, the Department of Treasury's Financial Management Service no longer includes personal identification numbers on the checks that it issues for benefit payments, federal income tax refund payments, and payments to businesses for goods and services provided to the federal government.

> When purchasing advertising space in a trade magazine in 2002, a Colorado man wrote his birth date and Social Security number on the payment check. The salesman who received the check then used this information to obtain surgery in the victim's name. Two years later, the victim received a collection notice demanding payment of over $40,000 for the surgery performed on the identity thief. In addition to the damage this caused to his credit rating, the thief's medical information was added to the victim's medical records.

More must be done to eliminate unnecessary uses of SSNs. In particular, it would be optimal to have a unified and effective approach or standard for use or display of SSNs by federal agencies. The Office of Personnel Management (OPM), which issues and uses many of the federal forms and procedures using the SSN, and the Office of Management and Budget (OMB), which oversees the management and administrative practices of federal agencies, can play pivotal roles in restricting the unnecessary use of SSNs, offering guidance on better substitutes that are less valuable to identity thieves, and establishing greater consistency when the use of SSNs is necessary or unavoidable.

RECOMMENDATION: DECREASE THE UNNECESSARY USE OF SOCIAL SECURITY NUMBERS IN THE PUBLIC SECTOR

To limit the unnecessary use of SSNs in the public sector— and to begin to develop alternative strategies for identity management—the Task Force recommends the following:

- Complete Review of use of SSNs. As recommended in the Task Force's interim recommendations, OPM undertook a review of the use of SSNs in its collection of human resource data from agencies and on OPM-based papers and electronic forms. Based on that review, which OPM completed in 2006, OPM should take steps to eliminate, restrict, or conceal the use of SSNs (including assigning employee identification numbers where practicable), in calendar year 2007. If necessary to implement this recommendation, Executive Order 9397, effective November 23, 1943, which requires federal agencies to use SSNs in "any system of permanent account numbers pertaining to individuals," should be partially rescinded. The use by federal agencies of SSNs for the purposes of employment and taxation, employment verification, and sharing of data for law enforcement purposes, however, is expressly authorized by statute and should continue to be permitted.
- Issue Guidance on Appropriate use of SSNs. Based on its inventory, OPM should issue policy guidance to the federal human capital management community on the appropriate and inappropriate use of SSNs in employee records, including the appropriate way to restrict, conceal, or mask SSNs in employee records and human resource management information systems. OPM should issue this policy in calendar year 2007.
- Require Agencies to Review use of SSNs. OMB has surveyed all federal agencies regarding their use of SSNs to determine the circumstances under which such use can be eliminated, restricted, or concealed in agency business processes, systems, and

paper and electronic forms, other than those authorized or approved by OPM. OMB should complete the analysis of these surveys in the second quarter of 2007[36]

- Establish a Clearinghouse for Agency Practices that Minimize Use of SSNs. Based on results from OMB's review of agency practices on the use of SSNs, the SSA should develop a clearinghouse for agency practices and initiatives that minimize use and display of SSNs to facilitate sharing of best practices—including the development of any alternative strategies for identity management—to avoid duplication of effort, and to promote interagency collaboration in the development of more effective measures. This should be accomplished by the fourth quarter of 2007.
- Work with State and Local Governments to Review use of SSNs. In the second quarter of 2007, the Task Force should begin to work with state and local governments—through organizations such as the National Governor's Association, the National

Association of Attorneys General, the National League of Cities, the National Association of Counties, the U.S. Conference of Mayors, the National District Attorneys Association, and the National Association for Public Health Statistics and Information Systems—to highlight and discuss the vulnerabilities created by the use of SSNs and to explore ways to eliminate unnecessary use and display of SSNs.

Recommendation: Develop Comprehensive Record on Private Sector Use of SSNs

SSNs are an integral part of our financial system. They are essential in matching consumers to their credit file, and thus essential in granting credit and detecting fraud, but their availability to identity thieves creates a possibility of harmto consumers. Beginning in 2007, the Task Force should develop a comprehensive record on the uses of the SSN in the private sector and evaluate their necessity. Specifically, the Task Force member agencies that have direct experience with the private sector use of SSNs, such as DOJ, FTC, SSA, and the financial regulatory agencies, should gather information from stakeholders—including the financial services industry, law enforcement agencies, the consumer reporting agencies, academics, and consumer advocates. The Task Force should then make recommendations to the President as to whether additional specific steps should be taken with respect to the use of SSNs. Any such recommendations should be made to the President by the first quarter of 2008.

2. Data Security in the Public Sector

While private organizations maintain consumer information for commercial purposes, public entities, including federal agencies, collect personal information about individuals for a variety of purposes, such as determining program eligibility and delivering efficient and effective services. Because this information often can be used to commit identity theft, agencies must guard against unauthorized disclosure or misuse of personal information.

A. Safeguarding of Information in the Public Sector

Two sets of laws and associated policies frame the federal government's responsibilities in the area of data security. The first specifically governs the federal government's information privacy program, and includes such laws as the Privacy Act, the Computer Matching and Privacy Protection Act, and provisions of the E-Government Act.[37] The other concerns the information and information technology security program. The Federal Information Security Management Act (FISMA), the primary governing statute for this program, establishes a comprehensive framework for ensuring the effectiveness of information security controls over information resources that support federal operations and assets, and provides for development and maintenance of minimum controls required to protect federal information and information systems. FISMA assigns specific policy and oversight responsibilities to OMB, technical guidance responsibilities to the National Institute of Standards and Technology (NIST), implementation responsibilities to all agencies, and an operational assistance role to the Department of Homeland Security (DHS). FISMA requires the head of each agency to implement policies and procedures to cost-effectively reduce information technology security risks to an acceptable level. It further requires agency operational program officials, Chief Information Officers (CIOs), and Inspectors General (IGs) to conduct annual reviews of the agency information security program and report the results to OMB. Additionally, as part of its oversight role, OMB issued several guidance memoranda last year on how agencies should safeguard sensitive information, including a memorandum addressing FISMA oversight and reporting, and which provided a checklist developed by NIST concerning protection of remotely accessed information, and that recommended that agencies, among other things, encrypt all data on mobile devices and use a "time-out" function for remote access and mobile devices.[38] The United States Computer Emergency Readiness Team (US-CERT) has also played an important role in public sector data security.[39]

Federal law also requires that agencies prepare extensive data collection analyses and report periodically to OMB and Congress. The President's Management Agenda (PMA) requires agencies to report quarterly to OMB on selected performance criteria for both privacy and security. Agency performance levels for both status and progress are graded on a PMA Scorecard.[40] Federal agency performance on information security has been uneven. As a result, OMB and the agencies have undertaken a number of initiatives to improve the government security programs. OMB and DHS are leading an interagency Information Systems Security Line of Business (ISS LOB) working group, exploring ways to improve government data security practices. This effort already has identified a number of key areas for improving government-wide security programs and making them more cost-effective.

Employee training is essential to the effectiveness of agency security programs. Existing training programs must be reviewed continuously and updated to reflect the most recent changes, issues, and trends. This effort includes the development of annual general security awareness training for all government employees using a common curriculum; recommended security training curricula for all employees with significant security responsibilities; an information-sharing repository/portal of training programs; and opportunities for knowledge-sharing (e.g., conferences and seminars). Each of these components builds elements of agency security awareness and practices, leading to enhanced protection of sensitive data.

B. Responding to Data Breaches in the Public Sector

Several federal government agencies suffered high-profile security breaches involving sensitive personal information in 2006. As is true with private sector breaches, the loss or compromise of sensitive personal information by the government has made affected individuals feel exposed and vulnerable and may increase the risk of identity theft. Until this Task Force issued guidance on this topic in September 2006, government agencies had no comprehensive formal guidance on how to respond to data breaches, and in particular, had no guidance on what factors to consider in deciding (1) whether a particular breach warrants notice to consumers, (2) the content of the notice, (3) which third parties, if any, should be notified, and (4) whether to offer affected individuals credit monitoring or other services.

The experience of the last year also has made one thing apparent: an agency that suffers a breach sometimes faces impediments in its ability to effectively respond to the breach by notifying persons and entities in a position to cooperate (either by assisting in informing affected individuals or by actively preventing or minimizing harms from the breach). For example, an agency that has lost data such as bank account numbers might want to share that information with the appropriate financial institutions, which could assist in monitoring for bank fraud and in identifying the account holders for possible notification. The very information that may be most necessary to disclose to such persons and entities, however, often will be information maintained by federal agencies that is subject to the Privacy Act. Critically, the Privacy Act prohibits the disclosure of any record in a system of records unless the subject individual has given written consent or unless the disclosure falls within one of 12 statutory exceptions.

Recommendation: Educate Federal Agencies on How to Protect Their Data and Monitor Compliance with Existing Guidance

To ensure that government agencies receive specific guidance on concrete steps that they can take to improve their data security measures, the Task Force recommends the following:

- Develop Concrete Guidance and Best Practices. OMB and DHS, through the current interagency Information Systems Security Line of Business (ISS LOB) task force, should (a) outline best practices in the area of automated tools, training, processes, and standards that would enable agencies to improve their security and privacy programs, and (b) develop a list of the most common 10 or 20 "mistakes" to avoid in protecting information held by the government. The Task Force made this recommendation as part of its interim recommendations to the President, and it should be implemented and completed in the second quarter of 2007.
- Comply With Data Security Guidance. OMB already has issued an array of data security regulations and standards aimed at urging agencies to better protect their data. Given that data breaches continue to occur, however, it is imperative that agencies continue to report compliance with its data security guidelines and

directives to OMB. If any agency does not comply fully, OMB should note that fact in the agency's quarterly PMA Scorecard.

- Protect Portable Storage and Communications Devices. Many of the most publicized data breaches in recent months involved losses of laptop computers. Because government employees increasingly rely on laptops and other portable communications devices to conduct government business, no later than the second quarter of 2007, all Chief Information Officers of federal agencies should remind the agencies of their responsibilities to protect laptops and other portable data storage and communication devices. If any agency does not fully comply, that failure should be reflected on the agency's PMA scorecard.

RECOMMENDATION: ENSURE EFFECTIVE, RISK-BASED RESPONSES TO DATA BREACHES SUFFERED BY FEDERAL AGENCIES

To assist agencies in responding to the difficult questions that arise following a data breach, the Task Force recommends the following:

- Issue Data Breach Guidance to Agencies. The Task Force developed and formally approved a set of guidelines, reproduced in Appendix A, that sets forth the factors that should be considered in deciding whether, how, and when to inform affected individuals of the loss of personal data that can contribute to identity theft, and whether to offer services such as free credit monitoring to the persons affected. In the interim recommendations, the Task Force recommended that OMB issue that guidance to all agencies and departments. OMB issued the guidance on September 20, 2006.
- Publish a "Routine use" Allowing Disclosure of Information Following a Breach. To allow agencies to respond quickly to data breaches, including by sharing information about potentially affected individuals with other agencies and entities that can assist in the response, federal agencies should, in accordance with the Privacy Act exceptions, publish a routine use that specifically permits the disclosure of information in connection with response and remediation efforts in the event of a data breach. Such a routine use would serve to protect the interests of the people whose information is at risk by allowing agencies to take appropriate steps to facilitate a timely and effective response, thereby improving their ability to prevent, minimize, or remedy any harms that may result from a compromise of data maintained in their systems of records. This routine use should not affect the existing ability of agencies to properly disclose and share information for law enforcement purposes. The Task Force offers the routine use that is reproduced in Appendix B as a model for other federal agencies to use in developing and publishing their own routine uses.[41] DOJ has now published such a routine use, which became effective as of January 24, 2007. The proposed routine use language reproduced in Appendix B should be reviewed and adapted by agencies to fit their individual systems of records.

3. Data Security in the Private Sector

Data protection in the private sector is the subject of numerous legal requirements, industry standards and guidelines, private contractual arrangements, and consumer and business education initiatives. But no system is perfect, and data breaches can occur even when entities have implemented appropriate data safeguards.

A. The Current Legal Landscape

Although there is no generally applicable federal law or regulation that protects all consumer information or requires that such information be secured, a variety of specific statutes and regulations impose data security requirements for particular entities in certain contexts. These include Title V of the GLB Act, and its implementing rules and guidance, which require financial institutions to maintain reasonable protections for the personal information they collect from customers [42;] Section 5 of the FTC Act, which prohibits unfair or deceptive practices [43]; the FCRA,[44] which restricts access to consumer reports and imposes safe disposal requirements, among other things [45]; HIPAA, which protects health information [46]; Section 326 of the Uniting and Strengthening America by Providing Appropriate Tools Required to Intercept and Obstruct Terrorism (USA PATRIOT) Act,[47] which requires verification of the identity of persons opening accounts with financial institutions; and the Drivers Privacy Protection Act of 1994 (DPPA), which prohibits most disclosures of drivers' personal information.[48] See Volume II, Part A, for a description of federal laws and regulations related to data security.

The federal bank regulatory agencies—the Federal Deposit Insurance Corporation (FDIC), Federal Reserve Board (FRB), National Credit Union Administration (NCUA), Office of the Comptroller of the Currency (OCC), and the Office of Thrift Supervision (OTS)—and the FTC and SEC, among others, have pursued active regulatory and enforcement programs to address the data security practices of those entities within their respective jurisdictions. Depending on the severity of a violation, the financial regulatory agencies have cited institutions for violations, without taking formal action when management quickly remedied the situation.

> BJ's Wholesale Club, Inc. suffered a data breach that led to the loss of thousands of credit card numbers and millions of dollars in unauthorized charges. Following the breach, the FTC charged the company with engaging in an unfair practice by failing to provide reasonable security for credit card information. The FTC charged that BJ's stored the information in unencrypted clear text without a business need to do so, failed to defend its wireless systems against unauthorized access, failed to use strong credentials to limit access to the information, and failed to use adequate procedures for detecting and investigating intrusions. The FTC also charged that these failures were easy to exploit by hackers, and led to millions of dollars in fraudulent charges.

In circumstances where the situation was not quickly remedied, the financial regulatory agencies have taken formal, public actions and sought civil penalties, restitution, and cease and desist orders. The FDIC has taken 17 formal enforcement actions between the beginning of 2002 and the end of 2006; the FRB has taken 14 formal enforcement actions since 2001; the OCC has taken 18 formal actions since 2002; and the OTS has taken eight formal enforcement actions in the past five years. Remedies in these cases have included substantial penalties and restitution, consumer notification, and restrictions on the use of customer information. Additionally, the FTC has obtained orders against 14 companies that allegedly failed to implement reasonable procedures to safeguard the sensitive consumer information they maintained. Most of these cases have been brought in the last two years. The SEC also has brought data security cases. See Volume II, Part B, for a description of enforcement actions relating to data security.

> In April 2004, the New York Attorney General settled a case with BarnesandNoble.com, fining the company $60,000 and requiring it to implement a data security program after an investigation revealed that an alleged design vulnerability in the company's Website permitted unauthorized access to consumers' personal information and enabled thieves to make fraudulent purchases. In addition, California, Vermont, and New York settled a joint action with Ziff Davis Media, Inc. involving security shortcomings that exposed the credit card numbers and other personal information of about 12,000 consumers.

In addition to federal law, every state and the District of Columbia has its own laws to protect consumers from unfair or deceptive practices. Moreover, 37 states have data breach notice laws,[49] and some states have laws relevant to data security, including safeguards and disposal requirements.

Trade associations, industry collaborations, independent organizations with expertise in data security, and nonprofits have developed guidance and standards for businesses. Topics include: incorporating basic security and privacy practices into everyday business operations; developing privacy and security plans; employee screening, training, and management; implementing electronic and physical safeguards; employing threat recognition techniques; safeguarding international transactions; and credit and debit card security.[50]

Some entities that use service providers also have begun using contractual provisions that require third-party service vendors with access to the institution's sensitive data to safeguard that data.[51] Generally, these provisions also address specific practices for contracting organizations, including conducting initial and follow-up security audits of a vendor's data center, and requiring vendors to provide certification that they are in compliance with the contracting organization's privacy and data protection obligations.[52]

> In 2006, the Federal Reserve Board issued a Cease and Desist Order against an Alabama-based financial institution for, among other things, failing to comply with an existing Board regulation that required implementation of an information security program.

B. Implementation of Data Security Guidelines and Rules

Many private sector organizations understand their vulnerabilities and have made significant strides in incorporating data security into their operations or improving existing security programs. See Volume II, Part C, for a description of education efforts for businesses on safeguarding data. For example, many companies and financial institutions now regularly require two-factor authentication for business conducted via computer or telephone; send dual confirmations when customers submit a change of address; limit access to non-public personal information to necessary personnel; regularly monitor websites for phishing and firewalls for hacking; perform assessments of network security to determine the adequacy of protection from intrusion, viruses, and other data security breaches; and post identity theft education materials on company web sites. Additionally, many firms within the consumer data industry offer services that provide companies with comprehensive background checks on prospective employees and tenants as permitted by law under the FCRA, and help companies verify the identity of customers.

Yet, as the reports of data breach incidents continue to show, further improvements are necessary. In a survey of financial institutions, 95 percent of respondents reported growth in their information security budget in 2005, with 71 percent reporting that they have a defined information security governance framework.[53] But many organizations also report that they are in the early stages of implementing comprehensive security procedures. For instance, in a survey of technology decision makers released in 2006, 85 percent of respondents indicated that their stored data was either somewhat or extremely vulnerable, while only 22 percent had implemented a storage security solution to prevent unauthorized access.[54] The same survey revealed that 58 percent of data managers responding believed their networks were not as secure as they could be.[55]

> In 2005, the FTC settled a law enforcement action with Superior Mortgage, a mortgage company, alleging that the company failed to comply with the GLB Safeguards Rule. The FTC alleged that the company's security procedures were deficient in the areas of risk assessment, access controls, document protection, and oversight of service providers. The FTC also charged Superior with misrepresenting how it applied encryption to sensitive consumer information. Superior agreed to undertake a comprehensive data security program and retain an independent auditor to assess and certify its security procedures every two years for the next 10 years.

Small businesses face particular challenges in implementing effective data security policies for reasons of cost and lack of expertise. A 2005 survey found that while many small businesses are accelerating their adoption and use of information technology and the Internet, many do not have basic security measures in place. [56] For example, of the small businesses surveyed,

- nearly 20 percent did not use virus scans for email, a basic information security safeguard;

- over 60 percent did not protect their wireless networks with even the simplest of encryption solutions;
- over 70 percent reported expectations of a more challenging environment for detecting security threats, but only 30 percent reported increasing information security spending in 2005; and
- 74 percent reported having no information security plan in place.

Further complicating matters is the fact that some federal agencies are unable to receive data from private sector entities in an encrypted form. Therefore, some private sector entities that have to transmit sensitive data to federal agencies—sometimes pursuant to law or regulations issued by agencies—are unable to fully safeguard the transmitted data because they must decrypt the data before they can send it to the agencies. The E-Authentication Presidential Initiative is currently addressing how agencies can more uniformly adopt appropriate technical solutions to this problem based on the level of risk involved, including, but not limited to, encryption.

> In 2004, an FDIC examination of a state-chartered bank disclosed significant computer system deficiencies and inadequate controls to prevent unauthorized access to customer information.
>
> The FDIC issued an order directing the bank to develop and implement an information security program, and specifically ordered the bank, among other things, to perform a formal risk assessment of internal and external threats that could result in unauthorized access to customer information.
>
> The bank also was ordered to review computer user access levels to ensure that access was restricted to only those individuals with a legitimate business need to access the information.

C. Responding to Data Breaches in the Private Sector

Although the link between data breaches and identity theft is unclear, reports of private sector data security breaches add to consumers' fear of identity thieves gaining access to sensitive consumer information and undermine consumer confidence. Pursuant to the GLB Act, the financial regulatory agencies require financial institutions under their jurisdiction to implement programs designed to safeguard customer information. In addition, the federal bank regulatory agencies (FDIC, FRB, NCUA, OCC, and OTS) have issued guidance with respect to breach notification. In addition, 37 states have laws requiring that consumers be notified when their information has been subject to a breach.[57] Some of the laws also require that the entity that experienced the breach notify law enforcement, consumer reporting agencies, and other potentially affected parties.[58] Notice to consumers may help them avoid or mitigate injury by allowing them to take appropriate protective actions, such as placing a fraud alert on their credit file or monitoring their accounts. In some cases, the organization experiencing the breach has offered additional assistance, including free credit monitoring services. Moreover, prompt notification to law enforcement allows for the investigation and deterrence of identity theft and related unlawful conduct.

The states have taken a variety of approaches regarding when notice to consumers is required. Some states require notice to consumers whenever there is unauthorized access to sensitive data. Other states require notification only when the breach of information poses a risk to consumers. Notice is not required, for example, when the data cannot be used to commit identity theft, or when technological protections prevent fraudsters from accessing data. This approach recognizes that excessive breach notification can overwhelm consumers, causing them to ignore more significant incidents, and can impose unnecessary costs on consumers, the organization that suffered the breach, and others. Under this approach, however, organizations struggle to assess whether the risks are sufficient to warrant consumer notification. Factors relevant to that assessment often include the sensitivity of the breached information, the extent to which it is protected from access (e.g., by using technological tools for protecting data), how the breach occurred (e.g., whether the information was deliberately stolen as opposed to accidentally misplaced), and any evidence that the data actually have been misused.

A number of bills establishing a federal notice requirement have been introduced in Congress. Many of the state laws and the bills in Congress address who should be notified, when notice should be given, what information should be provided in the notice, how notice should be effected, and the circumstances under which consumer notice should be delayed for law enforcement purposes.

Despite the substantial effort undertaken by the public and private sectors to educate businesses on how to respond to data breaches (see Volume II, Part D, for a description of education for businesses on responding to data breaches), there is room for improvement by businesses in planning for and responding to data breaches. Surveys of large corporations and retailers indicate that fewer than half of them have formal breach response plans. For example, an April 2006 cross-industry survey revealed that only 45 percent of large multinational corporations headquartered in the U.S. had a formal process for handling security violations and data breaches.[59] Fourteen percent of the companies surveyed had experienced a significant privacy breach in the past three years.[60] A July 2005 survey of large North American corporations found that although 80 percent of responding companies reported having privacy or data-protection strategies, only 31 percent had a formal notification procedure in the event of a data breach.[61] Moreover, one survey found that only 43 percent of retailers had formal incident response plans, and even fewer had tested their plans.[62]

> When an online retailer became the target of an elaborate fraud ring, the company looked to one of the major credit reporting agencies for assistance. By using shared data maintained by that agency, the retailer was able to identify applications with common data elements and flag them for further scrutiny. By using the shared application data in connection with the activities of this fraud ring, the company avoided $26,000 in fraud losses.

RECOMMENDATION: ESTABLISH NATIONAL STANDARDS EXTENDING DATA PROTECTION SAFEGUARDS REQUIREMENTS AND BREACH NOTIFICATION REQUIREMENTS

Several existing laws mandate protection for sensitive consumer information, but a number of private entities are not subject to those laws. The GLB Act, for example, applies to "financial institutions," but generally not to other entities that collect and maintain sensitive information. Similarly, existing federal breach notification standards do not extend to all entities that hold sensitive consumer information, and the various state laws that contain breach notification requirements differ in various respects, complicating compliance. Accordingly, the Task Force recommends the development of (1) a national standard imposing safeguards requirements on all private entities that maintain sensitive consumer information; and (2) a national standard requiring entities that maintain sensitive consumer information to provide notice to consumers and law enforcement in the event of a breach. Such national standards should provide clarity and predictability for businesses and consumers, and should incorporate the following important principles.

Covered data. The national standards for data security and for breach notification should cover data that can be used toperpetrate identity theft—in particular, any data or combination of consumer data that would allow someone to use, log into, or access an individual's account, or to establish a new account using the individual's identifying information. This identifying information includes a name, address, or telephone number paired with a unique identifier such as a Social Security number, a driver's license number, a biometric record, or a financial account number (together with a PIN or security code, if such PIN or code is required to access an account) (hereinafter "covered data"). The standards should not cover data, such as a name and address alone, that by itself typically would not cause harm. The definitions of covered data for data security and data breach notification requirements should be consistent.

Covered entities. The national standards for data security and breach notification should cover any private entity that collects, maintains, sells, transfers, disposes of, or otherwise handles covered data in any medium, including electronic and paper formats.

Unusable data. National standards should recognize that rendering data unusable to outside parties likely would prevent "acquisition" of the data, and thus ordinarily would satisfy an entity's legal obligations to protect the data and would not trigger notification of a breach. The standards should not endorse a specific technology because unusability is not a static concept and the effectiveness of particular technologies may change over time.

Risk-based standard for breach notification. The national breach notification standard should require that covered entities provide notice to consumers in the event of a data breach, but only when the risks to consumers are real—that is, when there is a significant risk of identity theft due to the breach. This "significant risk of identity theft" trigger for notification recognizes that excessive breach notification can overwhelm consumers, causing them to take costly actions when there is little risk, or conversely, to ignore the notices when the risks are real.

Notification to law enforcement. The national breach notification standard should provide for timely notification to law enforcement and expressly allow law enforcement to authorize a delay in required consumer notice, either for law enforcement or national security reasons (and either on its own behalf or on behalf of state or local law enforcement).

Relationship to current federal standards. The national standards for data security and breach notification should be drafted to be consistent with and so as not to displace any rules, regulations, guidelines, standards, or guidance issued under the GLB Act by the FTC, the federal bank regulatory agencies, the SEC, or the Commodity Futures Trading Commission (CFTC), unless those agencies so determine.

Preemption of state laws. To ensure comprehensive national requirements that provide clarity and predictability, while maintaining an effective enforcement role for the states, the national data security and breach notification standards should preempt state data security and breach notification laws, but authorize enforcement by the state Attorneys General for entities not subject to the jurisdiction of the federal bank regulatory agencies, the SEC, or the CFTC.

Rulemaking and enforcement authority. Coordinated rulemaking authority under the Administrative Procedure Act should be given to the FTC, the federal bank regulatory agencies, the SEC, and the CFTC to implement the national standards. Those agencies should be authorized to enforce the standards against entities under their respective jurisdictions, and should specifically be authorized to seek civil penalties in federal district court.

Pivate right of action. The national standards should not provide for or create a private right of action.

Standards incorporating such principles will prompt covered entities to establish and implement administrative, technical, and physical safeguards to ensure the security and confidentiality of sensitive consumer information; protect against any anticipated threats or hazards to the security or integrity of such information; and protect against unauthorized access to or use of such information that could result in substantial harm or inconvenience to any consumer. Because the costs associated with implementing safeguards or providing breach notice may be different for small businesses and larger businesses, or may differ based on the type of information held by a business, the national standard should expressly call for actions that are reasonable for the particular covered entity and should not adopt a one-size-fits-all approach to the implementation of safeguards.

> When a major consumer lending institution encountered a problem when the loss ratio on many of its loans —including mortgages and consumer loans— became excessively high due to fraud, the bank hired a leading provider of fraud prevention products to authenticate potential customers during the application process prior to extending credit. The result was immediate: two million dollars of confirmed fraud losses were averted within the first six months of implementation.

RECOMMENDATION: BETTER EDUCATE THE PRIVATE SECTOR ON SAFEGUARDING DATA

Although much has been done to educate the private sector on how to safeguard data, the continued proliferation of data breaches suggests that more needs to be done. While there is no perfect data security system, a company that is sensitized to the importance of data security, understands its legal obligations, and has the information it needs to secure its data adequately, is less likely to suffer a data compromise. The Task Force therefore makes the following recommendations concerning how to better educate the private sector:

- Hold Regional Seminars for Businesses on Safeguarding Information. By the fourth quarter of 2007, the federal financial regulatory agencies and the FTC, with support from other Task Force member agencies, should hold regional seminars and develop self-guided and online tutorials for businesses and financial institutions, about safeguarding information, preventing and reporting breaches, and assisting identity theft victims. The seminar's leaders should make efforts to include small businesses in these sessions and address their particular needs. These seminars could be co-sponsored by local bar associations, the Better Business Bureaus (BBBs), and other similar organizations. Self-guided tutorials should be made available through the Task Force's online clearinghouse at www.idtheft.gov.
- Distribute Improved Guidance for Private Industry. In the second quarter of 2007, the FTC should expand written guidance to private sector entities that are not regulated by the federal bank regulatory agencies or the SEC on steps they should take to safeguard information. The guidance should be designed to give a more detailed explanation of the broad principles encompassed in existing laws. Like the Information Technology Examination Handbook's Information Security Booklet issued under the auspices of the Federal Financial Institutions Examination Council,[63] the guidance should be risk-based and flexible, in recognition of the fact that different private sector entities will warrant different solutions.

> A leading payment processing and bill payment company recently deployed an automated fraud detection and case management system to more than 40 financial institutions. The system helps ensure that receiving and paying bills online remains a safe practice for consumers. To mitigate risk and reduce fraud for banks and consumers before it happens, the system combines the company's cumulative knowledge of payment patterns and a sophisticated analytics engine to help financial services organizations detect and stop unauthorized payments.

Recommendation: Initiate Investigations of Data Security Violations

Beginning immediately, appropriate government agencies should initiate investigations of and, if appropriate, take enforcement actions against entities that violate the laws governing data security. The FTC, SEC, and federal bank regulatory agencies have used regulatory and enforcement efforts to require companies to maintain appropriate information safeguards under the law. Federal agencies should continue and expand these efforts to ensure that such entities use reasonable data security measures. Where appropriate, the agencies should share information about those enforcement actions on www.idtheft.gov.

IV. Educating Consumers on Protecting Their Personal Information

The first line of defense against identity theft often is an aware and motivated consumer who takes reasonable precautions to protect his information. Every day, unwitting consumers create risks to the security of their personal information. From failing to install firewall protection on a computer hard drive to leaving paid bills in a mail slot, consumers leave the door open to identity thieves. Consumer education is a critical component of any plan to reduce the incidence of identity theft.

The federal government has been a leading provider of consumer information about identity theft. Numerous departments and agencies target identity theft-related messages to relevant populations. See Volume II, Part E, for a description of federal consumer education efforts. The FTC, through its Identity Theft Clearinghouse and ongoing outreach, plays a primary role in consumer awareness and education, developing information that has been co-branded by a variety of groups and agencies. Its website, www.ftc.gov/idtheft serves as a comprehensive one-stop resource in both English and Spanish for consumers. The FTC also recently implemented a national public awareness campaign centered around the themes of "Deter, Detect, and Defend," which seeks to drive behavioral changes in consumers that will reduce their risk of identity theft (Deter); encourage them to monitor their credit reports and accounts to alert them of identity theft as soon as possible after it occurs (Detect); and mitigate the damage caused by identity theft should it occur (Defend). This campaign, mandated in the FACT Act, consists of direct messaging to consumers as well as material written for organizations, community leaders, and local law enforcement. The Deter, Detect, and Defend materials have been adopted and distributed by hundreds of entities, both public and private.

The SSA and the federal regulatory agencies are among the many other government bodies that also play a significant role in educating consumers on how to protect themselves. For example, the SSA added a message to its SSN verification printout warning the public not to share their SSNs with others. This warning was especially timely in the aftermath of Hurricane Katrina, which necessitated the issuance of a large number of those printouts. Similarly, the Senior Medicare Patrol (SMP) program, funded by U.S. Administration on Aging in the Department of Health and Human Services, uses senior volunteers to educate their peers about protecting their personal information and preventing and identifying consumer and health care fraud. The SMP program also has worked closely with the Centers for Medicare and Medicaid Services to protect seniors from new scams aimed at defrauding them of their Medicare numbers and other personal information. And the U.S. Postal Inspection Service has produced a number of consumer education materials, including several videos, alerting the public to the problems associated with identity theft.

Significant consumer education efforts also are taking place at the state level. Nearly all of the state Attorneys General offer information on the prevention and remediation of identity theft on their web sites, and several states have conducted conferences and workshops focused on education and training in privacy protection and identity theft prevention. Over the past year, the Attorney General of Illinois and the Governors of New Mexico and California have hosted summit meetings, bringing together law enforcement, educators, victims' coordinators, consumer advocates, and the business community to develop better strategies for educating the public and fighting identity theft. The National Governors Association convened the National Strategic Policy Council on Cyber and Electronic Crime in September 2006 to trigger a coordinated education and prevention effort by federal, state, and local policymakers. The New York State Consumer Protection Board has conducted "Consumer Action Days," with free seminars about identity theft and other consumer protection issues.

Police departments also provide consumer education to their communities. Many departments have developed materials and make them available in police stations, in city government buildings, and on web sites.[64] As of this writing, more than 500 local police departments are using the FTC's "Deter, Detect, Defend" campaign materials to teach their communities about identity theft. Other groups, including the National Apartment

Association and the National Association of Realtors, also have promoted this campaign by distributing the materials to their membership.

Although most educational material is directed at consumers in general, some is aimed at and tailored to specific target groups. One such group is college students. For several reasons—including the vast amounts of personal data that colleges maintain about them and their tendency to keep personal data unguarded in shared dormitory rooms—students are frequent targets of identity thieves. According to one report, one-third to one-half of all reported personal information breaches in 2006 have occurred at colleges and universities.[65] In recognition of the increased vulnerability of this population, many universities are providing information to their students about the risks of identity theft through web sites, orientation campaigns, and seminars.[66]Federal, state, and local government agencies provide a great deal of identity theft-related information to the public through the Internet, printed materials, DVDs, and in-person presentations. The messages the agencies provide—how to protect personal information, how to recognize a potential problem, where to report a theft, and how to deal with the aftermath— are echoed by industry, law enforcement, advocates, and the media. See Volume II, Part F, for a description of private sector consumer education efforts. But there is little coordination among the agencies on current education programs. Dissemination in some cases is random, information is limited, and evaluation of effectiveness is almost nonexistent. Although a great deal of useful information is being disseminated, the extent to which the messages are reaching, engaging, or motivating consumers is unclear.

RECOMMENDATION: INITIATE A MULTI-YEAR PUBLIC AWARENESS CAMPAIGN

Because consumer education is a critical component of any plan to reduce the incidence of identity theft, the Task Force recommends that member agencies, in the third quarter of 2007, initiate a multi-year national public awareness campaign that builds on the FTC's current "AvoID Theft: Deter, Detect,

Defend" campaign, developed pursuant to direction in the FACT Act. This campaign should include the following elements:

- Develop a Broad Awareness Campaign. By broadening the current FTC campaign into a multi-year awareness campaign, and by engaging the Ad Council or similar entities as partners, important and empowering messages should be disseminated more widely and by more partners. The campaign should include public service announcements on the Internet, radio, and television, and in newspapers and magazines, and should address the issue from a variety of perspectives, from prevention through mitigation and remediation, and reach a variety of audiences.
- Enlist Outreach Partners. The agencies conducting the campaign should enlist as outreach partners national organizations either that have been active in helping consumers protect themselves against identity theft, such as the AARP, the Identity Theft Resource Center (ITRC), and the Privacy Rights Clearinghouse (PRC), or that may be well-situated to help in this area, such as the White House Office of Faith-Based and Community Initiatives.
- Increase Outreach to Traditionally underserved Communities. Outreach to underserved communities should include encouraging language translations of existing materials and involving community-based organizations as partners.
- Establish "Protect Your Identity Days." The campaign should establish "Protect Your Identity Days" to promote better data security by businesses and individual commitment to security by consumers. These "Protect Your Identity Days" should also build on the popularity of community "shred-ins" by encouraging community and business organizations to shred documents containing personal information.

RECOMMENDATION: DEVELOP AN ONLINE CLEARINGHOUSE" FOR CURRENT EDUCATIONAL RESOURCES

The Task Force recommends that in the third quarter of 2007, the Task Force member agencies develop an online "clearinghouse" for current identity theft educational resources for consumers, businesses, and law enforcement from a variety of sources at www.idtheft.gov. This would make the materials immediately available in one place to any public or private entity willing to launch an education program, and to any citizen interested in accessing the information. Rather than recreate content, entities could link directly to the clearinghouse for timely and accurate information. Educational materials should be added to the website on an ongoing basis.

A. PREVENTION: MAKING IT HARDER TO MISUSE CONSUMER DATA

Keeping valuable consumer data out of the hands of criminals is the first step in reducing the incidence of identity theft. But, because no security is perfect and thieves are resourceful, it is essential to reduce the opportunities for criminals to misuse the data they do manage to steal.

An identity thief who wants to open new accounts in a victim's name must be able to (1) provide identifying information to enable the creditor or other grantor of benefits to access information on which to base an eligibility decision, and (2) convince the creditor or other grantor of benefits that he is, in fact, the person he purports to be. For example, a credit card grantor processing an application for a credit card will use the SSN to access the consumer's credit report to check his creditworthiness, and may rely on photo documents, the SSN, and/or other proof to access other sources of information intended to "verify" the applicant's identity. Thus, the SSN is a critical piece of information for the thief, and its wide availability increases the risk of identity theft.

Identity systems follow a two-fold process: first, determining ("identification") and setting ("enrollment") the identity of an individual at the onset of the relationship; and second, later ensuring that the individual is the same person who was initially enrolled ("authentication"). With the exception of banks, savings associations, credit unions, some broker-dealers, mutual funds, futures commission merchants, and introducing brokers (collectively, "financial institutions"), there is no generally-applicable legal obligation on private sector entities to use any particular means of identification. Financial institutions are required to follow certain verification procedures pursuant to regulations promulgated by the federal bank regulatory agencies, the Department ofTreasury, the SEC, and the CFTC under the USA PATRIOT Act.67 The regulations require these financial institutions to establish a Customer Identification Program (CIP) specifying identifying information that will be obtained from each customer when accounts are opened (which must include, at a minimum, name, date of birth, address, and an identification number such as an S SN). The CIP requirement is intended to ensure that financial institutions form a reasonable belief that they know the true identity of each customer who opens an account. The government, too, is making efforts to implement new identification mechanisms. For example, REAL ID is a nationwide effort intended to prevent terrorism, reduce fraud, and improve the reliability and accuracy of identification documents that state governments issue.68 See Volume II, Part G, for a description of recent laws relating to identification documents.

The verification process can fail, however, in a number of ways. First, identity documents may be falsified. Second, checking the identifying information against other verifying sources of information can produce varying results, depending on the accuracy of the initial information presented and the accuracy or quality of the verifying sources. The process also can fail because employees are trained improperly or fail to follow proper procedures. Identity thieves exploit each of these opportunities to circumvent the verification process.[69]

Once an individual's identity has been verified, it must be authenticated each time he wants the access for which he was initially verified, such as access to a bank account. Generally, businesses authenticate an individual by requiring him to present some sort of credential to prove that he is the same individual whose identity was originally verified. A credential is generally one or more of the following:

- Something a person knows—most commonly a password, but also may be a query that requires specific knowledge only the customer is likely to have, such as the exact amount of the customer's monthly mortgage payment.
- Something a person has—most commonly a physical device, such as a Universal Serial Bus (USB) token, a smart card, or a password- generating device.[70]
- Something a person is—most commonly a physical characteristic, such as a fingerprint, iris, face, and hand geometry. This type of authentication is referred to as biometrics.[71]

Some entities use a single form of authentication—most commonly a password—but if it is compromised, there are no other fail-safes in the system. To address this problem, the federal bank regulatory agencies issued guidance promoting stronger customer authentication methods for certain high-risk transactions. Such methods are to include the use of multi-factor authentication, layered security, or other similar controlsreasonably calculated to mitigate the exposure from any transactions that are identified as high-risk. The guidance more broadly provides that banks, savings associations, and credit unions conduct risk-based assessments, evaluate customer awareness programs, and develop security measures to reliably authenticate customers remotely accessing Internet- based financial services.[72] Financial institutions covered by the guidance were advised that the agencies expected them to have completed the risk assessment and implemented risk mitigation activities by year-end 2006.[73] Along with the financial services industry, other industries have begun to implement new authentication procedures using different types of credentials.

SSNs have many advantages and are widely used in our current marketplace to match consumers with their records (including their credit files) and as part of the authentication process. Keeping the authentication process convenient for consumers and credit grantors without making it too easy for criminals to impersonate consumers requires a fine balance. Notwithstanding improvements in certain industries and companies, efforts to facilitate the development of better ways to authenticate consumers without undue burden would help prevent criminals from profiting from their crime.

RECOMMENDATION: HOLD WORKSHOPS ON AUTHENTICATION

Because developing more reliable methods of authenticating the identities of individuals would make it harder for identity thieves to open new accounts or access existing accounts using other individuals' information, the Task Force will hold a workshop or series of workshops, involving academics, industry, and entrepreneurs, focused on developing and promoting improved means of authenticating the identities of individuals. These experts will discuss the existing problem and examine the limitations of current processes of authentication. With that information, the Task Force will probe viable technological and other solutions that will reduce identity fraud, and identify needs for future research. Such workshops have been successful in developing creative and timely responses to consumer protection issues, and the workshops are expected to be useful for both the private and public sectors. For example, the federal government has an interest as a facilitator of the development of new technologies and in implementing technologies that better protect the data it handles in providing benefits and services, and as an employer.

As noted in the Task Force's interim recommendations to the President, the FTC and other Task Force member agencies will host the first such workshop in the second quarter of 2007.

The Task Force also recommends that a report be issued or subsequent workshops be held to report on any proposals or best practices identified during the workshop series.

RECOMMENDATION: DEVELOP COMPREHENSIVE RECORD ON PRIVATE SECTOR USE OF SSNS

As noted in Section III A 1, above, the Task Force recommends developing a comprehensive record on the uses of the SSN in the private sector and evaluating their necessity.

B. VICTIM RECOVERY: HELPING CONSUMERS REPAIR THEIR LIVES

Because identity theft can be committed despite the best of precautions, an essential step in the fight against this crime is ensuring that victims have the knowledge, tools, and assistance necessary to minimize the damage and begin the recovery process. Currently, consumers have a number of rights and available resources, but they may not be aware of them.

1. Victim Assistance: Outreach and Education

Federal and state laws offer victims of identity theft an array of tools to avoid or mitigate the harms they suffer. For example, under the FACT Act, victims can: (1) place alerts on their credit files; (2) request copies of applications and other documents used by the thief; (3)

request that the credit reporting agencies block fraudulent trade lines on credit reports; and (4) obtain information on the fraudulent accounts from debt collectors.

In some cases, the recovery process is relatively straightforward. Consumers whose credit card numbers have been used to make unauthorized purchases, for example, typically can get the charges removed without undue burden. In other cases, however, such as those involving new-account fraud, recovery can be an ordeal.

Widely-available guidance advises consumers of steps to take if they have become victims of identity theft, or if their personal information has been breached. For example, the FTC's web site, www.ftc.gov/idtheft, contains step-by-step recovery information for victims, as well as for those who may be at risk following a compromise of their data. Many other agencies and organizations link directly to the FTC site and themselves provide education and assistance to victims. State governments also provide assistance to victims. State consumer protection agencies, privacy agencies, and state Attorneys General provide victim information and guidance on their websites, and some provide personal assistance as well. A number of states have established hotlines, counseling, and other assistance for victims of identity theft. For example, the Illinois Attorney General's office has implemented an Identity Theft Hotline; each caller is assigned a consumer advocate to assist with the recovery process and to help prevent further victimization.

Fair and Accurate Credit Transaction Act (FACT Act) Rights

The Fair and Accurate Credit Transactions Act of 2003 added new sections to the Fair Credit Reporting Act that provide a number of new tools for victims to recover from identity theft. These include the right to place a fraud alert with the credit reporting agencies and receive a free copy of the credit report. An initial alert lasts for 90 days. A victim with an identity theft report documenting actual misuse of the consumer information is entitled to place a 7-year alert on his file. In addition, under the FACT Act, victims can request copies of documents relating to fraudulent transactions, and can obtain information from a debt collector regarding a debt fraudulently incurred in the victim's name. Victims who have a police report also can ask that fraudulent accounts be blocked from their credit report, and can prevent businesses from reporting information that resulted from identity theft to the credit reporting agencies.

Identity theft victims, and consumers who suspect that they may become victims because of lost data, are advised to act quickly to prevent or minimize harm. The steps are straightforward:

- Contact one of the three major credit reporting agencies to place a fraud alert on their credit file. The agencies are required to transmit this information to the other two companies. Consumers who place this 90-day alert are entitled to a free copy of their credit report. Fraud alerts are most useful when a consumer's SSN is compromised, creating the risk of new account fraud.
- Contact any creditors where fraudulent accounts were opened or charges were made to dispute these transactions, and follow up in writing.

- Report actual incidents of identity theft to the local police department and obtain a copy of the police report. This document will be essential to exercising other remedies.
- Report the identity theft incident to the ID Theft Data Clearinghouse by filing a complaint online at ftc.gov/idtheft, or calling toll free 877 ID THEFT. The complaint will be entered into the Clearinghouse and shared with the law enforcement agencies who use the database to investigate and prosecute identity crimes.

Some states provide additional protections to identity theft victims by allowing them to request a "credit freeze," which prevents consumers' credit reports from being released without their express consent. Because most companies obtain a credit report from a consumer before extending credit, a credit freeze will likely prevent the extension of credit in a consumer's name without the consumer's express permission.

A number of private sector organizations also provide critical victim assistance. Not-for-profit groups such as the Privacy Rights Clearinghouse (PRC) and the Identity Theft Resource Center (ITRC) offer counseling and assistance for identity theft victims who need help in going through the recovery process. The Identity Theft Assistance Center (ITAC), a victim assistance program established by the financial services industry, has helped approximately 13,000 victims resolve problems with disputed accounts and other fraud related to identity theft since its founding in 2004. Finally, many individual companies have established hotlines, distributed materials, and provided special services for customers whose information has been misused. Indeed, some companies rely on their identity theft services as marketing tools.

Despite this substantial effort by the public and private sectors to educate and assist victims, there is room for improvement. Many victims are not aware, or do not take advantage, of the resources available to them. For example, while the FTC receives roughly 250,000 contacts from victims every year, that number is only a small percentage of all identity theft victims. Moreover, although first responders could be a key resource for identity theft victims, the first responders often are overworked and may not have the information that they need about the steps for victim recovery. It is essential, therefore, that public and private outreach efforts be expanded, better coordinated, and better funded.

Recommendation: Provide Specialized Training about Victim Recovery to First Responders and Others Providing Direct Assistance to Identity Theft Victims

First responders and others who provide direct assistance and support to identity theft victims must be adequately trained. Accordingly, the Task Force recommends the following:

- Train Local Law Enforcement Officers. By the third quarter of 2007, federal law enforcement agencies, which could include the U.S. Postal Inspection Service, the FBI, the Secret Service, and the FTC, should conduct training seminars—delivered in person, online, or via video—for local law enforcement officers on available resources and providing assistance for victims.

- Provide Educational Materials for First Responders That Can Be Readily used as a Reference Guide for Identity Theft Victims. During the third quarter of 2007, the FTC and DOJ should develop a reference guide, which should include contact information for resources and information on first steps to recovery, and should make that guide available to law enforcement officers through the online clearinghouse at www.idtheft.gov. Such guidance would assist first responders in directing victims on their way to recovery.
- Distribute an Identity Theft Victim Statement of Rights. Federal law provides substantial assistance to victims of identity theft. From obtaining a police report to blocking fraudulent accounts in a credit report, consumers—as well as law enforcement, private businesses, and other parties involved in the recovery process—need to know what remedies are available. Accordingly, the Task Force recommends that, during the third quarter of 2007, the FTC draft an ID Theft Victim Statement of Rights, a short and simple statement of the basic rights victims possess under current law. This document should then be disseminated to victims through law enforcement, the financial sector, and advocacy groups, and posted at www.idtheft.gov.
- Develop Nationwide Training for Victim Assistance Counselors. Crime victims receive assistance through a wide array of federal and state-sponsored programs, as well as nonprofit organizations. Additionally, every United States Attorney's Office in the country has a victim-witness coordinator who is responsible for referring crime victims to the appropriate resources to resolve harms that resulted from the misuse of their information. All of these counselors should be trained to respond to the specific needs of identity theft victims, including assisting them in coping with the financial and emotional impact of identity crime. Therefore, the Task Force recommends that a standardized training curriculum for victim assistance be developed and promoted through a nationwide training campaign, including through DOJ's Office for Victims of Crime (OVC). Already, OVC has begun organizing training workshops, the first of which was held in December 2006. These workshops are intended to train not only victim- witness coordinators from U.S. Attorney's Offices, but also state, tribal, and local victim service providers. The program will help advocates learn how to assist victims in self-advocacy and how and when to intervene in a victim's recovery process. Training topics will include helping victims deal with the economic and emotional ramifications of identity theft, assisting victims with understanding how an identity theft case proceeds through the criminal justice system, and identity theft laws. Additional workshops should be held in 2007.

Recommendation: Develop Avenues for Individualized Assistance to Identity Theft Victims

Although many victims are able to resolve their identity theft- related issues without assistance, some individuals would benefit from individualized counseling. The availability of personalized assistance should be increased through national service organizations, such as those using retired seniors or similar groups, and pro bono activities by lawyers, such as those organized by the American Bar Association (ABA). In offering individualized assistance to identity theft victims, these organizations and programs should use the victim resource guides that are already available through the FTC and DOJ's Office for Victims of Crime. Specifically, the Task Force also recommends the following:

- Engage the American Bar Association to Develop a Program Focusing on Assisting Identity Theft Victims with recovery.

The ABA has expertise in coordinating legal representation in specific areas of practice through law firm volunteers. Moreover, law firms have the resources and expertise to staff an effort to assist victims of identity theft. Accordingly, the Task Force recommends that, beginning in 2007, the ABA, with assistance from the Department of Justice, develop a pro bono referral program focusing on assisting identity theft victims with recovery.

2. Making Identity Theft Victims Whole

Identity theft inflicts many kinds of harm upon its victims, making it difficult for them to feel that they ever will recover fully. Beyond tangible forms of harm, statistics cannot adequately convey the emotional toll that identity theft often exacts on its victims, who frequently report feelings of violation, anger, anxiety, betrayal of trust, and even self- blame or hopelessness. These feelings may continue, or even increase, as victims work through the credit recovery and criminal justice processes.

Embarrassment, cultural factors, or personal or family circumstances (e.g., if the victim has a relationship to the identity thief) may keep the victims from reporting the problem to law enforcement, in turn making them ineligible to take advantage of certain remedies. Often, these reactions are intensified by the ongoing, long-term nature of the crime. Criminals may not stop committing identity theft after having been caught; they simply use information against the same individual in a new way, or they sell the information so that multiple identity thieves can use it. Even when the fraudulent activity ceases, the effects of negative information on the victim's credit report can continue for years.

The many hours victims spend in attempting to recover from the harms they suffer often takes a toll on victims that is not reflected in their monetary losses. One reason that identity theft can be so destructive to its victims is the sheer amount of time and energy often required to recover from the offense, including having to correct credit reports, dispute charges with individual creditors, close and reopen bank accounts, and monitor credit reports for future problems arising from the theft.

> "I received delinquent bills for purchases she [the suspect] made. I spent countless hours on calls with creditors in Texas who were reluctant to believe that the accounts that had been opened were fraudulent. I spent days talking to police in Texas in an effort to convince them that I was allowed by Texas law to file a report and have her [the suspect] charged with the theft of my identity.... I had to send more than 50 letters to the creditors to have them remove the more than 60 inquiries that were made by this woman...."
>
> Nicole Robinson Testimony before House Ways and Means Committee, Subcommittee on Social Security May 22, 2001

In addition to losing time and money, some identity theft victims suffer the indignity of being mistaken for the criminal who stole their identities, and have been wrongfully arrested.74 In one case, a victim's driver's license was stolen, and the information from the license was used to open a fraudulent bank account and to write more than $10,000 in bad checks.

The victim herself was arrested when local authorities thought she was the criminal. In addition to the resulting feelings of trauma, this type of harm is a particularly difficult one for an identity theft victim to resolve.

Recommendation: Amend Criminal Restitution Statutes to Ensure that Victims Recover for the Value of Time Spent in Attempting to Remediate the Harms they Suffered

Restitution to victims from convicted thieves is available for the direct financial costs of identity theft offenses. However, there is no specific provision in the federal restitution statutes for compensation for the time spent by victims recovering from the crime, and court decisions interpreting the statutes suggest that such recovery would be precluded.

As stated in the Task Force's interim recommendations to the President, the Task Force recommends that Congress amend the federal criminal restitution statutes to allow for restitution from a criminal defendant to an identity theft victim, in an amount equal to the value of the victim's time reasonably spent attempting to remediate the intended or actual harm incurred from the identity theft offense. The language of the proposed amendment is in Appendix C. DOJ transmitted the proposed amendment to Congress on October 4, 2006.

Recommendation: Explore the Development of a National Program Allowing Identity Theft Victims to Obtain an Identification Document for Authentication Purposes

One of the problems faced by identity theft victims is proving that they are who they say they are. Indeed, some identity theft victims have been mistaken for the criminal who stole their identity, and have been arrested based on warrants issued for the thief who stole their personal data. To give identity theft victims a means to authenticate their identities in such a situation, several states have developed identification documents, or "passports," that authenticate identity theft victims. These voluntary mechanisms are designed to prevent the misuse of the victim's name in the criminal justice system when, for example, an identity thief uses his victim's name when arrested. These documents often use multiple factors for authentication, such as biometric data and a password. The FBI has established a similar system through the National Crime Information Center, allowing identity theft victims to place their name in an "Identity File." This program, too, is limited in scope. Beginning in 2007, the Task Force member agencies should lead an effort to study the feasibility of developing a nationwide system allowing identity theft victims to obtain a document that they can use to avoid being mistaken for the suspect who has misused their identity. The system should build on the programs already used by several states and the FBI.

3. Gathering Better Information on the Effectiveness of Victim Recovery Measures

Identity theft victims have been granted many new rights in recent years. Gathering reliable information about the utility of these new rights is critical to evaluating whether they are working well or need to be modified. Additionally, because some states have measures in place to assist identity theft victims that have no federal counterpart, it is important to assess the success of those measures to determine whether they should be adopted more widely. Building a record of victims' experiences in exercising their rights is therefore crucial to ensuring that any strategy to fight identity theft is well-supported.

RECOMMENDATION: ASSESS EFFICACY OF TOOLS AVAILABLE TO VICTIMS

The Task Force recommends the following surveys or assessments:

- Conduct Assessment of FACT Act Remedies under FCRA. The FCRA is among the federal laws that enable victims to restore their good name. The FACT Act amendments to the FCRA provide several new rights and tools for actual or potential identity theft victims, including the availability of credit file fraud alerts; the blocking of fraudulent trade lines on credit reports; the right to have creditors cease furnishing information relating to fraudulent accounts to credit reporting agencies; and the right to obtain business records relating to fraudulent accounts. Many of these rights have been in effect for a short time. Accordingly, the Task Force recommends that the agencies with enforcement authority for these statutory provisions assess their impact and effectiveness through appropriate surveys. Agencies should report on the results in calendar year 2008.
- Conduct Assessment of State Credit Freeze Laws. Among the state-enacted remedies without a federal counterpart is one granting consumers the right to obtain a credit freeze. Credit freezes make a consumer's credit report inaccessible when, for example, an identity thief attempts to open an account in the victim's name. State laws differ in several respects, including whether all consumers can obtain a freeze or only identity theft victims; whether credit reporting agencies can charge the consumer for unfreezing a file (which would be necessary when applying for credit); and the time allowed to the credit reporting agencies to unfreeze a file. These provisions are relatively new, and there is no "track record" to show how effective they are, what costs they may impose on consumers and businesses, and what features are most beneficial to consumers. An assessment of how these measures have been implemented and how effective they have been would help policy makers in considering whether a federal credit freeze law would be appropriate.

Accordingly, the Task Force recommends that the FTC, with support from the Task Force member agencies, assess the impact and effectiveness of credit freeze laws, and report on the results in the first quarter of 2008.

C. Law Enforcement: Prosecuting and Punishing Identity Thieves

The two keys to preventing identity theft are (1) preventing access to sensitive consumer information through better data security and increased education, and (2) preventing the misuse of information that may be obtained by would-be identity thieves. Should those mechanisms fail, strong criminal law enforcement is necessary to both punish and deter identity thieves.

The increased awareness about identity theft in recent years has made it necessary for many law enforcement agencies at all levels of government to devote additional resources to investigating identity theft-related crimes. The principal federal law enforcement agencies that investigate identity theft are the FBI, the United States Secret Service, the United States Postal Inspection Service, SSA OIG, and ICE. Other agencies, as well as other federal Inspectors General, also may become involved in identity theft investigations.

In investigating identity theft, law enforcement agencies use a wide range of techniques, from physical surveillance to financial analysis to computer forensics. Identity theft investigations are labor-intensive, and because no single investigator can possess all of the skill sets needed to handle each of these functions, the investigations often require multiple detectives, analysts, and agents. In addition, when a suspected identity theft involves large numbers of potential victims, investigative agencies may need additional personnel to handle victim-witness coordination and information issues.

> In September 2006, the Michigan Attorney General won the conviction of a prison inmate who had orchestrated an elaborate scheme to claim tax refunds owed to low income renters through the state's homestead property tax program. Using thousands of identities, the defendant and his cohorts were detected by alert U.S. Postal carriers who were suspicious of the large number of Treasury checks mailed to certain addresses.

During the last several years, federal and state agencies have aggressively enforced the laws that prohibit the theft of identities. All 50 states and the District of Columbia have some form of legislation that prohibits identity theft, and in all those jurisdictions, except Maine, identity theft can be a felony. See Volume II, Part H, for a description of state criminal law enforcement efforts. In the federal system, a wide range of statutory provisions is used to investigate and prosecute identity theft including, most notably, the aggravated identity theft statute [75] enacted in 2004, which carries a mandatory two-year prison sentence. Since then, DOJ has made increasing use of the aggravated identity theft statute: in Fiscal Year 2006, DOJ charged 507 defendants with aggravated identity theft, up from 226 defendants charged with aggravated identity theft in Fiscal Year 2005. In many of these cases, the courts have imposed substantial sentences. See Volume II, Part I, for a description of sentencing in federal identity theft prosecutions.

The Department of Justice also has initiated many special identity theft initiatives in recent years. The first of these, in May 2002, involved 73 criminal prosecutions by U.S. Attorney's Offices against 135 individuals in 24 federal districts. Since then, identity theft has played an integral part in several initiatives that DOJ and other agencies have directed at online economic crime. For example, "Operation Cyber Sweep," a November 2003 initiative targeting Internet-related economic crime, resulted in the arrest or conviction of more than 125 individuals and the return of indictments against more than 70 people involved in various types of Internet-related fraud and economic crime. See Volume II, Part J, for a description of special enforcement and prosecution initiatives.

> In a "Operation Firewall," the Secret Service was responsible for the first-ever takedown of a large illegal online bazaar. Using the website www.shadowcrew. com, the Shadowcrew organization had thousands of members engaged in the online trafficking of stolen identity information and documents, such as drivers' licenses, passports, and Social Security cards, as well as stolen credit card, debit card, and bank account numbers. The Shadowcrew members trafficked in at least 1.7 million stolen credit card numbers and caused total losses in excess of $4 million. The Secret
>
> Service successfully shut down the website following a year-long undercover investigation, which resulted in the arrests of 21 individuals in the United States on criminal charges in October 2004. Additionally, law enforcement officers in six foreign countries arrested or searched eight individuals.

1. Coordination and Intelligence/Information Sharing

Federal law enforcement agencies have recognized the importance of coordination among agencies and of information sharing between law enforcement and the private sector. Coordination has been challenging, however, for several reasons: identity theft data currently reside in numerous databases; there is no standard reporting form for all identity theft complaints; and many law enforcement agencies have limited resources. Given these challenges, law enforcement has responded to the need for greater cooperation by, among other things, forming interagency task forces and developing formal intelligence-sharing mechanisms. Law enforcement also has worked to develop methods of facilitating the timely receipt and analysis of identity theft complaint data and other intelligence.

A. Sources of Identity Theft Information

Currently, federal law enforcement has a number of sources of information about identity theft. The primary source of direct consumer complaint data is the FTC, which, through its Identity Theft Clearinghouse, makes available to law enforcement through a secure web site the complaints it receives. Internet-related identity theft complaints also are received by the Internet Crime Complaint Center (IC3), a joint venture of the FBI and National White Collar Crime Center. The IC3 develops case leads from the complaints it receives and sends them to law enforcement throughout the country. Additionally, a special component of the FBI that works closely with the IC3 is the Cyber Initiative and Resource Fusion Unit (CIRFU). The CIRFU, based in Pittsburgh, facilitates the operation of the National Cyber Forensic Training Alliance (NCFTA), a public/private alliance and fusion center, by maximizing intelligence development and analytical resources from law enforcement and critical industry partners. The U.S. Postal Inspection Service also hosts its Financial Crimes Database, a web-based national database available to U.S. Postal Service inspectors for use in analyzing mail theft and identity theft complaints received from various sources. These are but a few of the sources of identity theft data for law enforcement. See Volume II, Part K, for a description of how law enforcement obtains and analyzes identity theft data.

Private sector entities—including the financial services industry and credit reporting agencies—also are important sources of identity theft information for law enforcement agencies. They often are best positioned to identify early anomalies in various components of the e-commerce environment in which their businesses interact, which may represent the earliest indicators of an identity theft scenario. For this reason and others, federal law enforcement has undertaken numerous public- and private- sector collaborations in recent years to improve information sharing.

For example, corporations have placed analysts and investigators with IC3 in support of initiatives and investigations. In addition, ITAC, the cooperative initiative of the financial services industry, shares information with law enforcement and the FTC to help catch and convict the criminals responsible for identity theft. See Volume II, Part K, for a description of other private sector sources of identity theft data. Such alliances enable critical industry experts and law enforcement agencies to work together to more expeditiously receive and process information and intelligence vital both to early identification of identity theft schemes and rapid development of aggressive investigations and mitigation strategies, such as public service advisories. At the same time, however, law enforcement agencies report that they have encountered obstacles in obtaining support and assistance from key private-sector stakeholders in some cases, absent legal process, such as subpoenas, to obtain information.

One barrier to more complete coordination is that identity theft information resides in multiple databases, even within individual law enforcement agencies. A single instance of identity theft may result in information being posted at federal, state, and local law enforcement agencies, credit reporting agencies, credit issuers, financial institutions, telecommunications companies, and regulatory agencies. This, in turn, leads to the inefficient "stove-piping" of relevant data and intelligence. Additionally, in many cases, agencies do not or cannot share information with other agencies, making it difficult to determine whether an identity theft complaint is related to a single incident or a series of incidents. This problem may be even more pronounced at the state and local levels.

B. Format for Sharing Information and Intelligence

A related issue is the inability of the primary law enforcement agencies to communicate electronically using a standard format, which greatly impedes the sharing of criminal law enforcement information. When data collection systems use different formats to describe the same event or fact, at least one of the systems must be reprogrammed to fit the other program's terms. Where several hundred variables are involved, the programming resources required to connect the two databases can be an insurmountable barrier to data exchange.

To address that concern, several law enforcement organizations, including the International Association of Chiefs of Police's (IACP) Private Sector Liaison Committee and the Major Cities' Chiefs (MCC), have recommended developing a standard electronic identity theft police report form. Reports that use a standard format could be shared among law enforcement agencies and stored in a national repository for investigatory purposes.

C. Mechanisms for Sharing Information

Law enforcement uses a variety of mechanisms to facilitate information sharing and intelligence analysis in identity-theft investigations. See Volume II, Part L, for a description of federal law enforcement outreach efforts. As just one example, the Regional Information Sharing Systems (RISS) Program is a long-standing, federally-funded program to support regional law enforcement efforts to combat identity theft and other crimes. Within that program, law enforcement has established intelligence- sharing systems. These include, for example, the Regional Identity Theft Network (RITNET), created to provide Internet-accessible identity theft information for federal, state, and local law enforcement agencies within the Eastern District of Pennsylvania. RITNET is designed to include data from the FTC, law enforcement agencies, and the banking industry, and allow investigators to connect crimes committed in various jurisdictions and link investigators. It also will collect information on all reported frauds, regardless of size, thereby eliminating the advantage identity thieves have in keeping theft amounts low.

Multi-agency working groups and task forces are another successful investigative approach, allowing different agencies to marshal resources, share intelligence, and coordinate activities. Federal authorities lead or co- lead over 90 task forces and working groups devoted (in whole or in part) to identity theft. See Volume II, Part M, for a description of interagency working groups and task forces.

Despite these efforts, coordination among agencies can be improved. Better coordination would help law enforcement officers "connect the dots" in investigations and pool limited resources.

RECOMMENDATION: ESTABLISH A NATIONAL IDENTITY THEFT LAW ENFORCEMENT CENTER

The Task Force recommends that the federal government establish, as resources permit, an interagency National Identity Theft Law Enforcement Center to better consolidate, analyze, and share identity theft information among law enforcement agencies, regulatory agencies, and the private sector. This effort should be led by the Department of Justice and include representatives of federal law enforcement agencies, including the FBI, the Secret Service, the U.S. Postal Inspection Service, the SSA OIG, and the FTC. Leveraging existing resources, increased emphasis should be placed on the analysis of identity theft complaint data and other information and intelligence related to identity theft from public and private sources, including from identity theft investigations. This information should be made available to appropriate law enforcement at all levels to

aid in the investigation, prosecution, and prevention of identity theft crimes, including to target organized groups of identity thieves and the most serious offenders operating both in the United States and abroad. Effective mechanisms that enable law enforcement officers from around the country to share, access, and search appropriate law enforcement information aroundthe-clock, including through remote access, should also be developed. As an example, intelligence from documents seized during investigations could help facilitate the ability of agents and officers to "connect the dots" between various investigations around the country.

> In a case prosecuted by the United States Attorney's Office for the Eastern District of Pennsylvania, a gang purchased 180 properties using false or stolen names. The thieves colluded to procure inflated appraisals for the properties, obtained financing, and drained the excess profits for their own benefit, resulting in harm to the identity theft victims and to the neighborhood when most of the properties went into foreclosure.

Recommendation: Develop and Promote the Acceptance of a Universal Identity Theft Report Form

The Task Force recommended in its interim recommendations that the federal government, led by the FTC, develop and promote a universal police report like that recommended by the IACP and MCC—a standard document that an identity theft victim could complete, print, and take to any local law enforcement agency for verification and incorporation into the police department's report system. This would make it easier for victims to obtain these reports, facilitate entry of the information into a central database that could be used by law enforcement to analyze patterns and trends, and initiate more investigations of identity theft.

Criminal law enforcers, the FTC, and representatives of financial institutions, the consumer data industry, and consumer advocacy groups have worked together to develop a standard form that meets this need and captures essential information. The resulting Identity Theft Complaint ("Complaint") form was made available in October 2006 via the FTC's Identity Theft website, www.ftc.gov/idtheft. Consumers can print copies of their completed Complaint and take it to their police station, where it can be used as the basis for a police report. The Complaint provides much greater specificity about the details of the crime than would a typical police report, so consumers will be able to submit it to credit reporting agencies and creditors to assist in resolving their identity theft-related problems. Further, the information they enter into the Complaint will be collected in the FTC's Identity Theft Data

Clearinghouse, thus enriching this source of consumer complaints for law enforcement. This system also relieves the burden on local law enforcement because consumers are completing the detailed Complaint before filing their police report.

RECOMMENDATION: ENHANCE INFORMATION SHARING BETWEEN LAW ENFORCEMENT AND THE PRIVATE SECTOR

Because the private sector in general, and financial institutions in particular, are an important source of identity theft-related information for law enforcement, the Task Force recommends the following steps to enhance information sharing between law enforcement and the private sector:

- *Enhance Ability of Law Enforcement to receive Information From Financial Institutions.* Section 609(e) of the Fair Credit Reporting Act enables identity theft victims to receive identity theft-related documents and to designate law enforcement agencies to receive the documents on their behalf. Despite that fact, law enforcement agencies have sometimes encountered difficulties in obtaining such information without a subpoena. By the second quarter of 2007, DOJ should initiate discussions with the financial sector to ensure greater compliance with this law, and should include other law enforcement agencies in these discussions. DOJ, on an ongoing basis, should compile any recommendations that may result from those discussions and, where appropriate, relay those recommendations to the appropriate private or public sector entity for action.
- *Initiate Discussions With the Financial Services Industry on Countermeasures to Identity Thieves.* Federal law enforcement agencies, led by the U.S. Postal Inspection Service, should continue discussions with the financial services industry as early as the second quarter of 2007 to develop more effective fraud prevention measures to deter identity thieves who acquire data through mail theft. Discussions should include use of the Postal Inspection Service's current Financial Industry Mail Security Initiative. The Postal Inspection Service, on an ongoing basis, should compile any recommendations that may result from those discussions and, where appropriate, relay those recommendations to the appropriate private or public sector entity for action.
- *Initiate Discussions With Credit reporting Agencies On Preventing Identity Theft.* By the second quarter of 2007, DOJ should initiate discussions with the credit reporting agencies on possible measures that would make it more difficult for identity thieves to obtain credit based on access to a victim's credit report. The discussions should include other law enforcement agencies, including the FTC. DOJ, on an ongoing basis, should compile any recommendations that may result from the discussions and, where appropriate, relay the recommendations to the appropriate private or public sector entity for action.

V. Coordination with Foreign Law Enforcement

Federal enforcement agencies have found that a significant portion of the identity theft committed in the United States originates in other countries. Therefore, coordination and cooperation with foreign law enforcement is essential. A positive step by the United States in ensuringsuch coordination was the ratification of the Convention on Cybercrime (2001). The Cybercrime Convention is the first multilateral instrument drafted to address the problems posed by the spread of criminal activity on computer networks, including offenses that relate to the stealing of personal information and the exploitation of that information to commit fraud. The Cybercrime Convention requires parties to establish laws against these offenses, to ensure that domestic laws give law enforcement officials the necessary legal authority to gather electronic evidence, and to provide international cooperation to other parties in the fight against computer-related crime. The United States participated in the drafting of the Convention and, in November 2001, was an early signatory.

Because of the international nature of many forms of identity theft, providing assistance to, and receiving assistance from, foreign law enforcement on identity theft is critical for U.S. enforcement agencies. Under current law, the United States generally is able to provide such assistance, which fulfills our obligations under various treaties and enhances our ability to obtain reciprocal assistance from foreign agencies. Indeed, there are numerous examples of collaborations between U.S. and foreign law enforcement in identity theft investigations.

> The FBI Legal Attache in Bucharest recently contributed to the development and launch of www.efrauda.ro, a Romanian government website for the collection of fraud complaints based on the IC3 model. The IC3 also provided this Legal Attache with complaints received by U.S. victims who were targets of a Romanian Internet crime ring. The complaint forms provided to Romanian authorities via the Legal Attache assisted the Romanian police and Ministry of Justice with the prosecution of Romanian subjects.

Nevertheless, law enforcement faces several impediments in their ability to coordinate efforts with foreign counterparts. First, even though federal law enforcement agencies have successfully identified numerous foreign suspects trafficking in stolen consumer information, their ability to arrest and prosecute these criminals is very limited. Many countries do not have laws directly addressing identity theft, or have general fraud laws that do not parallel those in the United States. Thus, investigators in the United States may be able to prove violations of American identity theft statutes, yet be unable to show violations of the foreign country's law. This can impact cooperation on extradition or collection of evidence necessary to prosecute offenders in the United States. Additionally, some foreign governments are unwilling to cooperate fully with American law enforcement representatives, or may cooperate but fail to aggressively prosecute offenders or seize criminal assets.

Second, certain statutes governing foreign requests for electronic and other evidence—specifically, 18 U.S.C. § 2703 and 28 U.S.C. § 1782—fail to make clear whether, how, and in which court certain requests can be fulfilled. This jurisdictional uncertainty has impeded the ability of American law enforcement officers to assist their counterparts in other countries who are conducting identity theft investigations.

Recommendation: Encourage other Countries to Enact Suitable Domestic Legislation Criminalizing Identity Theft

The Department of Justice, after consulting with the Department of State, should formally encourage other countries to enact suitable domestic legislation criminalizing identity theft. A number of countries already have adopted, or are considering adopting, criminal identity-theft offenses. In addition, since 2005, the United Nations Crime Commission (UNCC) has convened an international Expert Group to examine the worldwide problem of fraud and identity theft. That Expert Group is drafting a report to the UNCC (for presentation in 2007) that is expected to describe the major trends in fraud and identity theft in numerous countries and to offer recommendations on best practices by governments and the private sector to combat fraud and identity theft. DOJ should provide input to the Expert Group concerning the need for the criminalization of identity theft worldwide.

Recommendation: Facilitate Investigation and Prosecution of International Identity Theft by Encouraging Other Nations to Accede to the Convention on Cybercrime, or to Ensure That Their Laws and Procedures Tre at Least as Comprehensive

Global acceptance of the Convention on Cybercrime will help to assure that all countries have the legal authority to collect electronic evidence and the ability to cooperate in trans-border identity theft investigations that involve electronic data. The U.S. government should continue its efforts to promote universal accession to the Convention and assist other countries in bringing their laws into compliance with the Convention's standards. The Department of State, in close coordination with the Department of Justice and Department of Homeland Security, should lead this effort through appropriate bilateral and multilateral outreach mechanisms. Other agencies, including the Department of Commerce and the FTC, should participate in these outreach efforts as appropriate. This outreach effort began years ago in a number of international settings, and should continue until broad international acceptance of the Convention on Cybercrime is achieved.

Recommendation: Identify Countries That Have Become Safe Havens for Perpetrators of Identity Theft and Target Them for Diplomatic and Enforcement Initiatives Formulated to Change Their Practices

Safe havens for perpetrators of identity theft and individuals who aid and abet such illegal activities should not exist. However, the inaction of law enforcement agencies in some countries has turned those countries into breeding grounds for sophisticated criminal networks devoted to identity theft. Countries that tolerate the existence of such criminal networks encourage their growth and embolden perpetrators to expand their operations. In 2007, the U.S. law enforcement community, with input from the international law enforcement community, should identify the countries that are safe havens for identity thieves. Once identified, the U.S. government should use appropriate diplomatic measures and any suitable enforcement mechanisms to encourage those countries to change their practices.

RECOMMENDATION: ENHANCE THE U.S. GOVERNMENT'S ABILITY TO RESPONDTO APPROPRIATE FOREIGN REQUESTS FOR EVIDENCE IN CRIMINAL CASES INVOLVING IDENTITY THEFT

The Task Force recommends that Congress clarify which courts can respond to appropriate foreign requests for electronic and other evidence in criminal investigations, so that the United States can better provide prompt assistance to foreign law enforcement in identity theft cases. This clarification can be accomplished by amending 18 U. S.C. § 2703 and making accompanying amendments to 18 U.S.C. §§ 2711 and 3127, and by enacting a new statute, 18 U.S.C. § 3512, which would supplement the foreign assistance authority of 28 U.S.C. § 1782. Proposed language for these legislative changes is available in Appendix D (text of amendments to 18 U.S.C. §§ 2703, 2711, and 3127, and text of new language for 18 U.S.C. § 3512).

RECOMMENDATION: ASSIST, TRAIN, AND SUPPORT FOREIGN LAW ENFORCEMEN

Because the investigation of major identity theft rings increasingly will require foreign cooperation, federal law enforcement agencies, led by DOJ, FBI, Secret Service, USPIS, and ICE, should assist, train, and support foreign law enforcement through the use of Internet intelligence-collection entities, including IC3 and CIRFU, and continue to make it a priority to work with other countries in joint investigations targeting identity theft. This work should begin in the third quarter of 2007.

A. PROSECUTION APPROACHES AND INITIATIVES

As part of its effort to prosecute identity theft aggressively, DOJ, since 2002, has conducted a number of enforcement initiatives that have focused, in whole or in part, on identity theft. In addition to broader enforcement initiatives led by DOJ, various individual U.S. Attorney's Offices have undertaken their own identity theft efforts. For example, the U.S. Attorney's Office in the District of Oregon has an identity theft "fast track" program that requires eligible defendants to plead guilty to aggravated identity theft and agree, without litigation, to a 24-month minimum mandatory sentence. Under this program, it is contemplated that defendants will plead guilty and be sentenced on the same day, without the need for a pre-sentence report to be completed prior to the guilty plea, and waive all appellate and post-conviction remedies. In exchange for their pleas of guilty, defendants are not charged with the predicate offense, such as bank fraud or mail theft, which would otherwise result in a consecutive sentence under the United States Sentencing Guidelines. In addition, two U.S. Attorney's Offices have collaborated on a special initiative to combat passport fraud, known as Operation Checkmate. See Volume II, Part J.

Notwithstanding these efforts, challenges remain for federal law enforcement. Because of limited resources and a shortage of prosecutors, many U.S. Attorney's Offices have monetary thresholds—i.e., requirements that a certain amount of monetary loss must have been suffered by the victims—before the U.S. Attorney's Office will open an identity theft case. When a U.S. Attorney's Office declines to open a case based on a monetary threshold, investigative agents cannot obtain additional information through grand jury subpoenas that could help to uncover more substantial monetary losses to the victims.

RECOMMENDATION: INCREASE PROSECUTIONS OF IDENTITY THEFT

The Task Force recommends that, to further increase the number of prosecutions of identity thieves, the following steps should be taken:

- *Designate An Identity Theft* Coordinator for Each united States Attorney's Office To Design a Specific Identity Theft Program for Each District. DOJ should direct that each U.S. Attorney's Office, by June 2007, designate one Assistant U.S. Attorney who should serve as a point of contact and source of expertise within that office for other prosecutors and agents. That Assistant U.S. Attorney also should assist each U.S. Attorney in making a district-specific determination about the areas on which to focus to best address the problem of identity theft. For example, in some southwest border districts, identity theft may be best addressed by stepping up efforts to prosecute immigration fraud. In other districts, identity theft may be best addressed by increasing prosecutions of bank fraud schemes or by making an effort to add identity theft violations to the charges that are brought against those who commit wire/mail/bank fraud schemes through the misappropriation of identities.
- *Evaluate Monetary Thresholds for Prosecution.* By June 2007, the investigative agencies and U.S. Attorney's Offices should re-evaluate current monetary thresholds for initiating identity theft cases and, specifically, should consider whether monetary thresholds for accepting such cases for prosecution should be lowered in light of the fact that investigations often reveal additional loss and additional victims, that monetary loss may not always adequately reflect the harm suffered, and that the aggravated identity theft statute makes it possible for the government to obtain significant sentences even in cases where precisely calculating the monetary loss is difficult or impossible.
- *Encourage State Prosecution of Identity Theft.* DOJ should explore ways to increase resources and training for local investigators and prosecutors handling identity theft cases. Moreover, each U.S. Attorney, by June 2007, should engage in discussions

with state and local prosecutors in his or her district to encourage those prosecutors to accept cases that do not meet appropriately-set thresholds for federal prosecution, with the understanding that these cases need not always be brought as identity theft cases.

- *Create Working Groups and Task Forces.* By the end of 2007, U.S. Attorneys and investigative agencies should create or make increased use of interagency working groups and task forces devoted to identity theft. Where funds for a task force are unavailable, consideration should be given to forming working groups with non-dedicated personnel.

Recommendation: Conduct Targeted Enforcement Initiatives

Law enforcement agencies should continue to conduct enforcement initiatives that focus exclusively or primarily on identity theft. The initiatives should pursue the following:

- Unfair or Deceptive Means to Make SSNs Available for Sale. Beginning immediately, law enforcement should more aggressively target the community of businesses on the Internet that sell individuals' SSNs or other sensitive information to anyone who provides them with the individual's name and other limited information. The SSA OIG and other agencies also should continue or initiate investigations of entities that use unlawful means to make SSNs and other sensitive personal information available for sale.
- Identity Theft Related to the Health Care System. HHS should continue to investigate identity theft related to Medicare fraud. As part of this effort, HHS should begin to work with state authorities immediately to provide for stronger state licensure and certification of providers, practitioners, and suppliers. Schemes to defraud Medicare may involve the theft of beneficiaries' and providers' identities and identification numbers, the opening of bank accounts in individuals' names, and the submission of fraudulent Medicare claims. Medicare payment is linked to state licensure and certification of providers, practitioners, and suppliers as business entities. Lack of state licensure and certification laws and/or laws that do not require identification and location information of owners and officers of providers, practitioners and suppliers, can hamper the ability of HHS to stop identity theft related to fraudulent billing of the Medicare program.
- Identity Theft By Illegal Aliens. Law enforcement agencies, particularly the Department of Homeland Security, should conduct targeted enforcement initiatives directed at illegal aliens who use stolen identities to enter or stay in the United States.

RECOMMENDATION: REVIEW CIVIL MONETARY PENALTY PROGRAMS

By the fourth quarter of 2007, federal agencies, including the SEC, the federal bank regulatory agencies, and the Department of Treasury, should review their civil monetary penalty programs to assess whether they adequately address identity theft. If they do not, analysis should be done as to what, if any, remedies, including legislation, would be appropriate, and any such legislation should be proposed by the first quarter of 2008. If a federal agency does not have a civil monetary penalty program, the establishment of such a program with respect to identity theft should be considered.

VI. STATUTES CRIMINALIZING IDENTITY-THEFT RELATED OFFENSES: THE GAPS

Federal law enforcement has successfully investigated and prosecuted identity theft under a variety of criminal statutes. Effective prosecution can be hindered in some cases, however, as a result of certain gaps in those statutes. At the same time, a gap in one aspect of the U.S. Sentencing Guidelines has precluded some courts from enhancing the sentences for some identity thieves whose conduct affected multiple victims. See Volume II, Part N, for an additional description of federal criminal statutes used to prosecute identity theft.

A. THE IDENTITY THEFT STATUTES

The two federal statutes that directly criminalize identity theft are the identity theft statute (18 U.S.C. § 1028(a)(7)) and the aggravated identity theft statute (18 U.S.C. § 1028A(a)). The identity theft statute generally prohibits the possession or use of a means of identification of a person in connection with any unlawful activity that either constitutes a violation of federal law or that constitutes a felony under state or local law.76 Similarly, the aggravated identity theft statute generally prohibits the possession or use of a means of identification of another person during the commission of, or in relation to, any of several enumerated federal felonies, and provides for enhanced penalties in those situations.

There are two gaps in these statutes, however. First, because both statutes are limited to the illegal use of a means of identification of "a person," it is unclear whether the government can prosecute an identity thief who misuses the means of identification of a corporation or organization, such as the name, logo, trademark, or employer identification number of a legitimate business. This gap means that federal prosecutors cannot use those statutes to charge identity thieves who, for example, create and use counterfeit documents or checks in the name of a corporation, or who engage in phishing schemes that use an organization's name. Second, the enumerated felonies in the aggravated identity theft statute do not include certain crimes that recur in identity theft and fraud cases, such as mail theft, uttering counterfeit securities, tax fraud, and conspiracy to commit certain offenses.

B. Computer-Related Identity Theft Statutes

Two of the federal statutes that apply to computer-related identity theft have similar limitations that preclude their use in certain important circumstances. First, 18 U.S.C. § 1030(a)(2) criminalizes the theft of information from a computer. However, federal courts only have jurisdiction if the thief uses an interstate communication to access the computer (unless the computer belongs to the federal government or a financial institution). As a result, the theft of personal information either by a corporate insider using the company's internal local networks, or by a thief intruding into a wireless network, generally would not involve an interstate communication and could not be prosecuted under this statute. In one case in North Carolina, for instance, an individual broke into a hospital computer's wireless network and thereby obtained patient information. State investigators and the victim asked the United States Attorney's Office to support the investigation and charge the criminal. Because the communications occurred wholly intrastate, however, no federal law criminalized the conduct.

A second limitation is found in 18 U. S.C. § 1030(a)(5), which criminalizes actions that cause "damage" to computers, i.e., that impair the "integrity or availability" of data or computer systems.[77] Absent special circumstances, the loss caused by the criminal conduct must exceed $5,000 to constitute a federal crime. Many identity thieves obtain personal information by installing malicious spyware, such as keyloggers, on many individuals' computers. Whether the programs succeed in obtaining the unsuspecting computer owner's financial data, these sorts of programs harm the "integrity" of the computer and data. Nevertheless, it is often difficult or impossible to measure the loss this damage causes to each computer owner, or to prove that the total value of these many small losses exceeds $5,000.

C. Cyber-Extortion Statute

Another federal criminal statute that may apply in some computer-related identity theft cases is the "cyber-extortion" provision of the Computer Fraud and Abuse Act, 18 U.S.C. § 1030(a)(7). This provision, which prohibits the transmission of a threat "to cause damage to a protected computer,"[78] is used to prosecute criminals who threaten to delete data, crash computers, or knock computers off of the Internet using a denial of service attack. Some cyber-criminals extort companies, however, without explicitly threatening to cause damage to computers. Instead, they steal confidential data and then threaten to make it public if their demands are not met. In other cases, the criminal causes the damage first—such as by accessing a corporate computer without authority and encrypting critical data—and then threatens not to correct the problem unless the victim pays. Thus, the requirement in section 1030(a)(7) that the defendant must explicitly "threaten to cause damage" can preclude successful prosecutions for cyber-extortion under this statute under certain circumstances.

D. Sentencing Guidelines Governing Identity Theft

In recent years, the courts have created some uncertainty about the applicability of the "multiple victim enhancement" provision of the U.S. Sentencing Guidelines in identity theft cases. This provision allows courts to increase the sentence for an identity thief who victimizes more than one person. It is unclear, however, whether this sentencing enhancement applies when the victims have not sustained actual monetary loss. For example, in some jurisdictions, when a financial institution indemnifies 20 victims of unauthorized charges to their credit cards, the courts consider the financial institution to be the only victim. In such cases, the identity thief therefore may not be penalized for having engaged in conduct that harmed 20 people, simply because those 20 people were later indemnified. This interpretation of the Sentencing Guidelines conflicts with a primary purpose of the Identity Theft and Assumption Deterrence Act of 1998: to vindicate the interests of individual identity theft victims.[79]

Recommendation: Close the Gaps in Federal Criminal Statutes Used to Prosecute Identity-Theft Related Offenses to Ensure Increased Federal Prosecution of These Crimes

The Task Force recommends that Congress take the following legislative actions:

- Amend the Identity Theft and Aggravated Identity Theft Statutes to Ensure That Identity Thieves Who Misappropriate Information Belonging to Corporations and Organizations Can Be Prosecuted. Proposed amendments to 18 U.S.C. §§ 1028 and 1028A are available in Appendix E.
- Add Several New Crimes to the List of Predicate Offenses for Aggravated Identity Theft Offenses. The aggravated identity theft statute, 18 U. S.C. § 1028A, should include other federal offenses that recur in various identity-theft and fraud cases—mail theft, uttering counterfeit securities, and tax fraud, as well as conspiracy to commit specified felonies already listed in 18 U.S.C. § 1028A—in the statutory list of predicate offenses for that offense. Proposed additions to 18 U.S.C. § 1028A are contained in Appendix E.
- Amend the Statute That Criminalizes the Theft of Electronic Data By Eliminating the Current Requirement That the Information Must Have Been Stolen Through Interstate Communications. The proposed amendment to 18 U.S.C. § 1030(a)(2) is available in Appendix F.
- Penalize Malicious Spyware and Keyloggers. The statutory provisions in 18 U.S.C. § 1030(a)(5) should be amended to penalize appropriately the use of malicious spyware and keyloggers, by eliminating the current requirement that the defendant's action must cause "damage" to computers and that the loss caused by the conduct must exceed $5,000. Proposed amendments to 18 U.S.C. §§ 1030(a)(5), (c), and (g), and the accompanying amendment to 18 U. S.C. § 2332b(g), are included in Appendix G.

- Amend the Cyber-Extortion Statute to Cover Additional, Alternate Types of Cyber-Extortion. The proposed amendment to 18 U.S.C. § 1030(a)(7) is available in Appendix H.

Recommendation: Ensure That an Identity Thief's Sentence Can be Enhanced When the Criminal Conduct Affects More Than One Victim

The Sentencing Commission should amend the definition of "victim," as that term is used under United States Sentencing Guideline section 2B 1.1, to state clearly that a victim need not have sustained an actual monetary loss. This amendment will ensure that courts can enhance the sentences imposed on identity thieves who cause harm to multiple victims, even when that harm does not result in any monetary loss to the victims. The proposed amendment to United States Sentencing Guideline section 2B 1.1 is available in Appendix I.

VII. Training of Law Enforcement Officers and Prosecutors

Training can be the key to effective investigations and prosecutions, and much has been done in recent years to ensure that investigators and prosecutors have been trained on topics relating to identity theft. In addition to ongoing training by U.S. Attorney's Offices, for example, several federal law enforcement agencies—including DOJ, the Postal Inspection Service, the Secret Service, the FTC, and the FBI—along with the American Association of Motor Vehicle Administrators (AAMVA) have sponsored jointly over 20 regional, one-day training seminars on identity fraud for state and local law enforcement agencies across the country. See Volume II, Part O, for a description of training by and for investigators and prosecutors.

Nonetheless, the amount, focus, and coordination of law enforcement training should be expanded. Identity theft investigations and prosecutions involve particular challenges—including the need to coordinate with foreign authorities, some difficulties with the application of the Sentencing Guidelines, and the challenges that arise from the inevitable gap in time between the commission of the identity theft and the reporting of the identity theft—that warrant more specialized training at all levels of law enforcement.

Recommendation: Enhance Training for Law Enforcement Officers and Prosecutors

- Develop Course at National Advocacy Center (NAC) Focused Solely on Investigation and Prosecution of Identity Theft. By the third quarter of 2007, DOJ's Office of Legal Education should complete the development of a course specifically focused on identity theft for prosecutors. The identity theft course should include, among other things: a review of the scope of the problem; a review of applicable statutes, forfeiture and sentencing guideline applications; an outline of investigative and case presentation techniques; training on addressing the unique needs of identity theft victims; and a review of programs for better utilizing collective resources (working groups, task forces, and any "model programs"— fast track programs, etc.).

- Increase Number of Regional Identity Theft Seminars. In 2006, the federal agencies and the AAMVA held a number of regional identity theft seminars for state and local law enforcement officers. In 2007, the number of seminars should be increased. Additionally, the participating entities should coordinate with the Task Force to provide the most complete, targeted, and up-to-date training materials.
- Increase Resources for Law Enforcement Available on the Internet. The identity theft clearinghouse site, www.idtheft.gov, should be used as the portal for law enforcement agencies to gain access to additional educational materials on investigating identity theft and responding to victims.
- Review Curricula to Enhance Basic and Advanced Training on Identity Theft. By the fourth quarter of 2007, federal investigative agencies should review their own training curricula, and curricula of the Federal Law Enforcement Training Center, to ensure that they are providing the most useful training on identity theft.

A. Measuring Success of Law Enforcement Efforts

One shortcoming in the federal government's ability to understand and respond effectively to identity theft is the lack of comprehensive statistical data about the success of law enforcement efforts to combat identity theft. Specifically, there are few benchmarks that measure the activities of the various components of the criminal justice system in their response to identity thefts occurring within their jurisdictions, little data on state and local enforcement, and little information on how identity theft incidents are being processed in state courts.

Addressing these questions requires benchmarks and periodic data collection. The Bureau of Justice Statistics (BJS) has platforms in place, as well as the tools to create new platforms, to obtain information about identity theft from victims and the response to identity theft from law enforcement agencies, state and federal prosecutors, and courts.

Recommendation: Enhance the Gathering of Statistical Data Measuring the Criminal Justice System's Response to Identity Theft

- Gather and Analyze Statistically Reliable Data from Identity Theft Victims. The BJS and FTC should continue to gather and analyze statistically reliable data from identity theft victims. The BJS should conduct its surveys in collaboration with subject matter experts from the FTC. BJS should add additional questions on identity theft to the household portion of its National Crime Victimization Survey (NCVS), and conduct periodic supplements to gather more in-depth information. The FTC should conduct a general identity theft survey approximately every three years, independently or in conjunction with BJS or other government agencies. The FTC also should conduct surveys focused more narrowly on issues related to the effectiveness of and compliance with the identity theft-related provisions of the consumer protection laws it enforces.

- Expand Scope of National Crime Victimization Survey (NCVS). The scope of the annual NCVS should be expanded to collect information about the characteristics, consequences, and extent of identity theft for individuals ages 12 and older. Currently, information on identity theft is collected only from the household respondent and does not capture data on multiple victims in the household or multiple episodes of identity theft.
- review of Sentencing Commission Data. DOJ and the FTC should systematically review and analyze U.S. Sentencing Commission identity theft-related case files every two to four years, and should begin in the third quarter of 2007.
- Track Prosecutions of Identity Theft and the Amount of resources Spent. In order to better track resources spent on identity theft cases, DOJ should, by the second quarter of 2007, create an "Identity Theft" category on the monthly report that is completed by all Assistant United States Attorneys, and should revise its departmental case tracking application to allow for the reporting of offenses by individual subsections of section 1028. Additionally, BJS should incorporate additional questions in the National Survey of Prosecutors to better understand the impact identity theft is having on prosecutorial resources.
- Conduct Targeted Surveys. In order to expand law enforcement knowledge of the identity theft response and prevention activities of state and local police, BJS should undertake new data collections in specified areas. Proposed details of those surveys are included in Appendix J.

VIII. Conclusion: The Way Forward

There is no magic bullet that will eradicate identity theft. To successfully combat identity theft and its effects, we must keep personal information out of the hands of thieves; take steps to prevent an identity thief from misusing any data that may end up in his hands; prosecute him vigorously if he succeeds in committing the crime; and do all we can to help the victims recover.

Only a comprehensive and fully coordinated strategy to combat identity theft—one that encompasses effective prevention, public awareness and education, victim assistance, and law enforcement measures, and that fully engages federal, state, and local authorities and the private sector—will have any chance of solving the problem. This proposed strategic plan strives to set out such a comprehensive approach to combating identity theft, but it is only the beginning. Each of the stakeholders—consumers, business and government—must fully and actively participate in this fight for us to succeed, and must stay attuned to emerging trends in order to adapt and respond to developing threats to consumer well being.

APPENDICES

Appendix A

Identity Theft Task Force's Guidance Memorandum on Data Breach Protocol

September 19, 2006

MEMORANDUM FROM THE IDENTITY THEFT TASK FORCE

Chair, Attorney General Alberto R. Gonzales
Co-Chair, Federal Trade Commission Chairman Deborah Platt Majoras

SUBJECT: Identity Theft Related Data Security Breach Notification Guidance

The Identity Theft Task Force ("Task Force") has considered the steps that a Department or agency should take in responding to a theft, loss, or unauthorized acquisition of personal information that poses a risk of subsequent identity theft. This memorandum reports the Task Force's recommended approach to such situations, without addressing other notification issues that may arise under the Privacy Act or other federal statutes when the data loss involves sensitive information that does not pose an identity theft risk.

I. Background

Identity theft, a pernicious crime that harms consumers and our economy, occurs when individuals' identifying information is used without authorization in an attempt to commit fraud or other crimes.[1] There are two primary forms of identity theft. First, identity thieves can use financial account identifiers, such as credit card or bank account numbers, to commandeer an individual's existing accounts to make unauthorized charges or withdraw money. Second, thieves can use accepted identifiers like social security numbers ("SSNs") to open new financial accounts and incur charges and credit in an individual's name, but without that person's knowledge.

This memorandum describes three related recommendations: (1) Agencies should immediately identify a core response group that can be convened in the event of a breach; (2) If an incident occurs, the core response group should engage in a risk analysis to determine whether the incident poses problems related to identity theft; (3) If it is determined that an identity theft risk is present, the agency should tailor its response (which may include advice to those potentially affected, services the agency may provide to those affected, and public notice) to the nature and scope of the risk presented. The memorandum provides a menu of steps for an agency to consider, so that it may pursue such a risk-based, tailored response. Ultimately, the precise steps to take must be decided in light of the particular facts presented, as there is no single response for all breaches. This memorandum is intended simply to assist those confronting such issues in developing an appropriate response.

---

[1]Federal laws define "identifying information" broadly. *See, e.g.*, The 1998 Identity Theft Assumption and Deterrence Act (Pub. L. No. 105-318, 112 Stat. 3007 (1998) (codified at 18 U.S.C. § 1028)) and the Fair and Accurate Credit Transactions Act (15 U.S.C. §§ 1681-1681x, as amended). This memorandum focuses on the type of identifying information generally used to commit identity theft.

II. Data Breach Planning

Given the volume of personal information appropriately collected to carry out myriad government functions, it is almost inevitable that some agencies will, on occasion, lose control of such information. Thus, an important first step in responding to a breach is for agencies to engage in advance planning for this contingency. We therefore recommend that each agency identify in advance a core management group that will be convened upon the identification of a potential loss of personal information. This core group would initially evaluate the situation to help guide any further response. Our experience suggests that such a core group should include, at minimum, an agency's chief information officer, chief legal officer, chief privacy officer (or their designees), a senior management official from the agency, and the agency's inspector general (or equivalent or designee). Such a group should ensure that the agency has brought together many of the basic competencies needed to respond, including expertise in information technology, legal authorities, the Privacy Act, and law enforcement. We recommend that this core group convene at least annually to review this memorandum and discuss likely actions should an incident occur.

III. Identifying an Incident That Presents Identity Theft Risk and the Level of Risk Involved

A loss of control over personal information, may, but need not necessarily, present a risk of identity theft. For example, a data report showing the name "John Smith," with little or no further identifying information related to John Smith, presents little or no risk of identity theft. Thus, the first steps in considering whether there is a risk of identity theft, and hence whether an "identity theft response" is necessary, are understanding the kind of information most typically used to commit identity theft and then determining whether that kind of information has been potentially compromised in the incident being examined. Because circumstances will differ from case to case, agencies should draw upon law enforcement expertise, including that of the agency Inspector General, in assessing the risk of identity theft from a data compromise and the likelihood that the incident is the result of or could lead to criminal activity.

An SSN standing alone can generate identity theft. Combinations of information can have the same effect. With a name, address, or telephone number, identity theft becomes possible, for instance, with any of the following: (1) any government-issued identification number (such as a driver's license number if the thief cannot obtain the SSN); (2) a biometric record; (3) a financial account number, together with a PIN or security code, if a PIN or security code is necessary to access the account; or (4) any additional, specific factor that adds to the personally identifying profile of a specific individual, such as a relationship with a specific financial institution or membership in a club. For further purposes of this memorandum, information posing a risk of identity theft will be described as "covered information." If a particular data loss or breach does not involve this type of information, the identity theft risk is minimal, and it is unlikely that further steps designed to address identity theft risks are necessary.[2]

Even where covered information has been compromised, various other factors should be considered in determining whether the information accessed could result in identity theft. Our experience suggests that in determining the level of risk of identity theft, the agency should consider not simply the data that was compromised, but all of the circumstances of the data loss, including

- how easy or difficult it would be for an unauthorized person to access the covered information in light of the manner in which the covered information was protected;[3]
- the means by which the loss occurred, including whether the incident might be the result of a criminal act or is likely to result in criminal activity;[4]
- the ability of the agency to mitigate the identity theft;[5] and
- evidence that the compromised information is actually being used to commit identity theft.

Considering these factors together should permit the agency to develop an overall sense of where

---

[2]OMB has promulgated guidance requiring certain notifications within the government, most notably to the United States Computer Emergency Readiness Team (US-CERT), whenever personal information is compromised, and which applies even where there is no identity theft risk. That reporting guidance remains in full effect.

[3]For example, information on a computer laptop that is adequately protected by encryption is less likely to be accessed, while "hard copies" of printed-out data are essentially unprotected.

[4]For example, as a general matter, the risk of identity theft is greater if the covered information was stolen by a thief who was targeting the data (such as a computer hacker) than if the information was inadvertently left unprotected in a public location, such as in a briefcase in a hotel lobby. Similarly, in some cases of theft, the circumstances might indicate that the data-storage device, such as a computer left in a car, rather than the information itself, was the target of the theft. An opportunistic criminal, of course, may exploit information once it comes into his possession, and this possibility must be considered when fashioning an agency response, along with the recognition that risks vary with the circumstances under which incidents occur. In making this assessment, it is crucial that federal law enforcement (which may include the agency's Inspector General) be consulted.

[5]The ability of an agency or other affected entities to monitor for and prevent attempts to misuse the covered information can be a factor in determining the risk of identity theft. For example, if the compromised information relates to disability beneficiaries, the agency can monitor its beneficiary database for requests for change of address, which may signal attempts to misuse the information, and take steps to prevent the fraud. Likewise, alerting financial institutions in cases of a data breach involving financial account information can allow them to monitor for fraud or close the compromised accounts.

along the continuum of identity-theft risk the risk created by the particular incident falls. That assessment, in turn, should guide the agency's further actions.

IV. Reducing Risk After Disclosure

While assessing the level of risk in a given situation, the agency should simultaneously consider options for attenuating that risk. It is important in this regard for the agency to understand certain standard options available to agencies and individuals to help protect potential victims:

A. Actions that Individuals Can Routinely Take

The steps that individuals can take to protect themselves will depend on the type of information that is compromised. In notifying the potentially affected individuals about steps they can take following a data breach, agencies should focus on the steps that are relevant to those individuals' particular circumstances, which may include the following:

- Contact their financial institution to determine whether their account(s) should be closed. This option is relevant only when financial account information is part of the breach.
- Monitor their financial account statements and immediately report any suspicious or unusual activity to their financial institution.
- Request a free credit report at www.AnnualCreditReport.com or by calling 1-877-322-8228. It might take a few months for most signs of fraudulent accounts to appear on the credit report, and this option is most useful when the data breach involves information that can be used to open new accounts. Consumers are entitled by law to obtain one free credit report per year from each of the three major credit bureaus – Equifax, Experian, and TransUnion – for a total of three reports every year. The annual free credit report can be used by individuals, along with the free report provided when placing a fraud alert (which is discussed below), to self-monitor for identity theft. The annual report also can be used as an alternative for those individuals who want to check their credit report, but do not want to place a fraud alert. Contact information for the credit bureaus should be provided, which can be found on the FTC's website.
- Place an initial fraud alert[6] on credit reports maintained by the three major credit bureaus noted above. This option is most useful when the breach includes information that can be used to open a new account, such as SSNs. After placing an initial fraud alert, individuals are entitled to a free credit report, which they should

[6]A fraud alert is a mechanism that signals to credit issuers who obtain credit reports on a consumer that they must take reasonable steps to verify the consumer's identity before issuing credit, making it harder for identity thieves to secure new credit lines. It should be noted that, although fraud alerts can help prevent fraudulent credit accounts from being opened in an individual's name, they also can delay that individual's own legitimate attempts to secure credit.

-4-

obtain beginning a few months after the breach and review for signs of suspicious activity.

- For residents of states in which state law authorizes a credit freeze, consider placing a credit freeze on their credit file.[7] This option is most useful when the breach includes information that can be used to open a new account, such as SSNs. A credit freeze cuts off third party access to a consumer's credit report, thereby effectively preventing the issuance of new credit in the consumer's name.
- For deployed members of the military, consider placing an active duty alert on their credit file.[8] This option is most useful when the breach includes information that can be used to open a new account, such as SSNs. Such active duty alerts serve a similar function as initial fraud alerts, causing creditors to be more cautious in extending new credit. However, unlike initial fraud alerts, they last for one year instead of 90 days. In addition, active duty alerts do not entitle the individual to a free credit report. Therefore, those placing an active duty alert should combine this option with a request for obtaining the annual free credit reports to which all individuals are entitled.
- Review resources provided on the FTC identity theft website, www.ftc.gov/idtheft. The FTC maintains a variety of consumer publications providing comprehensive information on breaches and identity theft.
- Be aware that the public announcement of the breach could itself cause criminals engaged in fraud, under the guise of providing legitimate assistance, to use various techniques, including email or the telephone, to deceive individuals affected by the breach into disclosing their credit card numbers, bank account information, SSNs, passwords, or other sensitive personal information. One common such technique is "phishing," a scam involving an email that appears to come from a bank or other organization that asks the individual to verify account information, and then directs him to a fake website whose only purpose is to trick the victim into divulging his personal information. Advice on avoiding such frauds is available on the FTC's web site http://www.ftc.gov/bcp/edu/pubs/consumer/alerts/alt166.htm.

---

[7]State laws vary with respect to usability and cost issues, which individuals will need to consider before deciding to place a credit freeze.

[8]A variety of factors may influence a service member's decision to place an active duty alert–for example, if there are stateside family members who need easy credit access, the alert would likely be counterproductive.

-5-

B. Actions that Agencies Can Take

If the breach involves government-authorized credit cards, the agency should notify the issuing bank promptly. If the breach involves individuals' bank account numbers to be used for the direct deposit of credit card reimbursements, government employee salaries, or any benefit payment, the agency should notify the bank or other entity that handles that particular transaction for the agency.

Agencies may take two other significant steps that can offer additional measures of protection – especially for incidents where the compromised information presents a risk of new accounts being opened – but which will involve additional agency expense. First, in recent years, some companies have developed technologies to analyze whether a particular data loss appears to be resulting in identity theft. This data breach analysis may be a useful intermediate protective action, especially where the agency is uncertain about whether the identity-theft risk warrants implementing more costly additional steps such as credit monitoring (see below) or where the risk is such that agencies wish to do more than rely on the individual action(s) identified above.

For two reasons, such technology may be useful for incidents involving data for large numbers of individuals. First, the cost of implementing credit monitoring (and the potential to have spent large sums unnecessarily if no identity theft materializes) can be substantial for large incidents because the cost of credit monitoring generally is a function of the number of individuals for whom credit monitoring is being provided. Second, subsequent to any large data breach that is reported publicly, it is likely that an agency will get reports of identity theft directly from individuals in the affected class. Yet, agencies should be aware that approximately 3.6% of the adult population reports itself annually as the victim of some form of identity theft. Thus, for any large breach, it is statistically predictable that a certain number of the potential victim class will be victims of identity theft through events *other than* the data security breach in question. Data-breach monitoring of the type described here can assist an agency in determining whether the particular incident it has suffered is truly a source of identity theft, or whether, instead, any such reports are the normal by-product of the routine incidence of identity theft.

Second, and typically at great expense, agencies may wish to provide credit-monitoring services. Credit monitoring is a commercial service that can assist individuals in early detection of instances of identity theft, thereby allowing them to take steps to minimize the harm (although credit monitoring cannot guarantee that identity theft will not occur). A credit-monitoring service typically notifies individuals of changes that appear in their credit report, such as creation of a new account or new inquiries to the file.[9]

---

[9]Various credit-monitoring services provide different features and their offerings are constantly evolving. Therefore, agencies may wish to consult with OMB or the FTC concerning the most current, available options.

In deciding whether to offer credit monitoring services and of what type and length, agencies should consider the seriousness of the risk of identity theft arising from the data breach. Particularly important are whether incidents have already been detected and the cost of providing the service. Such costs can be substantial, although rates are often subject to negotiation; bulk purchase discounts have been offered in many cases of large data breaches.[10] The length of time for which the service is provided may have an impact on cost as well. In addition, the agency should consider the characteristics of the affected individuals. Some affected populations may have more difficulty in taking the self-protective steps described earlier. For example, there may be groups who, because of their duties or their location, may warrant special protection from the distraction or effort of self-monitoring for identity theft.

Agencies should also be aware that, to assist the timely implementation of either data breach analysis or credit monitoring, the General Services Administration (GSA) is putting in place several government-wide contracting methods to provide these services if needed. Thus, an agency's contract officer, working with GSA, should be able promptly to secure such services and to develop cost estimates associated with such services.

Finally, it is important to note that notification to law enforcement is an important way for an agency to mitigate the risks faced by the potentially affected individuals. Because an agency data breach may be related to other breaches or other criminal activity, the agency's Inspector General should coordinate with appropriate federal law enforcement agencies to enable the government to look for potential links and to effectively investigate and punish criminal activity that may result from, or be connected to, the breach.

V. Implementing a Response Plan: Notice to Those Affected

Having identified the level of risk and bearing in mind the steps that can be taken by the agency or individual to limit that risk, the agency should then move to implement a response plan that incorporates elements of the above. Agencies should bear in mind that notice and the response it can generate from individuals is not "costless," a consideration that can be especially important where the risk of identity theft is low. The costs can include the financial expense and inconvenience that can arise from canceling credit cards, closing bank accounts, placing fraud alerts on credit files, and/or obtaining new identity documents. The private sector and other government agencies also incur costs in servicing these consumer actions. Moreover, frequent public notices of such incidents may be counterproductive, running the risk of injuring the public and, by making it more difficult to distinguish between serious and minor threats, causing citizens to ignore all notices, even of incidents that truly warrant heightened vigilance. Thus, weighing all the facts available, the risks to consumers caused by the data security breach warrant notice when notice would facilitate appropriate remedial action that is likely to be justified given the risk.

---

[10]In some instances, monitoring services may even be provided at no cost. Agencies should check the GSA contract schedule.

-7-

Assuming that an agency has made the decision to provide notice to those put at risk, agencies should incorporate the following elements into that notification process:

1. ***Timing:*** The notice should be provided in a timely manner, but without compounding the harm from the initial incident through premature announcement based on incomplete facts or in a manner likely to make identity theft more likely to occur as a result of the announcement. While it is important to notify promptly those who may be affected so that they can take protective steps quickly, false alarms or inaccurate alarms are counterproductive. In addition, sometimes an investigation of the incident (such as a theft) can be impeded if information is made public prematurely. For example, an individual who has stolen a password-protected laptop in order to resell it may be completely unaware of the nature and value of the information the laptop contains. In such a case, public announcement may actually alert the thief to what he possesses, increasing risk that the information will be misused. Thus, officials should consult with those law enforcement officials investigating the incident (which could include the agency's Inspector General) regarding the timing and content of any announcement, before making any public disclosures about the incident. Indeed, even when the decision has been made to notify affected individuals, under certain circumstances, law enforcement may need a temporary delay before such notice is given to ensure that a criminal investigation can be conducted effectively or for national security reasons. Similarly, if the data breach resulted from a failure in a security or information system, that system should be repaired and tested before disclosing details related to the incident.[11]

2. ***Source:*** Given the serious security and privacy concerns raised by data breaches, notification to individuals affected by the data loss should be issued by a responsible official of the agency, or, in those instances in which the breach involves a publicly known component of an agency, a responsible official of the component.

There may be some instances in which notice of a breach may appropriately come from an entity other than the actual agency that suffered the loss. For example, when the data security breach involves a federal contractor operating a system of records on behalf of the agency or a public-private partnership (for example, a federal agency/private-sector agreement to operate a program that requires the collection of covered information on members of the public), the responsibility for complying with these notification procedures should be established with the contractor or partner prior to entering the business relationship. Additionally, a federal agency that suffers a breach involving personal information may wish to determine, in conjunction with the regulated entity from which it obtained the information, whether notice is more appropriately given by the agency or by the regulated entity. Whenever possible, to avoid creating confusion and anxiety, the actual notice

[11] There may be other reasons related to law enforcement or national security that dictate that notice not be given to those who are affected. For example, if an agency suffers a breach of a database containing law enforcement sensitive data, immediate notification to potentially affected individuals may be inappropriate – even if the risk of identity theft resulting from that breach is significant – as such notification may result in the disclosure of law enforcement-sensitive or counter-terrorism data.

-8-

should come from the entity which the affected individuals are reasonably likely to perceive as the entity with which they have a relationship. In all instances, the agency is responsible for ensuring that its contractor or partner promptly notifies the agency of any data loss it suffers.

3. ***Contents***: The substance of the notice should be reduced to a stand-alone document and written in clear, concise, and easy-to-understand language, capable of individual distribution and/or posting on the agency's website and other information sites. The notice should include the following elements:

- a brief description of what happened;
- to the extent possible, a description of the types of personal information that were involved in the data security breach (e.g., full name, SSN, date of birth, home address, account number, disability code, etc.);
- a brief description of what the agency is doing to investigate the breach, to mitigate losses, and to protect against any further breaches;
- contact procedures for those wishing to ask questions or learn additional information, including a toll-free telephone number, website, and/or postal address;
- steps individuals should take to protect themselves from the risk of identity theft (see above for the steps available), including steps to take advantage of any credit monitoring or other service the agency intends to offer and contact information for the FTC website, including specific publications.

Given the amount of information needed to give meaningful notice, an agency may want to consider providing the most important information up front, with the additional details in a Frequently Asked Questions (FAQ) format or on its website. If an agency has knowledge that the affected individuals are not English speaking, notice should also be provided in the appropriate language(s).

4. ***Method of Notification***: Notification should occur in a manner calibrated to ensure that the individuals affected receive actual notice of the incident and the steps they should take. First-class mail notification to the last known mailing address of the individual should be the primary means by which the agency provides notification. Even when an agency has reason to doubt the continued accuracy of such an address or lacks an address, mailed notice may still be effective. The United States Postal Service (USPS) will forward mail to a new address for up to one year, or will provide an updated address via established processes.[12] Moreover, certain agencies, such as the Social Security Administration and the Internal Revenue Service, may sometimes possess address information that can be used to facilitate effective mailing. The notice should be

---

[12]Agencies may receive updated addresses as a mailer by becoming a direct licensee of the Postal Service or by using a USPS licensed NCOA Link service provider. A current list of service providers is available at http://ribbs.usps.gov/files/ncoalink/CERTIFIED%5FLICENSEES/. For information on address-update and delivery-validation services, contact the USPS at 1-800-589-5766.

sent separately from any other mailing so that it stands out to the recipient. If using another agency to facilitate mailing as referenced above, agencies should take care that the agency that suffered the loss is identified as the sender, not the facilitating agency.

Substitute means of notice such as broad public announcement through the media, website announcements, and distribution to public service and other membership organizations likely to have access to the affected individual class, should be employed to supplement direct mail notification or if the agency cannot obtain a valid mailing address. Email notification is discouraged, as the affected individuals could encounter difficulties in distinguishing the agency's email from a "phishing" email.

The agency also should give special consideration in providing notice to individuals who are visually or hearing impaired consistent with Section 504 of the Rehabilitation Act of 1973. Accommodations may include establishing a Telecommunications Device for the Deaf (TDD) or posting a large-type notice on the agency's web site.

5. ***Preparing for follow-on inquiries***: Those notified can experience considerable frustration if, in the wake of an initial public announcement, they are unable to find sources of additional accurate information. Agencies should be aware that the GSA has a stand-by capability through its "USA Services" operation to quickly put in place a 1-800-FedInfo call center staffed by trained personnel and capable of handling individual inquiries for circumstances in which the number of inquiries is likely to exceed the agency's native capacity. Thus, agencies may wish to consider briefly delaying a public announcement to allow them to implement a consolidated announcement strategy, as opposed to a hasty public announcement without any detailed guidance on steps to take. Such a strategy will permit public statements, website postings, and a call center staffed with individuals prepared to answer the most frequently asked questions all to be made simultaneously available.

6. ***Prepare counterpart entities that may receive a surge in inquiries***: Depending on the nature of the incident, certain entities, such as the credit-reporting agencies or the FTC, may experience a surge in inquiries also. For example, in incidents involving a substantial number of SSNs (e.g., more than 10,000), notifying the three major credit bureaus allows them to prepare to respond to requests from the affected individuals for fraud alerts and/or their credit reports. Thus, especially for large incidents, an agency should inform the credit bureaus and the FTC of the timing and distribution of any notices, as well as the number of affected individuals, in order to prepare.

-10-

Appendix B. Proposed Routine Use Language

Subsection (b)(3) of the Privacy Act provides that information from an agency's system of records may be disclosed without a subject individual's consent if the disclosure is "for a routine use as defined in subsection (a)(7) of this section and described under subsection (e)(4)(D) of this section." 5 U.S.C. § 552a(b)(3). Subsection (a)(7) of the Act states that "the term 'routine use' means, with respect to the disclosure of a record, the use of such record for a purpose which is compatible with the purpose for which it was collected." 5 U.S.C. § 552a(a)(7). The Office of Management and Budget, which pursuant to subsection (v) of the Privacy Act has guidance and oversight responsibility for the implementation of the Act by federal agencies, has advised that the compatibility concept encompasses (1) functionally equivalent uses, and (2) other uses that are necessary and proper. 52 Fed. Reg. 12,990, 12,993 (Apr. 20, 1987). In recognition of and in accordance with the Act's legislative history, OMB in its initial Privacy Act guidance stated that "[t]he term routine use. . . recognizes that there are corollary purposes 'compatible with the purpose for which [the information] was collected' that are appropriate and necessary for the efficient conduct of government and in the best interest of both the individual and the public." 40 Fed. Reg. 28,948, 28,953 (July 9, 1975). A routine use to provide for disclosure in connection with response and remedial efforts in the event of a breach of federal data would certainly qualify as such a necessary and proper use of information— a use that is in the best interest of both the individual and the public.

Subsection (e)(4)(D) of the Privacy Act requires that agencies publish notification in the Federal Register of "each routine use of the records contained in the system, including the categories of users and the purpose of such use." 5 U.S.C. § 552a(e)(4)(D). The Department of Justice has developed the following routine use that it plans to apply to its Privacy Act systems of records, and which allows for disclosure as follows:[80]

To appropriate agencies, entities, and persons when (1) the Department suspects or has confirmed that the security or confidentiality of information in the system of records has been compromised; (2) the Department has determined that as a result of the suspected or confirmed compromise there is a risk of harm to economic or property interests, identity theft or fraud, or harm to the security or integrity of this system or other systems or programs (whether maintained by the Department or another agency or entity) that rely upon the compromised information; and (3) the disclosure made to such agencies, entities, and persons is reasonably necessary to assist in connection with the Department's efforts to respond to the suspected or confirmed compromise and prevent, minimize, or remedy such harm.

Agencies should already have a published system of records notice for each of their Privacy Act systems of records. To add a new routine use to an agency's existing systems of records, an agency must simply publish a notice in the Federal Register amending its existing systems of records to include the new routine use.

Subsection (e)(1 1) of the Privacy Act requires that agencies publish a Federal Register notice of any new routine use at least 30 days prior to its use and "provide an opportunity for interested persons to submit written data, views, or arguments to the agency." 5 U.S.C. § 552a(e)(1 1). Additionally, subsection (r) of the Act requires that an agency provide Congress and OMB with "adequate advance notice" of any proposal to make a "significant change in a system of records." 5 U.S.C. § 552a(r). OMB has stated that the addition of a routine use qualifies as a significant change that must be reported to Congress and OMB and that such notice is to be provided at least 40 days prior to the alteration. See Appendix Ito OMB Circular No. A-130—Federal Agency Responsibilities for Maintaining Records About Individuals, 61 Fed. Reg. 6435, 6437 (Feb. 20, 1996). Once a notice is prepared for publication, the agency would send it to the Federal Register, OMB, and Congress, usually simultaneously, and the proposed change to the system (i.e., the new routine use) would become effective 40 days thereafter. See id. at 6438 (regarding timing of systems of records reports and noting that notice and comment period for routine uses and period for OMB and congressional review may run concurrently). Recognizing that each agency likely will receive different types of comments in response to its notice, the Task Force recommends that OMB work to ensure accuracy and consistency across the range of agency responses to public comments.

Appendix C. Text of Amendments to 18 U.S.C. §§ 3663(B) and 3663a(B) Proposed Language:

(a) Section 3663 of Title 18, United States Code, is amended by:

1) Deleting "and" at the end of paragraph (4) of subsection (b);
2) Deleting the period at the end of paragraph (5) of subsection (b) and inserting in lieu thereof "; and"; and
3) Adding the following after paragraph (5) of subsection (b): "(6) in the case of an offense under sections 1028(a)(7) or 1028A(a) of this title, pay an amount equal to the value of the victim's time reasonably spent in an attempt to remediate intended or actual harm incurred from the offense.".

Make conforming changes to the following:

(b) Section 3663A of Title 18, United States Code, is amended by: (1) Adding the following after Section 3663A(b)(4). "(5) in the case of an offense under this title, section 1028(a)(7) or 1028A(a), pay an amount equal to the value of the victim's time reasonably spent in an attempt to remediate intended or actual harm incurred from the offense.".

Section Analysis

These new subsections provide that defendants may be ordered to pay restitution to victims of identity theft and aggravated identity theft for the value of the victim's time spent remediating the actual or intended harm of the offense. Restitution could therefore include an amount equal to the value of the victim's time spent clearing a victim's credit report or resolving charges made by the perpetrator for which the victim has been made responsible.

New subsections 3663(b)(6) and 3663A(b)(5) of Title 18 would make clear that restitution orders may include an amount equal to the value of the victim's time spent remediating the actual or intended harm of the identity theft or aggravated identity theft offense. The federal courts of appeals have interpreted the existing provisions of Section 3663 in such a way that would likely preclude the recovery of such amounts, absent explicit statutory authorization. For example, in United States v. Arvanitis, 902 F.3d 489 (7th Cir. 1990), the court held that restitution ordered for offenses resulting in loss of property must be limited to recovery of property which is the subject of the offenses, and may not include consequential damages. Similarly, in Similarly, in United States v. Husky, 924 F.2d 223

(11th Cir. 1991), the Eleventh Circuit held that the list of compensable expenses in a restitution statute is exclusive, and thus the district court did not have the authority to order the defendant to pay restitution to compensate the victim for mental anguish and suffering. Finally, in United States v. Schinnell, 80 F.3d 1064 (5th Cir. 1996), the court held that restitution was not allowed for consequential damages involved in determining the amount of loss or in recovering those funds; thus, a victim of wire fraud was not entitled to restitution for accounting fees and costs to reconstruct bank statements for the time period during which the defendant perpetuated the scheme, for the cost of temporary employees to reconstruct monthly bank statements, and for the costs incurred in borrowing funds to replace stolen funds. These new subsections will provide statutory authority for inclusion of amounts equal to the value of the victim's time reasonably spent remediating the harm incurred as a result of the identity theft offense.

Appendix D. Text of Amendments to 18 U.S.C. §§ 2703, 2711 and 3127, and Text of New Language for 18 U.S.C. § 3512

The basis for these proposals is set forth in Section III.2 of the strategic plan, which describes coordination with foreign law enforcement.

Proposed Language:

§ 2703. Required disclosure of customer communications or records

1) Contents of wire or electronic communications in electronic storage.—A governmental entity may require the disclosure by a provider of electronic communication service of the contents of a wire or electronic communication, that is in electronic storage in an electronic communications system for one hundred and eighty days or less, only pursuant to a warrant issued using the procedures described in the Federal Rules of Criminal Procedure by a court with jurisdiction over the offense under investigation by a court of competent jurisdiction or an equivalent State warrant. A governmental entity may require the disclosure by a provider of electronic communications services of the contents of a wire or electronic communication that has been in electronic storage in an electronic communications system for more than one hundred and eighty days by the means available under subsection (b) of this section.
2) Contents of wire or electronic communications in a remote computing service.—(1) A governmental entity may require a provider of remote computing service to disclose the contents of any wire or electronic communication to which this paragraph is made applicable by paragraph (2) of this subsection—

(a) without required notice to the subscriber or customer, if the governmental entity obtains a warrant issued using the procedures described in the Federal Rules of Criminal Procedure by a court with jurisdiction over the offense under investigation by a court of competent jurisdiction or equivalent State warrant; or

(b) with prior notice from the governmental entity to the subscriber or customer if the governmental entity—

I uses an administrative subpoena authorized by a Federal or State statute or a Federal or State grand jury or trial subpoena; or

II obtains a court order for such disclosure under subsection (d) of this section; except that delayed notice may be given pursuant to section 2705 of this title.

(c) Records concerning electronic communication service or remote computing service.—(1) A governmental entity may require a provider of electronic communication service or remote computing service to disclose a record or other information pertaining to a subscriber to or customer of such service (not including the contents of communications) only when the governmental entity—

(A) obtains a warrant issued using the procedures described in the Federal Rules of Criminal Procedure by a court with jurisdiction over the offense under investigation by a court of competent jurisdiction or equivalent State warrant;

§ 2711. Definitions for Chapter as Used in this Chapter—

1) the terms defined in section 2510 of this title have, respectively, the definitions given such terms in that section;
2) the term "remote computing service" means the provision to the public of computer storage or processing services by means of an electronic communications system; and
3) the term "court of competent jurisdiction" has the meaning assigned by section 3127, and includes any Federal court within that definition, without geographic limitation means—

(A) any district court of the United States (including a magistrate judge of such a court) or any United States court of appeals that–

(i) has jurisdiction over the offense being investigated;
(ii) is in or for a district in which the provider of electronic communication service is located or in which the wire or electronic communications, records, or other information are stored; or
(iii) is acting on a request for foreign assistance pursuant to section 3512 of this title; or

(B) a court of general criminal jurisdiction of a State authorized by the law of that State to issue search warrants.

§ 3127. Definitions for Chapter as Used in this Chapter—

1) the terms "wire communication", "electronic communication", "electronic communication service", and "contents" have the meanings set forth for such terms in section 2510 of this title;
2) the term "court of competent jurisdiction" means—

(A) any district court of the United States (including a magistrate judge of suchacourt) or any United States court of appeals having jurisdiction over the offense being investigated that–

(i) has jurisdiction over the offense being investigated;
(ii) is in or for a district in which the provider of electronic communication service is located;
(iii) is in or for a district in which a landlord, custodian, or other person subject to 3124(a) or (b) is located; or
(iv) is acting on a request for foreign assistance pursuant to section 3512 of this title; or

(B) a court of general criminal jurisdiction of a State authorized by the law of that State to enter orders authorizing the use of a pen register or a trap and trace device;

§ 3512. Foreign Requests for Assistance in Criminal Investigations and Prosecutions:

A) Upon application of an attorney for the government, a Federal judge may issue such orders as may be necessary to execute a request from a foreign authority for assistance in the investigation or prosecution of criminal offenses, or in proceedings related to the prosecution of criminal offenses including but not limited to proceedings regarding forfeiture, sentencing, and restitution. Such orders may include the issuance of a search warrant as provided under Rule 41 of the Federal Rules of Criminal Procedure, a warrant or order for contents of stored wire or electronic communications or for records related thereto as provided under 18 U.S. C. § 2703, an order for a pen register or trap and trace device as provided under 18 U.S. C. § 3123, or an order requiring the appearance of a person for the purpose of providing testimony or a statement, or requiring the production of documents or other things, or both.
B) In response to an application for execution of a request from a foreign authority as described in subsection (a) , a Federal judge may also issue an order appointing a person to direct the taking of testimony or statements or of the production of documents or other things, or both. A person so appointed may be authorized to –

1) issue orders requiring the appearance of a person, or the production of documents or other things, or both;
2) administer any necessary oath; and
3) take testimony or statements and receive documents or other things.

(c) Except as provided in subsection (d), an application for execution of a request from a foreign authority under this section may be filed –

1) in the district in which a person who may be required to appear resides or is located or in which the documents or things to be produced are located;
2) in cases in which the request seeks the appearance of persons or production of documents or things that may be located in multiple districts, in any one of the districts in which such a person, documents or things may be located; or
3) in any case, the district in which a related Federal criminal investigation or prosecution is being conducted, or in the District of Columbia.

(d) An application for a search warrant under this section, other than an application for a warrant issued as provided under 18 U.S.C. § 2703, must be filed in the district in which the place or person to be searched is located.
(e) A search warrant may be issued under this section only if the foreign offense for which the evidence is sought involves conduct that, if committed in the United States, would be considered an offense punishable by imprisonment for more than one year under federal or state law.
(f) Except as provided in subsection (d), an order or warrant issued pursuant to this section may be served or executed in any place in the United States.
(g) This section does not preclude any foreign authority or an interested person from obtaining assistance in a criminal investigation or prosecution pursuant to 28 U.S.C. § 1782.
(h) As used in this section –

1) the term "foreign authority" means a foreign judicial authority, a foreign authority responsible for the investigation or prosecution of criminal offenses or for proceedings related to the prosecution of criminal offenses, or an authority designated as a competent authority or central authority for the purpose of making requests for assistance pursuant to an agreement or treaty with the United States regarding assistance in criminal matters; and
2) the terms "Federal judge" and "attorney for the Government" have the meaning given such terms for the purposes of the Federal Rules of Criminal Procedure.

Appendix E. Text of Amendments to 18 U.S.C. §§ 1028 and 1028a

The basis for these proposed amendments is set forth in Section III.D.4.a of the strategic plan, which describes gaps in the identity theft statutes.

Proposed Amendment to Aggravated Identity Theft Statute to Add Predicate Offenses

Congress should amend the aggravated identity theft offense (18 U.S.C. § 1028A) to include other federal offenses that recur in various identity-theft and fraud cases, specifically, mail theft (18 U.S.C. § 1708), uttering counterfeit securities (18 U.S.C. § 513), and tax fraud (26 U.S.C. §§ 7201, 7206, and 7207), as well as conspiracy to commit specified felonies already listed in section 1 028A—in the statutory list of predicate offenses for that offense (18 U.S.C. § 1028A(c)).

Proposed Additions to Both Statutes to Include Misuse of Identifying Information of Organizations

1) Section 1028(a) of Title 18, United States Code, is amended by inserting in paragraph (7) the phrase "(including an organization as defined in Section 18 of this Title)" after the word "person".
2) Section 1028A(a) of Title 18, United States Code, is amended by inserting in paragraph (1) the phrase "(including an organization as defined in Section 18 of this Title)" after the word "person".
3) Section 1028(d)(7) of Title 18, United States Code, is amended by inserting in paragraph (7) the phrase "or other person" after the word "individual".

Rationale:

Corporate identity theft whereby criminals assume the identity of corporate entities to cloak fraudulent schemes in a misleading and deceptive air of legitimacy have become rampant. Criminals routinely engage in unauthorized "appropriation" of legitimate companies' names and logos in a variety of contexts: misrepresenting themselves as officers or employees of a corporation, sending forged or counterfeit documents or financial instruments to victims to improve their aura of legitimacy, and offering nonexistent benefits (e.g., loans and credit cards) in the names of companies.

One egregious example of corporate identity theft is represented on the Internet by the practice commonly known as "phishing," whereby criminals electronically assume the identity of a corporation in order to defraud unsuspecting recipients of email solicitations to voluntarily disclose identifying and financial account information. This personal information is then used to further the underlying criminal scheme—for example, toscavenge the bank and credit card accounts of these unwitting consumer victims. Phishing is just one example of how criminals in mass-marketing fraud schemes incorporate corporate identity theft into their schemes, though phishing also is designed with individual identity theft in mind.

Phishing has become so routine in many major fraud schemes that no particular corporation can be easily singled out as having suffered a special "horror story" which stands above the rest. In August 2005, the "AntiPhishing Working Group" determined in just that month alone, there were 5,259 unique phishing websites around the world. By December 2005, that number had increased to 7,197, and there were 15,244 unique phishing reports. It was also reported in August 2005, that 84 corporate entities' names (and even logos and web content) were "hijacked" (i.e., misused) in phishing attacks, though only 3 of these corporate brands accounted for 80 percent of phishing campaigns. By December 2005 the number of victimized corporate entities had increased to 120. The financial sector is and has been the most heavily targeted industry sector in phishing schemes, accounting for nearly 85 percent of all phishing attacks. See, e.g. http://antiphishing.org/apwg_ phishing_activity_ report_ august_05.pdf.

In addition, major companies have reported to the Department of Justice that their corporate names, logos, and marks are often being misused in other types of fraud schemes. These include telemarketing fraud schemes in which communications purport to come from legitimate banks or companies or offer products or services from legitimate banks and companies, and West African fraud schemes that misuse legitimate banks and companies' names in commu-nications with victims or in counterfeit checks.

Uncertainty has arisen as to whether Congress intended Sections 1028(a)(7) and 1028A(a) of Title 18, United States Code to apply only to "natural" persons or to also protect corporate entities. These two amendments would clarify that Congress intended that these statute apply broadly and may be used against phishing directed against victim corporate entities.

Appendix F. Text of Amendment to 18 U.S.C. § 1030(A)(2)

The basis for this proposed amendment is set forth in Section III.D.4.b of the strategic plan, which describes gaps in the computer-related identity theft statutes.

Proposed Language:

1030(a) Whoever—

1) intentionally accesses a computer without authorization or exceeds authorized access, and thereby obtains–
A) information contained in a financial record of a financial institution, or of a card issuer as defined in section 1602(n) of title 15, or contained in a file of a consumer reporting agency on a consumer, as such terms are defined in the Fair Credit Reporting Act (15 U.S.C. 1681 et seq.);
B) information from any department or agency of the United States; or
C) information from any protected computer if the conduct involved an interstate or foreign communication.

Appendix G. Text of Amendments to 18 U.S.C. §§ 1030(A)(5), (C), and (G), and to 18 U.S.C. § 2332b

The basis for these proposed amendments is set forth in Section III.D.4.b of the strategic plan, which describes gaps in the computer-related identity theft statutes.

Proposed Language: 18 U.S.C. § 1030

(a) Whoever—

(5)

A) knowingly causes the transmission of a program, information, code, or command, and as a result of such conduct, intentionally causes damage without authorization, to a protected computer;
B) intentionally accesses a protected computer without authorization, and as a result of such conduct, recklessly causes damage; or
C) intentionally accesses a protected computer without authorization, and as a result of such conduct, causes damage; and
D) by conduct described in clause (i), (ii), or (iii) of subparagraph (A) , caused (or, in the case of an attempted offense, would, if completed, have caused)—

(i) loss to 1 or more persons during any 1-year period (and, for purpose s of an investigation, prosecution, or other proceeding brought by the United States only, loss resulting from a related course of conduct affecting 1 or more other protected computers) aggregating at least $ 5,000 in value;
(ii) the modification or impairment, or potential modification ormpairment, of the medical examination, diagnosis, treatment, or care of 1 or more individuals;
(iii) physical injury to any person;
(iv) a threat to public health or safety; or
(v) damage affectingacomputer system used by or for a government entity in furtherance of the administration of justice, national defense, or national security;

(c) The punishment for an offense under subsection (a) or (b) of this section is—

(2) (A) except as provided in subparagraph (B), a fine under this title or imprisonment for not more than one year, or both, in the case of an offense under subsection (a)(2), (a)(3), (a)(5)(A)(iii), or (a)(6) of this section which does not occur after a conviction for another offense under this section, or an attempt to commit an offense punishable under this subparagraph;

(3) ...(B) a fine under this title or imprisonment for not more than ten years, or both, in the case of an offense under subsection (a)(4), (a)(5)(A)(iii), or (a)(7) of this section which occurs after a conviction for another offense under this section, or an attempt to commit an offense punishable under this subparagraph;

(4) (A) except as provided in paragraph (5), a fine under this title, imprisonment for not more than 10 years, or both, in the case of an offense under subsection (a)(5)(A)(i) , or an attempt to commit an offensepunishable under that subsection;

(i) a fine under this title, imprisonment for not more than 5 years, or both, in the case of an offense under subsection (a)(5)(A)(ii), or an attempt to commit an offense punishable under that subsection;
(ii) except as provided in paragraph (5), a fine under this title, imprisonment for not more than 20 years, or both, in the case of an
(iii) offense under subsection (a)(5)(A)(i) or (a)(5)(A)(ii), or an attempt to commit an offense punishable under either subsection, that occurs after a conviction for another offense under this section; and

(5) (A) if the offender knowingly or recklessly causes or attempts to cause serious bodily injury from conduct in violation of subsection (a)(5)(A)(i), a fine under this title or imprisonment for not more than 20 years, or both; and

(B) if the offender knowingly or recklessly causes or attempts to cause death from conduct in violation of subsection (a)(5)(A)(i), a fine under this title or imprisonment for any term of years or for life, or both.

(4) (A) a fine under this title, imprisonment for not more than 5 years, or both, in the case of an offense under subsection (a)(5)(B), which does not occur after a conviction for another offense under this section, if the offense caused (or, in the case of an attempted offense, would, if completed, have caused)—

(i) loss to 1 or more persons during any 1-year period (and, for purposes of an investigation, prosecution, or other proceeding brought by the United States only, loss resulting from a related course of conduct affecting 1 or more other protected computers) aggregating at least $5,000 in value;
(ii) the modification or impairment, or potential modification or impairment, of the medical examination, diagnosis, treatment, or care of 1 or more individuals;
(iii) physical injury to any person;
(iv) a threat to public health or safety;
(v) damage affecting a computer used by or for a government entity in furtherance of the administration of justice, national defense, or national security; or
(vi) damage affecting ten or more protected computers during any 1-year period;
(vii) or an attempt to commit an offense punishable under this subparagraph;

B) except as provided in subparagraphs (c)(4)(D) and (c)(4)(E), a fine under this title, imprisonment for not more than 10 years, or both, in the case of an offense under subsection (a)(5)(A), which does not occur after a conviction for another offense under this section, if the offense caused (or, in the case of an attempted offense, would, if completed, have caused) a harm provided in subparagraphs (c)(4)(A)(i) through (vi), or an attempt to commit an offense punishable under this subparagraph;

C) a fine under this title, imprisonment for not more than 20 years, or both, in the case of an offense under subsection (a)(5) that occurs after a conviction for another offense under this section, or an attempt to commit an offense punishable under this subparagraph;

D) if the offender attempts to cause or knowingly or recklessly causes serious bodily injury from conduct in violation of subsection (a)(5)(A), a fine under this title or imprisonment for not more than 20 years, or both;

E) if the offender attempts to cause or knowingly or recklessly causes death from conduct in violation of subsection (a)(5)(A), a fine under this title or imprisonment for any term of years or for life, or both; or

F) a fine under this title, imprisonment for not more than one year, or both, for any other offense under subsection (a)(5), or an attempt to commit an offense punishable under this subparagraph.

G) Any person who suffers damage or loss by reason of a violation of this section may maintain a civil action against the violator to obtain compensatory damages and injunctive relief or other equitable relief. A civil action for a violation of this section may be brought only if the conduct involves 1 of the factors set forth in clause (i), (ii), (iii), (iv), or (v) of subsection (a)(5)(B) subparagraph (c)(4)(A). Damages for a violation involving only conduct described in subsection (a)(5)(B)(i) subparagraph (c)(4)(A)(i) are limited to economic damages. No action may be brought under this subsection unless such action is begun within 2 years of the date of the act complained of or the date of the discovery of the damage. No action may be brought under this subsection for the negligent design or manufacture of computer hardware, computer software, or firmware.

18 U.S.C. § 2332b(g)(5)(B)(I)

...1030(a)(5)(A)(i) resulting in damage as defined in 1 030(a)(5)(B)(ii) through (v) 1 030(c) (4)(A)(ii) through (vi) (relating to protection of computers)

Appendix H. Text of Amendments to 18 U.S.C. § 1030(A)(7) The Basis for This Proposed Amendment Is Set Forth in Section III.D.4.C of the Strategic Plan, Which Describes Gaps in the Cyber-Extortion Statute

Proposed Language:

18 U.S.C. § 1030(a)(7).

(7) with intent to extort from any person any money or other thing of value, transmits in interstate or foreign commerce any communication containing any –

a) threat to cause damage to a protected computer;
b) threat to obtain information from a protected computer without authorization or in excess of authorization or to impair the confidentiality of information obtained from a protected computer without authorization or by exceeding authorized access; or
c) demand or request for money or other thing of value in relation to damage to a protected computer, where such damage was caused to facilitate the extortion;

Appendix I. Text of Amendment to United States Sentencing Guideline § 2b1.1

The basis for this proposed amendment is set forth in Section III.D.4.d of the strategic plan, which describes the Sentencing Guidelines provision governing identity theft.

Proposed Language for United States Sentencing Guidelines § 2B1.1, Comment.(N.1):

"Victim" means (A) any person who sustained any harm, whether monetary or non-monetary, as a result of the offense. Harm is intended to be an inclusive term, and includes bodily injury, non-monetary loss such as the theft of a means of identification, invasion of privacy, reputational damage, and inconvenience. "Person" includes individuals, corporations, companies, associations, firms, partnerships, societies, and joint stock companies.

Appendix J. Description of Proposed Surveys

In order to expand law enforcement knowledge of the identity theft response and prevention activities of state and local police, the Bureau of Justice Statistics (BJS) should undertake new data collections in three areas: (1)a survey of law enforcement agencies focused on the response to identity theft; (2) enhancements to the existing Law Enforcement Management and Administrative Statistics (LEMAS) survey platform; and (3) enhancements to the existing training academy survey platform. Specifically, BJS should undertake to do the following:

- New survey of state and local law enforcement agencies. A new study focused on state and local law enforcement responses to identity theft should seek to document agency personnel, operations, workload, and policies and programs related to the handling of this crime. Detail on the organizational structure, if any, associated with identity theft response should be included (for example, the use of special units devoted to identity theft). The study should inquire about participation in regional identity theft task forces, community outreach and education efforts, as well as identity theft prevention programs. Information collected should also include several summary measures of identity theft in the agencies' jurisdictions (offenses known, arrests, referrals, outcomes), with the goal of producing some standardized metrics with which to compare jurisdictions.
- Enhancement to existing LEMAS survey. BJS should develop a special battery of questions for the existing LEMAS survey platform. The LEMAS survey, conducted roughly every three years since 1987, collects detailed administrative information from a nationally representative sample of about 3,000 agencies. The sample includes all agencies with 100 or more officers, and a stratified random sample of smaller agencies as well as campus law enforcement agencies. Information collected should include whether agencies presently enforce identity theft laws, utilize special units, have designated personnel, participate in regional identity theft task forces, and have policies and procedures in place related to the processing of identity theft incidents. The survey should also inquire whether agencies collect summary measures of identity theft in their jurisdictions, including offenses known, arrests, referrals, and any outcome measures. Finally, this study should also collect information on whether agencies are engaged in community outreach, education, and prevention activities related to identity theft.
- Enhancement to existing law enforcement training academy survey. BJS should develop a special battery of questions for the existing law enforcement training academy survey platform. A section of the data collection instrument should be devoted to the types of training, if any, being provided by basic academies across the country in the area of identity theft. BJS should subsequently provide statistics on the number of recruits who receive training on identity theft, as well as the nature and

content of the training. In-service training provided to active-duty officers should also be covered.

- The Bureau of Justice Statistics should revise both the State Court Processing Statistics (SCPS) and National Judicial Reporting Program (NJRP) programs so that they are capable of distinguishing identity theft from other felony offenses. In addition, the scope of these surveys should be expanded to include misdemeanor identity theft offenders. If SCPS and NJRP were able to follow identity theft offenders, then a variety of different types of court-specific information could be collected. These include how many offenders are charged with identity theft in the Nation's courts, what percentage of these offenders are released at pretrial, and how are the courts adjudicating (e.g., convicting or dismissing) identity theft offenders. Among those convicted identity theft offenders, data should be collected on how many are being sentenced to prison, jail, or probation. These projects should also illuminate the prior criminal histories or rap sheets of identity theft offenders. Both projects should also allow for the post conviction tracking of identity theft offenders for the purposes of examining their overall recidivism rates.
- BJS should ensure that other state court studies that it funds are reconfigured to analyze the problem of identity theft. For example, State Court Organization (SCO) currently surveys the organizational structure of the Nation's state courts. This survey could be supplemented with additional questionnaires that measure whether special courts similar to gun, drug, or domestic violence courts are being created for identity theft offenders. Also, SCO should examine whether courts are training or funding staff equipped to handle identity theft offenders.
- BJS should ensure that the Civil Justice Survey of State Courts, which examines civil trial litigation in a sample of the Nation's state courts, is broadened to identify and track various civil enforcement procedures and their utilization against identity thieves.

REFERENCES

[1] Public Law 105-318, 112 Stat. 3007 (Oct. 30, 1998). The Identity Theft Assumption and Deterrence Act provides an expansive definition of identity theft. It includes the misuse of any identifying information, which could include name, SSN, account number, password, or other information linked to an individual, to commit a violation of federal or state law. The definition thus covers misuse of existing accounts as well as creation of new accounts.

[2] The federal financial regulatory agencies include the banking and securities regulators, namely, the Federal Deposit Insurance Corporation, the Federal Reserve Board, the National Credit Union Administration, the Office of the Comptroller of the Currency, the Office of Thrift Supervision, the Commodity Futures Trading Commission, and the Securities and Exchange Commission.

[3] The public comments are available at www.idtheft.gov.

[4] Testimony of John M. Harrison, June 19, 2003, Senate Banking Committee, "The Growing Problem of Identity Theft and its Relationship to the Fair Credit Reporting Act."
[5] See U.S. Attorney's Office, Western District of Michigan, Press Release (July 5, 2006), available at http://www.usdoj.gov/usao/miw/press/JMiller_ Others10172006.html.
[6] Javelin Strategy and Research, 2007 Identity Fraud Survey Report: Identity Fraud is Dropping, Continued Vigilance Necessary (Feb 2007), summary available at http:// www.javelinstrategy.com; Bureau of Justice Statistics (DOJ) (2004), available at http://www.ojp.usdoj.gov/bjs/pub/pdf/it04.pdf; Gartner, Inc. (2003), available at http://www.gartner.com/5_about/press_releases/pr21july2003a.jsp; FTC 2003 Survey Report (2003), available at http://www.consumer.gov/idtheft/pdf/ synovate_report.pdf.
[7] See Business Software Alliance, Consumer Confidence in Online Shopping Buoyed by Security Software Protection, BSA Survey Suggests (Jan. 12, 2006), available at http:// www.bsacybersafety.com/news/2005-Online-Shopping-Confidence.cfm.
[8] See Cyber Security Industry Alliance, Internet Security Voter Survey (June 2005) at 9, available at https://www.csialliance.org/publications/surveys_and_polls/CSIA_ Internet_Security_Survey_June_2005.pdf.
[9] See U.S. Attorney's Office, Southern District of Florida, Press Release (July 19, 2006), available at http://www.usdoj.gov/usao/fls/PressReleases/060719-01.html.
[10] See, e.g., John Leland, Meth Users, Attuned to Detail, Add Another Habit: ID Theft, New York Times, July 11, 2006, available at http://www.nytimes. com/2006/07/11/us/11meth.html?ex=1153540800anden=7b6c7773afa880beandei=50 70; Byron Acohido and Jon Swartz, Meth addicts' other habit: Online Theft, USA Today, December 14, 2005, available at http://www.usatoday.com/tech/news/ internetprivacy/2005-12-14-meth-online-theft_x.htm
[11] Bob Mims, Id Theft Is the No. 1 Runaway U.S. Crime, The Salt Lake Tribune, May 3, 2006, available at 2006 WLNR 7592526.
[12] Dennis Tomboy, Meth Addicts Stealing Mail, Deseret Morning News, April 28, 2005, http://deseretnews.com/dn/view/0,1249,600129714,00.html.
[13] Stephen Mihm, Dumpster-Diving for Your Identity, New York Times Magazine, December 21, 2003, available at http://www.nytimes.com/2003/12/21/magazine/ 21IDENTITY.html?ex=1387342800anden=b693eef01223bc3bandei=5007andpartner= US ERLAND.
[14] Pub. L. No. 108-159, 117 Stat. 1952.
[15] The FACT Act required merchants to comply with this truncation provision within three years of the Act's passage with respect to any cash register or device that was in use before January 1, 2005, and within one year of the Act's passage with respect to any cash register or device that was first put into use on or after January 1, 2005. 15 U.S.C. § 168 1c(g)(3).
[16] Overview of Attack Trends, CERT Coordination Center 2002, available at http:// www.cert.org/archive/pdf/attack_trends.pdf.
[17] Lanowitz, T., Gartner Research ID Number G00 127407: December 1, 2005.
[18] "Vishing" Is Latest Twist In Identity Theft Scam, Consumer Affairs, July 24, 2006, available at http://www.consumeraffairs.com/news04/2006/07/scam_vishing.html.
[19] Fraudsters have recently used pretexting techniques to obtain phone records, see, e.g., Jonathan Krim, Online Data Gets Personal: Cell Phone Records For Sale, Washington

Post, July 13, 2005, available at 2005 WLNR 10979279, and the FTC is pursuing enforcement actions against them. See http://www.ftc.gov/opa/2006/05/phonerecords.htm.

[20] The FTC brought three cases after sting operations against financial pretexters. Information on the settlement of those cases is available at http://www.ftc.gov/opa/2002/03/pretextingsettlements.htm.

[21] See, e.g., Computers Stolen with Data on 72,000 Medicaid Recipients, Cincinnati Enquirer, June 3, 2006.

[22] 15 U.S.C. § 1681e; 15 U.S.C. § 6802(a).

[23] Although the FACT Act amendments to the Fair Credit Reporting Act require merchants to truncate credit account numbers, allowing only the final five digits to appear on an electronically generated receipt, 15 U.S.C. § 1618c(g), manually created receipts might still contain the full account number.

[24] See http://www.bizjournals.com/philadelphia/stories/2006/07/24/daily30.html. See also Identity Theft Resource Center, Fact Sheet 126: Checking Account Takeover and Check Fraud, http://www.idtheftcenter.org/vg126.shtml.

[25] For example, the Securities and Exchange Commission instituted proceedings against a 19-year-old internet hacker after the hacker illicitly accessed an investor's online brokerage account. His bogus transactions saved the hacker approximately $37,000 in trading losses. The SEC also obtained an emergency asset freeze to halt an Estonia-based "account intrusion" scheme that targeted online brokerage accounts in the U.S. to manipulate the markets. See Litigation Release No. 19949 (Dec. 19, 2006), available at http://www.sec.gov/litigation/ litreleases/2006/lr19949.htm.

[26] For unauthorized credit card charges, the Fair Credit Billing Act limits consumer liability to a maximum of $50 per account. 15 U.S.C. § 1643. For bank account fraud, different laws determine consumers' legal remedies based on the type of fraud that occurred. For example, applicable state laws protect consumers against fraud committed by a thief using paper documents, like stolen or counterfeit checks. If, however, the thief used an electronic fund transfer, federal law applies. The Electronic Fund Transfer Act limits consumer liability for unauthorized transactions involving an ATM or debit card, depending on how quickly the consumer reports the loss or theft of his card: (1) if reported within two business days of discovery, the consumer's losses are limited to a maximum of $50; (2) if reported more than two business days after discovery, but within 60 days of the transmittal date of the account statement containing unauthorized transactions, he could lose up to $500; and (3) if reported more than 60 days after the transmittal date of the account statement containing unauthorized transactions, he could face unlimited liability. 15 U.S.C. § 1693g. As a matter of policy, some credit and debit card companies waive liability under some circumstances, freeing the consumer from fraudulent use of his credit or debit card.

[27] See John Leland, Some ID Theft Is Not For Profit, But to Get a Job, N.Y. Times, Sept. 4, 2006.

[28] See World Privacy Forum, Medical Identity Theft: The Information Crime That Can Kill You (May 3, 2006), available at worldprivacyforum.org/pdf/wpf_medicalidtheft2006.pdf.

[29] See http://www.idanalytics.com/news_and_events/20051208.htm. Some other organizations have begun conducting statistical analyses to determine the link between data breaches and identity theft. These efforts are still in their early stages, however.

[30] Government Accounting Office, Social Security Numbers: Government Could Do More to Reduce Display in Public Records and On Identity Cards (November 2004), at 2, available at http://www.gao.gov/new.items/d0559.pdf.

[31] 15 U.S.C. §§ 6801 et seq.; 42 U.S.C. §§ 1320d et seq.; 18 U.S.C. §§ 2721 et seq.

[32] 5 U.S.C. § 552a.

[33] See, e.g., Ariz. Rev. Stat. § 44-1373.

[34] Social Security Numbers: Federal and State Laws Restrict Use of SSNs, Yet Gaps Remain, GAO - 05-1016T, September 15, 2005.

[35] See, e.g., www.wpsic.com/edi/comm_sub_p.shtml?mm=3, Non-SSN Member Numbers to Be Assigned for Privacy Protection.

[36] Except where expressly noted, all references to years in this strategic plan are intended to refer to calendar years, rather than fiscal years.

[37] The federal government's overall information privacy program derives primarily from five statutes that assign OMB policy and oversight responsibilities, and agencies responsibility for implementation. The Privacy Act of 1974 (5 U. S.C. § 552a) sets collection, maintenance, and disclosure conditions; access and amendment rights and notice and record-keeping requirements with respect to personally identifiable information retrieved by name or personal identifier. The Computer Matching and Privacy Protection Act of 1988 (5 U.S.C. § 552a note) amended the Privacy Act to provide a framework for the electronic comparison of personnel and benefits-related information systems. The Paperwork Reduction Act of 1995 (44 U.S.C. § 3501 et seq.) and the Information Technology Management Reform Act of 1996 (also known as Clinger-Cohen Act; 41 U.S.C. § 251 note) linked agency privacy activities to information technology and information resources management, and assigned to agency Chief Information Officers (CIO) the responsibility to ensure implementation of privacy programs within their respective agencies. Finally, Section 208 of the E-Government Act of 2002 (44 U.S.C. § 3501 note) included provisions requiring agencies to conduct privacy impact assessments on new or substantially altered information technology systems and electronic information collections, and post web privacy policies at major entry points to their Internet sites. These provisions are discussed in OMB memorandum 0 3-22, "OMB Guidance for Implementing the Privacy Provisions of the E-Government Act of 2002."

[38] See Protection of Sensitive Agency Information, Memorandum from Clay Johnson III, Deputy Director for Management, OMB, to Heads of Departments and Agencies, M-06-16 (June 23, 2006).

[39] The United States Computer Emergency Readiness Team (US-CERT) has played an important role in public sector data security. US-CERT is a partnership between DHS and the public and private sectors. Established in 2003 to protect the nation's Internet infrastructure, US-CERT coordinates defense against and responses to cyber attacks across the nation. The organization interacts with federal agencies, state and local governments, industry professionals, and others to improve information sharing and incident response coordination and to reduce cyber threats and vulnerabilities. US-CERT provides the following support: (1) cyber security event monitoring; (2)

advanced warning on emerging threats; (3) incident response capabilities for federal and state agencies; (4) malware analysis and recovery support; (5) trends and analysis reporting tools; and (6) other support services in the area of cyber security. US-CERT also provides consumer and business education on Internet and information security.

[40] See http://www.whitehouse.gov/results/agenda/scorecard.html.

[41] The proposed routine use language set forth in Appendix B differs slightly from that included in the Task Force's interim recommendations in that it further clarifies, among other things, the categories of users and the circumstances under which disclosure would be "necessary and proper" in accordance with the OMB's guidance on this issue.

[42] 15 U.S.C. §§ 6801-09; 16 C.F.R. Part 313 (FTC); 12 C.F.R. Part 30, App. B (OCC, national banks); 12 C.F.R. Part 208, App. D-2 and Part 225, App. F (FRB, state member banks and holding companies); 12 C.F.R. Part 364, App. B (FDIC, state non-member banks); 12 C.F.R. Part 570, App. B (OTS, savings associations); 12 C.F.R. Part 748, App. A (NCUA, credit unions); 16 C.F.R. Part 314 (FTC, financial institutions that are not regulated by the FRB, FDIC, OCC, OTS, NCUA, CFTC, or SEC); 17 C.F.R. Part 248.30 (SEC); 17 C.F.R. Part 160.30 (CFTC).

[43] 15 U.S.C. § 45(a). Further, the federal bank regulatory agencies have authority to enforce Section 5 of the FTC Act against entities over which they have jurisdiction. See 15 U.S.C. §§ 6801-09.

[44] 15 U.S.C. §§ 1681-1681x, as amended.

[45] Pub. L. No. 108-159, 117 Stat. 1952.

[46] 42 U.S.C. §§ 1320d et seq.

[47] 31 U.S.C. § 53 18(l).

[48] 18 U.S.C. §§ 2721 et seq.

[49] http://www.ncsl.org/programs/lis/cip/priv/breachlaws.htm.

[50] http://www.bbb.org/securityandprivacy/SecurityPrivacyMadeSimpler.pdf;www. staysafeonline.org/basics/company/basic_tips.html;The Financial Services Roundtable, Voluntary Guidelines for Consumer Confidence in Online Financial Services, available at www.bitsinfo.org/downloads/Publications%20Page/bitsconscon.pdf; www.realtor. org/realtororg.nsf/files/NARInternetSecurityGuide.pdf/$FILE/ NARInternetSecurityGuide.pdf; www.antiphishing.org/reports/bestpracticesforisps. pdf; www.uschamber.com/sb/security/default.htm; www.truste.org/pdf/ Security Guidelines.pdf; www.the-dma. org/privacy/informationsecurity.shtml; http://www. staysafeonline.org/basics/company/basic_tips.html.

[51] These changes may be attributable to requirements contained in the regulations implementing Title V of the GLB Act. See 12 C.F.R. Part 30, App. B (national banks); 12 C.F.R. Part 208, App. D-2 and Part 225, App. 5 (state member banks and holding companies); 12 C.F.R. Part 364, App. B (state non-member banks); 12 C.F.R. Part 570, App. B (savings associations); 12 C.F.R. Part 748, App. A and B, and 12 C.F.R. Part 717 (credit unions); 16 C.F.R. Part 314 (financial institutions that are not regulated by the FDIC, FRB, NCUA, OCC, or OTS).

[52] See, e.g., http://www.truste.org/pdf/SecurityGuidelines.pdf; http://www.the-dma. org/privacy/informationsecurity.shtml.

[53] Deloitte Financial Services, 2006 Global Security Survey, available at http://singe. rucus.net/blog/archives/756-Deloitte-Security-Surveys.html.

[54] Datalink, Data Storage Security Study, March 2006, available at www.datalink.com/security/.

[55] Id.

[56] See Small Business Technology Institute, Small Business Information Security Readiness (July 2005).

[57] See, e.g., California (Cal. Civ. Code § 1798.82 (2006)); Illinois (815 Ill. Comp. Stat 530/5 (2005)); Louisiana (La. Rev. Stat. 51:3074 (2006)); Rhode Island (R.I. Gen. Laws § 11-49.2.3 (2006)).

[58] See, e.g., Colorado (Colo. Rev. Stat. § 6-1-7 16 (2006)); Florida (Fla. Stat. § 817.5681 (2005)); New York (NY CLS Gen. Bus. § 889-aa (2006)); Ohio (Ohio Rev. Code Ann. § 1349.19 (2006)).

[59] Ponemon Institute LLC, Benchmark Study of European and U.S. Corporate Privacy Practices, p. 16 (Apr. 26, 2006).

[60] Id.

[61] Ponemon Institute, LLC, 2005 Benchmark Study of Corporate Privacy Practices (July 11, 2005).

[62] MultiChannel Merchant, Retailers Need to Provide Greater Data Security, Survey Says (Dec. 1, 2005), available at http://multichannelmerchant.com/opsandfulfillment/advisor/retailers_data_security_1201/index.html.

[63] See Information Technology Examination Handbook's Information Security Booklet, available at http://www.ffiec.gov/guides.htm.

[64] See, e.g., http://www.pvkansas.com/police/crime/iden_theft.shtml (Prairie Village, Kansas), http://phoenix.gov//POLICE/dcd1.html (Phoenix, Arizona); www.co.arapahoe.co.us/departments/SH/index.asp (Arapahoe County, Colorado).

[65] Colleges Are Textbook Cases of Cybersecurity Breaches, USA TODAY, August 1, 2006.

[66] Examples of this outreach include a wide-scale effort at the University of Michigan which launched Identity Web, a comprehensive site based on the recommendations of a graduate class in fall of 2003. The State University of New York's Orange County Community College offers identity theft seminars, the result of a student who fell victim to a scam. A video at student orientation sessions at Drexel University in Philadelphia warns students of the dangers of identity theft on social networking sites. Bowling Green State University in Kentucky emails campus-wide "fraud alerts" when it suspects that a scam is being targeted to its students. In recent years, more colleges and universities have hired chief privacy officers, focusing greater attention on the harms that can result from the misuse of students' information.

[67] See 31 C.F.R. § 103.121 (banks, savings associations, credit unions, and certain non-federally regulated banks); 31 C.F.R. § 103.122 (broker-dealers); 17 C.F.R. § 270.0-11, 31 C.F.R. § 103.131 (mutual funds); and 31 C.F.R. § 103.123 (futures commission merchants and introducing brokers).

[68] See http://www.dhs.gov/xprevprot/laws/gc_1172765386179.shtm.

[69] A primary reason criminals use other people's identities to commit identity theft is to enable them to operate with anonymity. However, in committing identity theft, the suspects often leave telltale signs that should trigger concern for alert businesses. Section 114 of the FACT Act seeks to take advantage of businesses' awareness of these patterns, and requires the federal bank regulatory agencies and the FTC to develop

regulations and guidelines for financial institutions and creditors addressing identity theft. In developing the guidelines, the agencies must identify patterns, practices, and specific forms of activity that indicate the possible existence of identity theft. 15 U.S.C. § 168 1m. Those agencies have issued a set of proposed regulations that would require each financial institution and creditor to develop and implement an identity theft prevention program that includes policies and procedures for detecting, preventing, and mitigating identity theft in connection with account openings and existing accounts. The proposed regulations include guidelines listing patterns, practices, and specific forms of activity that should raise a "red flag" signaling a possible risk of identity theft. Recognizing these "red flags" can enable businesses to detect identity theft at its early stages before too much harm is done. See 71 Fed. Reg. 40786 (July 18, 2006) to be codified at 12 C.F.R. Parts 41(OCC), 222 (FRB), 334 and 364 (FDIC), 571 (OTS), 717 (NCUA), and 16 C.F.R. Part 681 (FTC), available at http://www.occ.gov /fr/fedregister/71fr40786.pdf.

[70] USB token devices are typically small vehicles for storing data. They are difficult to duplicate and are tamper-resistant. The USB token is plugged directly into the USB port of a computer, avoiding the need for any special hardware on the user's computer. However, a login and password are still required to access the information contained on the device. Smart cards resemble a credit card and contain a microprocessor that allows them to store and retain information. Smart cards are inserted into a compatible reader and, if recognized, may require a password to perform a transaction. Finally, the common token system involves a device that generates a one-time password at predetermined intervals. Typically, this password would be used in conjunction with other login information such as a PIN to allow access to a computer network. This system is frequently used to allow for remote access to a work station for a telecommuter.

[71] Biometrics are automated methods of recognizing an individual based on measurable biological (anatomical and physiological) and behavioral characteristics. Biometrics commonly implemented or studied include: fingerprint, face, iris, voice, signature, and hand geometry. Many other modalities are in various stages of development and assessment. Additional information on biometric technologies, federal biometric programs, and associated privacy considerations can be found at www.biometrics.gov.

[72] See Authentication in an Internet Banking Environment (October 12, 2005), available at http://www.ffiec.gov/pdf/authentication_guidance.pdf.

[73] See FFIEC Frequently Asked Questions on FFIEC Guidance on Authentication in an Internet Banking Environment (August 15, 2006), available at http://www.ffiec. gov/pdf/authentication_faq.pdf.

[74] See Kristin Davis and Jessica Anderson, But Officer, That Isn't Me, Kiplinger's Personal Finance (October 2005); Bob Sullivan, The Darkest Side of ID Theft, MSNBC.com (Dec. 1, 2003); David Brietkopf, State of Va. Creates Special Cards for Crime Victims, The American Banker (Nov. 18, 2003).

[75] 18 U.S.C. § 1028A.

[76] 18 U.S.C. § 1028(d)(7).

[77] See 18 U.S.C. § 1030(e)(8).

[78] 18 U.S.C. § 1030(a)(7).

[79] S. Rep. No. 105-274, at 9 (1998).

[80] As this Task Force has been charged with considering the federal response to identity theft, this routine use notice does not include all possible triggers, such as embarrassment or harm to reputation. However, after consideration of the Strategic Plan and the work of other groups charged with assessing Privacy Act considerations, OMB may determine that a routine use that takes into account other possible triggers may be preferable.

In: Identity Theft Breaches
Editor: Cary S. Logweller

ISBN 978-1-60692-227-9

Chapter 2

FEDERAL TRADE COMMISSION: 2006 IDENTITY THEFT SURVEY REPORT

EXECUTIVE SUMMARY

Identity theft (ID theft) is an issue that continues to plague consumers, businesses, and law enforcement. To provide greater insight into the prevalence and cost of ID theft, the Federal Trade Commission (FTC) has sponsored its second ID theft survey of US adults. The specific objectives of the survey were to:

- Estimate the prevalence of ID theft victimization
- Measure the impacts of ID theft on the victims
- Identify actions taken by victims
- Explore measures that may help victims of future cases of ID theft

The study was conducted through telephone interviews using a Random-Digit-Dialing (RDD) sampling methodology. This system was designed to obtain a random sample of U.S. adults age 18 and older. A total of 4,917 interviews were conducted between March 27 and June 11, 2006.

The Prevalence of ID Theft

- A total of 3.7 percent of survey participants indicated that they had discovered they were victims of ID theft in 2005. This result suggests that approximately 8.3 million U.S. adults discovered that they were victims of some form of ID theft in 2005.[3] (See Table 1.)
- In this report, victims of ID theft are classified as belonging to one of three categories based on the most serious problem the victim reported. Each of these categories represents a form of identity theft as it is defined by federal law. The survey confirmed prior data indicating that the magnitude of harm to consumers, as a general matter, correlates with the kind of ID theft suffered by the victim. In order of the magnitude of harm, from least to most, the three categories are: "Existing Credit

Card Only," "Existing Non-Credit Card Account," and "New Accounts and Other Frauds."

- For the calendar year 2005:

Table 1.Prevalence of ID Theft in 2005, by Category of Misuse

	Percent of Adult Population1[1]	Number of Persons (millions)[2]
New Accounts and Other Fraud	0.8 % (0.5 % – 1.2%) 1.5 %	1.8 (1.2 – 2.8) 3.3
Misuse of Existing Non-Credit Card Account or Account Number	(1.1% – 2.1%) 1.4 %	(2.4 – 4.6) 3.2
Misuse of Existing Credit Card or Credit Card Number	(1.0 % - 2.1%)	(2.1 – 4.6)
Total Victims in 2005	3.7 % (3.0% - 4.6%)	8.3 (6.6 – 10.3)

- 1.4 percent of survey participants, representing 3.2 million American adults, reported that the misuse of their information was limited to the misuse of one or more of their existing credit card accounts in 2005.[4] These victims were placed in the "Existing Credit Cards Only" category because they did not report any more serious form of identity theft.
- 1.5 percent of participants, representing 3.3 million American adults, reported discovering in 2005 the misuse of one or more of their existing accounts other than credit cards—for example, checking or savings accounts or telephone accounts—but not experiencing the most serious form of identity theft. These victims were placed in the "Existing Non-Credit Card Accounts" category.
- 0.8 percent of survey participants, representing 1.8 million American adults, reported that in 2005 they had discovered that their personal information had been misused to open new accounts or to engage in types of fraud other than the misuse of existing or new financial accounts in the victim's name. These victims were placed in the "New Accounts and Other Fraud" category, whether or not they also experienced another type of identity theft.

This consumer survey may not capture all types of identity theft or their associated costs. Situations in which someone creates a fictitious identity by combining personal information from one or more consumers with invented information, rather than using the identity of an existing individual, may not have been captured. This form of fraud, called synthetic ID theft, is not always detectable by the consumer(s) whose information was used.

Table 2. Costs of ID Theft, Misuse Discovered Since 2001

	New Accounts and Other Frauds	Existing Non-Credit Card Accounts	Existing Credit Cards Only	All ID Theft
Value of Goods and Services Obtained by Identity Thieves				
Median	$1,350	$457	$350	$500
90th Percentile	$15,000	$3,800	$4,000	$6,000
95th Percentile	$30,000	$6,000	$7,000	$13,000
Victims' Out-of-Pocket Expenses				
Median	$40	$0	$0	$0
90th Percentile	$3,000	$900	$132	$1,200
95th Percentile	$5,000	$1,200	$400	$2,000
Hours Victims Spent Resolving Their Problems				
Median	10	4	2	4
90th Percentile	100	44	25	55
95th Percentile	1,200	96	60	130
Sample size n =	138	164	257	559

Table 2 presents various measures of the costs of ID theft. Rather than average values, the table uses median values (the point at which half the victims fell above the number and half below). A minority of ID thefts result in much greater harm than the typical case. Because these large values have a significant impact on the average value, the median better represents the typical experience. To capture the experiences of those who suffer the most serious harm, the table also reports values for the 90th percentile and 95th percentile of harms reported.

Financial Value Obtained by Thief

- The median value of goods and services obtained by the identity thieves for all categories of ID theft was $500. Ten percent of victims reported that the thief obtained $6,000 or more, while 5 percent reported that the thief obtained at least $13,000 in goods and services. (See Table 2.)
- Where the identity thieves opened new accounts or committed other frauds (the "New Accounts and Other Frauds" category), the median value of goods and services obtained by the thieves was $1,350. Ten percent of these victims reported that the thief obtained $15,000 or more in goods and services; in the top 5 percent, the thief obtained at least $30,000 in goods and services. Victims in the New Accounts and Other Frauds category were three times as likely to report that the thieves obtained more than $5,000 as victims in the other two categories of ID theft (23% vs. 7%).
- Where the ID theft was limited to the misuse of existing accounts – either credit card or noncredit card – the median value of goods and services obtained was less than $500. However, much higher amounts were obtained in some cases. Ten percent of victims in the "Existing Credit Card Only" category reported that the thief obtained $4,000 or more in goods and services. In the "Existing Non-Credit Card Accounts" category, the comparable figure was $3,800.

The Costs of ID Theft to Victims

- In more than 50 percent of ID thefts, victims incurred no out-of-pocket expenses. (Out-of- pocket expenses include any lost wages, legal fees, any payment of fraudulent debts, and miscellaneous expenses such as notarization, copying, and postage.)[5] In the New Accounts and Other Frauds category, the median value of out-of-pocket expenses was $40.
- However, some victims do incur substantial out-of-pocket expenses. Ten percent of all victims reported out-of-pocket expenses of $1,200 or more. For the New Accounts and Other Frauds category, the top 10 percent of the victims incurred expenses of at least $3,000, and the top 5 percent incurred expenses of at least $5,000. One-quarter of victims in the New Accounts and Other Frauds category reported paying out-of-pocket expenses of at least $1,000.
- Victims of all types of ID theft spent hours of their time resolving the various problems that result from ID theft. The median value for the number of hours spent

resolving problems by all victims was 4. However, 10 percent of all victims spent at least 55 hours resolving their problems. The top 5 percent of victims spent at least 130 hours.

- Victims in the New Accounts and Other Frauds category spent the greatest amount of time resolving problems. In the top 10 percent in this category, victims reported spending 100 hours or more resolving problems. The top 5 percent reported spending at least 1,200 hours.
- Almost one-quarter of all victims were able to resolve any problems experienced as a result of ID theft within one day of discovering that their personal information had been misused. This refers to the amount of time that passed from when they discovered the crime to when their problems where resolved, not to the number of hours spent resolving their problems.
- Thirty-seven percent of victims reported experiencing problems other than out-of-pocket expenses or the expenditure of time resolving issues as a result of having their personal information misused. The problems victims reported include, among other things, being harassed by collections agents, being denied new credit, being unable to use existing credit cards, being unable to obtain loans, having their utilities cut off, being subject to a criminal investigation or civil suit, being arrested, and having difficulties obtaining or accessing bank accounts.
- Victims of New Accounts and Other Frauds were more than twice as likely to report having one or more of these other types of problems (68%) than were victims in the Existing Non-Credit Card Accounts category (32%,) and four times as likely as victims in the Existing Credit Cards Only category (17%).

COMPARISON TO THE 2003 ID THEFT SURVEY

The FTC conducted a similar telephone survey of consumers in 2003, the first national survey to measure the prevalence and cost of identity theft. Based on the knowledge gained from conducting and analyzing the 2003 survey, FTC staff changed certain elements of the survey methodology for the 2006 survey, to more accurately capture consumers' identity theft experiences. Because of these methodological changes, estimates of the losses from ID theft in the two surveys cannot be directly compared.

- Prevalence. The 2003 survey found that 4.6% of the survey population had experienced ID theft during the one year period before the survey was conducted. The 2006 survey found that 3.7% of the survey population had experienced ID theft during 2005. The difference between the rates is not statistically significant.[6] Given the sample sizes and the variances within the samples, one cannot conclude that the apparent difference between the two figures is the result of a real decrease in ID theft rather than a result of random variation.
- Average amount obtained by the thief. Both the 2003 and 2006 surveys asked victims for their best recollection of the amount of money obtained by the thief. In the 2006 survey, the average amount obtained by the thief was $1,882, whereas the average was $4,789 in the 2003 survey.

Although these results appear to show a dramatic change in the amount obtained by the thief, some of this difference may be explained by several changes in the survey methodology. First, in the 2003 survey, the amounts reported by victims were only recorded as falling within a specified range – e.g., between $100 and $499. In estimating the average amount obtained by thieves, each individual response was assumed to be equal to the mid-point of the specified range selected by that individual. For example, if the consumer chose the category "$100 - $499," the value used in the estimate was $300. In contrast the 2006 survey recorded the actual values reported by victims. This difference between using actual values versus the mid-point of a range of values could lead to differences in the results.[7]

Second, the average value is highly influenced by a small number of "outlier" victims who claimed to have suffered exceptionally large losses. (See Table 2, above.) In estimating average and total amounts obtained by identity thieves, this report excludes the responses of two individuals whose extremely high estimates were suspect.[8]No such exclusions were made in the 2003 survey report.

Third, the 2006 report adopted a new way to account for instances where more than one individual may have been victimized by a single theft of personal information because the misuse involved accounts that were jointly held by two people. In the 2003 report, the total amount obtained by the thief was attributed to each of the victims, whereas in the 2006 report, the total was divided amongst the victims (e.g., attributing half of the loss to each of two joint victims).

Although we believe that these methodological changes improve the reliability of the estimated values, they tend to cause lower estimates as compared to the 2003 survey. Thus, the differences in the estimates between 2003 and 2006 may, at least in part, be due to the changes in methodology as opposed to changes in consumers' actual experiences. We cannot, therefore, be confident that the difference between the 2003 and 2006 estimates represents an actual drop in the average amount obtained by identity thieves.

- Total amount obtained by thieves.

Similarly, the estimate of total losses from ID theft in the 2006 survey - $15.6 billion – is considerably lower than the estimate of $47.6 billion in the 2003 survey. This reflects lower estimates of both the prevalence of ID theft and the average loss per incident. As discussed above, however, some of these differences result from the changes in survey methodology. Thus, we cannot determine whether total losses have actually dropped significantly between 2003 and 2006.

- Average consumer out-of-pocket expenses.

The 2003 survey found that victims had, on average, out-of-pocket expenses of $500. In the 2006 survey, the average victim loss was $371. The same methodological differences that pertain to the amount the thief obtained also apply to these average loss estimates, that is, measuring loss as a range versus actual amount and how we accounted for joint victims.

PREVALENCE OF IDENTITY THEFT[9]

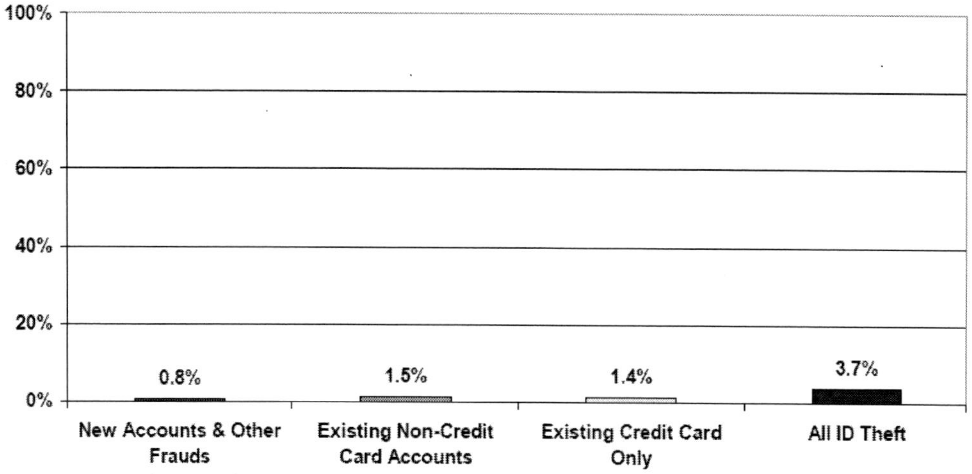

Figure 1. 3.7% of respondents (3.0% – 4.6%)[10] said they became aware of being a victim of ID theft during 2005. This suggests that 8.3 million American adults (6.6 million – 10.3 million) discovered they were ID theft v3 ictims in 2005.[11]

Categorizing ID Theft

- This report classifies ID theft victims in one of three categories: New Accounts and Other Frauds, Existing Non-Credit Card Accounts, and Existing Credit Cards Only. They are placed in the category that includes the most serious type of ID theft they reported. ID theft is considered more serious if it causes the victim more harm, measured by factors such as the amount of time it takes to recover, the out-of-pocket expenses incurred, and the additional problems they experience.
- The "New Accounts and Other Frauds" category is considered to be the most serious, followed by the "Existing Non-Credit Card Accounts" category. "Existing Credit Cards Only" is considered the least serious type of victimization. Placing victims in only one category means that, for example, victims who reported that a new account had been opened using their information and also that one of their existing non-credit card accounts had been misused are placed in the "New Accounts and Other Frauds" category, not in the "Existing Non-Credit Card Accounts" category.
- 1.4% of respondents (1.0% - 2.1%) fall into the category labeled "Existing Credit Cards Only." This category includes victims who reported the misuse of only their existing credit cards and no other misuse of their personal information.
- 1.5% of respondents (1.1% - 2.1%) fall into the category of ID theft that includes the misuse of existing accounts other than a credit card, "Existing Non-Credit Card Accounts."
- 0.8% of respondents (0.5% - 1.2%) fall into the category labeled "New Accounts and Other Frauds." This category includes victims whose personal information had been used to open new accounts (for example, new credit card or bank accounts, telephone or wireless service, or loans) or commit other frauds (for example, the thief giving

the victim's name and identifying information when charged with a crime, renting an apartment or a house, or obtaining medical care).

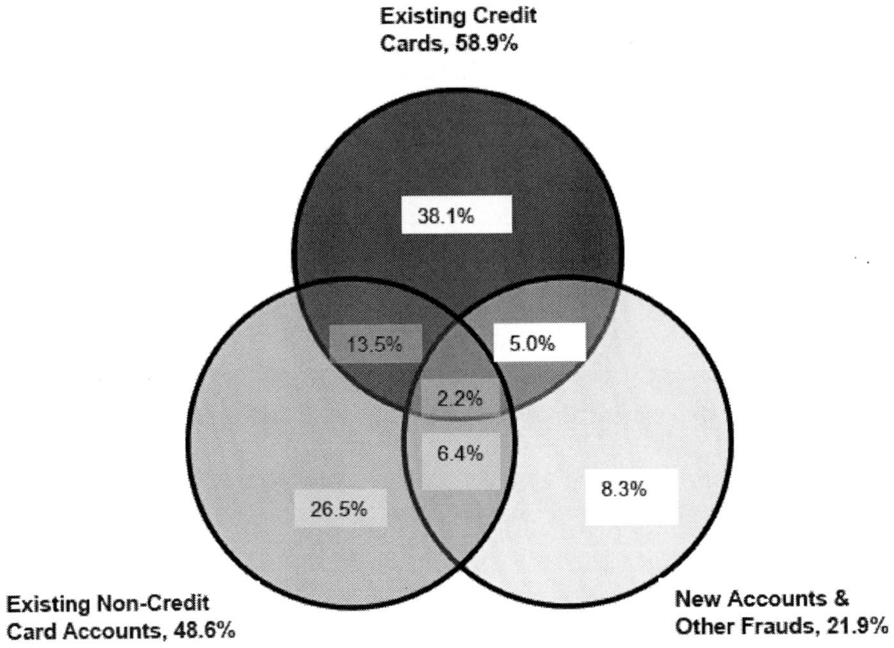

Figure 2. Display of 2005 ID Theft Victim Overlap Among Categories.

- For most purposes, this report groups victims according to the most serious form of ID theft that they suffered. However, many victims suffer multiple types of ID theft, and this diagram illustrates the overlap in types.
- 58.9% of all victims experienced the misuse of an existing credit card.
- A total of 48.6% of victims experienced the misuse of existing accounts other than existing credit card accounts.
- 21.9% of victims had their personal information used to open a new account or commit some other kind of fraud.
- For 38.1% of all victims (1.4% of all respondents), the misuse of an existing credit card was the only form of ID theft suffered.
- Approximately one-third of victims who experienced the misuse of an existing credit card also experienced another type of ID theft. Therefore, these victims are counted in one of the other two, more serious, categories of ID theft.
- Victims who experienced the misuse of existing accounts other than credit card accounts are included in the Existing Non-Credit Card Accounts category (1.5% of all respondents), unless new accounts were opened or other frauds were committed using their information.

- 13.5% of victims experienced both the misuse of existing non-credit accounts and the misuse of existing credit accounts, but not new accounts or other frauds.
- All victims whose personal information was used to open new accounts or commit other frauds are included in the New Accounts and Other Frauds category. That is, all of the 21.9% of victims in the yellow circle of the diagram (0.8% of all adult Americans) are included in this category. This category includes:
-
- 6.4% of victims who, in addition to new accounts or other frauds, had existing non-credit card accounts, but not existing credit card accounts, misused.
- 5.0% of victims who, in addition to new accounts or other frauds, had existing credit card accounts, but not existing non-credit card accounts, misused.
- 2.2% of victims who had both existing credit and non-credit card accounts misused, in addition to new accounts and other frauds.

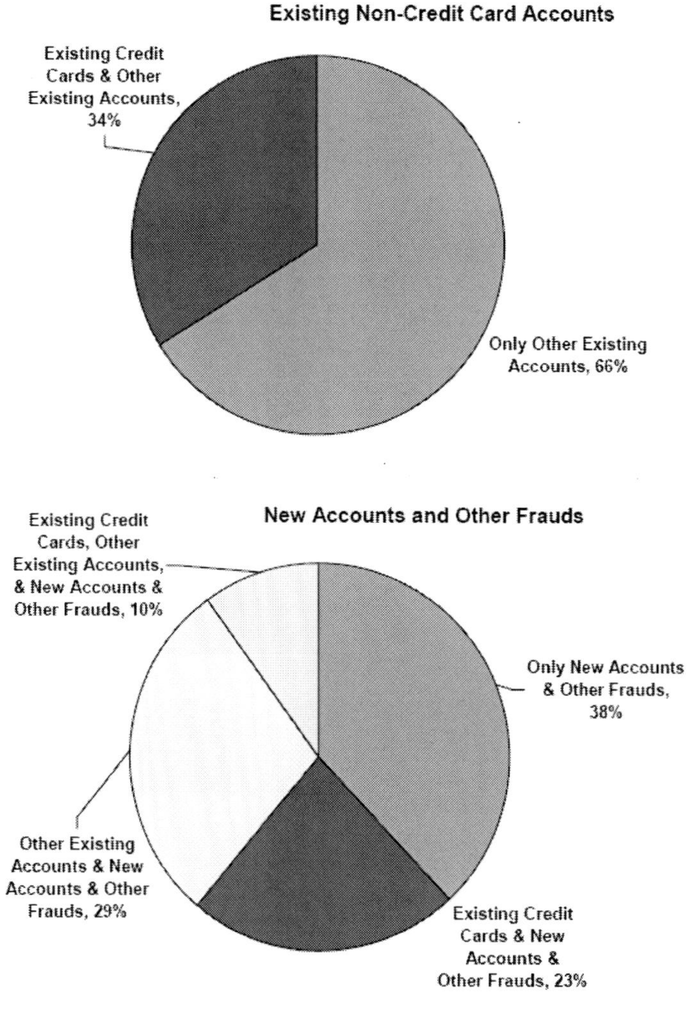

Figure 3. Display of Breakout of 2005 ID Theft Victims within Categories.

- As mentioned above, each victim is classified as belonging to only one of the categories of ID Theft, based on the most serious problem the victim reported. Some victims in the two more serious categories have had their information misused in ways that relate to more than one category.
- Approximately 34% of victims in the "Existing Non-Credit Card Accounts" category also experienced the misuse of an existing credit card account.
- Similarly, 62% of those who discovered that they had experienced "New Accounts and Other Frauds" ID Theft in 2005 also experienced the misuse of an existing credit card or other account: 23% experienced the misuse of an existing credit card, 29% experienced the misuse of an existing non-credit card account, and 10% experienced both the misuse of existing credit cards and the misuse of existing non-credit card accounts.

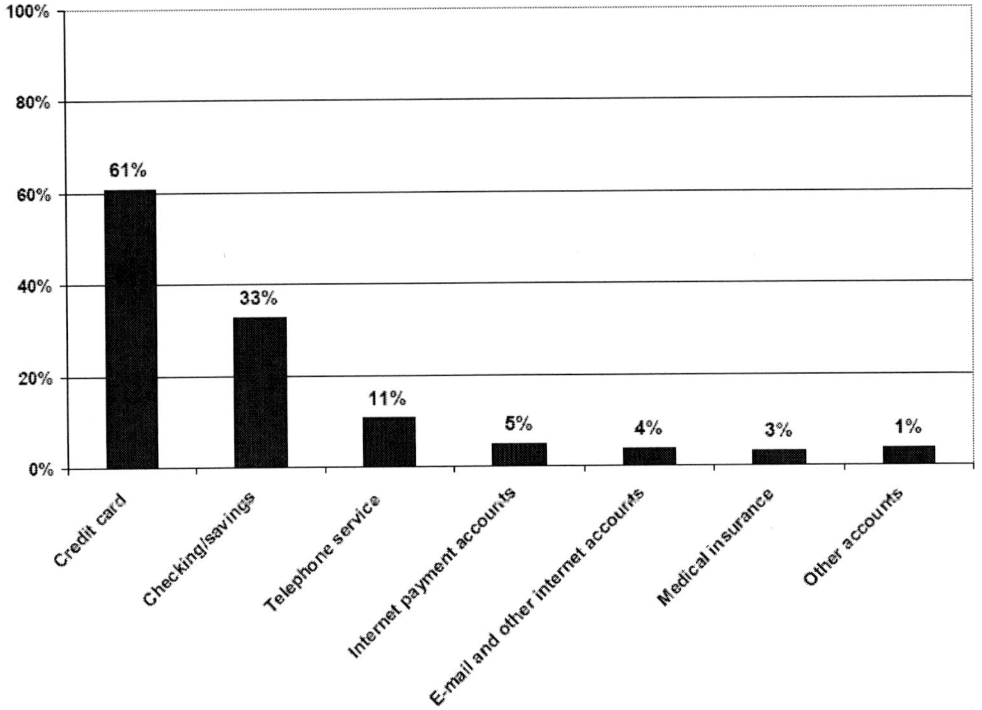

The figures on this and the succeeding pages are based on the responses of all survey participants who reported discovering the misuse of their personal information between the beginning of 2001 and when they were interviewed—a total of 559 individuals. The data in Figures 1-3 are based only on those who discovered the misuse of their information in 2005.

Figure 4. Q1 / Q29: Existing Accounts Misused [12].

- Eighty-five percent of all ID theft victims reported that one or more of their existing accounts had been misused.[13] This figure includes both credit card and non-credit card accounts.
- Sometimes identity thieves take additional steps to facilitate their unauthorized use of the victim's existing accounts. They may change the billing or mailing address in order to conceal their unauthorized use, or add their names as authorized users to

obtain a card in their name from the card issuer. These types of actions are known as "account takeover."

- Account takeover was reported by 9% of victims who experienced existing credit card misuse and 11% of victims who experienced existing non-credit card account misuse.[14] Because new account fraud involves the creation of an entirely new account rather than the misuse of an existing one, account takeover does not apply to that type of identity theft.

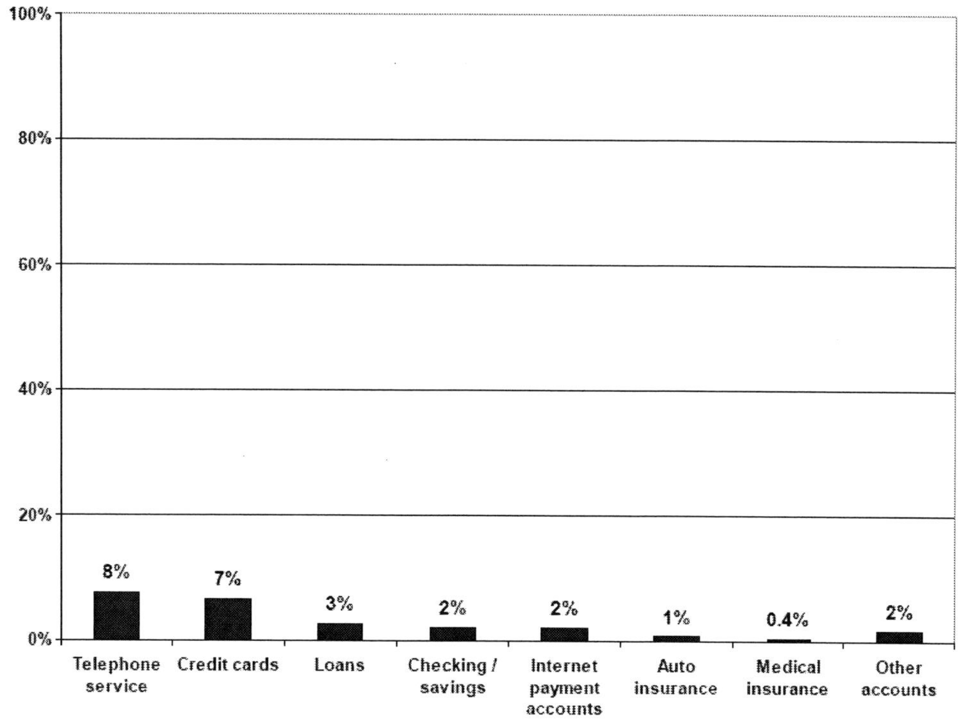

Figure 5. Q32 / Q33 – New Accounts Opened by Identity Thieves [15]

- Seventeen percent of all ID theft victims said the thief used their personal information to open at least one new account.[16]
- The two most common type of accounts victims reported thieves opening were telephone service accounts (including both landline and wireless phone accounts) and credit card accounts (8% and 7% of all victims, respectively).
- Just over half of victims who reported that new accounts were opened said that a single new account was opened.[17]
- One-quarter of victims who had new accounts opened reported that 3 or more accounts were opened.

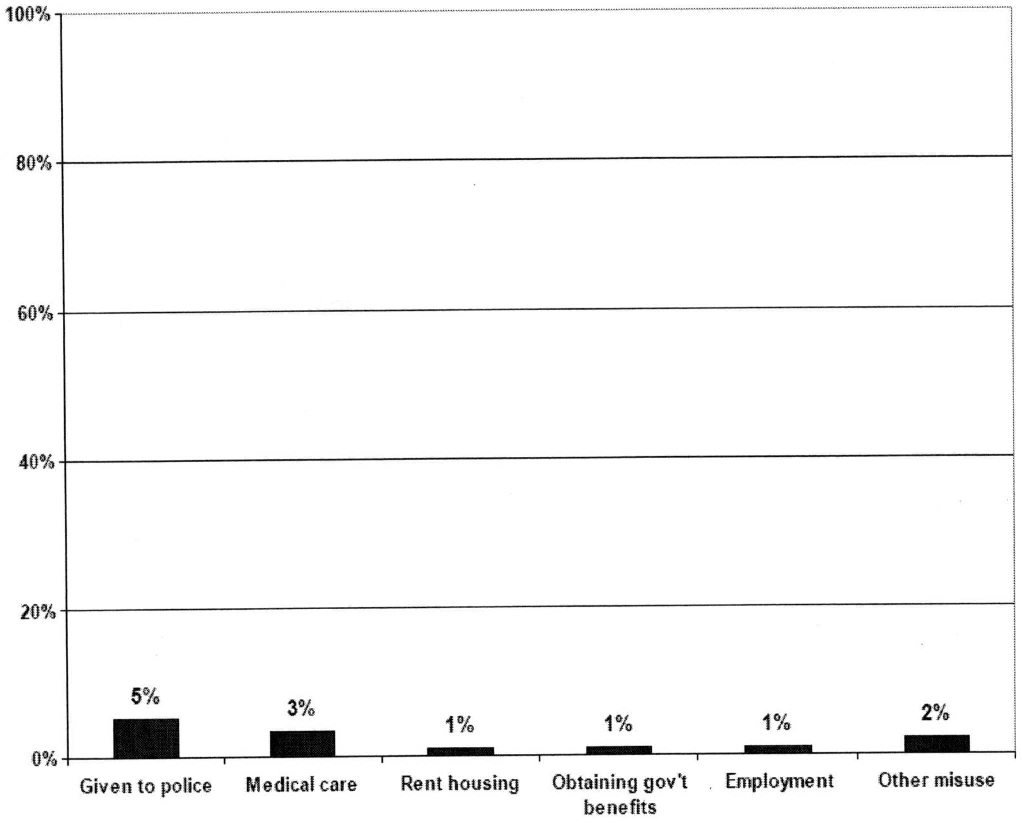

Figure 6. Q34 – Other Misuses of Personal Information [18].

Twelve percent of victims reported one or more misuse other than accessing new or existing financial accounts in the victim's name, and specified what type(s) of fraudulent activities were committed. The most common forms of non-account misuse were:

- Five percent of victims said that they were aware that their name and/or personal information were given to the police when the thief was stopped or charged with a crime.
- Three percent of victims said the thief had obtained medical treatment, services, or supplies using their personal information.

TIME CONSIDERATIONS [19]

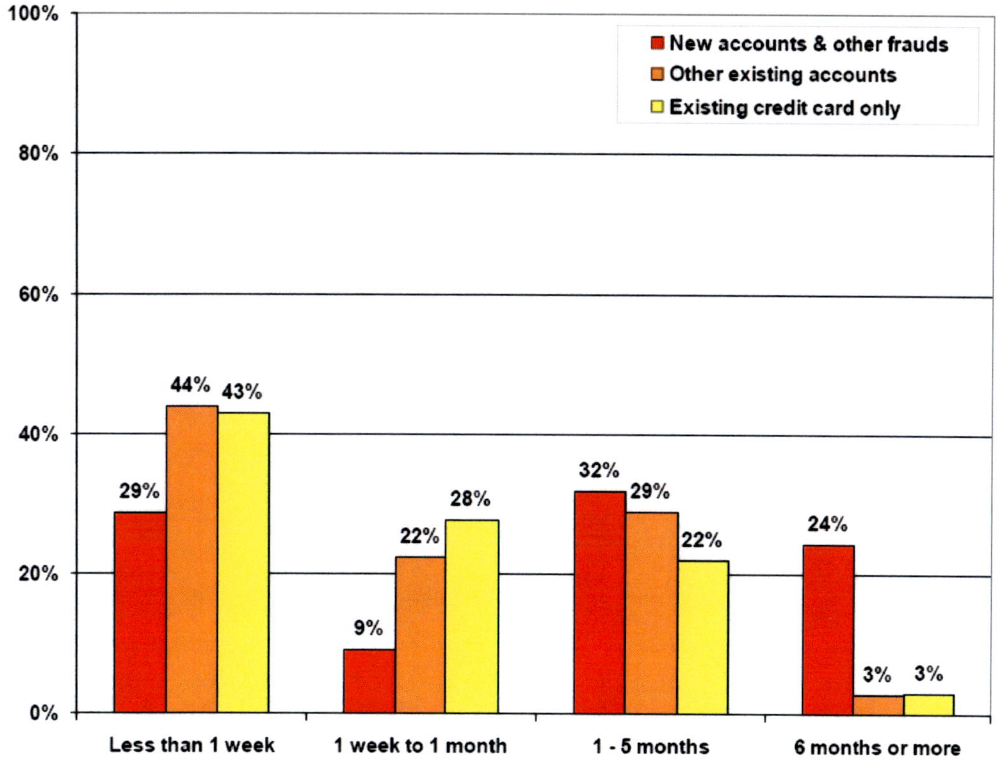

Figure 7. Q16 – Length of Time to Discover Misuse[19].

- o Nearly one-quarter (24%) of New Accounts and Other Frauds victims did not find out about the misuse of their information until at least 6 months after it started – compared to just 3% of Existing Credit Cards Only and Existing Non-Credit Card Accounts victims.
- o In the Existing Credit Cards Only and Existing Non-Credit Card Accounts categories, the median amount of time that elapsed before victims discovered that their personal information was being misused was between 1 week and 1 month. For the New Accounts and Other Frauds category, the median value was between 1 and 2 months.
- o • Where discovery of the misuse occurred more quickly, victims reported lower out-of-pocket losses and thieves obtained less: [20]
- o Thirty percent of those who discovered that their personal information was being misused 6 months or more after it started had to spend $1,000 or more, compared to 10% of those who found the misuse within 6 months.
- o Sixty-nine percent of those who discovered the misuse within 6 months spent fewer than 10 hours compared to 32% of those who took 6 months or more to discover it.
- o Thirty-one percent of those who discovered the misuse of their information 6 months or more after it started reported that the thief obtained $5,000 or more, compared to 10% of those who found out in less than 6 months.

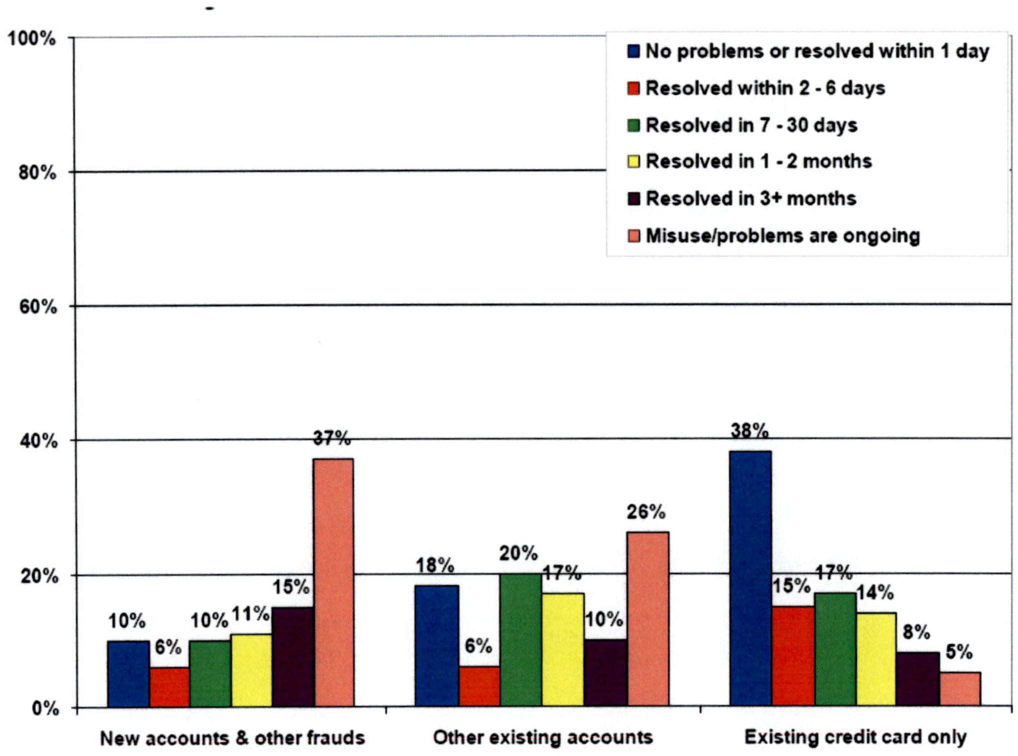

Figure 8. Q17 / Q19 / Q20 – Problem Resolution[21].

- Almost one-quarter of all victims (23%) said that either they had no problems or they were able to resolve any problems experienced as a result of being a victim of ID theft within one day of discovering that their personal information was being misused.
- While 38% of victims in the Existing Credit Cards Only category either had no problems or were able to resolve any problems within one day, only 10% of victims in the New Accounts and Other Frauds category were able to do so.
- Eleven percent of all victims said that it had taken 3 or more months to resolve their problems after they discovered that their information was being misused.
- o While 15% of victims in the New Accounts and Other Frauds category took 3 months or longer to resolve the problems, only 8% of victims in the Existing Credit Cards Only category took this long to resolve problems.
- • Twenty-one percent of all victims indicated that they were either continuing to experience problems related to the misuse of their information or that the misuse was continuing.
- o This was the case for 37% of those who had experienced New Accounts and Other Frauds ID theft, as compared to only 5% of victims in the Existing Credit Card Only category.

OFFENDERS' MEANS OF ACCESS

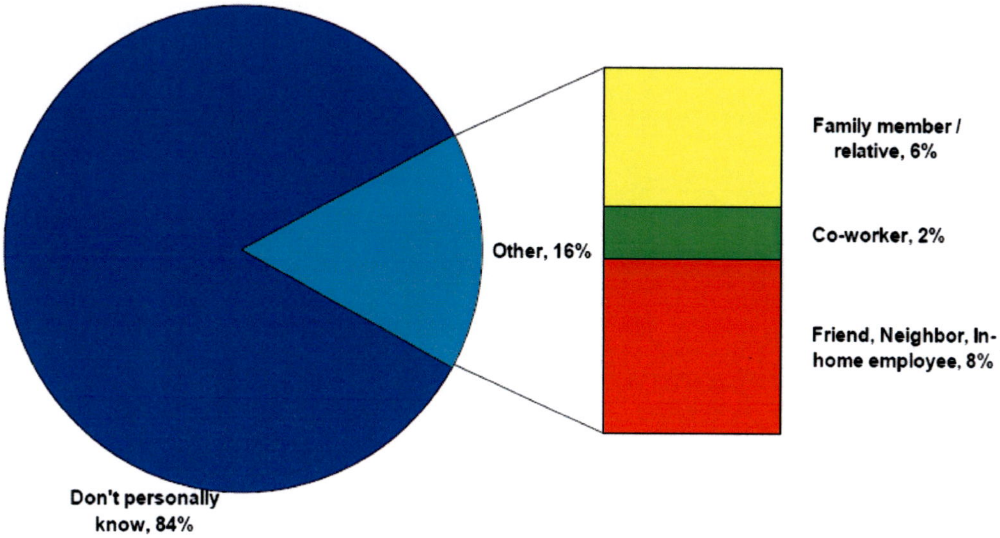

Figure 9. Q23 – Personal Relationship with Thief [22].

- ID theft victims generally are either unaware of the identity of the thief or do not personally know the thief. Over three-quarters of all ID theft victims (84%) reported that he or she did not personally know the thief, regardless of whether they had information about the thief's identity.
- Sixteen percent of all victims said that they personally knew the thief: o Six percent of victims knew that a family member or relative was the thief.
- Eight percent of victims knew that a friend, neighbor, or in-home employee was the thief.
- Two percent of victims reported that someone known to the victim from the workplace was the thief.
- Victims in the New Accounts and Other Frauds (24%) and the Existing Non-Credit Card Account (21%) categories were nearly 5 times as likely to know the thief personally as victims in the Existing Credit Card Only category (5%).[23].

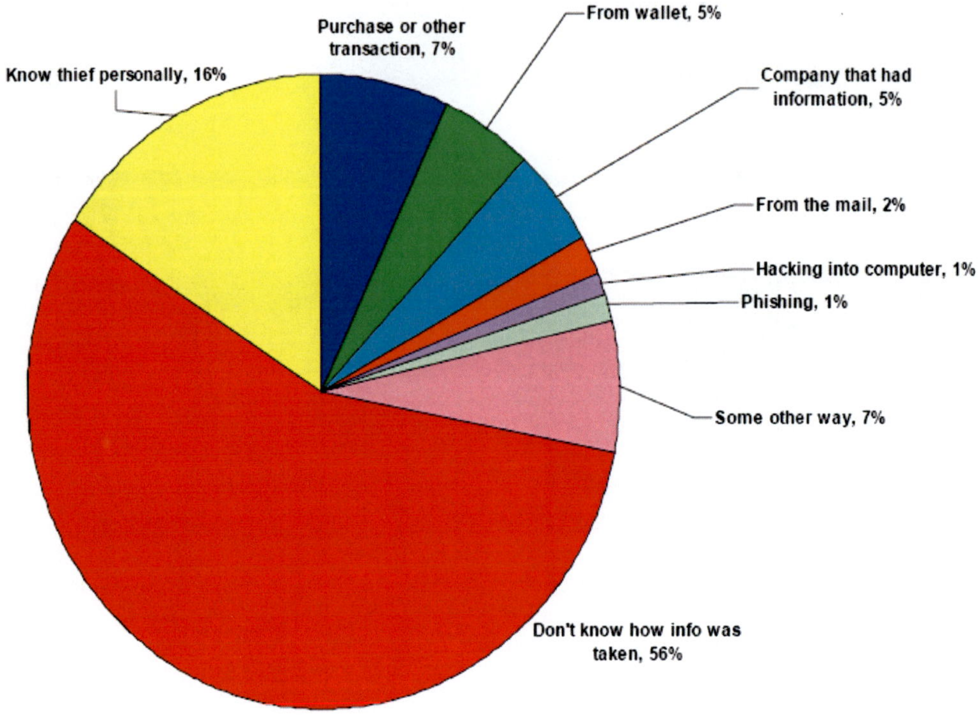

Figure 10. Q23 / Q25 / Q26 / Q27 – How Information Was Obtained [24].

- The majority of victims (56%) did not know how their information was stolen. Forty-three percent of victims were aware of who took their information or how it was taken.[25]
- Among those who knew how their information was taken, the most common factor was that their information was stolen by someone they personally knew. Sixteen percent of all victims indicated that their information was taken by someone they personally knew.
- Seven percent of all victims reported that their personal information was stolen during a purchase or financial transaction, including transactions conducted in a store, online, and through the mail.
- Five percent of all victims cited theft of a wallet or purse, and another 5% cited theft from a company that maintained their information.

TOLL OF VICTIMIZATION

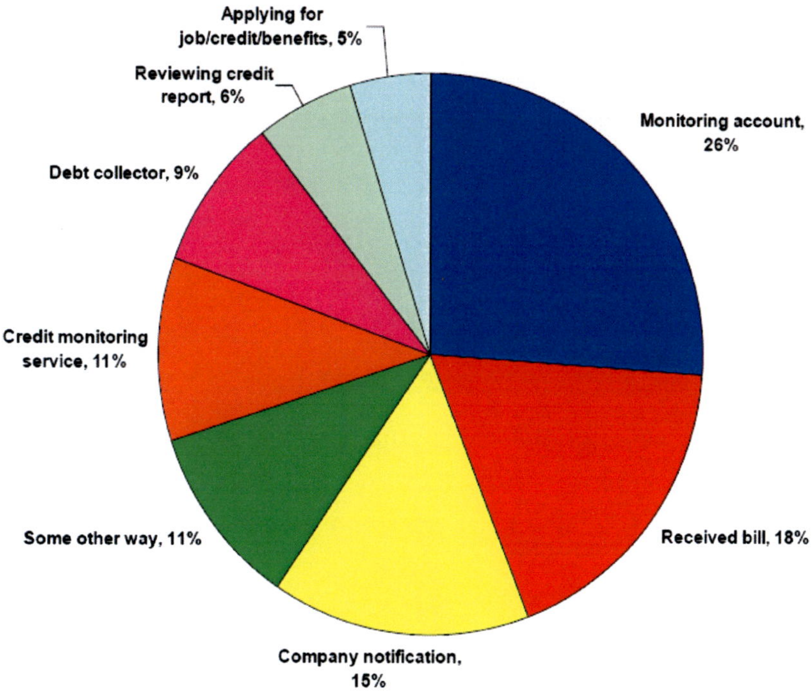

Figure 11. Q21 / Q21a – How Victims Discovered ID Theft [26]

- The most common way victims discovered the misuse of their personal information was by monitoring the activity in their accounts (37% of all victims).
- This includes victims using electronic means (12%), paper statements (6%), and those who could not recall whether they first found out electronically or by looking at a paper statement (8%). It also includes victims who used a credit monitoring service to detect unusual activity in their accounts (11%).
- How a victim was most likely to discover the misuse of their information depended on the category of ID theft suffered by the victim.
- When the misuse was limited to Existing Credit Cards Only, victims most commonly discovered their information was being misused when they received a bill with fraudulent charges (25%), by monitoring their accounts (24%), or when they were notified of unusual account activity by the company affected (23%).[27]
- In the Existing Non-Credit Card Accounts category, 41% of victims said that they discovered the misuse by monitoring their accounts.
- For New Accounts and Other Frauds victims, the most commonly mentioned means of discovery was being contacted by a debt collector (23%).
- Account monitoring was significantly more likely to be the way the fraud was detected for victims in the Existing Non-Credit Card Accounts (41%) and the Existing Credit Cards Only (24%) categories than for those in the New Accounts and Other Frauds category (11%).

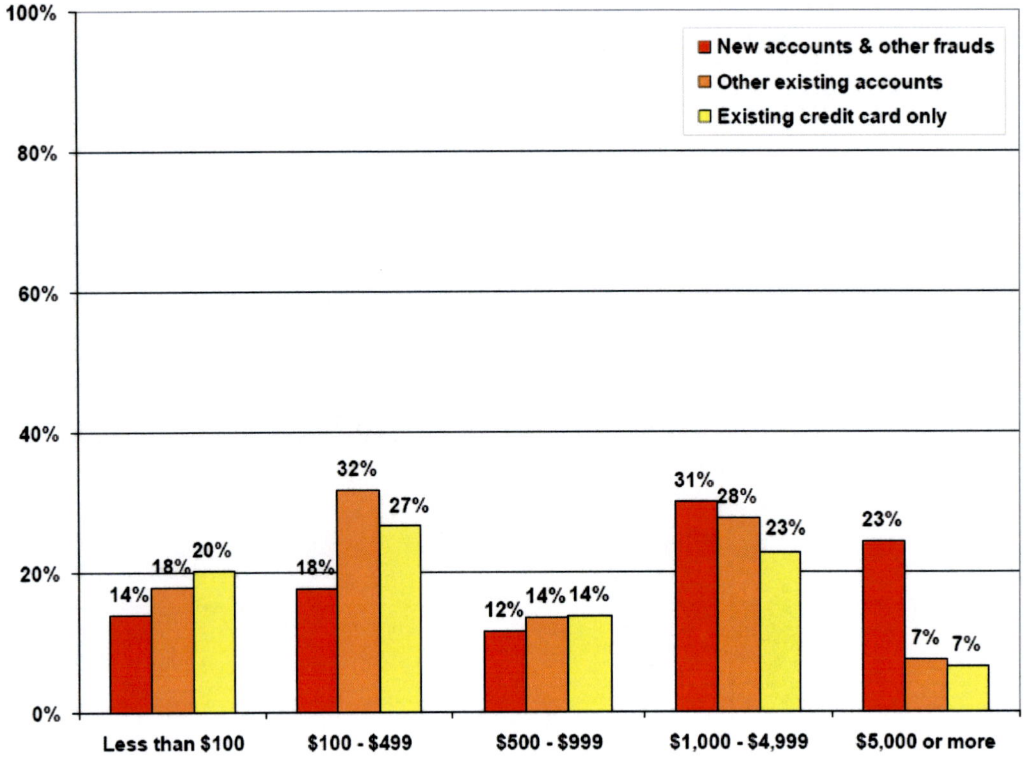

Figure 12. Q36 / Q39 / Q40 – Value Thief Obtained. [28]

- Victims were asked to estimate the value of the goods and services that the thief obtained from businesses, including financial institutions, using the victim's personal information. These figures include amounts where the business assumed the loss and amounts where the victim actually paid the debt created by the thief.
- The median value obtained by thieves was $500.
- The median values of goods and services obtained by the thief varied with the category of the identity theft.
- The median value obtained by thieves in the New Accounts and Other Frauds category was $1,350.
- The median value in the Existing Non-Credit Card Accounts category was $457. o The median value in the Existing Credit Cards Only category was $350.
- Eighteen percent of victims reported that the thieves obtained goods or services worth less than $100.
- Twelve percent of victims reported that the thieves obtained goods or services valued at $5,000 or more.
- Victims in the New Accounts and Other Frauds category were three times as likely to report that the thieves obtained more than $5,000 as victims in the other two categories of ID theft (23% vs. 7%).

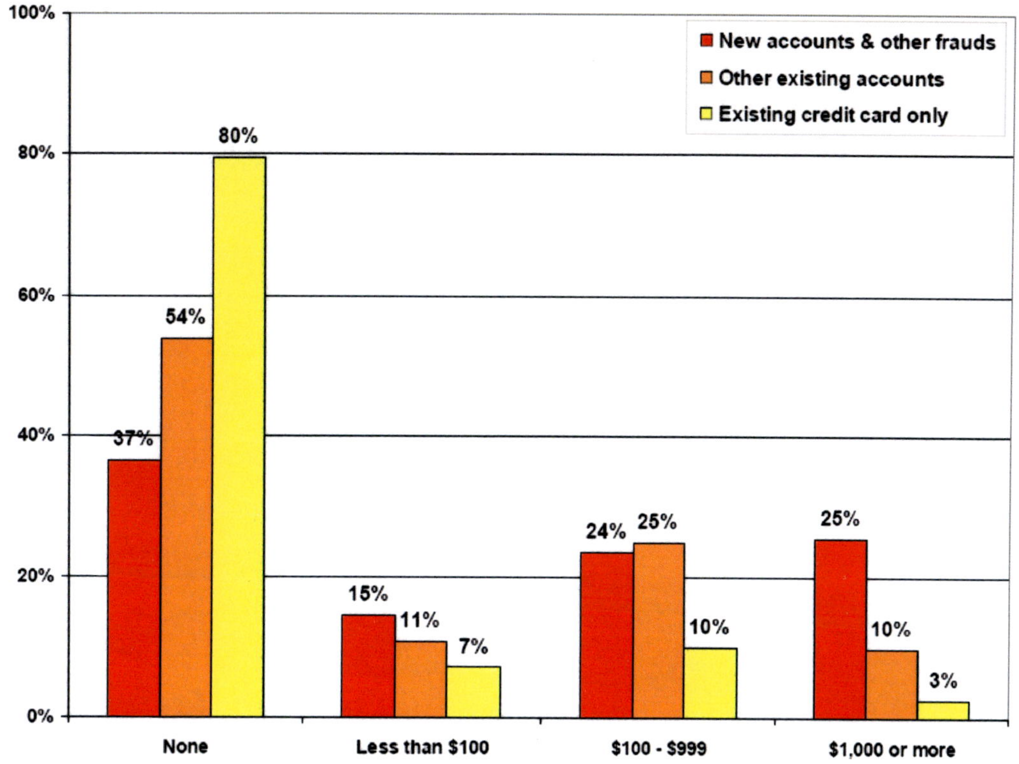

Figure 13. Q41 / Q44 / Q45 – Out-of-Pocket Payments by Victims [29]

- Survey participants were asked about their total out-of-pocket expenses, which include lost wages, legal fees, and payments of any fraudulent debts, as well as miscellaneous expenses such as postage and notarization fees.
- The majority of victims (59%) incurred no out-of-pocket expenses.
- More than three-quarters (80%) of victims in the Existing Credit Cards Only category paid no out-of-pocket expenses, compared to 37% for victims in the New Accounts and Other Frauds category and 54% for the Existing Non-Credit Card Accounts category.
- One-quarter of victims in the New Accounts and Other Frauds category reported paying out- of-pocket expenses of at least $1,000. They are two and one-half times as likely as Existing Non-Credit Card Accounts victims (10%) and eight times as likely as Existing Credit Cards Only victims (3%), to pay this amount.
- Thirty percent of victims who had no out-of-pocket expenses nonetheless reported other types of costs in resolving their ID theft incident.[30]
- Nineteen percent said that they spent 10 or more hours resolving problems related to ID theft.
- Nineteen percent said that they experienced one or more of the other types of problems included in Figure 15.
- Eight percent reported both that they spent more than 10 hours resolving problems and they experienced one or more of the other problems.

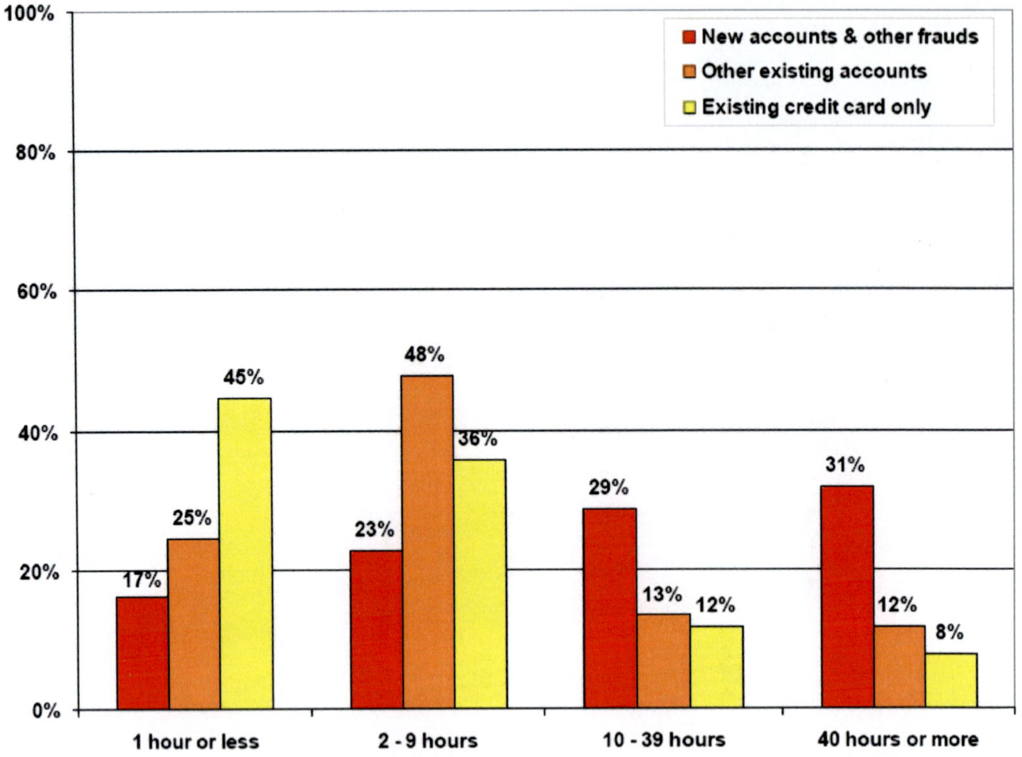

Figure 14. Q48 / Q51 / Q52 – Time Spent Resolving Problems. [31]

- This graph shows the estimated hours spent by victims in resolving problems stemming from ID theft. It does not refer to the amount of time that passed from when the victims discovered the crime to when their problems where resolved.
- When asked about the amount of time spent resolving problems stemming from the misuse of personal information, the median amount of time reported for all victims was 4 hours.
- Thirty percent of victims reported that they spent one hour or less resolving problems that resulted from their ID theft.
- Victims in the Existing Credit Cards Only category (45%) were most likely to report spending one hour or less resolving problems. Those in the Existing Non-Credit Card Accounts category (25%) and in the New Accounts and Other Frauds category (17%) were less likely to report one hour or less.
- Sixty percent of New Accounts and Other Frauds victims reported spending 10 or more hours resolving problems resulting from their ID theft. They were more than twice as likely as Existing Non-Credit Card Accounts victims (25%), and three times as likely as Existing Credit Card Only victims (20%), to spend this much time.

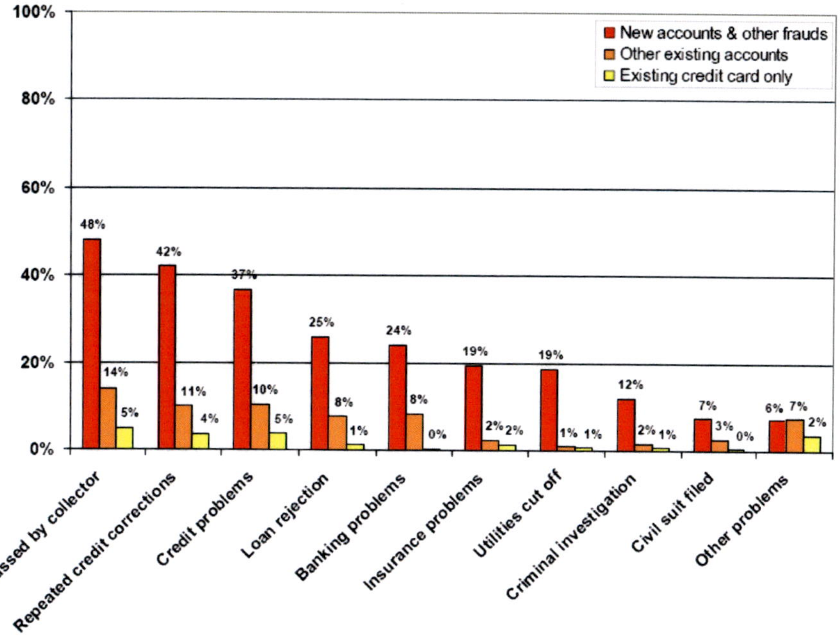

Figure 15. Q67 – Problems Experienced [32].

- Victims were asked whether they had experienced various types of problems, other than dollars and time expended, as a result of having their personal information misused. These included having problems obtaining or using a credit card, being turned down for a loan, or having problems opening a bank account or cashing checks.
- 16% of ID theft victims reported having credit problems, such as being rejected for credit or having a credit card refused by a merchant.
- 10% of ID theft victims reported suffering banking problems, such as being refused for a checking account or having checks rejected.
- 7% of victims reported having insurance problems, such as having been turned down for insurance or having to pay higher rates.
- A total of 37% of all ID theft victims reported having at least one of the problems identified; 21% of victims reported having more than one of these problems.
- Victims in the New Accounts & Other Frauds category were more than twice as likely to report having one or more of these problems (68%) as those in the Existing Non-Credit Card Accounts category (32%) and four times as likely as those in the Existing Credit Cards Only category (17%).
- Victims who reported that they had experienced one or more of these problems tended also to report incurring greater out-of-pocket expenses and spending more time to resolve their problems.[33]
- Among victims who had experienced one or more of these problems, 26% said that they had out-of-pocket expenses of $1,000 or more. Only 3% of victims who did not experience these problems incurred out-of-pocket expenses of $1,000 or more.

- Thirty-three percent of victims who had experienced one or more of these problems said that they had spent 40 hours or more resolving problems related to their ID theft. Only 6% of victims who did not experience these problems reported spending 40 hours or more resolving problems.

ACTIONS TAKEN

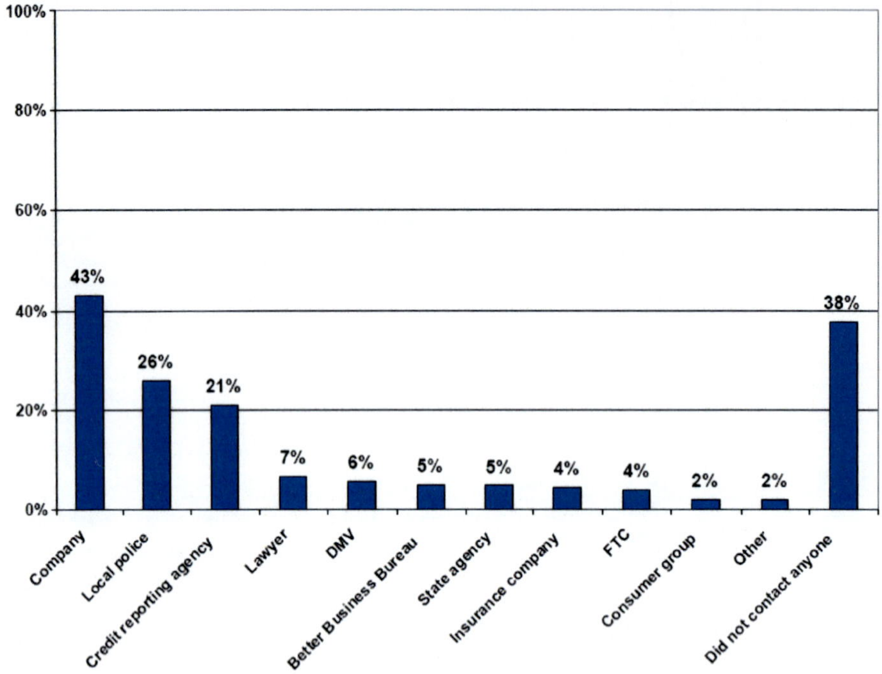

Figure 16. Q53 / Q53a/ Q54 / Q60 – Victim Contacts with Selected Parties [34]

- Forty-three percent of victims said that they contacted or were contacted by a company where an account was opened in their name or where an existing account was misused.[35]
- Twenty-six percent of victims said that they had contacted the police.
- While only 9% victims in the Existing Credit Cards Only category contacted thepolice, 44% of victims in the New Accounts & Other Frauds category did so.[36]
- Twenty-one percent of victims reported contacting one or more credit reporting agencies.
- While only 15% of victims in the Existing Credit Cards Only category and 12% of the Existing Non-Credit Card Accounts category contacted a credit reporting agency, 41% of those in the New Accounts & Other Frauds category made such contact.
- Victims were more likely to contact a credit reporting agency when the thief obtained a higher dollar amount. Twenty-nine percent of victims contacted at least one credit reporting agency when the value was over $1,000, compared to 16% when the value was less than $1,000.[37].

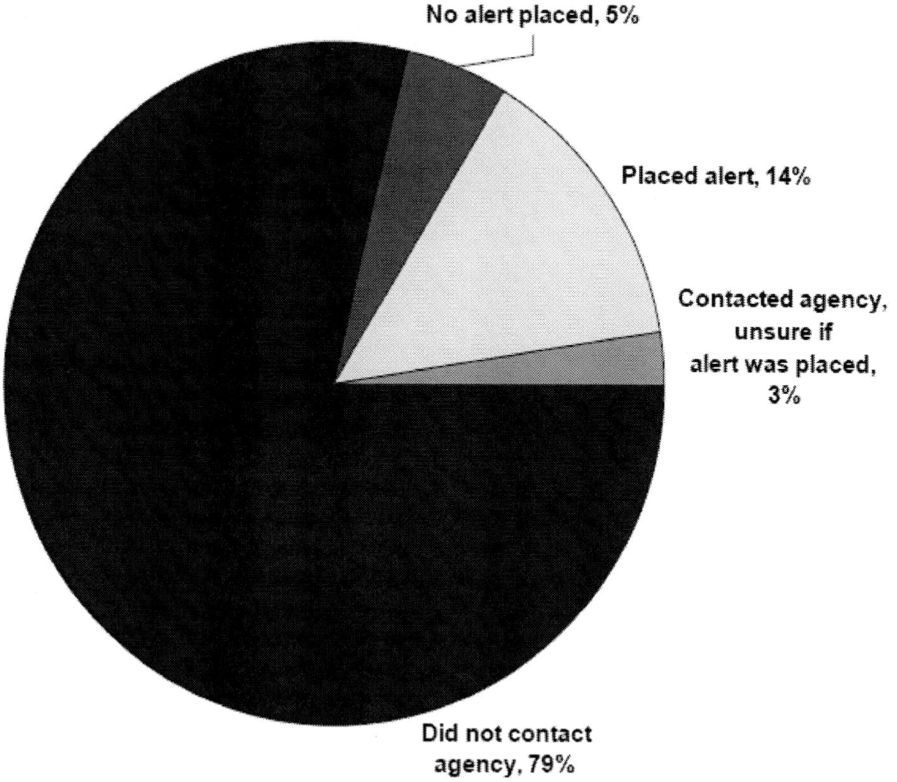

Figure 17. Q54 / Q63 –Initial 90-day Fraud Alert Placed [38]

- Since December 2004, the Fair Credit Reporting Act has allowed consumers who have a good faith suspicion that they have been or are about to become victims of ID theft to place an initial "fraud alert" on their credit file that will appear on credit reports issued to potential users of the report. The initial fraud alert remains in place for 90 days and notifies potential users that the consumer may be a victim of ID theft. A potential creditor that receives a credit report containing a fraud alert is required to take reasonable steps to verify the identity of the person applying for credit.[39]
- Fourteen percent of victims said they placed an initial 90-day fraud alert on their credit reports following the discovery of the misuse of their information.[40]
- Twenty-nine percent of victims in the New Accounts and Other Frauds category placed such alerts on their credit reports.
- Six percent of victims in the Existing Credit Cards Only category reported placing initial fraud alerts on their credit reports.

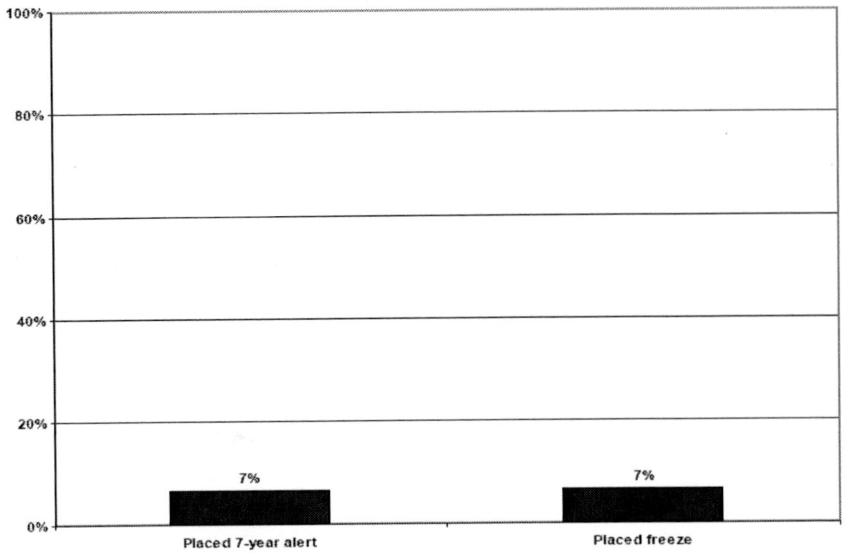

Figure 18. Q66 / Q61 – Further Measures Taken By Victims [41]

If a consumer has become an ID Theft victim, the Fair Credit Reporting Act since December 2004 has allowed the victim to place an extended, seven-year fraud alert on his or her credit file. The extended alert appears on all credit reports about the victim, notifying any potential user that the consumer has been a victim of ID theft. The extended alert also contains a telephone number at which the consumer may be reached, and any potential creditor is required to contact the consumer either at this number or in person before extending any additional credit in the consumer's name.[42] To get an extended alert, the consumer must provide the credit reporting agencies with an "Identity Theft Report," which is a detailed report that has been filed with a law enforcement agency.

In addition, some states allow ID theft victims to request a "credit freeze," which prevents their credit reports from being accessed without their express consent.[43] Because most companies obtain a credit report from a consumer before extending credit to a consumer, a credit freeze generally prevents the creation of new credit accounts in a consumer's name without the consumer's express permission. At the time this survey was conducted, credit freezes were available to consumers in 10 states.[44] As of the date of publication, most states have enacted credit freeze laws. Also, the three nationwide credit reporting agencies have offered freezes to consumers, even in states without specific credit freeze laws.

- Relatively few ID Theft victims took advantage of either extended alerts or credit freezes:
- Seven percent of ID Theft victims placed extended alerts on their credit reports.
- Seven percent of ID Theft victims placed a freeze on their credit reports.
- Each of these actions was taken by 15% of those in the New Accounts and Other Frauds category, but only by 3% to 4% of those in the Existing Accounts categories.[45]

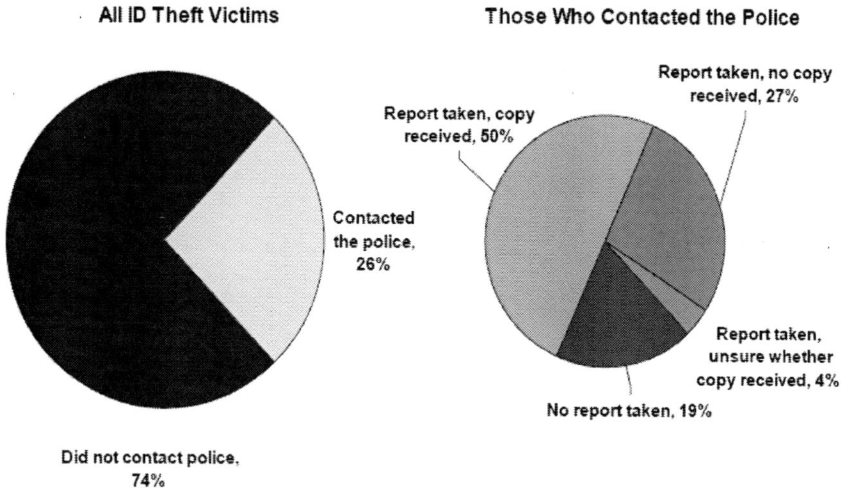

Figure 19. Q54 / Q55 / Q56 – Contact with Local Law Enforcement [46]

- A total of 26% of all victims contacted a local law enforcement agency.
- Although only 9% of victims in the Existing Credit Card Only category contacted the police, the police were contacted by 44% of those in the New Accounts & Other Frauds category.[47]
- Eighty-one percent of victims who contacted a local law enforcement agency reported that the police took a report (21% of all victims).40
- The police did not take a report from 19% of victims who contacted them (5% of all victims).
- Where the local police took a report, 60% of victims reported receiving a copy of the report (13% of all victims). However, 40% of victims did not get a copy or could not recall if they got a copy (7% of all victims, and 1% of all victims, respectively).

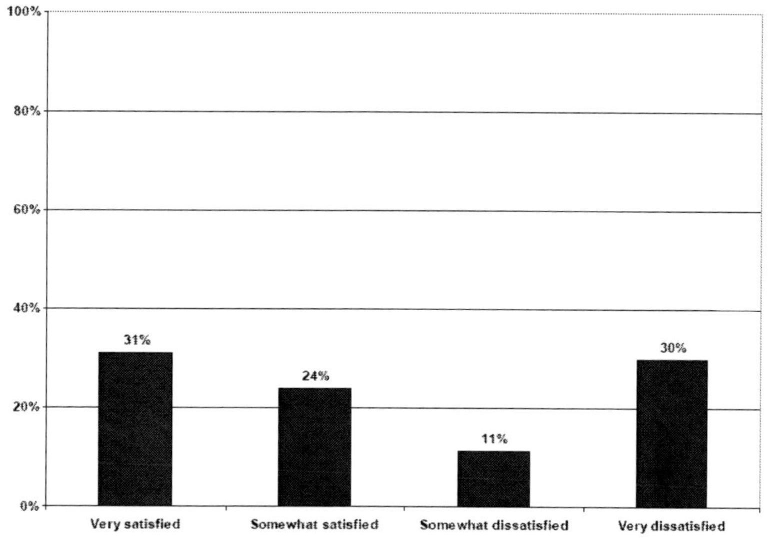

Figure 20. Q57 – Satisfaction with Local Law Enforcement Response [49]

Of the victims who contacted local law enforcement, 55% said they were "very" or "somewhat" satisfied, whereas, 41% of the victims who contacted local law enforcement were either "very" or "somewhat" dissatisfied with the response of local law enforcement.[50]

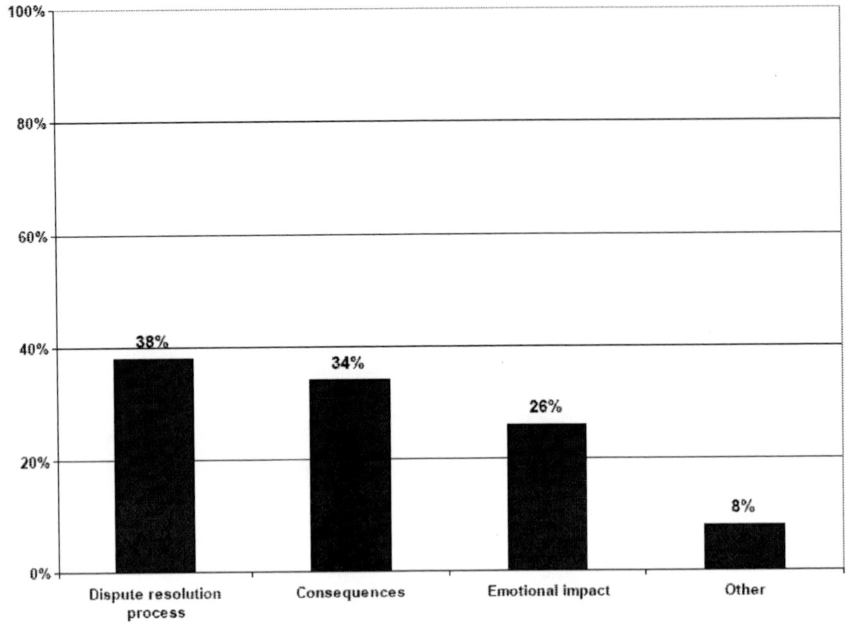

Figure 21. Q68 – Biggest Challenges of Experience. [51]

- Respondents who had spent 10 or more hours resolving problems were asked to describe in their own words the most difficult part of their experience. These respondents represent 31% of all ID Theft victims.
- Nearly 4-in-10 of these victims (38%) said that going through the dispute resolution process, itself, was the most difficult part. The dispute resolution process involves communicating with consumer reporting agencies and the companies where the thief committed the fraud to have the debts absolved and the credit reports corrected. It also involves the procedure of replacing credit cards and other key documents. Respondents also mentioned the sheer amount of time the dispute resolution process took.
- About one-third (34%) of these victims mentioned dealing with the practical consequences of the thief's actions, rather than the process of resolving disputes, as the most difficult part of their experience. Victims must cope with losing money, being unable to use their credit and bank accounts, or having their utilities shut off. Victims also reported being unable to open new accounts and other consequences flowing from the damage to their credit reports.
- Twenty-six percent of these victims said they were most affected by the emotional impact of the ID theft including the effects of stress on their lives and their health or the emotional toll resulting from the realization that they were vulnerable or had been betrayed.

Breach Notification

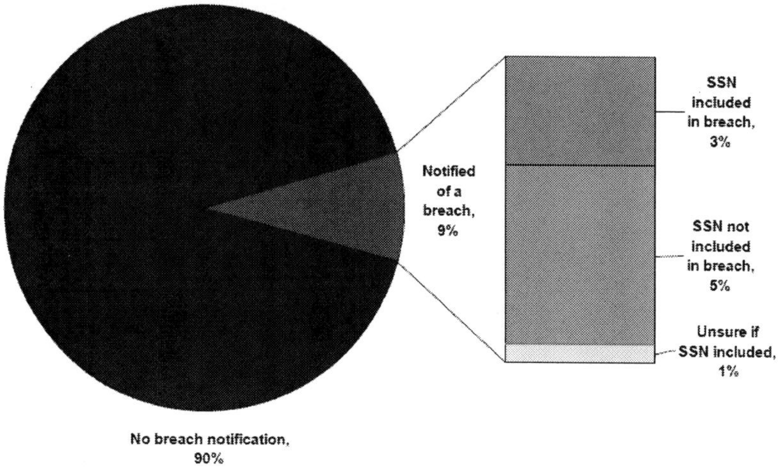

Figure 22. Q10 / Q10aa – Breach Notification Since 2001.[52]

- All survey participants, including those who were not identity theft victims, were asked if they had received notice of a breach of their personal information. A breach notification involves a company, agency, or some other organization notifying consumers that there has been a breach of the security of their data files, and that the consumer's personal information is among the information that has been compromised. It does not demonstrate any misuse of the information, just that the information has been compromised.[53]
- Nine percent of all respondents indicated they had been notified about a breach of their personal information since 2001[54]

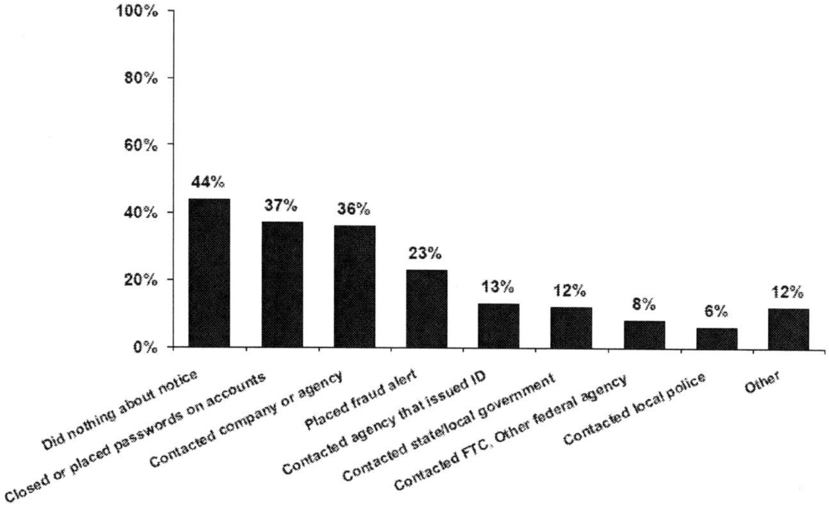

Figure 23. Q12 / Q13 – Actions Taken Following Breach Notification [55]

- Most people (55%) who received a notice about a breach of their information took action to understand or proactively address the situation.[56] Note that respondents could mention more than one action, so the sum of the specific steps taken displayed in the graph above will be greater than 55%.
- Most of those who were notified of a breach and did take action either called the company or agency that sent the notice (36% of those who received a breach notice) or closed an affected account or placed a password on it (37%).

FREE CREDIT REPORTS

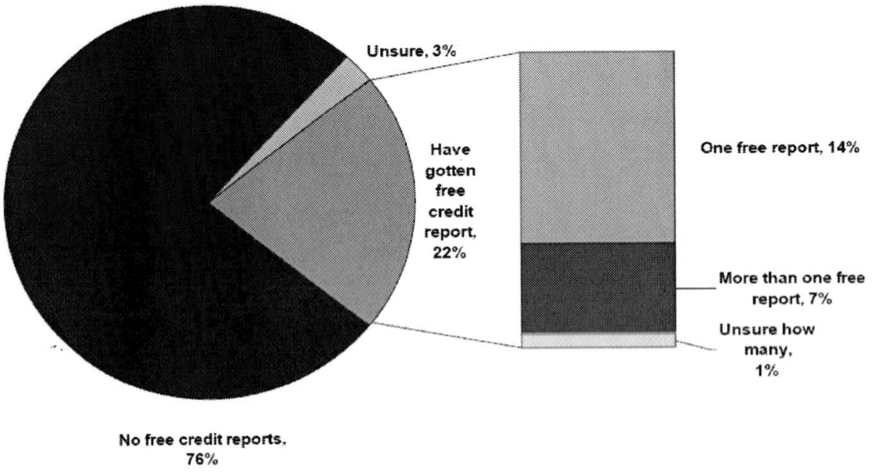

Figure 24. Q13a/Q13b – Free Credit Reports Since 2004 [57]

All consumers are entitled to receive a free copy of their credit report from each of the three nationwide credit reporting agencies ("CRAs") (Experian, Equifax, and TransUnion), as well as from various nationwide specialty CRAs, every twelve months.[58] Additionally, placing a fraud alert entitles consumers to immediately request free copies of their credit reports regardless of the timing of their previous requests.[59] Consumers who have had an extended fraud alert placed on their credit reports are entitled to request two free copies of their credit report from each of the CRAs in the twelve months following the date the extended alert was placed.[60]

- Just over 1-in-5 respondents in the overall sample (22%) said they had availed themselves of a free credit report since the annual free credit reports began to become available in parts of the country on December 1, 2004.[61] Annual free credit reports became available nationwide on September 1, 2005.
- Those with more than a high school education were nearly twice as likely as those with a high school education or less to request a free credit report (27% vs. 14%).[62]
- Respondents between the ages of 25 and 44 were most likely to request a free credit report (29%), while those age 65 and over were least likely to do so (1 3%).[63]

VICTIMS OF NON-ACCOUNT ID THEFT

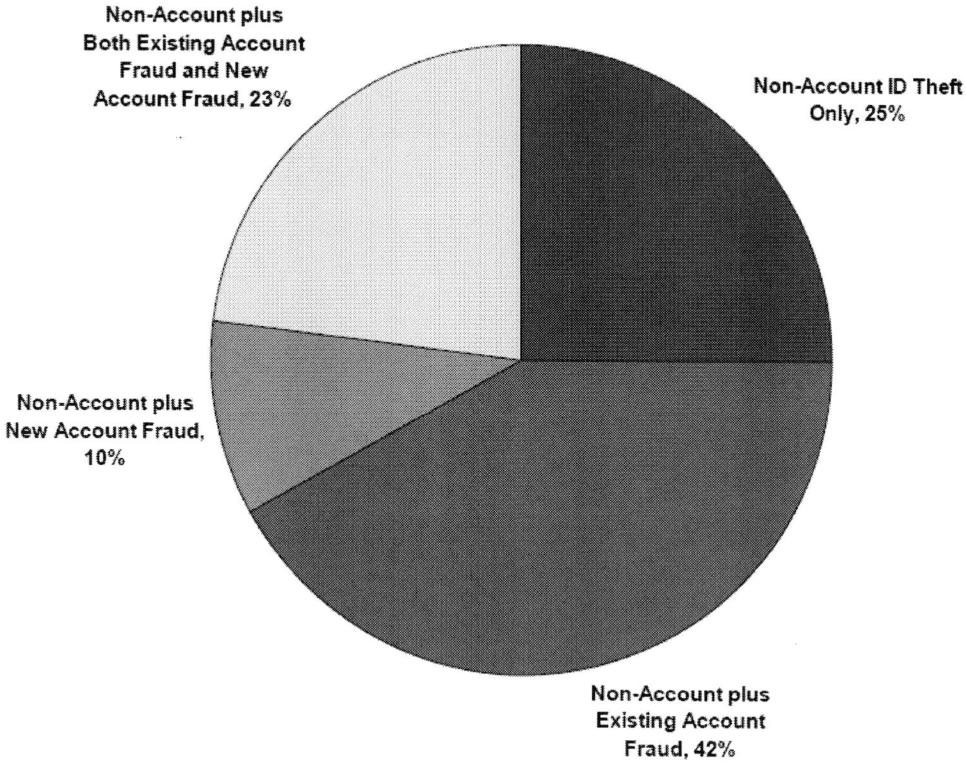

Figure 25. Q9 / Q34 – Non-Account ID Theft.

Overall, the experiences of 20% of ID theft victims included having their personal information used in "Non-Account ID Theft," which is fraud that does not involve accessing the victim's existing accounts or creating new financial accounts in the victim's name.[64] For example, the thief might provide the victim's name and information to employers for employment purposes, to the government to obtain disaster relief or benefits, or to police when being charged with a crime.

Among Non-Account ID Theft victims, 61% reported a specific way that their information had been misused – Figure 6 describes their responses. The remaining 39% indicated that their information had been misused to commit this type of fraud, but did not indicate the specific way it had been misused. Among the specific offenses committed by thieves using their information:

- Twenty-seven percent had their name given to law enforcement when the perpetrator was stopped or charged with a crime.
- Eighteen percent had their information used by the thief to obtain medical treatment, services, or supplies.
- Renting housing and obtaining government benefits were each reported by 6% of these victims, and obtaining employment was reported by 5%.

- Many Non-Account ID Theft victims also experienced types of ID theft that involve financial accounts: 65% experienced the misuse of existing accounts, and 33% had one or more new accounts opened in their name.[65]
  - Forty-three percent had an existing checking or savings account misused. o Thirty-four percent had an existing credit card misused.
  - Twenty-five percent had existing telephone (cellular or conventional) accounts misused and 18% had new telephone accounts opened in their name.
  - Fourteen percent had new credit card accounts opened in their name.

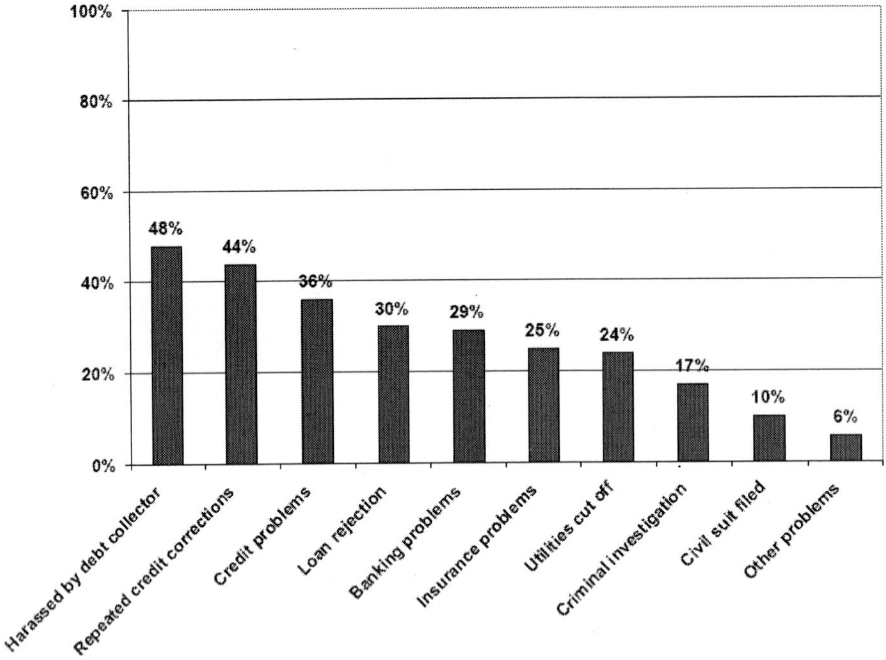

Figure 26. Q67 – Non-Account ID Theft Victim Experience.

- Approximately two-thirds (70%) of all ID Theft victims whose experiences included Non- Account ID theft encountered one or more of the problems in the above graph. This is nearly two and one-half times the rate for those whose experiences did not include Non- Account ID Theft (29%).
- The most frequently reported problems were:

  - Forty-eight percent of Non-Account ID Theft victims reported being harassed by a debt collector.
  - Forty-four percent said they needed to repeatedly correct information on their credit report.
  - Thirty-six percent said they experienced credit problems. o Thirty percent had been turned down for a loan.
  - Twenty-nine percent reported having banking problems.

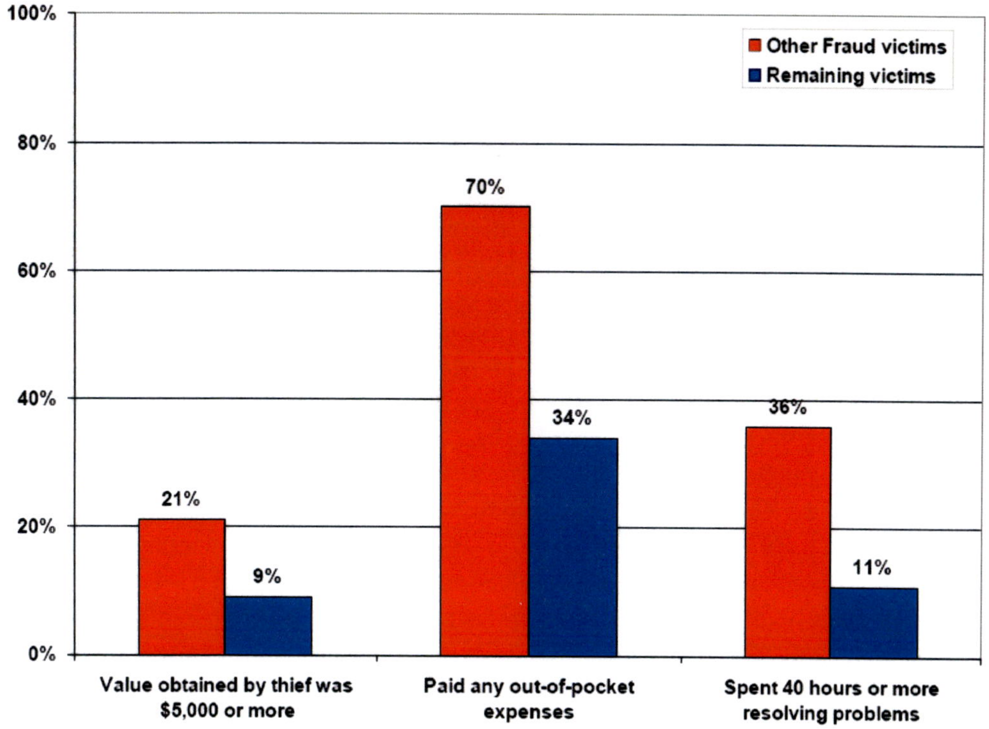

Figure 27. Q36 / Q41 / Q48 – Costs of Non-Account ID Theft.

- Where the victim's experience included Non-Account ID Theft, the value obtained by the thief was more than twice as likely to be $5,000 or more (21%) than for cases that did not involve this kind of misuse (9%).
- Victims whose experiences included Non-Account ID Theft were more likely than the remaining ID Theft victims to suffer costs associated with their experience.
  - Non-Account ID Theft victims were more than twice as likely to have actual, out-of-pocket expenses associated with their experience (70% of Non-Account ID Theft victims had to pay out of pocket expenses vs. 34% of the remaining victims).
  - Victims of Non-Account ID Theft were over three times more likely than the remaining victims to spend 40 hours or more resolving their problems (36% vs. 11%).

Appendix A: Methodology Report

I. Background and Objectives

The Federal Trade Commission (FTC) commissioned a study to gather information on consumer experiences with Identity Theft building upon similar research conducted in 2003. Since that time, more has become known about Identity Theft, the ways people are victimized, the costs, and the toll taken on its victims. The previous survey instrument was updated based on a review of 2003 results and the updated information will help policymakers, organizations, and citizens combat Identity Theft.

The survey was conducted through telephone interviews using a Random-Digit-Dialing (RDD) sampling methodology. The sampling scheme was designed to obtain a random sample of U.S. adults age 18 and older. A total of 4,917 interviews were conducted between March 27 and June 11, 2006.

The results contained in this report are based generally on the responses of those people who discovered that their personal information was being misused—that is, that they were victims of ID theft—between the beginning of 2001 and when they were interviewed. The data on the number of people who discovered they were victims of ID theft in 2005 and the data in the sections on breach notification and free credit reports are based on the responses of all survey participants from whom demographics were collected.[1] The data in Figure 2 and 3 are based on the responses of those who discovered that their personal information was being misuse d in 2005.

For many of the survey questions, there were a few respondents who either did not know the answer to the question or who refused to answer the question. In computing the figures in the report, those who answered “don’t know” or refused to answer have not been eliminated. Rather, they are included and simply recorded as not giving any of the indicated responses to a particular question. As a result, the responses to a question may total to less than 100 percent even where the question called for each participant to give only one response.

II. Methodology

A. Sampling Frame

The sampling frame consisted of all blocks of telephone numbers with at least one listed residential telephone number. A block of telephone numbers consisted of 100 numbers having the same first eight digits. The survey employed the GENESYS sampling system which randomly generates representative single-stage samples of telephone numbers. It generates each telephone number by randomly selecting a block known to contain at least one listed residential telephone number and then randomly generating the two final digits to complete the number. The advantage of beginning with blocks containing a known residential number is that it avoids generating numbers in blocks that are assigned exclusively to businesses or are unassigned. The resulting sample of telephone numbers represents all households in the U.S. with telephones, both listed and unlisted, without bias and with the efficiency of a single-stage sample.

The sampling frame was stratified to meet the goals of the sampling plan. The strata were constructed such that the resulting sample would provide a nationally representative statistical sample of US households in the 50 states and the District of Columbia.

Eight strata were defined and compiled by Census Region and urban/non-urban requirements. The top three classes of Metropolitan Statistical Areas as defined by the Census Bureau were categorized as urban, while the bottom two classes were categorized as non-urban.

The strata and the number of sample records dialed in each stratum are listed in the table below:

Identity Theft Study 2006 Starting Sample Distribution	
Region	Sample records
Northeast / urban	6,228
Northeast / non-urban	1,854
Midwest / urban	6,498
Midwest / non-urban	2,224
South / urban	16,136
South / non-urban	2,952
West / urban	10,986
West / non-urban	2,222
TOTAL	49,100

B. Questionnaire Design

The initial draft questionnaire was designed by the Federal Trade Commission, and subsequent drafts were developed collaboratively by the FTC and Synovate.

To ensure that all aspects of the survey instrument and protocol were working as designed, pilot testing was performed early in the field period with a limited number of interviewers dialing households. The pilot testing involved trained interviewers and the fully developed survey instrument programmed into the Computer Assisted Telephone Interviewing (CATI) system. The survey was deemed to be working as intended from a substantive and technical perspective, and the fieldwork continued.

A copy of the final questionnaire appears in Appendix C.

C. Telephone Data Collection

Interviewing began on March 27, 2006 and continued through June 11, 2006. Interviews were conducted between 9 a.m. and 9 p.m. Monday through Friday, between 9 a.m. and 8 p.m. on Saturdays, and between 11 a.m. and 8 p.m. on Sundays (all times local to the households being called).

Interviewers were monitored for quality and provided with guidance and correction when necessary. In addition, project management reports were generated by computer on a daily basis in order to track sample disposition and production rates.

Synovate's CATI system was used for data collection. The questionnaire was programmed into the system, and telephone interviewers read questions as they were logically fed in predetermined order from the computer to a viewing screen. Answers were sent back to the computer through the keyboard. This system reduced interviewer (non-random) error, such as not adhering to skip patterns, thus enhancing the quality of the data.

D. Respondent Eligibility

To be eligible to participate in the study the respondent had to be age 18 or older. The person who answered the telephone was asked to identify the household member, age 18 or older, with the most recent birthday, who then served as the randomly selected respondent.

E. Procedures to Maximize Response Rates

Several procedures were undertaken in order to maximize the response rates and to reduce the chance of interpretive error or bias associated with low response rates. The procedures were:

- Experienced interviewers were assigned to the project.
- Telephone interviews were conducted at different times of the day and days of the week in order to increase the likelihood of locating available respondents at times convenient for them. When possible, callbacks were scheduled at specific times requested by respondents.
- Every telephone number that did not result in contact with a respondent (this excludes business numbers, disconnects, faxes and modems) was dialed up to 7 times in order to increase the chances of finding a potential respondent.
- Production rates, interview length, and sample dispositions were monitored closely every other day.
- Project management personnel received weekly reports containing the number of refusals received and hours dialed by each interviewer. These reports were closely monitored and interviewers with a high refusal to hours-dialed ratio were removed from dialing. Those interviewers who had a ratio above the average were provided corrective feedback and monitored more closely by quality control supervisors. In addition, those who demonstrated the lowest refusal to hours-dialed ratio were selected for conversion dialing.

F. Non-Response Follow-up Results

All people who declined to take the survey were re-contacted by telephone one to two weeks following the initial contact in order to secure their cooperation. The contact was made by more experienced interviewers, specially trained in refusal avoidance techniques. Those respondents who requested they not be contacted again were omitted from these dialing efforts.

In order to assess the extent of any bias due to non-response, a random subset of those who refused for a second time during the conversion attempt answered a few key questions. The results of this interviewing are discussed in Appendix B.

G. Final Sample Dispositions and Response Rates

The table below shows the final dispositions for the entire random digit dial (RDD) sample generated by GENESYS for the FTC Identity Theft Survey. The classification of each sample piece was based on the most significant attempt. For example, if a respondent was not available on the first attempt and subsequent attempts resulted in a no answer, the final disposition was Respondent Not Available. If a respondent refused to participate during the first phase of dialing and the number was found to be an answering machine on a subsequent conversion attempt, it was categorized as a Refusal. Interviews completed during the conversion phase of the study were included in the calculation of the final response rates.

The response rate was computed using the AAPOR Outcome Rate Calculator Version 2.1, formula AAPOR RR3.

Identity Theft Study 2006 Final Overall Sample Disposition		
	Total	
	Frequency	Percent
Interview - Category 1		
Completed screening interviews	4,917	10.01
Partial interviews	353	0.72
Total	5,270	10.73
Eligible, non-interview, Category 2		
Refusal and break off	3,801	7.74
Total	3,801	7.74
Unknown Eligibility, non-interview, Category 3		
Always busy	533	1.09
No answer	12,417	25.29
Answering machine-don't know if household	2,998	6.11
Call blocking	595	1.21
No screener completed	8,980	18.29
Total	25,523	51.98
No Eligible, Category 4		
Fax/data line	2,296	4.68
Disconnected number	5,780	11.77
Non-working number	1,620	3.30
Temporarily out of service	150	0.31
Number changed	60	0.12
Cell phone	30	0.06
Business, govt. office, other organization	3,744	7.63
No eligible respondent	826	1.68
Total	14,506	29.54
TOTAL PHONE NUMBERS USED	49,100	100.0
AAPOR Response Rate		
Response Rate 3		26%

H. Data Preparation and Processing

Data cleaning and quality control checks were automatically performed during the interviewing process on the CATI system. Final cleaning runs checked all questionnaire logic and relationships among items.

I. Weighting

The basic survey design for the FTC Identity Theft Study consisted of the following: The study sampled U.S. adults, 18 years or older, by calling a random sample of U.S. telephone households. Through a series of screening questions, the respondent was identified as either a victim of identity theft or not. If the respondent was a victim, he or she completed an extensive interview. A random portion of respondents who were not victims were asked a series of demographic questions.

Those that were not asked these questions were thanked and no further questions were asked.

Sample weights were constructed based on the survey design to provide unbiased estimates for total national demographics and for victims of identity theft. The sample weights include a design weight – the correction for the random selection of non-victims to be asked demographic questions and a post-stratified adjustment weight to correct for different rates of contact and cooperation among different age groups, genders, educational groups, race/ethnicity groups and regions.

The design weights were calculated using the information in the following table. The goal is to recreate an unbiased national sample representative of the U.S. population. The total sample of 4,916 respondents would be an unbiased national sample. By including the design weights, the 1,496 respondents for whom demographic information was collected are also an unbiased national sample.

Sample Subgroups	Number in Sample[2]	Number in Sample with Demographic Information	Design Weight to adjust for sub-sampling
Identity Theft Victims (including minor victims)	915	915	915/915 = 1.000000
Non-identity Theft Victims	4,001	581	4001/581=6.886403
Total	4,916	1,496	--

The next step is to produce a final weight using post-stratified adjustments to account for different contact and cooperation rates among different demographic groups. The post-stratified adjustment used iterative proportional fitting to marginal population distributions for Gender, Age, Race, Region, and Hispanic Ethnicity within Region. This methodology is also referred to as sample balancing, raking or rim weighting. For this study, the estimates from the March 2005 Supplement of the Current Population Survey were used as the population marginal distribution.

The target population percentages for Gender, Age, Race, Region, and Hispanic Ethnicity within Region are summarized in the following table.

	Region	Population Percentage
1	Northeast	18.89
2	Midwest	22.34
3	South	36.03
4	West	22.74

	Age	Population Percentage
1	18 to 24	12.86
2	25 to 34	18.09
3	35 to 44	19.95
4	45 to 54	19.31
5	55 to 64	13.59
6	65 plus	16.20

	Gender	Population Percentage
1	Male	48.29
2	Female	51.71

	Region	Hispanic Origin	Population Percentage
1	Northeast	Yes	1.96
2		No	16.59
3	Midwest	Yes	1.20
4		No	21.08
5	South	Yes	5.03
6		No	31.06
7	West	Yes	6.18
8		No	16.90

	African-American	Population Percentage
1	Yes	11.88
0	No	88.12

	Asian	Population Percentage
1	Yes	4.54
0	No	95.46

White		Population Percentage
1	Yes	82.03
0	No	17.97

	Native American	Population Percentage
1	Yes	1.69
0	No	98.31

An additional marginal was set based on an interim review of the data. This review revealed that some respondents were considering credit card fraud as identity theft. The questionnaire was adjusted to isolate credit card fraud only and this adjusted questionnaire was fielded using nationally representative replicates. Based on these interviews, a marginal distribution of credit card only victims, other victims and non-victims was created, summarized as:

- 7.1% - Existing Credit Card only victims,
- 10.7% - All other victims, and
- 82.2% - Non-victims

These percentages were used as the targets for the final marginal in the post-stratification adjustments to the weights.

The distribution of the final weights is summarized in this table.

N	Mea	Su	Standar deviati	Minim	Maximum
1,496	3.28	4,	4.5738	0.0310	55.4446

Appendix B: Drop-out and Refused Report

As with any survey of a sample of a population, the results of this survey may differ from what one would find if all adult Americans – the population covered by this survey – were interviewed. There are a number of reasons for this. First, uncertainty is introduced because only a sample of the population was interviewed and their experiences may differ somewhat from those of others in the relevant population. Perhaps a smaller or larger percentage of this particular group of individuals experienced ID theft than was true of the population as a whole. The degree of uncertainty resulting from the use of a sample rather than a census is a function of the number of people who were asked a particular set of questions and is captured by standard statistical methods in standard errors of the estimates which are included in the figures on the prevalence of the various types of ID theft.

However, additional problems can arise because not everyone who was asked to participate in the survey agreed to do so. In addition, some of those who began the survey failed to complete it. The results reported in the body of this study are based on the responses of those who participated in and completed the survey. Therefore, if the experiences of either those who refused to participate in the survey or those who failed to complete the survey differ from the experiences of those who completed the survey, the results will not be completely representative of the population as a whole in ways that are not captured in the number of interviews completed and the standard errors of the estimates. This appendix preliminarily considers how the inability to include these two groups in the survey may have affected the results – particularly the estimates of the prevalence of ID theft.

Incomplete Interviews

As shown in the Methodology Report in Appendix A, 5,270 interviews were begun, and of these, 353 were not completed. Of these 353 people, 79 completed enough of the interview to allow determination of whether they had ever been a victim of ID theft and, if so, the type of ID theft they experienced – that is, they participated at least through Q9; 274 did not complete enough of the survey to be able to determine whether or not they had ever been victims of ID theft. By comparing the prevalence figures based on only the 4,916 completed interviews with the figures based on both complete interviews and the 79 interviews that were incomplete but provide enough information to determine whether the person had ever experienced ID theft, one can get some idea of how the failure to complete the interview affected the results This assumes that those who quit after Q9 also are representative of those who quit prior to Q9.

As shown in Table 1, inclusion of these incomplete interviews does result in a slightly higher measure of the percentage of people who have experienced some form of ID theft at some point in their lives – 19.5 percent with the incomplete interviews included compared to 18.5 percent including only the completed interviews.[1] Similar increases – a few tenths of a percentage point – are found for each of the three types of ID theft.

Refused to Participate

The figures in this appendix cannot be compared with the figures in the body of the report. There are at least two reasons for this. First, these data measure the percentage of people whose survey answers indicated that they had been a victim of ID theft at some point in their lives, not just in 2005. Second, the data here are not weighted to adjust for differences between those who were interviewed and the population at largeA second problem that can cause the results of a survey to differ from the actual experiences of the population being surveyed is the fact that not everyone who is asked to participate agrees to do so. Indeed, as shown in the Methodological Report, the response rate for this survey was 26 percent. While steps, including the use of random digit dialing to locate survey participants, were used to ensure that the sample was as random as possible, if those who did not agree to participate differ in some relevant way from those who were actually interviewed, the survey results may not reflect the actual experiences of the population as a whole.

In order to get some idea of possible differences between those who refused to participate in the survey and those who did participate, the contractor persuaded a sample of 100 people who were unwilling to participate in the survey to answer a few questions – including the questions about whether the person had ever been a victim of ID theft. (This sample is referred to as the "Conversion Sample.") Comparing the prevalence figures for these 100 people to those of the people who did agree to participate in the survey can provide some measure of any possible bias introduced by the fact that not everyone was willing to participate in the survey.

Table 3 contains the relevant figures for the Conversion Sample as well as for the complete and incomplete interviews. In general, the responses of the Conversion Sample suggest that those who refused to participate in the survey may be somewhat more likely to have experienced ID theft than those who agreed to participate in the survey.[2] However, one must be careful in drawing conclusions from these data. The Conversion Sample consists of only 100 observations and the observed differences are not statistically significant.

Table 3. Comparison of Prevalence of ID Theft, Complete Interviews Only, Complete and Incomplete Interviews, and Conversion Partial Interviews, Ever a Victim

	Complete Interviews Only	Complete & Incomplete Interviews	Conversion Sample
Victim of Any Kind of ID Theft	18.5%	19.5%	25.0%
Only Misuse of an Existing Credit Card	8.9%	9.2%	11.0%
Misuse of Other Existing Accounts	5.1%	5.6%	6.0%
New Accounts & Other Frauds	4.5%	4.8%	8.0%
n =	4,916	4,995	100

Note. The data in this table cannot be compared with the data in the body of the report for at least two reasons. First, these data measure the percentage of people who indicate that they have been a victim of ID theft at some point in their lives, not in 2005. Second, the data here are not weighted to adjust for differences between those who were interviewed and the population at large.

Appendix C: Questionnaire
Federal Trade Commission
Incidence Of Identity Theft Study

2006 Identity Theft Survey Instrument

Hello, I'm .... of Synovate. I am calling on behalf of the Federal Trade Commission, a U.S. government agency that enforces a number of consumer protection laws. We are conducting a research survey today. We are not selling anything, and no sales calls will be made. The survey is anonymous and you will not be asked for any personal information.

(READ ONLY IF NECESSARY:) For your information, under the Paperwork Reduction Act, as amended, an agency may not conduct or sponsor, and a person is not required to respond to, a collection of information unless it displays a currently valid OMB control number. For this survey, that number is 3084 - 0124.

A. In order to interview the right person, I need to speak with the member of your household who is aged 18 or over and has had the most recent birthday. Would that be you?

1. YES (**CONTINUE TO QUESTION 1**)
2. NO

IF QA:2 (NO) THEN ASK:

May I please speak to the person in your household who is 18 years of age or older and has had the most recent birthday?

IF THAT PERSON IS NOT HOME, THEN ASK:

When would be a convenient time for me to call him or her back?

(REPEAT INTRODUCTION AND QUESTION A WITH NEW RESPONDENT)

10. Have you ever been notified by a company, government agency, or other organization that it had lost your personal information, such as an account number or your social security number, or that the information had been stolen or hacked?

1. Yes
2. No - **SKIP TO Q13a**
3. Don't Know - **SKIP TO Q13a**
4. Refused - **SKIP TO Q13a**

If Q10:1, Read: **IF YOU RECEIVED MORE THAN ONE NOTIFICATION ABOUT THE LOSS OR THEFT OF YOUR INFORMATION, PLEASE THINK ABOUT THE MOST RECENT NOTIFICATION YOU RECEIVED IN ANSWERING THE NEXT FIVE QUESTIONS.**

10a. When did you receive that notification?

1. Since the beginning of 2006
2. In the last 6 months of 2005
3. In the first 6 months of 2005
4. In 2004
5. In 2003
6. In 2002
7. In 2001
8. Before 2001
9. Don't know
10. Refused

10aa. Did the notification indicate that your Social Security Number was included in the information that was lost or stolen?

1. Yes
2. No
3. Don't Know
4. Refused

12. After receiving this notification, did you do anything about the loss or theft of your information?

    1. Yes
    2. No - **SKIP TO Q11**
    3. Don't Know - **SKIP TO Q11**
    4. Refused - **SKIP TO Q11**

13. What did you do about the loss or theft of your information after receiving this notification? Did you (**INSERT AND RANDOMIZE**) (**CAN BE MULTIPLES.**)

    1. Consult a lawyer or other professional
    2. Contact the company or agency that sent the notification
    3. Place a fraud alert on your credit report
    4. Close or put a password on your affected accounts
    5. Contact the State Attorney General or a state or local consumer agency
    6. Contact your local police or the local police in another jurisdiction
    7. Contact the government agency that issued the identification number that was lost or stolen, such as contacting the DMV if your drivers license number was lost or stolen

    (**ALWAYS ASK IN THIS ORDER**)

    9. Contact the Federal Trade Commission
    10. Contact another federal agency (SPECIFY)______ (CAN BE MULTIPLES).

    11. (**ASK LAST**) Or contact someone else (SPECIFY)______.
    12. Don't Know
    13. Refused

11. Did you discover that someone had misused your information after you received the notification?

    1. Yes
    2. No
    3. Don't Know
    4. Refused

13a. Have you gotten any free annual credit reports since December 1, 2004?

1. Yes
2. No - **SKIP TO INSTRUCTION BEFORE Q1**
3. Don't Know - **SKIP TO INSTRUCTION BEFORE Q1**
4. Refused - **SKIP TO INSTRUCTION BEFORE Q1**

13b. How many free annual credit reports did you get?

1. One
2. Two
3. Three
4. More than three
5. Don't know
6. Refused

(IF "YES" ON Q10, READ: "Now I would like to learn about any actual misuse of your information whether in connection with the data breach we discussed earlier or as a separate incident.")

1. Has anyone ever placed charges on you existing credit card account without your permission?

    1. Yes
    2. No
    3. Don't know
    4. Refused

2. **(THERE IS NO Q2)**
3. **(THERE IS NO Q3)**
4. **(THERE IS NO Q4)**
6. (THERE IS NO Q6)

7. Has anyone ever placed charges on or taken money from any of your existing accounts OTHER THAN a credit card account without your permission? This could include misusing an existing wireless telephone account or an ATM or check card to take money from your banking account.

1. Yes
2. No
3. Don't know
4. Refused

(ASK IF Q1 = 1 OR IF Q7 = 1; ELSE GO TO Q8)

5. Did someone change the billing address or have themselves added as an authorized user of . . . ?

(READ. ENTER SINGLE RESPONSE FOR EACH TYPE OF ACCOUNT.)

1. **(READ IF Q1 = 1)** any of the credit card account(s) that were misused, or
2. **(READ IF Q7 = 1)** any of the existing account(s) that were misused OTHER THAN credit card accounts

8. Has anyone ever opened NEW credit card accounts, bank accounts, or other accounts using your personal information such as your Social Security number or date of birth without your permission?

1. Yes
2. No
3. Don't Know
4. Refused

9. Has anyone ever used your personal information without your permission for some other fraudulent purpose, such as giving your information to the police when they were cited for a traffic violation or charged with a crime; obtaining government benefits, medical care, or a job; or renting an apartment or house?

1. Yes
2. No
3. Don't Know
4. Refused

IF "YES" ON Q1, Q7, Q8, OR Q9, ASK Q14; OTHERWISE GO TO QD5 BEFORE Q69

14. I would like to learn some more about the misuse of your personal information. This might include the misuse of any of your existing accounts, the opening of new accounts, or any

other fraud committed using your personal information. First of all, has your personal information been MISUSED within the last five years?

1. Yes
2. No
3. Don't Know
4. Refused

15. Can you tell me when you DISCOVERED that your personal information had been misused? **(READ LIST IF NECESSARY. ENTER SINGLE RESPONSE.) (INTERVIEWER NOTE: IF "DON'T KNOW" OR "REFUSED," PROBE:** Please give me your best estimate.)

1. Since the beginning of 2006
2. In the last 6 months of 2005
3. In the first 6 months of 2005
4. In 2004
5. In 2003
6. In 2002
7. In 2001
8. Before 2001 – **SKIP TO QD5 BEFORE Q69**
9. Don't know - **SKIP TO QD5 BEFORE Q69**
10. Refused - **SKIP TO QD5 BEFORE Q69**

16. From the time the misuse of your information first began, how long did it take you to discover it was being misused? **(READ LIST IF NECESSARY. ENTER SINGLE RESPONSE.)**

1. One day or less
2. More than a day but less than a week
3. At least a week, but less than one month
4. 1 to 2 months
5. 3 to 5 months
6. 6 to 11 months,
7. 1 year to less than 2 years
8. 2 years to less than 3 years
9. Or, 3 years or more
10. Don't know
11. Refused

17. Has the misuse of your personal information stopped, or is someone still misusing your personal information?

1. Misuse has stopped
2. Still Misusing information - **SKIP TO Q21**
3. Don't Know - **SKIP TO Q21**
4. Refused - **SKIP TO Q21**

18. **(THERE IS NO Q18)**

19. Is the misuse of your personal information still causing you problems? For example, are you still spending time clearing up your accounts or your credit report? Or, have you managed to resolve all of the problems caused by the misuse of your information?

1. Still experiencing problems - **SKIP TO Q21**
2. All problems resolved
3. Did not experience any problems - **SKIP TO Q21**
4. Don't know - **SKIP TO Q21**
5. Refused - **SKIP TO Q21**

20. Can you tell me how long it took you to resolve the problems after you discovered that your information was being misused? (**READ LIST IF NECESSARY. ENTER SINGLE RESPONSE.**)

1. One day or less
2. More than a day but less than a week
3. At least a week, but less than one month
4. 1 to 2 months
5. 3 to 5 months
6. 6 to 11 months
7. 1 year to less than 2 years
8. 2 years to less than 3 years
9. Or, 3 years or more
10. Don't know
11. Refused

21. How did you first find out someone had misused your personal information? Was it…(**READ AND RANDOMIZE**)? (**ENTER SINGLE RESPONSE.**)

1. By monitoring your accounts
2. When notified by your credit monitoring service
3. When notified of unusual account activity **(PROG NOTE: ALWAYS ASK 3 AFTER 2 AND 4.)**
4. When contacted by a debt collector
5. When you received a bill you did not owe
6. When you applied for credit, employment, or other services or benefits
7. When you reviewed your credit report
8. (**ASK LAST AND ONLY IF PERSON DOES NOT SELECT ONE OF RESPONSES 1 - 7.**) Or, did you find out some other way? (SPECIFY) ______________
9. Don't know
10. Refused

IF Q21:1 - "By monitoring your accounts" - ask Q21a; ELSE GO TO Q23

21a. You said that you first discovered someone had misused your personal information by monitoring your accounts. Was that through:
(**READ AND RANDOMIZE. ENTER SINGLE RESPONSE.**)?

1. Paper statements
2. The Internet, an ATM, or other electronic means
3. Don't know
4. Refused

22. (THERE IS NO Q22)

23. Was the person who misused your personal information…
(**READ AND RANDOMIZE LIST UNTIL AN ANSWER IS GIVEN. ENTER SINGLE RESPONSE.**)?

1. Someone you don't personally know (**ALWAYS READ FIRST; PAUSE BEFORE GOING ON**)
2. A Family Member or Relative (**IF YOU ARE ASKED, THE DEFINITION INCLUDES PRESENT & FORMER FAMILY MEMBERS, INCLUDING IN-LAWS AND STEP-FAMILY MEMBERS**)
3. A co-worker who you know
4. A Friend, Neighbor or In Home Employee
5. (**ASK LAST AND ONLY IF THE PERSON DOES NOT SELECT ONE OF RESPONSES 1-4**) Or someone else (**SPECIFY**) ______________
6. Don't know
7. Refused

IF Q23: 1, 5, 6, or 7, ASK Q25; OTHERWISE SKIP TO Q24

25. Do you know anything about HOW your personal information was obtained?

1. Yes
2. No - **GO TO INSTRUCTION BEFORE Q29**
3. Don't know - **GO TO INSTRUCTION BEFORE Q29**
4. Refused - **GO TO INSTRUCTION BEFORE Q29**

26. How was your personal information obtained? Was it stolen (**READ AND RANDOMIZE**)? (**ENTER SINGLE RESPONSE.**)

1. From your wallet or checkbook
2. From your postal mail
3. As a result of a fraudulent change of address
4. From *your* garbage
5. During a purchase or other transaction
6. From your employer
7. From someone hacking into *your* computer
8. As a result of a scam e-mail that you responded to
9. From an office or company that had your personal information in its files
10. (**ASK LAST AND ONLY IF PERSON DOES NOT SELECT ONE OF RESPONES 1-9**) Or, was it obtained some other way (**SPECIFY**)_____
11. I don't know how my information was obtained
12. Refused

24. Did any police or government official inform you that the person who stole your information was . . .?
(READ ITEMS A – B IN ORDER. READ ITEM B, "CONVICTED," WHETHER THE PERSON SAYS "YES" OR "NO" TO ITEM A, "CAUGHT". READ ITEM C ONLY IF THE ANSWER TO ITEM A = "YES" AND THE ANSWER TO ITEM B = "NO" RECORD YES/NO FOR EACH ITEM A – C THAT IS ASKED.)

		Yes	No	DK	Ref
A.	Caught				
B.	Convicted				
C.	Not prosecuted				

IF Q23 = 2,3,4, ASK Q26a AND POP-IN RESPONSE FROM Q23, THEN GO TO INSTRUCTION BEFORE Q29.
IF Q23 = 1,5,6 OR 7, AND Q26 = 1 THROUGH 10, READ Q26b, AND POP-IN RESPONSE FROM Q26.
IF Q26 = 11 OR 12, SKIP TO INSTRUCTION BEFORE Q29

26a. Can you briefly explain how you know that [READ RESPONSE TO Q23] misused your personal information? (**RECORD RESPONSE VERBATIM**)

26b. Can you briefly explain how you know that your personal information was obtained [READ RESPONSE TO Q26] [IFQ26 = 10, READ "in the way you described]? (**RECORD RESPONSE VERBATIM**)

IF Q26:5 – "During a purchase or other transaction" – ASK Q27. ELSE GO TO INSTRUCTION BEFORE Q29

27. You indicated that your information was obtained during a purchase or other transaction. Was the transaction (**READ AND RANDOMIZE**)? (**ENTER SINGLE RESPONSE.**)

1. An Online purchase
2. An In store purchase
3. A Mail Order or telephone purchase
4. An Online financial transaction such as checking your account balances or paying bills
5. (**ASK LAST AND ONLY IF PERSON DOES NOT SELECT ONE OF RESPONSES 1-4**)
   Or, Some other type of transaction (**SPECIFY**) ______________
6. Don't know
7. Refused

IF Q26:9 – "From an office or company that had your personal information in its files" – ASK Q27a. ELSE GO TO INSTRUCTION BEFORE Q29

27a. You indicated that your information was obtained from **an office or company that had your personal information in its files**. Was the person who stole the information someone who had been employed by that office or company?

1. Yes
2. No
3. Other (Specify) __________ **(DO NOT READ)**
4. Don't know
5. Refused

28. (THERE IS NO Q28)

ASK Q29 - Q31 IF "YES" TO Q7; OTHERWISE GO TO INSTRUCTIONS BEFORE Q32

29. You said that one or more of your **existing** accounts, **other than credit card** accounts, had been misused. Did the person run up charges on, take money from, or otherwise misuse, any of the following accounts? (READ AND RANDOMIZE) **(ENTER SINGLE RESPONSE FOR EACH ACCOUNT.)**

ACCOUNTS:
Checking or Savings Accounts, including misuse of an ATM or debit card
Medical Insurance Accounts
Internet or Email Accounts
Telephone Accounts, Whether Conventional or Cell Phone
Email Payments Accounts, such as Paypal or Bidpay
Other accounts (SPECIFY)____________

30. **(THERE IS NO Q30)**

31. **ASK IF YES TO CHECKING OR SAVINGS ACCOUNT ON Q29. ELSE, SKIP TO INSTRUCTION BEFORE Q32.** You said that one or more of your **checking or savings** accounts had been misused. How did the person take money from, make payments from, or otherwise misuse, your checking or savings accounts? Was it ...? **(READ AND RANDOMIZE) (CAN BE MULTIPLES)**

1. By paper transactions, such as checks
2. By card-based transactions, such as an ATM or payment card
3. By electronic transactions, such as an electronic transfer or ACH payment
4. Don't know
5. Refused

(Read: Now I would like to learn more about any NEW accounts that may have been opened, rather than existing accounts that you already had that were misused.)

32. Did the person use your personal information to obtain any (**INSERT AND RANDOMIZE ACCOUNTS**)

1. New Credit Card Accounts
2. New Checking or Savings Accounts
3. New Loans
4. New Medical Insurance Policies
5. New Automobile Insurance Policies
6. New Email payments Accounts, such as Paypal or Bidpay
7. New Telephone Accounts, Whether Conventional or Cell Phone
8. (**ASK LAST**) Other new accounts (SPECIFY)____________

(FOR EACH TYPE OF ACCOUNT FOR WHICH THE PERSON ANSWERS "YES" ON Q32, ASK Q33)

33. How many (**INSERT ACCOUNT**) were obtained using your information?

1. #_________ **(VALID RANGE 1 TO 25)**
2. Don't know
3. Refused

IF Q1 is NOT EQUAL TO YES AND Q7 IS NOT EQUAL TO YES AND Q8 IS NOT EQUAL TO YES AND THERE AREN'T ANY YES RESPONSES TO Q32, SKIP TO INSTRUCTION BEFORE Q34.

35. Were any of the existing accounts that were misused or new accounts that were opened joint accounts with your spouse or another adult?

1. Yes **(GO TO Q35a)**
2. No **(GO TO INSTRUCTION BEFORE Q33a)**
3. Don't know **(GO TO INSTRUCTION BEFORE Q33a)**
4. Refused **(GO TO INSTRUCTION BEFORE Q33a)**

35a. Do you know whose name was used when the joint account or accounts were misused? Was it: (READ CODES 1 Ц4)

1. Only your name that was used
2. Only the name of the other person on the account that was used
3. The names of both persons were used
4. Someone else's name was used
8. Don't know
9. Refused

IF "Yes" on any of the accounts identified in Q32 and Q8:2, 3, or 4, ASK; ELSE GO TO INSTRUCTION BEFORE Q34:

33a. I notice that you just said that **[INSERT RESPONSE(S) TO Q32 TO WHICH THE PERSON ANSWERED "YES"]** had been opened using your personal information. However, when we asked earlier if someone had used your personal information to obtain NEW credit cards, bank accounts, loans or other accounts, you answered **[INSERT RESPONSE TO Q8]**. Can you briefly explain why you answered these two questions in this way? (**RECORD RESPONSE VERBATIM**)

IF "YES" to Q7, Q8, OR Q9, ASK Q34; ELSE GO TO Q36.

34. As far as you know, did the person use your information in any of the following ways? Did the person **(INSERT AND RANDOMIZE) (CAN BE MULTIPLES)**?

1. File a fraudulent tax return
2. Obtain medical treatment, services, or supplies
3. Obtain employment
4. Provide your identifying information to law enforcement when they were stopped or charged with a crime
5. RENT an apartment or house
6. Obtain government benefits, such as Social Security, Medicare, Disaster Relief, Food Stamps, etc.
7. **(ASK LAST)** Use your information in any other way **(SPECIFY)** ____________.
8. Don't Know
9. Refused

(IF "Yes" on any of the fraudulent uses identified in Q34 and Q9:2, 3, or 4, ASK Q34a; ELSE GO TO Q36:

34a. I notice that you just said that your personal information had been used to **[INSERT RESPONSE(S) TO Q34 TO WHICH THE PERSON ANSWERED "YES"]**. However, when we asked earlier if someone had used your personal information for some other fraudulent purpose, such as to obtain government documents, medical care, or a job, you answered **[INSERT RESPONSE TO Q9]**. Can you briefly explain why you answered these two questions in this way? **(RECORD RESPONSE VERBATIM)**

36. What is the approximate total dollar value of what the person obtained while misusing your information? In answering this question, include the value of credit, loans, cash, services, and anything else the person may hav e obtained.

1. RECORD EXACT AMOUNT. __________. **(IF OVER $1,000, PROBE:** I just want to verify that the total amount is **(INSERT AMOUNT RESPONDENT INDICATED)**

IF PERSON SAYS DON'T KNOW OR DECLINES TO PROVIDE AN AMOUNT ON Q36, ASK Q37; ELSE GO TO INSTRUCTION BEFORE Q67:

37. Can you tell me whether (READ RESPONSES 1-3 IN ORDER. ENTER SINGLE RESPONSE)

    1. The thief got $1,000 or more - **GO TO Q40**
    2. The thief got less than $1,000, or - **GO TO Q39**
    3. You don't know if the thief got more or less than $1,000 - **GO TO INSTRUCTION BEFORE Q67**
    4. Refused - **GO TO INSTRUCTION BEFORE Q67**

38. DELETE Q38

39. Was the value

    1. Less than $100
    2. $100 - $499
    3. $500 - $999
    4. Don't know
    5. Refused

GO TO INSTRUCTION BEFORE Q67

40. Was the value

    1. $1,000 - $4,999
    2. $5,000 - $9,999
    3. $10,000 - $24,999
    4. $25,000 - $49,999
    5. $50,000 - $99,999
    6. $100,000 or more
    7. Don't know
    8. Refused

IF "YES" ON Q35, THEN READ: You indicated that one or more of the accounts that were misused or opened were joint accounts with another adult. In answering the rest of the questions, please consider both actions taken or amounts paid by yourself and by the person with whom you held the joint accounts.

67. What other types of problems, IF ANY, have you experienced as a result of the misuse of your personal information? Have you (**INSERT AND RANDOMIZE**)?

1. Been turned down for a loan
2. Had banking problems, such as being turned down for a checking account, or having checks rejected
3. Had credit problems, such as being turned down for a credit card, or having a card rejected
4. Had phone or utilities cut off, or been denied new service
5. Been turned down for insurance or had to pay higher rates
6. Been harassed by a debt collector or collections department
7. Had a lawsuit filed or a judgment entered against you
8. Been the subject of a criminal proceeding
9. Had to repeatedly correct the same information on your credit reports
10. (**ASK LAST**) Had any other types of problems (**SPECIFY**) ____________
11. Don't know
12. Refused

41. How much money did you pay out of your pocket as a result of the misuse of your personal information? In thinking about this answer, include costs for things such as lost wages, legal fees, or payment of any fraudulent debts. Also include miscellaneous expenses such as postage, and notarizing documents.

    1. **RECORD EXACT AMOUNT**. __________. (**IF OVER $1,000, PROBE**: I just want to verify that the total amount is (**INSERT AMOUNT RESPONDENT INDICATED**)

IF RESPONSE IS $0, GO TO Q48
IF PERSON GIVES AN AMOUNT GREATER THAN $0, GO TO INSTRUCTION BEFORE Q46
IF PERSON SAYS DON'T KNOW OR DECLINES TO PROVIDE AN AMOUNT ON Q41, ASK Q42:

42. Would you say out of your own pocket you had to pay… (**READ RESPONSES 1 TO 3 IN ORDER, ENTER SINGLE RESPONSE.**)

    1. $500 or more – **GO TO Q45**
    2. Less than $500, or – **GO TO Q44**
    3. You don't know if you had to pay more or less than $500 – **GO TO INSTRUCTION BEFORE Q46**
    4. Refused – **GO TO INSTRUCTION BEFORE Q46**

43. DELETE Q43

44. Was the amount

1. $0 - **(GO TO Q48)**
2. Less than $50 **(GO TO INSTRUCTION BEFORE Q46)**
3. $50 - $99 **(GO TO INSTRUCTION BEFORE Q46)**
4. $100 - $499 **(GO TO INSTRUCTION BEFORE Q46)**
5. Don't know **(GO TO INSTRUCTION BEFORE Q46)**
6. Refused **(GO TO INSTRUCTION BEFORE Q46)**

45. Was the amount

1. $500 - $999
2. $1,000 - $4,999
3. $5,000 - $9,999
4. $10,000 or more
5. Don't know
6. Refused

IF Q1 = 1, ASK Q46; ELSE GO TO Q47

46. How much, if any, did your credit card company require you to pay in connection with the unauthorized purchases on your card? **(READ LIST IF NECESSARY. ENTER SINGLE RESPONSE)** (**IF OVER $1,000, PROBE**: I just want to verify that the total amount is (**INSERT AMOUNT RESPONDENT INDICATED**)?

1. Nothing
2. $1 to $49
3. $51 - $99
4. $100 - $249
5. $250 - $499
6. $500 - $999
7. $1,000 or more
8. Don't know
9. Refused

47. Did you pay any money to a debt collection agency to resolve any unauthorized purchases or expenditures?

1. Yes
2. No
3. Don't know
4. Refused

48. How many hours of your own time have you spent resolving credit, financial, and other problems caused by the theft of your information? In estimating the amount of time you spent, please include any time that you spent at work and any time spent while on leave from work. **(INTERVIEWER: CODE ANYTHING LESS THAN ONE HOUR AS "1")**

   1. RECORD EXACT NUMBER OF HOURS. __________. **(IF OVER 80 HOURS, PROBE**: I just want to verify that the total amount is **(INSERT NUMBER OF HOURS RESPONDENT INDICATED)**

IF PERSON SAYS DON'T KNOW OR DECLINES TO PROVIDE A NUMBER OF HOURS ON Q48, ASK Q49; ELSE GO TO Q53:

49. To resolve any problems you had, would you say that you had to spend. **(READ CODES 1 – 3 IN ORDER; RECORD SINGLE RESPONSE)**

   1. 40 hours or more - **GO TO Q52**
   2. Less than 40 hours, or - **GO TO Q51**
   3. You don't know if it took more or less than 40 hours to resolve these problems - **GO TO Q53**
   4. Refused - **GO TO Q53**

50. DELETE Q50

51. Was the number of hours **(READ CODES 1 – 3; RECORD SINGLE RESPONSE)**

   1. 1 hour or less
   2. 2 to 9 hours
   3. 10 to 39 hours
   4. Don't know
   5. Refused

GO TO Q53

52. Was the number of hours **(READ CODES 1 – 4; RECORD SINGLE RESPONSE)**

   1. 40 to 79 hours
   2. 80 to 159 hours
   3. 160 to 239 hours
   4. 240 hours or more
   5. Don't know
   6. Refused

53. Did you contact anyone - such as a credit card company, a local police department, a credit bureau, or a lawyer- in attempting to report the theft or misuse of your personal information or resolve the problems caused by the misuse of your information?

1. Yes - **GO TO Q54**
2. No - **GO TO INSTRUCTIONS BEFORE Q53a**
3. Don't know - **GO TO INSTRUCTION BEFORE Q68**
4. Refused - **GO TO INSTRUCTION BEFORE Q68**

IF Q7 = 1 OR Q8 = 1, OR Q9 = 1, ASK Q53a;
IF Q41 IS $1 OR MORE AND Q46 = CODES 2 - 7, ASK Q53a;
IF Q48 = 2 OR MORE, ASK Q53a.

ELSE GO TO INSTRUCTION BEFORE Q68

53a. Can you briefly explain why you did not contact anyone to report the misuse of your personal information or resolve any problems that it caused? I am particularly interested in why you did not contact your local police department or the credit reporting agencies. (**RECORD RESPONSE VERBATIM**)

GO TO INSTRUCTION BEFORE Q68

54. Did you contact **(INSERT AND RANDOMIZE)**? **(CAN BE MULTIPLES)**

1. A lawyer or other professional
2. One or more Credit Reporting Agencies
3. The Department of Motor Vehicles
4. The Better Business Bureau
5. A consumer group, such as National Consumers League or Call for Action
6. One or more companies where an account was opened or misused, including a credit card issuer
7. The State Attorney General or a state or local consumer agency
8. Your local police or the local police in another jurisdiction
9. The insurance company where you have identity theft insurance

(ALWAYS ASK IN THIS ORDER):

10. The Federal Trade Commission
11. Another federal agency (**SPECIFY**)______.
12. (**ASK LAST**) Someone else (**SPECIFY**)______.
13. Don't Know
14. Refused

IF Q54:8 – "Notify your local police or the local police in another jurisdiction – IS "YES," GO TO Q55. ELSE GO TO NEXT INSTRUCTION.

IF Q7 = 1 OR Q8 = 1, OR Q9 = 1, ASK Q54a;
IF Q41 IS $1 OR MORE AND Q46 = CODES 2 – 7, ASK Q54a;
IF Q48 = 2 OR MORE, ASK Q54a.
ELSE GO TO INSTRUCTION BEFORE Q58

Q54a: I'd like to learn more about why identity theft victims do not report to the police. Can you briefly explain why you did not contact your local police or the local police in another jurisdiction? (**RECORD RESPONSE VERBATIM**)

GO TO INSTRUCTION BEFORE Q58.

55. Did the police take a police report from you about the misuse of your information?

1. Yes
2. No – **GO TO 57**
3. Don't know – **GO TO 57**
4. Refused – **GO TO 57**

56. Did you get a copy of the report?

1. Yes
2. No
3. Don't know
4. Refused

57. How satisfied were you with the response of your local police when you reported that your personal information had been misused? (**READ LIST. ENTER SINGLE RESPONSE.**)

4. Very Satisfied
3. Somewhat Satisfied
2. Somewhat Dissatisfied, or
1. Very Dissatisfied
5. Don't Know
6. Refused

IF Q57:1 OR 2; ASK Q57a; OTHERWISE GO TO INSTRUCTION BEFORE Q58

57a. Can you briefly explain why you were [INSERT RESPONSE TO Q57] with the response of your local police? (RECORD RESPONSE VERBATIM)

IF Q54:3 - "Notify the Department of Motor Vehicles, Q54:7 - "Notify the State Attorney General or a state or local consumer agency," OR Q54:10 - "Notify another federal agency," ASK Q58; OTHERWISE GO TO INSTRUCTION BEFORE Q60

58. Did the [**POP-IN "Department of Motor Vehicles if Q54:3, "State Attorney General or state or local consumer agency" if Q54:7 or "Federal agency" if Q54:10**] you contacted take a report about the misuse of your personal information?

1. Yes
2. No - **GO TO INSTRUCTION BEFORE Q60**
3. Don't know - **GO TO INSTRUCTION BEFORE Q60**
4. Refused - **GO TO INSTRUCTION BEFORE Q60**

59. Did you get a copy of the report?

1. Yes
2. No
3. Don't know
4. Refused

(ASK Q60 IF Q54:2 - "Notify one or more credit reporting agencies;" IF Q54 DOES NOT :2, ASK 66a)

60. You indicated that you notified one or more credit reporting agencies. How many credit reporting agencies did you contact? (**ENTER SINGLE RESPONSE.**)

1. One
2. Two
3. Three, or
4. More than three
5. Don't know
6. Refused

IF Q60 = 1, ASK Q62; ELSE GO TO Q63.

62. How many, if any, additional credit reporting agencies contacted you after you notified the one agency? (**ENTER SINGLE RESPONSE.**)

1. None
2. One
3. Two
4. Three, or
5. More than three
6. Don't know
7. Refused

63. Were "temporary" or initial 90-day fraud alerts placed on your credit reports at the credit reporting agencies you contacted or that contacted you?
(DO NOT READ LIST. ENTER SINGLE RESPONSE.) (IF CLARIFICATION NEEDED, "INITIAL 90-DAY" FRAUD ALERTS MIGHT HAVE BEEN CALLED "TEMPORARY" FRAUD ALERTS AND MIGHT HAVE LASTED MORE THAN 90 DAYS PRIOR TO 2005.)

1. Yes
2. No - **GO TO Q66**
3. Don't Know - **GO TO Q66**
4. Refused - **GO TO Q66**

64. (THERE IS NO Q64)

65. Were any new accounts opened after the initial 90-day fraud alerts were placed on your credit reports? **(DO NOT READ ANSWER LIST. ENTER SINGLE RESPONSE.)**

1. Yes
2. No
3. Don't know
4. Refused

66. Have you placed 7-year or permanent fraud alerts on your credit reports? **(IF CLARIFICATION NEEDED, "7-YEAR" FRAUD ALERTS MAY ALSO BE CALLED "PERMANENT" FRAUD ALERTS)**

1. Yes
2. No
3. Don't Know
4. Refused

61. Did you place a freeze on your credit reports at the credit reporting agencies you contacted? That is, did you tell any of the credit reporting agencies to not share your credit report with anyone, such as a potential creditor, unless you "unfreeze" it for that specific purpose?

1. Yes
2. No
3. Don't Know
4. Refused

IF Q53 does not :2 "No, did not contact anyone," and Q54 DOES NOT :2 – "Notify one or more credit reporting agencies;" ask Q66a

Q66a: I would like to know more about why identity theft victims do not notify credit reporting agencies. Can you briefly explain why you did not contact any credit reporting agencies? (**RECORD RESPONSE VERBATIM**)

ASK Q68 IF Q48 is 10 HOURS OR GREATER OR IF Q50:1 OR Q51:3

68. What was the hardest part of your experience with the misuse of your personal information? (**RECORD VERBATIM. PROBE FOR CLARIFICATION. IF RESPONDENT IS UNSURE, ENCOURAGE BEST GUESS**)

ASK IF Q1 = 1 AND Q7 IS NOT EQUAL TO YES AND Q8 IS NOT EQUAL TO YES AND Q9 IS NOT EQUAL TO YES.

Q68b. Which of the following best describes the misuse of your existing credit card? **(READ, RANDOMIZE CODES 1 – 4; ACCEPT ONE MENTION ONLY)**

1. A company I had given my card or card number to charged me for a product that I had not agreed to purchase
2. A company I had given my card or card number to charged me more or for something different than what I had agreed to purchase
3. I gave my card number to someone who claimed to be with a company where I had an account and they used it to obtain cash, goods, or services for themselves
4. Someone took my card or card number and used it to obtain cash, goods, or services for themselves
5. Other (SPECIFY)
6. Don't know
7. Refused

QD5. How many people in your household are:

1. Under 18 years old. Record exact number _____ **(IF 0, GO TO INSTRUCTIONS BEFORE QD1.)**
2. Between 13 and 17. Record exact number ______
3. Refused

IF ANSWER TO QD5 IS "ONE" OR MORE, ASK Q69. ELSE, GO TO INSTRUCTIONS BEFORE QD1.

69. Has any member of your household who is currently under the age of 18 experienced any form of misuse of their personal information?

1. Yes
2. No -**GO TO INSTRUCTION BEFORE QD1**
3. Don't Know - **GO TO INSTRUCTION BEFORE QD1**
4 .Refused - **GO TO INSTRUCTION BEFORE QD1**

69a. How many members of your household currently under the age of 18 have experienced any form of misuse of their personal information?

1. #________________ (VALID RANGE 1 - 6)

IF 69a: ONE, READ Q70; IF 69a: TWO OR MORE, READ Q70a
IF Q69A IS DON'T KNOW OR REFUSED, READ Q70A

70. How long ago was it first discovered that the minor's personal information had been misused?

70a. For the minor who most recently discovered that their personal information was being misused, how long ago was the misuse first discovered? **(USE ANSWERS BELOW FOR WHICHEVER QUESTION IS ASKED)**

1. Since the beginning of 2006
2. In the last 6 months of 2005
3. In the first 6 months of 2005
4. In 2004
5. In 2003
6. In 2002
7. In 2001
8. Before 2001
9. Don't Know
10. Refused

71. (THERE IS NO Q71)

ASK QD1 - QD9 if Q1=1, Q7=1, Q8=1, Q9=1, OR Q69=1.

ASK QD1 - QD9 OF A RANDOM SAMPLE OF 600 OTHER SURVEY PARTICIPANTS.

IF Q1 NOT EQUAL TO YES, AND Q7 NOT EQUAL TO YES AND Q8 NOT EQUAL TO YES AND Q9 NOT EQUAL TO YES AND Q69 NOT EQUAL TO YES, AND NOT SELECTED FOR DEMOGRAPHICS, THANK AND TERMINATE.

Now, for statistical purposes only

QD1. May I please have your age as of your last birthday? (**DO NOT READ LIST UNLESS RESPONDENT HESITATES**)

1. Under 25
2. 25 to 34
3. 35 to 44
4. 45 to 49
5. 50 to 54
6. 55 to 59
7. 60 to 64
8. 65 to 69
9. 70 to 74
10. 75 to 84
11. 85 or older
12. Refused

QD2. What was the last grade of school you completed? (**DO NOT READ**)

1. Completed grade school or less
2. Some high school, not completed
3. Completed high school
4. Some college, not completed
5. Completed college
6. Post graduate work (such as a masters degree, PhD, MD or law degree, whether started or completed)
7. Refused

QD3. Are you married?

1. Yes
2. No
3. Refused

QD4. How many people live in your household at the present time? Please include yourself and any children.

1. Record exact number ______
2. Refused

QD6. Are you of Hispanic or Latino origin?

1. Yes
2. No
3. Don't know
4. Refused

QD7. I am going to read a list of racial categories. Please choose one or more categories that best indicates your race. Are you? **(READ AND RANDOMIZE 1 – 5. ENTER YES/NO FOR EACH. IF PERSON REFUSES TO ANSWER ON FIRST TWO RACES READ, CODE "REFUSED" ON REMAINING RACES AND SKIP TO QD8)**

1. White
2. Black or African American
3. American Indian or Alaska Native
4. Asian
5. Native Hawaiian or Other Pacific Islander
6. Some other race **(ASK ONLY IF NO OR DK OR REF TO ALL PARTS 1 - 5)**
7. Don't Know
8. Refused

QD8. Now I would like to read a series of income groups. Please stop me when I read the group which describes your total household income, from all sources, over the past year.

1. Under $15,000
2. $15,000 to less than $20,000
3. $20,000 to less than $25,000
4. $25,000 to less than $30,000
5. $30,000 to less than $40,000
6. $40,000 to less than $50,000
7. $50,000 to less than $75,000
8. $75,000 to less than $100,000
9. $100,000 or more
10. Don't know
11. Refused

QD9. What is your gender? (By Observation)

1. Male
2. Female

THANK THE PERSON FOR THEIR PARTICIPATION AND TERMINATE

REFERENCES

[1] Figures in parentheses are 95% confidence intervals.

[2] Based on U.S. population age 18 and over of 222.94 million as of July 1, 2005. (http://www.census.gov/popest/states/asrh/tables/SC-EST2005-01 Res.xls (visited August 15, 2006))

[3] The difference between the 3.7% overall prevalence figure found in this survey and the 4.6% rate in the FTC's 2003 survey is not statistically significant using standard statistical analysis.

[4] Identity theft is defined both by statute (ID Theft Act, 18 U.S.C. § 1028(a)(7), 1029(e)) and by FTC rule (16 C.F.R. § 603.2), and includes the misuse or attempted misuse of any identifying information – such as the SSN, biometric data, or an existing credit card account number - to commit fraud

[5] In most cases, victims are not legally responsible for the cost of fraudulent transaction by identity thieves using their personal information. A variety of laws limit consumers' liability in these situations. Such laws include the Truth in Lending Act, 15 U.S.C. § 1601 et seq., implemented by Regulation Z, 12 C.F.R. § 226; see especially 15 U.S.C. § 1643; 12 C.F.R. § 226.12(b) (limits consumer liability for unauthorized credit card charges to a maximum of $50), and the Electronic Fund Transfer Act, 15 U.S.C. § 1693 et seq., implemented by Regulation E, 12 C.F.R. § 205; see especially 15 U.S.C. § 1693g; 12 C.F.R. § 205.6(b) (limits consumer liability for unauthorized electronic fund transfers depending upon the timing of consumer notice to the applicable financial institution). Consumer liability for losses associated with checking account fraud and loan fraud are typically limited by state statute or common law, although consumers are sometimes held liable.

[6] It should also be noted that, prior to asking whether they had experienced ID theft, the 2006 survey asked participants whether they had been notified that a company, government agency, or other organization had lost their personal information. Questions about breach notices were not included in the 2003 survey, and this change may affect participants' responses in unknown ways.

[7] To test this proposition, the 2006 "actual value" responses were put into the ranges used in 2003. For most of the ranges, the average of "actual value" responses was lower than the midpoint of the range.

[8] In one instance, a person who was interviewed claimed to be a victim of ID theft and reported that the thief had obtained goods or services worth $999,999. However, a closer reading of the entire interview record indicated that this person was describing the theft of intellectual property, rather than ID theft. In the second instance, the person reported that the value obtained by the thief was $485,000. While this person did appear to be describing ID theft, the record seemed

[9] In computing prevalence figures for 2005, individuals who reported that they had discovered that their personal information was being misused since the beginning of 2006 were eliminated from the sample. While these people discovered that their information was being misused in 2006, there is no way to know whether or not they had discovered a separate incident of ID theft in 2005.See Appendix B for a discussion

of the effect of consumers who declined to participate in or who began but did not complete the survey.

[10] Figures in parentheses are 95% confidence intervals. As with any survey, this study is subject to sampling error. While a survey of all adults in the U.S. might give results that differ somewhat from the figures reported here, there is a 95% probability that the figure would lie within the range of values represented by the figures in parentheses.

[11] In some cases, the misuse of an individual's personal information included the misuse of jointly held accounts. In these cases, the estimates of the prevalence of ID theft may include both account holders as victims. This seems appropriate since both individuals are likely to have been negatively impacted by the misuse. In other places in the report, the experiences of both victims are combined as a single victim response. In particular, when asked about the out-of-pocket expenses incurred and the time spent resolving problems, interviewees were asked to include the total amount of money or time expended by both themselves and the other individual included on the joint account. In addition, because the data reported here are the results of a survey of consumers, the data may not capture situations in which someone creates a new identity, rather than using the identity of an existing individual, and uses that fictitious identity to obtain goods or services, i.e. synthetic identity fraud. Whether such instances of synthetic identity fraud will be captured in a consumer survey will depend on whether the actions have been attached to a real person – perhaps the individual whose Social Security number was used in creating the fictitious identity.

[12] The figures on this and the succeeding pages are based on the responses of all survey participants who reported discovering the misuse of their personal information between the beginning of 2001 and when they were interviewed— a total of 559 individuals. The data in Figures 1-3 are based only on those who discovered the misuse of their information in 2005.

[13] Victims were asked what types of existing accounts were misused by the thief. The percentages for each category of misuse reflect each discrete misuse reported by the victim. Unlike in Figure 1, victims can be counted in more than one response category in this graph

[14] The data on takeovers of existing credit card accounts is based on the responses to question 5a of 379 individuals who indicated that their existing credit card accounts had been misused between 2001 and the time they were interviewed. The data on takeovers of existing non-credit card accounts are based on the responses to question 5b of 217 individuals who indicated that one or more of their existing non-credit card accounts had been misused

[15] Overall figures are based on the responses of the 559 individuals surveyed who indicated that their personal information had been misused between 2001 and the date they were interviewed.

[16] Victims were asked what types of accounts were opened. This graph shows several specific types of accounts they mentioned. The percentages reflect each time a victim mentioned that type, and, unlike in Figure 1, a victim can be counted more than once.

[17] These figures are based on the responses of 94 individuals who indicated that new accounts had been opened using their personal information.

[18] Based on the responses of the 559 individuals surveyed who indicated that their personal information had been misused between 2001 and the date they were interviewed.

[19] Overall figures are based on the responses of the 559 individuals surveyed who indicated that their personal information had been misused between 2001 and the date they were interviewed. Figures for Existing Credit Cards Only, Existing Non-Credit Card Accounts, and New Accounts & Other Frauds are based on the responses of the 257, 164, and 138 individuals, respectively, who indicated that they had experienced these types of ID theft during this period of time.

[20] Figures for those who discovered the misuse less than 6 months after it began are based on 485 observations; figures for those who discovered the misuse 6 or more months after the misuse began are based on 50 observations.

[21] Overall figures are based on the responses of the 559 individuals surveyed who indicated that their personal information had been misused between 2001 and the date they were interviewed. Figures for Existing Credit Cards. Only, Existing Non-Credit Card Accounts, and New Accounts & Other Frauds are based on the responses of the 257, 164, and 138 individuals, respectively, who indicated that they had experienced these types of ID theft during this period of time

[22] Overall figures are based on the responses of the 559 individuals surveyed who indicated that their personal information had been misused between 2001 and the date they were interviewed.

[23] Figures for Existing Credit Cards Only, Existing Non-Credit Card Accounts, and New Accounts & Other Frauds are based on the responses of the 257, 164, and 138 individuals, respectively, who indicated that they had experienced these types of ID theft between 2001 and the date they were interviewed.

[24] Based on the responses of the 559 individuals surveyed who indicated that their personal information had been misused between 2001 and the date they were interviewed.

[25] The remaining 1% of respondents either refused to answer or stated that they did not know whether they knew how their information was obtained.

[26] Overall figures are based on the responses of the 559 individuals surveyed who indicated that their personal information had been misused between 2001 and the date they were interviewed

[27] Figures for Existing Credit Cards Only, Existing Non-Credit Card Accounts, and New Accounts & Other Frauds are based on the responses of the 257, 164, and 138 individuals, respectively, who indicated that they had experienced these types of ID theft.

[28] Overall figures are based on the responses of the 559 individuals surveyed who indicated that their personal information had been misused between 2001 and the date they were interviewed. Figures for Existing Credit Cards Only, Existing Non-Credit Card Accounts, and New Accounts & Other Frauds are based on the responses of the 257, 164, and 138 individuals, respectively, who indicated that they had experienced these types of ID theft during this period of time.

[29] 21 Overall figures are based on the responses of the 559 individuals surveyed who indicated that their personal information had been misused between 2001 and the date they were interviewed. Figures for Existing Credit Cards Only, Existing Non-Credit

Card Accounts, and New Accounts & Other Frauds are based on the responses of the 257, 164, and 138 individuals, respectively, who indicated that they had experienced these types of ID theft during this period of time.

[30] Figures for those who incurred no out-of-pocket expenses are based on the responses of 359 individuals.

[31] Overall figures are based on the responses of the 559 individuals surveyed who indicated that their personal information had been misused between 2001 and the date they were interviewed. Figures for Existing Credit Cards Only, Existing Non-Credit Card Accounts, and New Accounts & Other Frauds are based on the responses of the 257, 164, and 138 individuals, respectively, who indicated that they had experienced these types of ID theft during this period of time.

[32] Overall figures are based on the responses of the 559 individuals surveyed who indicated that their personal information had been misused between 2001 and the date they were interviewed. Figures for Existing Credit Cards Only, Existing Non-Credit Card Accounts, and New Accounts & Other Frauds are based on the responses of the 257, 164, and 138 individuals, respectively, who indicated that they had experienced these types of ID theft during this period of time.

[33] Figures for those who experienced one or more of the problems discussed here are based on 177 observations; figures for those experienced none of the problems are based on 382 observations.

[34] Overall figures are based on the responses of the 559 individuals surveyed who indicated that their personal information had been misused between 2001 and the date they were interviewed

[35] This figure may not include all respondents who had contact with the company where an account was opened or misused. The 43% figure includes victims who indicated such contact in Q54, or who in answer to Q53, indicated that they had not contacted anyone, but whose verbatim responses when asked why they had not contacted anyone (Q53a) indicated that there had, in fact, been contact with a company or credit card company. However, many victims who said they had not contacted anyone were not asked Q53a and therefore remain in the "Did not contact anyone" group. Therefore, the survey is likely to underestimate the number of consumers who had contact with the companycontacted someone, but then in response to Q54 indicated that they had not contacted any of the identified entities, including “someone else.”

[36] Figures for Existing Credit Cards Only, Existing Non-Credit Card Accounts, and New Accounts & Other Frauds are based on the responses of the 257, 164, and 138 individuals, respectively, who indicated that they had experienced these types of ID theft between 2001 and the date they were interviewed.

[37] Figures for instances where the thief obtained goods and services with a value of less than $1,000 are based on 329 observations and where the value was $1,000 or more are based on 201 observations.

[38] Overall figures are based on the responses of the 559 individuals surveyed who indicated that their personal information had been misused between 2001 and the date they were interviewed.

[39] See Fair Credit Reporting Act, § 605A(h); 15 U.S.C. § 1681c-1(h).

[40] Figures for Existing Credit Cards Only, Existing Non-Credit Card Accounts, and New Accounts & Other Frauds are based on the responses of the 257, 164, and 138

individuals, respectively, who indicated that they had experienced these types of ID theft between 2001 and the date they were interviewed.

[41] Overall figures are based on the responses of the 559 individuals surveyed who indicated that their personal information had been misused between 2001 and the date they were interviewed.

[42] See Fair Credit Reporting Act § 605A(b), 15 U.S.C. § 1681c-1(b).

[43] Some states permit all consumers to obtain credit freezes, regardless of whether they are identity theft victims.

[44] See, e.g. California Civil Code § 1785.11.2, Connecticut General Statutes § 36a-701 a; Louisiana Statutes Annotated § 9.3571 (H) to (Y); North Carolina General Statutes §75-63.

[45] Figures for Existing Credit Cards Only, Existing Non-Credit Card Accounts, and New Accounts & Other Frauds are based on the responses of the 257, 164, and 138 individuals, respectively, who indicated that they had experienced these types of ID theft between 2001 and the date they were interviewed.

[46] Overall figures are based on the responses of the 559 individuals surveyed who indicated that their personal information had been misused between 2001 and the date they were interviewed.

[47] Figures for Existing Credit Cards Only, Existing Non-Credit Card Accounts, and New Accounts & Other Frauds are based on the responses of the 257, 164, and 138 individuals, respectively, who indicated that they had experienced these types of ID theft between 2001 and the date they were interviewed.

[48] Figures on the experiences of victims who contacted a local police department are based on 127 observations, while those where a police report was taken are based on 107 victims.

[49] These figures are based on the responses of 127 participants who said that they had contacted a local police department.

[50] These figures do not total 100% because some victims indicated either that they did not know whether they were satisfied with the response of the police or refused to answer the question.

[51] These figures are based on 172 responses of victims who said that they spent 10 hours or more resolving problems associated with being a victim of ID theft.

[52] Percentage of people receiving a breach notification is based on 1,496 observations. Based on the survey design, demographic characteristics were only collected for 1,496 of the 4,916 people interviewed, including all of those who reported being a victim of ID theft and a random sample of those who were not victims. Weights could only be computed for these observations with weights adjusted to reflect the fact that only a sample of non-victims would be included in weighted calculations. (See Methodological Appendix.)

[53] The practice of notifying consumers of data breaches is a relatively recent development. In 2003, California passed a law (Civil Code § 1798.92) requiring any business that stores data concerning California residents to notify those residents in the event of any actual or suspected data breach. Since the passage of the California statute, over 30 other states have passed some form of breach notice law. As a result of these laws, breach notices, and the resulting publicity regarding breaches, have become more

common. Because breach notices were not a common occurrence prior to the passage of the California law, the 2003 FTC Survey did not include questions about them

[54] This figure may overstate slightly the share of survey participants who received breach notices. Respondents who were contacted by a credit card or other company about actual misuse of their individual accounts may have answered that they had received a "breach notice," even though breach notices are not generally considered to include this type of contact. In addition, recent testing of a similar survey question suggests that some respondents who experienced ID theft may mistakenly have answered "yes" to the question because they discovered that their "information had been lost or stolen," even though they had not "been notified by a company, government agency, or other organization" of this fact.

[55] Based on responses of 187 individuals who said that they had received a breach notification since 2001.

[56] The figures for those that took some sort of action in response to a breach notice (55%) and those that took no action (44%) do not total 100%. This is because 1% of respondents refused to answer or stated that they did not know whether they took any action

[57] Based on 1,496 observations. Demographic characteristics were only collected for 1,496 of the 4,916 people interviewed, including all of those who reported being a victim of ID theft and a random sample of those who were not victims. Weights could only be computed for these observations with weights adjusted to reflect the fact that only a sample of non-victims would be included in weighted calculations. (See Methodological Appendix.)

[58] FCRA § 612(a), 15 U.S.C. § 1681j(1).

[59] FCRA § 605A(a)(2), 15 U.S.C. § 1681c-1(a)(2).

[60] FCRA § 605A(b)(2)(A), 15 U.S.C. § 1681c-1(b)(2)(A).

[61] Although respondents were asked whether they had received any "free annual credit reports," some respondents may have answered "yes" for credit reports received through other means, such as reports received as a result of placing a fraud alert.

[62] Based on responses of 453 individuals who were high school graduates or had not completed high school and 993 individuals who had attended at least some college.

[63] Based on responses of 428 individuals between 25 and 44 years of age and 309 individuals age 65 or over

[64] This figure cannot be compared directly with those in Figure 2 on page 14. As noted in footnote 11, Figures 1 – 3 are based on responses of people who discovered that their information was being misused in 2005, while the rest of the report is based on the responses of people who discovered that their information was being misused between the beginning of 2001 and the time they were interviewed.

[65] Based on the responses of 84 survey participants who indicated that they had experienced non-account ID theft.

Appndix A

[1] See Section II.I, for a discussion of the collection of demographic data and the weighting of the resulting responses to ensure that the resulting analysis was representative of the population of U.S. adults as a whole.

[2] In total, 4,917 individuals were contacted and completed the screening portion of the survey. In retrospect, one respondent did not answer appropriately, so they were subsequently dropped. This reduced the total sample to 4,916 completed screens with 915 respondents reporting Identity Theft for themselves or a minor child in the household

Appendix B

[1] The figures in this appendix cannot be compared with the figures in the body of the report. There are at least two reasons for this. First, these data measure the percentage of people whose survey answers indicated that they had been a victim of ID theft at some point in their lives, not just in 2005. Second, the data here are not weighted to adjust for differences between those who were interviewed and the population at large.

[2] Again, these figures are unweighted and reflect whether the person had ever experienced ID theft. Therefore, they cannot be compared directly with the figures in the body of the report.

In: Identity Theft Breaches
Editor: Cary S. Logweller

ISBN 978-1-60692-227-9

Chapter 3

TAKE CHARGE: FIGHTING BACK AGAINST IDENTITY THEFT

INTRODUCTION

In the course of a busy day, you may write a check at the grocery store, charge tickets to a ball game, rent a car, mail your tax returns, change service providers for your cell phone, or apply for a credit card. Chances are you don't give these everyday transactions a second thought. But an identity thief does.

Identity theft is a serious crime. People whose identities have been stolen can spend months or years – and thousands of dollars – cleaning up the mess the thieves have made of a good name and credit record. In the meantime, victims of identity theft may lose job opportunities, be refused loans for education, housing, or cars, and even get arrested for crimes they didn't commit. Humiliation, anger, and frustration are among the feelings victims experience as they navigate the process of rescuing their identity.

Working with other government agencies and organizations, the Federal Trade Commission (FTC) has produced this booklet to help you remedy the effects of an identity theft. It describes what steps to take, your legal rights, how to handle specific problems you may encounter on the way to clearing your name, and what to watch for in the future.

HOW IDENTITY THEFT OCURS

> I first was notified that someone had used my Social Security number for their taxes in February 2004. I also found out that this person opened a checking account, cable and utility accounts, and a cell phone account in my name. I'm still trying to clear up everything and just received my income tax refund after waiting four to five months. Trying to work and get all this cleared up is very stressful.

From a consumer's complaint to the FTC, July 9, 2004.

Despite your best efforts to manage the flow of your personal information or to keep it to yourself, skilled identity thieves may use a variety of methods to gain access to your data.

How Identity Thieves Get Your Personal Information

- They get information from businesses or other institutions by:
  - stealing records or information while they're on the job
  - bribing an employee who has access to these records
  - hacking these records
  - conning information out of employees

- They may steal your mail, including bank and credit card statements, credit card offers, new checks, and tax information.
- They may rummage through your trash, the trash of businesses, or public trash dumps in a practice known as "dumpster diving."
- They may get your credit reports by abusing their employer's authorized access to them, or by posing as a landlord, employer, or someone else who may have a legal right to access your report.
- They may steal your credit or debit card numbers by capturing the information in a data storage device in a practice known as "skimming." They may swipe your card for an actual purchase, or attach the device to an ATM machine where you may enter or swipe your card.
- They may steal your wallet or purse.
- They may steal personal information they find in your home.
- They may steal personal information from you through email or phone by posing as legitimate companies and claiming that you have a problem with your account. This practice is known as "phishing" online, or "pretexting" by phone.

How Identity Thieves Use Your Personal Information

- They may call your credit card issuer to change the billing address on your credit card account. The imposter then runs up charges on your account. Because your bills are being sent to a different address, it may be some time before you realize there's a problem.
- They may open new credit card accounts in your name. When they use the credit cards and don't pay the bills, the delinquent accounts are reported on your credit report.
- They may establish phone or wireless service in your name.
- They may open a bank account in your name and write bad checks on that account.
- They may counterfeit checks or credit or debit cards, or authorize electronic transfers in your name, and drain your bank account.
- They may file for bankruptcy under your name to avoid paying debts they've incurred under your name, or to avoid eviction.
- They may buy a car by taking out an auto loan in your name.
- They may get identification such as a driver's license issued with their picture, in your name.

- They may get a job or file fraudulent tax returns in your name.
- They may give your name to the police during an arrest. If they don't show up for their court date, a warrant for arrest is issued in your name.

If Your Personal Information Has Been Lost or Stolen

If you've lost personal information or identification, or if it has been stolen from you, taking certain steps quickly can minimize the potential for identity theft.

- Financial accounts:Close accounts, like credit cards and bank accounts, immediately. When you open new accounts, place passwords on them. Avoid using your mother's maiden name, your birth date, the last four digits of your Social Security number (SSN) or your phone number, or a series of consecutive numbers.
- social security number:Call the toll-free fraud number of any of the three nationwide consumer reporting companies and place an initial fraud alert on your credit reports. An alert can help stop someone from opening new credit accounts in your name. For consumer reporting company contact information, see page 5. For more information about fraud alerts, see page 6.
- Driver's license/other government-issued identification: Contact the agency that issued the license or other identification document. Follow its procedures to cancel the document and to get a replacement. Ask the agency to flag your file so that no one else can get a license or any other identification document from them in your name.

Once you've taken these precautions, watch for signs that your information is being misused. See staying Alert, page 27.

If your information has been misused, file a report about the theft with the police, and file a complaint with the Federal Trade Commission, as well. If another crime was committed – for example, if your purse or wallet was stolen or your house or car was broken into – report it to the police immediately.

Identity Theft Victims: Immediate Steps

If you are a victim of identity theft, take the following four steps as soon as possible, and keep a record with the details of your conversations and copies of all correspondence.

1. Place a Eraud Alert on Your Credit Reports, and Review Your Credit Reports

Fraud alerts can help prevent an identity thief from opening any more accounts in your name. Contact the toll-free fraud number of any of the three consumer reporting companies below to place a fraud alert on your credit report. You only need to contact one of the three companies to place an alert. The company you call is required to contact the other two, which will place an alert on their versions of your report, too.

- Equifax:1-800-525-6285; www.equifax.com; P.O. Box 740241, Atlanta, GA 30374-0241
- Experian:1-888-EXPERIAN (1-888-397-3742); www.experian.com; P.O. Box 9532, Allen, TX 75013
- Transunion: 1-800-680-7289; www.transunion.com; Fraud Victim Assistance Division, P.O. Box 6790, Fullerton, CA 92834-6790

Once you place the fraud alert in your file, you're entitled to order free copies of your credit reports, and, if you ask, only the last four digits of your SSN will appear on your credit reports.

Once you get your credit reports, review them carefully. Look for inquiries from companies you haven't contacted, accounts you didn't open, and debts on your accounts that you can't explain. Check that information like your SSN, address(es), name or initials, and employers are correct. If you find fraudulent or inaccurate information, get it removed. See correcting credit Reports, page 17 to learn how. Continue to check your credit reports periodically, especially for the first year after you discover the identity theft, to make sure no new fraudulent activity has occurred.

Fraud Alerts

There are two types of fraud alerts: an initial alert, and an extended alert.

- An initial alert stays on your credit report for at least 90 days. you may ask that an initial fraud alert be placed on your credit report if you suspect you have been, or are about to be, a victim of identity theft. An initial alert is appropriate if your wallet has been stolen or if you've been taken in by a "phishing" scam. when you place an initial fraud alert on your credit report, you're entitled to one free credit report from each of the three nationwide consumer reporting companies.
- An extended alert stays on your credit report for seven years. you can have an extended alert placed on your credit report if you've been a victim of identity theft and you provide the consumer reporting company with an "identity theft report" (see page 9). when you place an extended alert on your credit report, you're entitled to two free credit reports within 12 months from each of the three nationwide consumer reporting companies. In addition, the consumer reporting companies will remove your name from marketing lists for pre-screened credit offers for five years – unless you ask them to put your name back on the list before then.

To place either of these alerts on your credit report, you will be required to provide appropriate proof of your identity, which may include your ssn, name, address and other personal information requested by the consumer reporting company. To remove the fraud alert, you will need a copy of an identity theft report and proof of your identity.

When a business sees the alert on your credit report, they must verify your identity before issuing you credit. As part of this verification process, the business may try to contact you directly. This may cause some delays if you're trying to obtain credit.

To compensate for possible delays, you may wish to include a cell phone number, where you can be reached easily, in your alert. Remember to keep all contact infor mation in your alert current.

2. Close the Accounts that You Know, or Believe, Have Been Tampered with or Opened Fraudulently

Call and speak with someone in the security or fraud department of each company. Follow up in writing, and include copies (NOT originals) of supporting documents. It's important to notify credit card companies and banks in writing. Send your letters by certified mail, return receipt requested, so you can document what the company received and when. Keep a file of your correspondence and enclosures.

When you open new accounts, use new Personal Identification Numbers (PINs) and passwords. Avoid using easily available information like your mother's maiden name, your birth date, the last four digits of your SSN or your phone number, or a series of consecutive numbers.

If the identity thief has made charges or debits on your accounts, or on fraudulently opened accounts, ask the company for the forms to dispute those transactions:

- For charges and debits on existing accounts, ask the representative to send you the company's fraud dispute forms. If the company doesn't have special forms, use the sample letter on page 20 to dispute the fraudulent charges or debits. In either case, write to the company at the address given for "billing inquiries," NOT the address for sending your payments.
- For new unauthorized accounts, ask if the company accepts the ID Theft Affidavit (see page 37). If not, ask the representative to send you the company's fraud dispute forms.
- If the company already has reported these accounts or debts on your credit report, dispute this fraudulent information. See correcting credit Reports, page 17 to learn how.

Once you have resolved your identity theft dispute with the company, ask for a letter stating that the company has closed the disputed accounts and has discharged the fraudulent debts. This letter is your best proof if errors relating to this account reappear on your credit report or you are contacted again about the fraudulent debt.

PROVING YOU'RE A VICTIM

applications or other transaction records related to the theft of your identity may help you prove that you are a victim. for example, you may be able to show that the signature on an application is not yours. These documents also may contain information about the identity thief that is valuable to law enforcement. by law, companies must give you a copy of the application or other business transaction records relating to your identity theft if you submit your request in writing. be sure to ask the company representative where you should mail your request. Companies must provide these records at no charge to you within 30 days of receipt of your request and your supporting documents. you also may give permission to any law enforcement agency to get these records, or ask in your written request that a copy of these records be sent to a particular law enforcement officer.

The company can ask you for:

- proof of your identity. This may be a photocopy of a government-issued Id card, the same type of information the identity thief used to open or access the account, or the type of information the company usually requests from applicants or customers, and
- a police report and a completed affidavit, which may be the Identity Theft affidavit (see page 37) or the company's own affidavit.

3. File a Report with Your Local Police or the Police in the Community Where the Identity Theft Took Place

Then, get a copy of the police report or at the very least, the number of the report. It can help you deal with creditors who need proof of the crime. If the police are reluctant to take your report, ask to file a "Miscellaneous Incidents" report, or try another jurisdiction, like your state police. You also can check with your state Attorney General's office to find out if state law requires the police to take reports for identity theft. Check the Blue Pages of your telephone directory for the phone number or check www.naag.org for a list of state Attorneys General.

4. File a Complaint with the Federal Trade Commission

By sharing your identity theft complaint with the FTC, you will provide important information that can help law enforcement officials across the nation track down identity thieves and stop them. The FTC can refer victims' complaints to other government agencies and companies for further action, as well as investigate companies for violations of laws the agency enforces.

You can file a complaint online at www.consumer.gov/idtheft. If you don't have Internet access, call the FTC's Identity Theft Hotline, toll-free: 1-877-IDTHEFT (1-877-438-4338); TTY: 1-866-653-4261; or write: Identity Theft Clearinghouse, Federal Trade Commission, 600 Pennsylvania Avenue, NW, Washington, DC 20580.

Be sure to call the Hotline to update your complaint if you have any additional information or problems.

The Identity Theft Report

An identity theft report may have two parts:

part one is a copy of a report filed with a local, state, or federal law enforcement agency, like your local police department, your State Attorney General, the FBI, the U.S. Secret Service, the FTC, and the U.S. Postal Inspection Service. There is no federal law requiring a federal agency to take a report about identity theft; however, some state laws require local police departments to take reports. When you file a report, provide as much information as you can about the crime, including anything you know about the dates of the identity theft, the fraudulent accounts opened, and the alleged identity thief.

Note: Knowingly submitting false information could subject you to criminal prosecution for perjury.

part Two of an identity theft report depends on the policies of the consumer reporting company and the information provider (the business that sent the information to the consumer reporting company). That is, they may ask you to provide information or documentation in addition to that included in the law enforcement report which is reasonably intended to verify your identity theft. They must make their request within 15 days of receiving your law enforcement report, or, if you already obtained an extended fraud alert on your credit report, the date you submit your request to the credit reporting company for information blocking. The consumer reporting company and information provider then have 15 more days to work with you to make sure your identity theft report contains everything they need. They are entitled to take five days to review any information you give them. For example, if you give them information 11 days after they request it, they do not have to make a final decision until 16 days after they asked you for that information. If you give them any information after the 15-day deadline, they can reject your identity theft report as incomplete; you will have to resubmit your identity theft report with the correct information.

You may find that most federal and state agencies, and some local police departments, offer only "automated" reports – a report that does not require a face-to-face meeting with a law enforcement officer. Automated reports may be submitted online, or by telephone or mail. If you have a choice, do not use an automated report. The reason? It's more difficult for the consumer reporting company or information provider to verify the information. Unless you are asking a consumer reporting company to place an extended fraud alert on your credit report, you probably will have to provide additional information or documentation when you use an automated report.

Tips for Organizing Your Case

Accurate and complete records will help you to resolve your identity theft case more quickly.

- • Have a plan when you contact a company. Don't assume that the person you talk to will give you all the information or help you need. Prepare a list of questions to ask the representative, as well as information about your identity theft. Don't end the call until you're sure you understand everything you've been told. If you need more help, ask to speak to a supervisor.

- Write down the name of everyone you talk to, what he or she tells you, and the date the conversation occurred. Use Chart Your Course of Action on page 11 to help you.
- Follow up in writing with all contacts you've made on the phone or in person. Use certified mail, return receipt requested, so you can document what the company or organization received and when.
- Keep copies of all correspondence or forms you send.
- Keep the originals of supporting documents, like police reports and letters to and from creditors; send copies only.
- Set up a filing system for easy access to your paperwork.
- Keep old files even if you believe your case is closed. Once resolved, most cases stay resolved, but problems can crop up.

CHART YOUR COURSE OF ACTION

Use this form to record the steps you've taken to report the fraudulent use of your identity. Keep this list in a safe place for reference.

NATIONWIDE CONSUMER REPORTING COMPANIES – REPORT FRAUD

Consumer Reporting Company	Phone Number	Date Contacted	Contact Person	Comments
Equifax	1.800.525.6285			
Experian	1.888.EXPERIAN (397.3742)			
TransUnion	1.800.680.7289			

BANKS, CREDIT CARD ISSUERS AND OTHER CREDITORS (Contact each creditor promptly to protect your legal rights.)

Creditor	Address and Phone Number	Date Contacted	Contact Person	Comments

LAW ENFORCEMENT AUTHORITIES – REPORT IDENTITY THEFT

Agency/ Department	Phone Number	Date Contacted	Contact Person	Report Number	Comments

RESOLVING SPECIFIC PROBLEMS

I received a copy of my credit report and saw about a half a dozen items that I didn't know anything about. It's affected my credit rating so badly that I couldn't get a student loan. I didn't realize there was a problem until my student loan application was denied.

—From a consumer's complaint to the FTC, May 25, 2004

While dealing with problems resulting from identity theft can be time-consuming and frustrating, most victims can resolve their cases by being assertive, organized, and knowledgeable about their legal rights. Some laws require you to notify companies within specific time periods. Don't delay in contacting any companies to deal with these problems, and ask for supervisors if you need more help than you're getting.

BANK ACCOUNTS AND ERAUDULENT WITHDRAWALS

Different laws determine your legal remedies based on the type of bank fraud you have suffered. For example, state laws protect you against fraud committed by a thief using paper documents, like stolen or counterfeit checks. But if the thief used an electronic fund transfer, federal law applies. Many transactions may seem to be processed electronically but are still considered "paper" transactions. If you're not sure what type of transaction the thief used to commit the fraud, ask the financial institution that processed the transaction.

Fraudulent Electronic Withdrawals

The Electronic Fund Transfer Act provides consumer protections for transactions involving an ATM or debit card, or another electronic way to debit or credit an account. It also limits your liability for unauthorized electronic fund transfers.

You have 60 days from the date your bank account statement is sent to you to report in writing any money withdrawn from your account without your permission. This includes instances when your ATM or debit card is "skimmed" – that is, when a thief captures your account number and PIN without your card having been lost or stolen.

- If your ATM or debit card is lost or stolen, report it immediately because the amount you can be held responsible for depends on how quickly you report the loss.
- If you report the loss or theft within two business days of discovery, your losses are limited to $50.
- If you report the loss or theft after two business days, but within 60 days after the unauthorized electronic fund transfer appears on your statement, you could lose up to $500 of what the thief withdraws.
- If you wait more than 60 days to report the loss or theft, you could lose all the money that was taken from your account after the end of the 60 days.

Note: Most card issuers voluntarily have agreed to limit or waive consumers' liability for unauthorized use of their debit cards, no matter how much time has elapsed since the discovery of the loss or theft of the card. Contact your card issuer for more information.

The best way to protect yourself in the event of an error or fraudulent transaction is to call the financial institution and follow up in writing – by certified letter, return receipt requested – so you can prove when the institution received your letter. Keep a copy of the letter you send for your records.

After receiving your notification about an error on your statement, the institution generally has 10 business days to investigate. The institution must tell you the results of its investigation within three business days after completing it and must correct an error within one business day after determining that it occurred. If the institution needs more time, it may take up to 45 days to complete the investigation – but only if the money in dispute is returned to your account and you are notified promptly of the credit. At the end of the investigation, if no error has been found, the institution may take the money back if it sends you a written explanation. For more information, see Electronic Banking and Credit, ATM and Debit Cards: What To Do If They're Lost or Stolen at www.consumer.gov/idtheft.

Fraudulent Checks and Other "Paper" Transactions

In general, if an identity thief steals your checks or counterfeits checks from your existing bank account, stop payment, close the account, and ask your bank to notify Chex Systems, Inc., (contact information on page 15) or the check verification service with which it does business. That way, retailers can be notified not to accept these checks. While no federal law limits your losses if someone uses your checks with a forged signature, or uses another type of "paper" transaction such as a demand draft, state laws may protect you. Most states hold the bank responsible for losses from such transactions. At the same time, most states require you to take reasonable care of your account. For example, you may be held responsible for the forgery if you fail to notify the bank in a timely manner that a check was lost or stolen. Contact your state banking or consumer protection agency for more information.

You can contact major check verification companies directly for the following services:

- To request that they notify retailers who use their databases not to accept your checks, call:
  - TeleCheck at 1-800-710-9898 or 1-800-927-0188
  - Certegy, Inc. (previously Equifax Check Systems) at 1-800-437-5120

- To find out if the identity thief has been passing bad checks in your name, call:
  - SCAN: 1-800-262-7771

If your checks are rejected by a merchant, it may be because an identity thief is using the Magnetic Information Character Recognition (MICR) code (the numbers at the bottom of checks), your driver's license number, or another identification number. The merchant who rejects your check should give you its check verification company contact information so you can find out what information the thief is using. If you find that the thief is using your MICR code, ask your bank to close your checking account, and open a new one.

If you discover that the thief is using your driver's license number or some other identification number, work with your DMV or other identification issuing agency to get new identification with new numbers. Once you have taken the appropriate steps, your checks should be accepted.

Note:

- The check verification company may or may not remove the information about the MICR code or the driver's license/identification number from its database because this information may help prevent the thief from continuing to commit fraud.
- If the checks are being passed on a new account, contact the bank to close the account. Also contact Chex Systems, Inc., to review your consumer report to make sure that no other bank accounts have been opened in your name
- Dispute any bad checks passed in your name with merchants so they don't start any collections actions against you.

Fraudulent New Accounts

If you have trouble opening a new checking account, it may be because an identity thief has been opening accounts in your name. Chex Systems, Inc., produces consumer reports specifically about checking accounts, and as a consumer reporting company, is subject to the Fair Credit Reporting Act. You can request a free copy of your consumer report by contacting Chex Systems, Inc. If you find inaccurate information on your consumer report, follow the procedures under correcting credit Reports (see page 17) to dispute it. Contact each of the banks where account inquiries were made, too. This will help ensure that any fraudulently opened accounts are closed.

*Chex systems, inc.: 1-800-428-9623;*www.chexhelp.com
Fax: 602-659-2197
Chex Systems, Inc.
Attn: Consumer Relations
7805 Hudson Road, Suite 100
Woodbury, MN 55125

Where to Find Help

If you have trouble getting a financial institution to help you resolve your banking-related identity theft problems, including problems with bank-issued credit cards, contact the agency that oversees your bank (see list below).

If you're not sure which of these agencies is the right one, call your bank or visit the National Information Center of the Federal Reserve System at www.ffiec.gov/nic/ and click on "Institution Search."

Federal Deposit Insurance Corporation (FDIC) – www.fdic.gov

The FDIC supervises state-chartered banks that are not members of the Federal Reserve System, and insures deposits at banks and savings and loans.

Call the FDIC Consumer Call Center toll-free: 1-800-934-3342; or write: Federal Deposit Insurance Corporation, Division of Compliance and Consumer Affairs, 550 17th Street, NW, Washington, DC 20429.

FDIC Publications

- Classic Cons... And How to Counter Them www.fdic.gov/consumers /consumer /news/cnsprg98/cons.html
- A Crook Has Drained Your Account. Who Pays? www.fdic.gov/consumers /consumer/news/cnsprg98/crook.html
- Your Wallet: A Loser's Manual www.fdic.gov/consumers/consumer /news /cnfall97 /wallet.html

F*ederal reserve system (Fed) – www.federalreserve.gov*

The Fed supervises state-chartered banks that are members of the Federal Reserve System.

Call: 202-452-3693; or write: Division of Consumer and Community Affairs, Mail Stop 801, Federal Reserve Board, Washington, DC 20551; or contact the Federal Reserve Bank in your area. The Reserve Banks are located in Boston, New York, Philadelphia, Cleveland, Richmond, Atlanta, Chicago, St. Louis, Minneapolis, Kansas City, Dallas, and San Francisco.

National credit union administration (ncua) – www.ncua.gov

The NCUA charters and supervises federal credit unions and insures deposits at federal credit unions and many state credit unions.

Call: 703-518-6360; or write: Compliance Officer, National Credit Union Administration, 1775 Duke Street, Alexandria, VA 22314.

Office of the comptroller of the currency (occ) – www.occ.treas.gov The OCC charters and supervises national banks. If the word "national" appears in the name of a bank, or the initials "N.A." follow its name, the OCC oversees its operations.

Call toll-free: 1-800-613-6743 (business days 9:00 a.m. to 4:00 p.m. CST); fax: 713-336-4301; or write: Customer Assistance Group, 1301 McKinney Street, Suite 3710, Houston, TX 77010.

OCC Publications

- Check Fraud: A Guide to Avoiding Losses – www.occ.treas.gov/chckfrd/chckfrd.pdf
- How to Avoid Becoming a Victim of Identity Theft – www.occ.treas.gov/idtheft.pdf
- Identity Theft and Pretext Calling Advisory Letter 2001-4 – www.occ.treas.gov /ftp /advisory/2001-4.doc

Office of Thrift Supervision (OTS) – www.ots.treas.gov

The OTS is the primary regulator of all federal, and many state-chartered, thrift institutions, including savings banks and savings and loan institutions.

Call: 202-906-6000; or write: Office of Thrift Supervision, 1700 G Street, NW, Washington, DC 20552.

Bankruptcy Fraud

U.S. Trustee (usT) – www.usdoj.gov/ust

If you believe someone has filed for bankruptcy in your name, write to the U.S. Trustee in the region where the bankruptcy was filed. A list of the U.S. Trustee Programs' Regional Offices is available on the UST website, or check the Blue Pages of your phone book under U.S. Government Bankruptcy Administration.

In your letter, describe the situation and provide proof of your identity. The U.S. Trustee will make a criminal referral to law enforcement authorities if you provide appropriate documentation to substantiate your claim. You also may want to file a complaint with the U.S. Attorney and/or the FBI in the city where the bankruptcy was filed. The U.S. Trustee does not provide legal representation, legal advice, or referrals to lawyers. That means you may need to hire an attorney to help convince the bankruptcy court that the filing is fraudulent. When you or your attorney ask the bankruptcy court to dismiss the fraudulently filed bankruptcy case, you also should request that the bankruptcy court include

in its order of dismissal facts that will help you repair your credit, including a statement that you did not file this bankruptcy case and that the case was filed by an imposter as the result of identity theft. Ask the bankruptcy court to send a copy of the dismissal order to each consumer reporting company; if the court will not do so, you should send the order to the consumer reporting companies yourself. Some courts will even provide you with several official copies of the order at no charge so that you can send them to creditors or use them in case of future problems. The U.S. Trustee does not provide consumers with copies of court documents. You can get them from the bankruptcy clerk's office for a fee.

Correcting Fraudulent Information in Credit Reports

The Fair Credit Reporting Act (FCRA) establishes procedures for correcting fraudulent information on your credit report and requires that your report be made available only for certain legitimate business needs.

Under the FCRA, both the consumer reporting company and the information provider (the business that sent the information to the consumer reporting company), such as a bank or credit card company, are responsible for correcting fraudulent information in your report. To protect your rights under the law, contact both the consumer reporting company and the information provider.

Consumer Reporting Company Obligations

Consumer reporting companies will block fraudulent information from appearing on your credit report if you take the following steps: Send them a copy of an identity theft report (see page 9) and a letter telling them what information is fraudulent. The letter also should state that the information does not relate to any transaction that you made or authorized. In addition, provide proof of your identity that may include your SSN, name, address, and other personal information requested by the consumer reporting company.

The consumer reporting company has four business days to block the fraudulent information after accepting your identity theft report. It also must tell the information provider that it has blocked the information. The consumer reporting company may refuse to block the information or remove the block if, for example, you have not told the truth about your identity theft. If the consumer reporting company removes the block or refuses to place the block, it must let you know.

The blocking process is only one way for identity theft victims to deal with fraudulent information. There's also the "reinvestigation process," which was designed to help all consumers dispute errors or inaccuracies on their credit reports. For more information on this process, see How to Dispute Credit Report Errors and Your Access to Free Credit Reports, two publications from the FTC at www.consumer.gov/idtheft.

SAMPLE BLOCKING LETTER – CONSUMER REPORTING COMPANY

Date
Your Name
Your Address
Your City, State, Zip Code
Complaint Department
Name of Consumer Reporting Company Address
City, State, Zip Code
Dear Sir or Madam:

I am a victim of identity theft. I am writing to request that you block the following fraudulent information in my file. This information does not relate to any transaction that I have made. The items also are circled on the attached copy of the report I received. (Identify item(s) to be blocked by name of source, such as creditors or tax court, and identify type of item, such as credit account, judgment, etc.)

Enclosed is a copy of the law enforcement report regarding my identity theft. Please let me know if you need any other information from me to block this information on my credit report.

Sincerely, Your name

Enclosures: (List what you are enclosing.

Information Provider Obligations

Information providers stop reporting fraudulent information to the consumer reporting companies once you send them an identity theft report and a letter explaining that the information they're reporting resulted from identity theft. But you must send your identity theft report and letter to the address specified by the information provider. Note that the information provider may continue to report the information if it later learns that the information does not result from identity theft.

If a consumer reporting company tells an information provider that it has blocked fraudulent information in your credit report, the information provider may not continue to report that information to the consumer reporting company. The information provider also may not hire someone to collect the debt that relates to the fraudulent account, or sell that debt to anyone else who would try to collect it.

Credit Cards

The Fair Credit Billing Act establishes procedures for resolving billing errors on your credit card accounts, including fraudulent charges on your accounts. The law also limits your liability for unauthorized credit card charges to $50 per card. To take advantage of the law's consumer protections, you must:

- write to the creditor at the address given for "billing inquiries," NOT the address for sending your payments. Include your name, address, account number, and a description of the billing error, including the amount and date of the error. A sample letter is on page 20.
- send your letter so that it reaches the creditor within 60 days after the first bill containing the error was mailed to you. If an identity thief changed the address on your account and you didn't receive the bill, your dispute letter still must reach the creditor within 60 days of when the creditor would have mailed the bill. This is one reason it's essential to keep track of your billing statements, and follow up quickly if your bills don't arrive on time.

You should send your letter by certified mail, and request a return receipt. It becomes your proof of the date the creditor received the letter. Include copies (NOT originals) of your police report or other documents that support your position. Keep a copy of your dispute letter.

The creditor must acknowledge your complaint in writing within 30 days after receiving it, unless the problem has been resolved. The creditor must resolve the dispute within two billing cycles (but not more than 90 days) after receiving your letter.

For more information, see Fair Credit Billing and Avoiding Credit and Charge Card Fraud, two publications from the FTC at www.consumer.gov/idtheft.

Criminal Violations

Procedures to correct your record within criminal justice databases can vary from state to state, and even from county to county. Some states have enacted laws with special procedures for identity theft victims to follow to clear their names. You should check with the office of your state Attorney General, but you can use the following information as a general guide.

Sample Dispute Letter for Existing Accounts

> Date
> Your Name
> Your Address
> Your City, State, Zip Code Your Account Number
> Name of Creditor Billing Inquiries
> Address
> City, State, Zip Code
> Dear Sir or Madam:
>
> I am writing to dispute a fraudulent (charge or debit) on my account in the amount of $. I am a victim of identity theft, and I did not make this (charge or debit). I am requesting that the (charge be removed or the debit reinstated), that any finance and other charges related to the fraudulent amount be credited, as well, and that I receive an accurate statement.
>
> Enclosed are copies of (use this sentence to describe any enclosed information, such as a police report) supporting my position. Please investigate this matter and correct the fraudulent (charge or debit) as soon as possible.
>
> Sincerely, Your name
>
> Enclosures: (List what you are enclosing.)

If wrongful criminal violations are attributed to your name, contact the police or sheriff's department that originally arrested the person using your identity, or the court agency that issued the warrant for the arrest. File an impersonation report with the police/sheriff's department or the court, and confirm your identity: Ask the police department to take a full set of your fingerprints, photograph you, and make a copies of your photo identification documents, like your driver's license, passport, or travel visa. To establish your innocence, ask the police to compare the prints and photographs with those of the imposter.

If the arrest warrant is from a state or county other than where you live, ask your local police department to send the impersonation report to the police department in the jurisdiction where the arrest warrant, traffic citation, or criminal conviction originated.

The law enforcement agency should then recall any warrants and issue a "clearance letter" or "certificate of release" (if you were arrested/booked). You'll need to keep this document with you at all times in case you're wrongly arrested again. Ask the law enforcement agency to file the record of the follow-up investigation establishing your innocence with the district attorney's (D.A.) office and/or court where the crime took place. This will result in an amended complaint. Once your name is recorded in a criminal database, it's unlikely that it will be completely removed from the official record. Ask that the "key name" or "primary name" be changed from your name to the imposter's name (or to "John Doe" if the imposter's true identity is not known), with your name noted as an alias.

You'll also want to clear your name in the court records. To do so, you'll need to determine which state law(s) will help you with this and how. If your state has no formal procedure for clearing your record, contact the D.A.'s office in the county where the case was originally prosecuted. Ask the D.A.'s office for the appropriate court records needed to clear your name. You may need to hire a criminal defense attorney to help you clear your name. Contact Legal Services in your state or your local bar association for help in finding an attorney.

Finally, contact your state Department of Motor Vehicles (DMV) to find out if your driver's license is being used by the identity thief. Ask that your files be flagged for possible fraud.

DEBT COLLECTORS

The Fair Debt Collection Practices Act prohibits debt collectors from using unfair or deceptive practices to collect overdue bills that a creditor has forwarded for collection, even if those bills don't result from identity theft.

You can stop a debt collector from contacting you in two ways:

- Write a letter to the collection agency telling them to stop. Once the debt collector receives your letter, the company may not contact you again – with two exceptions: They can tell you there will be no further contact, and they can tell you that the debt collector or the creditor intends to take some specific action.
- Send a letter to the collection agency, within 30 days after you received written notice of the debt, telling them that you do not owe the money. Include copies of documents that support your position. Including a copy (NOT original) of your police report may be useful. In this case, a collector can renew collection activities only if it sends you proof of the debt.

If you don't have documentation to support your position, be as specific as possible about why the debt collector is mistaken. The debt collector is responsible for sending you proof that you're wrong. For example, if the debt you're disputing originates from a credit card you never applied for, ask for a copy of the application with the applicant's signature. Then, you can prove that it's not your signature.

If you tell the debt collector that you are a victim of identity theft and it is collecting the debt for another company, the debt collector must tell that company that you may be a victim of identity theft.

While you can stop a debt collector from contacting you, that won't get rid of the debt itself. To dispute the debt, it's important to contact the company that originally opened the account, otherwise that company may send it to a different debt collector, report it on your credit report, or initiate a lawsuit to collect on the debt.

For more information, see Fair Debt Collection, a publication from the FTC at www.consumer.gov/idtheft.

Driver's License

If you think your name or SSN is being used by an identity thief to get a driver's license or a non-driver's ID card, contact your state DMV. If your state uses your SSN as your driver's license number, ask to substitute another number.

Investment Fraud

U.S.Ssecurities and Exchange Commission (SEC) – www.sec.gov

The SEC's Office of Investor Education and Assistance serves investors who complain to the SEC about investment fraud or the mishandling of their investments by securities professionals. If you believe that an identity thief has tampered with your securities investments or a brokerage account, immediately report it to your broker or account manager and to the SEC. You can file a complaint with the SEC's Complaint Center at www.sec.gov/complaint.shtml. Include as much detail as possible. If you don't have Internet access, write to the SEC at: SEC Office of Investor Education and Assistance, 100 F Street, NE, Washington, DC 20549. For answers to general questions, call 202-551-6551.

Mail Theft

u.s. postal inspection service (uspis) – www.usps.gov/websites/depart/inspect

The USPIS is the law enforcement arm of the U.S. Postal Service, and investigates cases of identity theft. The USPIS has primary jurisdiction in all matters infringing on the integrity of the U.S. mail. If an identity thief has stolen your mail to get new credit cards, bank or credit card statements, pre-screened credit offers, or tax information, or has falsified change-of-address forms or obtained your personal information through a fraud conducted by mail, report it to your local postal inspector.

You can locate the USPIS district office nearest you by calling your local post office, checking the Blue Pages of your telephone directory, or visiting www.usps.gov/websites /depart/inspect.

Passport Fraud

United States Department of State (USDS) – *www.travel.state.gov/passport/passport_ 1738.html*

If you've lost your passport, or believe it was stolen or is being used fraudulently, contact the USDS through their website, or call a local USDS field office. Local field offices are listed in the Blue Pages of your telephone directory.

Phone Fraud

If an identity thief has established phone service in your name, is making unauthorized calls that seem to come from – and are billed to – your cellular phone, or is using your calling card and PIN, contact your service provider immediately to cancel the account and/or calling card. Open new accounts and choose new PINs. If you're having trouble getting fraudulent phone charges removed from your account or getting an unauthorized account closed, contact the appropriate agency below.

- For local service, contact your state Public Utility Commission.
- For cellular phones and long distance, contact the Federal Communications Commission (FCC) at www.fcc.gov. The FCC regulates interstate and international communications by radio, television, wire, satellite, and cable. Call: 1-888-CALL-FCC; TTY: 1-888-TELL-FCC; or write: Federal Communications Commission, Consumer Information Bureau, 445 12th Street, SW, Room 5A863, Washington, DC 20554. You can file complaints online at www.fcc.gov, or e-mail your questions to fccinfo@fcc.gov.

Social Security Number Misuse

Social Security Administration (SSA) – sww.ssa.gov

If you have specific information of SSN misuse that involves the buying or selling of Social Security cards, may be related to terrorist activity, or is designed

to obtain Social Security benefits, contact the SSA Office of the Inspector General. You may file a complaint online at www.socialsecurity.gov/oig,

call toll-free: 1-800-269-0271, fax: 410-597-0118, or write: SSA Fraud Hotline, P.O. Box 17768, Baltimore, MD 21235.

You also may call SSA toll-free at 1-800-772-1213 to verify the accuracy of the earnings reported on your SSN, request a copy of your Social Security Statement, or get a replacement SSN card if yours is lost or stolen. Follow up in writing.

SSA Publications:

- *SSA Fraud Hotline for Reporting Fraud* www.ssa.gov/oig/guidelin.htm
- *Social Security: Your Number and Card (SSA Pub. No. 05-10002)* www.ssa.gov/pubs/10002.html
- *Identity Theft And Your Social Security Number (SSA Pub. No. 05-10064)* www.ssa.gov/pubs/10064.html

Student Loans

Contact the school or program that opened the student loan to close the loan. At the same time, report the fraudulent loan to the U.S. Department of Education. Call the Inspector General's Hotline toll-free at 1-800-MIS-USED; visit www.ed.gov/about/offices/list

/oig/hotline. html?src=rt; or write: Office of Inspector General, U.S. Department of Education, 400 Maryland Avenue, SW, Washington, DC 20202-15 10.

Tax Fraud

Internal Revenue Service (IRS) – www.treas.gov/irs/ci

The IRS is responsible for administering and enforcing tax laws. Identity fraud may occur as it relates directly to your tax records. Visit www.irs.gov and type in the IRS key word "Identity Theft" for more information.

If you have an unresolved issue related to identity theft, or you have suffered or are about to suffer a significant hardship as a result of the administration of the tax laws, visit the IRS Taxpayer Advocate Service website www.irs.gov/advocate/ or call toll-free: 1-877-777-4778.

If you suspect or know of an individual or company that is not complying with the tax law, report it to the Internal Revenue Service Criminal Investigation Informant Hotline by calling toll-free: 1-800-829-0433 or visit www.irs.gov and type in the IRS key word "Tax Fraud."

For More Information

Federal Trade Commission (FTC) – ftc.gov

The FTC wants consumers and businesses to know about the importance of personal information privacy. To request free copies of brochures, visit www.consumer.gov/idtheft or call 1-877-FTC-HELP (1-877-382-4357).

FTC Publications:

- ID Theft: What It's All About ftc.gov/bcp/conline/pubs/credit/idtheftmini.htm
- Avoiding Credit and Charge Card Fraud ftc.gov/bcp/conline/pubs/credit/cards.htm
- Credit, ATM and Debit Cards: What to Do If They're Lost or Stolen ftc.gov /bcp/conline/pubs/credit/atmcard.htm
- Credit Card Loss Protection Offers: They're The Real Steal ftc.gov/bcp/conline/pubs /alerts/lossalrt.htm
- Electronic Banking ftc.gov/bcp/conline/pubs/credit/elbank.htm
- Fair Credit Billing ftc.gov/bcp/conline/pubs/credit/fcb.htm
- Fair Debt Collection ftc.gov/bcp/conline/pubs/credit/fdc.htm
- Getting Purse-onal: What To Do If Your Wallet or Purse Is Stolen ftc.gov/bcp /conline/pubs/alerts/getpurse.htm
- How to Dispute Credit Report Errors ftc.gov/bcp/conline/pubs/credit/crdtdis.htm
- Identity Crisis... What to Do If Your Identity Is Stolen ftc.gov/bcp/conline /pubs /alerts/idenalrt.htm
- Identity Thieves Can Ruin Your Good Name: Tips for Avoiding Identity Theft ftc.gov/bcp/conline/pubs/credit/idthieves.htm
- Your Access to Free Credit Reports ftc.gov/bcp/conline/pubs/credit/freereports.htm

Department of Justice (DOJ) – www.usdoj.gov

The DOJ and its U.S. Attorneys prosecute federal identity theft cases. Information on identity theft is available at www.usdoj.gov/criminal/fraud/idtheft.html.

Federal Bureau of investigation (FBi) – www.fbi.gov

The FBI, a criminal law enforcement agency, investigates cases of identity theft. The FBI recognizes that identity theft is a component of many crimes, including bank fraud, mail fraud, wire fraud, bankruptcy fraud, insurance fraud, fraud against the government, and terrorism. Local field offices are listed in the Blue Pages of your telephone directory.

u.s. secret service (usss) – www.treas.gov/usss

The U.S. Secret Service investigates financial crimes, which may include identity theft. Although the Secret Service generally investigates cases where the dollar loss is substantial, your information may provide evidence of a larger pattern of fraud requiring their involvement.

Local field offices are listed in the Blue Pages of your telephone directory. Financial Crimes Division – www.treas.gov/usss/financial_crimes.shtml

STAYING ALERT

Once resolved, most cases of identity theft stay resolved. But occasionally, some victims have recurring problems. To help stay on top of the situation, continue to monitor your credit reports and read your financial account statements promptly and carefully. You may want to review your credit reports once every three months in the first year of the theft, and once a year thereafter. And stay alert for other signs of identity theft, like:

- failing to receive bills or other mail. Follow up with creditors if your bills don't arrive on time. A missing bill could mean an identity thief has taken over your account and changed your billing address to cover his tracks.
- receiving credit cards that you didn't apply for.
- being denied credit, or being offered less favorable credit terms, like a high interest rate, for no apparent reason.
- getting calls or letters from debt collectors or businesses about merchandise or services you didn't buy.

Getting Your Credjt Report

Free Annual Credit Reports

The Fair Credit Reporting Act requires each of the nationwide consumer reporting companies – Equifax, Experian, and TransUnion – to provide you with a free copy of your credit report, at your request, once every 12 months.

To order your free annual report from one or all the national consumer reporting companies, visit www.annualcreditreport.com, call toll-free 1-877-322-8228, or complete the Annual Credit Report Request Form and mail it to: Annual Credit Report Request Service,

P.O. Box 105281, Atlanta, GA 30348-5281. The form is at the back of this booklet, or you can print it from ftc.gov/credit. Do not contact the three nationwide consumer reporting companies individually. They provide free annual credit reports only through www.annualcreditreport.com, 1-877-322-8228, and Annual Credit Report Request Service, P.O. Box 105281, Atlanta, GA 30348-5281.

The FTC advises consumers who order their free annual credit reports online to be sure to correctly spell www.annualcreditreport.com, or link to it from the FTC's website to avoid being misdirected to other websites that offer supposedly free reports, but only with the purchase of other products. While consumers may be offered additional products or services while on the authorized website, they are not required to make a purchase to receive their free annual credit reports.

For more information, see Your Access to Free Credit Reports, a publication from the FTC, at ftc.gov/credit.

Other Consumer Rights to Free Reports

Under federal law, you're entitled to a free report if a company takes adverse action against you, such as denying your application for credit, insurance, or employment, and you request your report within 60 days of receiving notice of the action. The notice will give you the name, address, and phone number of the consumer reporting company. You're also entitled to one free report a year if you're unemployed and plan to look for a job within 60 days; you're on welfare; or your report is inaccurate because of fraud. Otherwise, a consumer reporting company may charge you up to $9.50 for another copy of your report within a 12-month period.

To buy a copy of your report, contact:

- *Equifax*: 1-800-685-1111; www.equifax.com
- *Experian:* 1-888-EXPERIAN (1-888-397-3742); www.experian.com
- *Transunion*: 1-800-916-8800; www.transunion.com

Under state law, consumers in Colorado, Georgia, Maine, Maryland, Massachusetts, New Jersey, and Vermont already have free access to their credit reports.

MINIMIZING RECURENCES

> Last week I noticed that I was getting products in the mail that I hadn't ordered. Then I noticed charges on my credit card statement that I hadn't made. I spent a whole day calling the vendors' numbers listed on my statement to let them know someone was using my credit card to make purchases without my permission.
>
> I don't know what else this person may be doing with my accounts and/or my name, and I'm worried about that.
>
> From a consumer's complaint to the FTC, January 7, 2004

When it comes to identity theft, you can't control whether you will become a victim. But there are certain steps you can take to minimize recurrences.

What to Do Today

- Place passwords on your credit card, bank, and phone accounts. Avoid using easily available information like your mother's maiden name, your birth date, the last four digits of your SSN or your phone number, or a series of consecutive numbers. When opening new accounts, you may find that many businesses still have a line on their applications for your mother's maiden name. Ask if you can use a password instead.
- Secure personal information in your home, especially if you have roommates, employ outside help, or are having work done in your home.
- Ask about information security procedures in your workplace or at businesses, doctor's offices, or other institutions that collect your personally identifying information. Find out who has access to your personal information and verify that it is handled securely. Ask about the disposal procedures for those records as well. Find out if your information will be shared with anyone else. If so, ask how your information can be kept confidential.

ACTIVE DUTY ALERTS FOR MILITARY PERSONNEL

If you are a member of the military and away from your usual duty station, you may place an active duty alert on your credit reports to help minimize the risk of identity theft while you are deployed. Active duty alerts are in effect on your report for one year. If your deployment lasts longer, you can place another alert on your credit report when you place an active duty alert, you'll be removed from the credit reporting companies' marketing list for pre-screened credit card offers for two years unless you ask to go back on the list before then.

For contact information for the consumer reporting companies, see page 5. The process for getting and removing an alert, and a business's response to your alert, are the same as that for an initial alert (see page 6). you may use a personal representative to place or remove an alert.

Maintaining Vigilance

- Don't give out personal information on the phone, through the mail, or on the Internet unless you've initiated the contact or are sure you know who you're dealing with. Identity thieves are clever, and have posed as representatives of banks, Internet service providers (ISPs), and even government agencies to get people to reveal their SSN, mother's maiden name, account numbers, and other identifying information. Before you share any personal information, confirm that you are dealing with a legitimate organization. Check an organization's website by typing its URL in the address line, rather than cutting and pasting it. Many companies post scam alerts when their name is used improperly. Or call customer service using the number listed on your account statement or in the telephone book. For more information, see How Not to Get Hooked by a 'Phishing' Scam, a publication from the FTC at www.consumer.gov/idtheft.

- Treat your mail and trash carefully. Deposit your outgoing mail in post office collection boxes or at your local post office, rather than in an unsecured mailbox. Promptly remove mail from your mailbox. If you're planning to be away from home and can't pick up your mail, call the U.S. Postal Service at 1-800-275-8777 to request a vacation hold. The Postal Service will hold your mail at your local post office until you can pick it up or are home to receive it.
- To thwart an identity thief who may pick through your trash or recycling bins to capture your personal information, tear or shred your charge receipts, copies of credit applications, insurance forms, physician statements, checks and bank statements, expired charge cards that you're discarding, and credit offers you get in the mail. To opt out of receiving offers of credit in the mail, call: 1-888-5-OPTOUT (1-888-567-8688). The three nationwide consumer reporting companies use the same toll-free number to let consumers choose not to receive credit offers based on their lists. *Note:* You will be asked to provide your SSN which the consumer reporting companies need to match you with your file.
- Don't carry your SSN card; leave it in a secure place.
- Give your SSN only when absolutely necessary, and ask to use other types of identifiers. If your state uses your SSN as your driver's license number, ask to substitute another number. Do the same if your health insurance company uses your SSN as your policy number.
- Carry only the identification information and the credit and debit cards that you'll actually need when you go out.
- Be cautious when responding to promotions. Identity thieves may create phony promotional offers to get you to give them your personal information.
- Keep your purse or wallet in a safe place at work; do the same with copies of administrative forms that have your sensitive personal information.
- When ordering new checks, pick them up from the bank instead of having them mailed to your home mailbox.

A SPECIAL WORD ABOUT SOCIAL SECURITY NUMBERS

Your employer and financial institutions will need your ssN for wage and tax reporting purposes. other businesses may ask you for your ssN to do a credit check if you are applying for a loan, renting an apartment, or signing up for utilities. sometimes, however, they simply want your ssN for general record keeping. If someone asks for your ssN, ask:

- Why do you need my SSN?
- How will my ssN be used?
- How do you protect my ssN from being stolen?
- What will happen if I don't give you my SSN?

If you don't provide your ssN, some businesses may not provide you with the service or benefit you want. Getting satisfactory answers to these questions will help you decide whether you want to share your ssN with the business. The decision to share is yours.

THE DOORS AND WINDOWS ARE LOCKED, BUT . . .

You may be careful about locking your doors and windows, and keeping your personal papers in a secure place. Depending on what you use your personal computer for, an identity thief may not need to set foot in your house to steal your personal information. You may store your SSN, financial records, tax returns, birth date, and bank account numbers on your computer. These tips can help you keep your computer – and the personal information it stores – safe.

- Virus protection software should be updated regularly, and patches for your operating system and other software programs should be installed to protect against intrusions and infections that can lead to the compromise of your computer files or passwords. Ideally, virus protection software should be set to automatically update each week. The Windows XP operating system also can be set to automatically check for patches and download them to your computer.
- Do not open files sent to you by strangers, or click on hyperlinks or download programs from people you don't know. Be careful about using file-sharing programs. Opening a file could expose your system to a computer virus or a program known as "spyware," which could capture your passwords or any other information as you type it into your keyboard. For more information, see File Sharing: A Fair Share? Maybe Not and Spyware, publications from the FTC at www.consumer.gov/idtheft.
- Use a firewall program, especially if you use a high-speed Internet connection like cable, DSL or T-1 that leaves your computer connected to the Internet 24 hours a day. The firewall program will allow you to stop uninvited access to your computer. Without it, hackers can take over your computer, access the personal information stored on it, or use it to commit other crimes.
- Use a secure browser – software that encrypts or scrambles information you send over the Internet – to guard your online transactions. Be sure your browser has the most up-to-date encryption capabilities by using the latest version available from the manufacturer. You also can download some browsers for free over the Internet. When submitting information, look for the "lock" icon on the browser's status bar to be sure your information is secure during transmission.
- Try not to store financial information on your laptop unless absolutely necessary. If you do, use a strong password – a combination of letters (upper and lower case), numbers, and symbols. A good way to create a strong password is to think of a memorable phrase and use the first letter of each word as your password, converting some letters into numbers that resemble letters. For example, "I love Felix; he's a good cat," would become 1LFHA6c. Don't use an automatic log-in feature that saves your user name and password, and always log off when you're finished. That way, if your laptop is stolen, it's harder for a thief to access your personal information.
- Before you dispose of a computer, delete all the personal information it stored. Deleting files using the keyboard or mouse commands or reformatting your hard drive may not be enough because the files may stay on the computer's hard drive, where they may be retrieved easily. Use a "wipe" utility program
- to overwrite the entire hard drive.

- Look for website privacy policies. They should answer questions about maintaining accuracy, access, security, and control of personal information collected by the site, how the information will be used, and whether it will be provided to third parties. If you don't see a privacy policy – or if you can't understand it – consider doing business elsewhere.

For more information, see Site-Seeing on the Internet: A Traveler's Guide to Cyberspace, a publication from the FTC at ftc.gov

APPENDIX

It's the Law

Federal Law

The Identity Theft and Assumption Deterrence Act, enacted by Congress in October 1998 (and codified, in part, at 18 U.S.C. §1028) makes identity theft a federal crime.

Under federal criminal law, identity theft takes place when someone "knowingly transfers, possesses or uses, without lawful authority, a means of identification of another person with the intent to commit, or to aid or abet, or in connection with, any unlawful activity that constitutes a violation of federal law, or that constitutes a felony under any applicable state or local law."

Under this definition, a name or Social Security number is considered a "means of identification." So is a credit card number, cellular telephone electronic serial number, or any other piece of information that may be used alone or in conjunction with other information to identify a specific individual.

Violations of the federal crime are investigated by federal law enforcement agencies, including the U.S. Secret Service, the FBI, the U.S. Postal Inspection Service, and the Social Security Administration's Office of the Inspector General. Federal identity theft cases are prosecuted by the U.S. Department of Justice.

For the purposes of the law, the FCRA defines identity theft to apply to consumers and businesses.

State Laws

Many states have passed laws making identity theft a crime or providing help in recovery from identity theft; others are considering such legislation. Where specific criminal identity theft laws do not exist, the practices may be prohibited under other laws. Contact your state Attorney General (for a list of state offices, visit www.naag.org) or local consumer protection agency for laws related to identity theft, or visit www.consumer.gov/idtheft.

INSTRUCTIONS FOR COMPLETING THE ID THEFT AFFIDAVIT

To make certain that you do not become responsible for any debts incurred by an identity thief, you must prove to each of the companies where accounts were opened or used in your name that you didn't create the debt.

A group of credit grantors, consumer advocates, and attorneys at the Federal Trade Commission (FTC) developed an ID Theft Affidavit to make it easier for fraud victims to report information. While many companies accept this affidavit, others require that you submit more or different forms. Before you send the affidavit, contact each company to find out if they accept it.

It will be necessary to provide the information in this affidavit anywhere a new account was opened in your name. The information will enable the companies to investigate the fraud and decide the outcome of your claim. If someone made unauthorized charges to an existing account, call the company for instructions.

This affidavit has two parts:

- *Part One* — the ID Theft Affidavit — is where you report general information about yourself and the theft.
- *Part Two* — the Fraudulent Account Statement — is where you describe the fraudulent account(s) opened in your name. Use a separate Fraudulent Account Statement for each company you need to write to.

When you send the affidavit to the companies, attach copies (NOT originals) of any supporting documents (for example, driver's license or police report). Before submitting your affidavit, review the disputed account(s) with family members or friends who may have information about the account(s) or access to them.

Complete this affidavit as soon as possible. Many creditors ask that you send it within two weeks. Delays on your part could slow the investigation.

Be as accurate and complete as possible. You may choose not to provide some of the information requested. However, incorrect or incomplete information will slow the process of investigating your claim and absolving the debt. Print clearly.

When you have finished completing the affidavit, mail a copy to each creditor, bank, or company that provided the thief with the unauthorized credit, goods, or services you describe. Attach a copy of the Fraudulent Account Statement with information only on accounts opened at the institution to which you are sending the packet, as well as any other supporting documentation you are able to provide.

Send the appropriate documents to each company by certified mail, return receipt requested, so you can prove that it was received. The companies will review your claim and send you a written response telling you the outcome of their investigation. Keep a copy of everything you submit.

If you haven't already done so, report the fraud to the following organizations:

1. Any one of the nationwide consumer reporting companies to place a fraud alert on your credit report. Fraud alerts can help prevent an identity thief from opening any more accounts in your name. The company you call is required to contact the other two, which will place an alert on their versions of your report, too.

Equifax: 1 -800-525-6285; www.equifax.com

Experian: 1 -888-EXpERIAN (1 -888-397-3742); www.experian.com

Transunion: 1 -800-680-7289; www.transunion.com

In addition to placing the fraud alert, the three consumer reporting companies will send you free copies of your credit reports, and, if you ask, they will display only the last four digits of your social security number on your credit reports.

2. The security or fraud department of each company where you know, or believe, accounts have been tampered with or opened fraudulently. Close the accounts. Follow up in writing, and include copies (NoT originals) of supporting documents. It's important to notify credit card companies and banks in writing. send your letters by certified mail, return receipt requested, so you can document what the company received and when. Keep a file of your correspondence and enclosures when you open new accounts, use new personal Identification Numbers (pINs) and pass words. Avoid using easily available information like your mother's maiden name, your birth date, the last four digits of your social security number or your phone number, or a series of consecutive numbers.

3. your local police or the police in the community where the identity theft took place to file a report. Get a copy of the police report or, at the very least, the number of the report. It can help you deal with creditors who need proof of the crime. If the police are reluctant to take your report, ask to file a "Miscellaneous Incidents" report, or try another jurisdiction, like your state police. you also can check with your state Attorney General's office to find out if state law requires the police to take reports for identity theft. Check the Blue pages of your telephone directory for the phone number or check www.naag.org for a list of state Attorneys General.

4. The Federal Trade Commission. By sharing your identity theft complaint with the FTC, you will provide important information that can help law enforcement officials across the nation track down identity thieves and stop them. The FTC also can refer victims' complaints to other government agencies and companies for further action, as well as investigate companies for violations of laws that the FTC enforces you can file a complaint online at www.consumer.gov/idtheft. If you don't have Internet access, call the FTC's Identity Theft Hotline, toll-free: 1 -877-IDTHEFT (1 -877-438-4338); TTy:

1-866-653-4261; or write: Identity Theft Clearinghouse, Federal Trade Commission, 600 pennsylvania Avenue, Nw, washington, DC 20580.

If you are unable to complete the affidavit, a legal guardian or someone with power of attorney may complete it for you. Except as noted, the information you provide will be used only by the company to process your affidavit, investigate the events you report, and help stop further fraud. If this affidavit is requested in a lawsuit, the company might have to provide it to the requesting party. Completing this affidavit does not guarantee that the identity thief will be prosecuted or that the debt will be cleared.

DO NOT SEND AFFIDAVIT TO THE FTC OR ANY OTHER GOVERNMENT AGENCY

Name ______________________________ Phone number ________________ Page 1

ID Theft Affidavit

Victim Information

(1) My full legal name is ____
(First) (Middle) (Last) (Jr., Sr., III)

(2) (If different from above) When the events described in this affidavit took place, I was known as

____
(First) (Middle) (Last) (Jr., Sr., III)

(3) My date of birth is ______________________
(day/month/year)

(4) My Social Security number is______________________

(5) My driver's license or identification card state and number are____________________

(6) My current address is ____

City ______________________ State ____________ Zip Code __________

(7) I have lived at this address since ______________
(month/year)

(8) (If different from above) When the events described in this affidavit took place, my address was

______________________ ______________________________

City ______________________ State ____________ Zip Code __________

(9) I lived at the address in Item 8 from ______________ until ______________
(month/year) (month/year)

(10) My daytime telephone number is (_______)____________________

My evening telephone number is (_______)____________________

Name ______________________ Phone number ______________ Page 2

How the Fraud Occurred

Check all that apply for items 11 - 17:

(11) ❑ I did not authorize anyone to use my name or personal information to seek the money, credit, loans, goods or services described in this report.

(12) ❑ I did not receive any benefit, money, goods or services as a result of the events described in this report.

(13) ❑ My identification documents (for example, credit cards; birth certificate; driver's license; Social Security card; etc.) were ❑ stolen ❑ lost on or about ______________.
(day/month/year)

(14) ❑ To the best of my knowledge and belief, the following person(s) used my information (for example, my name, address, date of birth, existing account numbers, Social Security number, mother's maiden name, etc.) or identification documents to get money, credit, loans, goods or services without my knowledge or authorization:

______________________	______________________
Name (if known)	Name (if known)
______________________	______________________
Address (if known)	Address (if known)
______________________	______________________
Phone number(s) (if known)	Phone number(s) (if known)
______________________	______________________
Additional information (if known)	Additional information (if known)

(15) ❑ I do NOT know who used my information or identification documents to get money, credit, loans, goods or services without my knowledge or authorization.

(16) ❑ Additional comments: (For example, description of the fraud, which documents or information were used or how the identity thief gained access to your information.)

____

____

____

____

____

(Attach additional pages as necessary.)

Do Not Send Affidavit to the FTC or Any Other Government Agency

Name ______________________________ Phone number ________________ Page 3

Victim's Law Enforcement Actions

(17) (check one) I ❑ am ❑ am not willing to assist in the prosecution of the person(s) who committed this fraud.

(18) (check one) I ❑ am ❑ am not authorizing the release of this information to law enforcement for the purpose of assisting them in the investigation and prosecution of the person(s) who committed this fraud.

(19) (check all that apply) I ❑ have ❑ have not reported the events described in this affidavit to the police or other law enforcement agency. The police ❑ did ❑ did not write a report. In the event you have contacted the police or other law enforcement agency, please complete the following:

______________________ **(Agency #1)**	______________________ (Officer/Agency personnel taking report)
______________________ (Date of report)	______________________ (Report number, if any)
______________________ (Phone number)	______________________ (email address, if any)
______________________ **(Agency #2)**	______________________ (Officer/Agency personnel taking report)
______________________ (Date of report)	______________________ (Report number, if any)
______________________ (Phone number)	______________________ (email address, if any)

Documentation Checklist

Please indicate the supporting documentation you are able to provide to the companies you plan to notify. Attach copies (NOT originals) to the affidavit before sending it to the companies.

(20) ❑ A copy of a valid government-issued photo-identification card (for example, your driver's license, state-issued ID card or your passport). If you are under 16 and don't have a photo-ID, you may submit a copy of your birth certificate or a copy of your official school records showing your enrollment and place of residence.

(21) ❑ Proof of residency during the time the disputed bill occurred, the loan was made or the other event took place (for example, a rental/lease agreement in your name, a copy of a utility bill or a copy of an insurance bill).

Do Not Send Affidavit to the FTC or Any Other Government Agency

Name ________________________________ Phone number ________________ Page 4

(22) ❑ A copy of the report you filed with the police or sheriff's department. If you are unable to obtain a report or report number from the police, please indicate that in Item 19. Some companies only need the report number, not a copy of the report. You may want to check with each company.

Signature

I certify that, to the best of my knowledge and belief, all the information on and attached to this affidavit is true, correct, and complete and made in good faith. I also understand that this affidavit or the information it contains may be made available to federal, state, and/or local law enforcement agencies for such action within their jurisdiction as they deem appropriate. I understand that knowingly making any false or fraudulent statement or representation to the government may constitute a violation of 18 U.S.C. §1001 or other federal, state, or local criminal statutes, and may result in imposition of a fine or imprisonment or both.

________________________________ ________________________________

(signature) (date signed)

____

(Notary)

[Check with each company. Creditors sometimes require notarization. If they do not, please have one witness (non-relative) sign below that you completed and signed this affidavit.]

Witness:

________________________________ ________________________________

(signature) (printed name)

________________________________ ________________________________

(date) (telephone number)

Do Not Send Affidavit to the FTC or Any Other Government Agency

Name ______________________ Phone number ______________ Page 5

Fraudulent Account Statement

Completing this Statement

- Make as many copies of this page as you need. **Complete a separate page for each company you're notifying and only send it to that company.** Include a copy of your signed affidavit.
- List only the account(s) you're disputing with the company receiving this form. **See the example below.**
- If a collection agency sent you a statement, letter or notice about the fraudulent account, attach a copy of that document (**NOT** the original).

I declare (check all that apply):

❑ As a result of the event(s) described in the ID Theft Affidavit, the following account(s) was/were opened at your company in my name without my knowledge, permission or authorization using my personal information or identifying documents:

Creditor Name/Address (the company that opened the account or provided the goods or services)	Account Number	Type of unauthorized credit/goods/services provided by creditor (if known)	Date issued or opened (if known)	Amount/Value provided (the amount charged or the cost of the goods/services)
Example Example National Bank 22 Main Street Columbus, Ohio 22722	01234567-89	auto loan	01/05/2002	$25,500.00

❑ During the time of the accounts described above, I had the following account open with your company:

Billing name ______________________

Billing address ______________________

Account number ______________________

Do Not Send Affidavit to the FTC or Any Other Government Agency

EQUIFAX experian TransUnion

Annual Credit Report Request Form

You have the right to get a free copy of your credit file disclosure, commonly called a credit report, once every 12 months, from each of the nationwide consumer credit reporting companies - Equifax, Experian and TransUnion.

For instant access to your free credit report, visit www.annualcreditreport.com.

For more information on obtaining your free credit report, visit www.annualcreditreport.com or call 877-322-8228.

Use this form if you prefer to write to request your credit report from any, or all, of the nationwide consumer credit reporting companies. The following information is required to process your request. **Omission of any information may delay your request.**

Once complete, fold (do not staple or tape), place into a #10 envelope, affix required postage and mail to:
Annual Credit Report Request Service P.O. Box 105281 Atlanta, GA 30348-5281.

Please use a Black or Blue Pen and write your responses in PRINTED CAPITAL LETTERS without touching the sides of the boxes like the examples listed below:

A B C D E F G H I J K L M N O P Q R S T U V W X Y Z 0 1 2 3 4 5 6 7 8 9

Social Security Number: ___ - __ - ____

Date of Birth: __ / __ / ____
Month Day Year

Fold Here — Fold Here

First Name M.I.

Last Name JR, SR, III, etc.

Current Mailing Address:

House Number Street Name

Apartment Number / Private Mailbox For Puerto Rico Only: Print Urbanization Name

City State ZipCode

Previous Mailing Address (complete only if at current mailing address for less than two years):

House Number Street Name

Fold Here — Fold Here

Apartment Number / Private Mailbox For Puerto Rico Only: Print Urbanization Name

City State ZipCode

Shade Circle Like This → ●
Not Like This →

I want a credit report from (shade each that you would like to receive):
○ Equifax
○ Experian
○ TransUnion

○ Shade here if, for security reasons, you want your credit report to include no more than the last four digits of your Social Security Number.

31238

If additional information is needed to process your request, the consumer credit reporting company will contact you by mail.

Your request will be processed within 15 days of receipt and then mailed to you.

THE FTC'S PRIVACY POLICY

When you contact the FTC with complaints or requests for information, you can do it online at www.consumer.gov/idtheft; by telephone, toll-free at 1-877-ID-THEFT (1-877-438-4338); or by mail: Federal Trade Commission, Identity Theft Clearinghouse, 600 Pennsylvania Avenue, NW, Washington, DC 20580. Before you contact us, there are a few things you should know.

We enter the information you send into the Identity Theft Clearinghouse, an electronic database. The Clearinghouse is a system of records covered under the Privacy Act of 1974. In general, the Privacy Act prohibits unauthorized disclosures of the records it protects. It also gives individuals the right to review records about themselves. Learn more about your Privacy Act rights and the FTC's Privacy Act procedures by contacting the FTC's Freedom of Information Act Office: 202-326-2430; ftc.gov/foia/privacy_act.htm.

The information you submit is shared with FTC attorneys and investigators. It also may be shared with employees of various federal, state, or local law enforcement or regulatory authorities. The FTC also may share your information with some private entities, such as consumer reporting companies and any companies you may have complained about, where it believes that doing so might help resolve identity theft-related problems. You may be contacted by the FTC or any of the agencies or private entities to whom your complaint has been referred. In some limited circumstances, including requests from Congress, the FTC may be required by law to disclose information you submit.

You have the option to submit your information anonymously. However, if you do not provide your name and contact information, law enforcement agencies and other organizations will not be able to contact you for more information to help in identity theft investigations and prosecutions.

In: Identity Theft Breaches
Editor: Cary S. Logweller
ISBN 978-1-60692-227-9

Chapter 4

PROTECTING PERSONAL INFORMATION: A GUIDE FOR BUSINESS (FEDERAL TRADE COMMISSION)

Most companies keep sensitive personal information in their files—names, Social Security numbers, credit card, or other account data—that identifies customers or employees.

This information often is necessary to fill orders, meet payroll, or perform other necessary business functions. However, if sensitive data falls into the wrong hands, it can lead to fraud, identity theft, or similar harms. Given the cost of a security breach—losing your customers' trust and perhaps even defending yourself against a lawsuit—safeguarding personal information is just plain good business

A sound data security plan is built on 5 key principles:

1. Take stock. Know what personal information you have in your files and on your computers.
2. Scale down. Keep only what you need for your business.
3. Lock it. Protect the information that you keep.
4. Pitch it. Properly dispose of what you no longer need.
5. Plan ahead. Create a plan to respond to security incidents.

Use the checklists on the following pages to see how your company's practices measure up and where changes are necessary.

1. TAKE STOCK: KNOW WHAT PERSONAL INFORMATION YOU HAVE IN YOUR FILES AND ON YOUR COMPUTERS

Effective data security starts with assessing what information you have and identifying who has access to it. Understanding how personal information moves into, through, and out of your business and who has or could have access to it is essential to assessing security vulnerabilities. You can determine the best ways to secure the information only after you've traced how it flows.

- Inventory all computers, laptops, flash drives, disks, home computers, and other equipment to find out where your company stores sensitive data. Also inventory the information you have by type and location. Your file cabinets and computer systems are a start, but remember: your business receives personal information in a number of ways—through websites, from contractors, from call centers, and the like. What about information saved on laptops, employees' home computers, flash drives, and ell phones? No inventory is complete until you check everywhere sensitive data might be stored.
- Track personal information through your business by talking with your sales department, information technology staff, human resources office, accounting personnel, and outside service providers. Get a complete picture of:
- *Who sends sensitive personal information to your business.* Do you get it from customers? Credit card companies? Banks or other financial institutions? Credit bureaus? Other businesses?
- *How your business receives personal information.* Does it come to your business through a website? By email? Through the mail? Is it transmitted through cash registers in stores?
- *What kind of information you collect at each entry point.* Do you get credit card information online? Does your accounting department keep information about customers' checking accounts?
- *Where you keep the information you collect at each entry point.* Is it in a central computer database? On individual laptops? On disks or tapes? In file cabinets? In branch offices? Do employees have files at home?
- *Who has—or could have—access to the information.* Which of your employees has permission to access the information? Could anyone else get a hold of it? What about vendors who supply and update software you use to process credit card transactions? Contractors operating your call center?
  - Different types of information present varying risks. Pay particular attention to how you keep personally identifying information: Social Security numbers, credit card or financial information, and other sensitive data. That's what thieves use most often to commit fraud or identity theft

Security Check

Question:
Are there laws that require my company to keep sensitive data secure?

Answer:
yes. While you're taking stock of the data in your files, take stock of the law, too. Statutes like the Gramm-Leach-Bliley Act, the Fair Credit Reporting Act, and the Federal Trade Commission Act may require you to provide reasonable security for sensitive information.

To find out more, visit www.ftc.gov/privacy.

2. Scale Down: Keep Only What You Need for Your Business

If you don't have a legitimate business need for sensitive personally identifying information, don't keep it. In fact, don't even collect it. If you have a legitimate business need for the information, keep it only as long as it's necessary.

- Use Social Security numbers only for required and lawful purposes— like reporting employee taxes. Don't use Social Security numbers unnecessarily—for example, as an employee or customer identification number, or because you've always done it.

Security Check

Question:

We like to have accurate information about our customers, so we usually create a permanent file about all aspects of their transactions, including the information we collected from the magnetic stripe on their credit cards. Could this practice put their information at isk?

Answer:

yes. Keep sensitive data in your system only as long as you have a business reason to have it. Once that business need is over, properly dispose of it. If it's not in your system, it can't be stolen by hackers. It's as simple as that.

- Don't keep customer credit card information unless you have a business need for it. For example, don't retain the account number and expiration date unless you have an essential business need to do so. Keeping this information or keeping it longer than necessary raises the risk that the information could be used to commit fraud or identity theft.
- Check the default settings on your software that reads customers' credit card numbers and processes the transactions. Sometimes it's preset to keep information permanently. Change the default setting to make sure you're not inadvertently keeping information you don't need.
- If you must keep information for business reasons or to comply with the law, develop a written recordsretention policy to identify what information must be kept, how to secure it, how long to keep it, and how to dispose of it securely when you no longer need it.
- Don't keep customer credit card information unless you have a business need for it. For example, don't retain the account number and expiration date unless you have an essential business need to do so. Keeping this information or keeping it longer than necessary raises the risk that the information could be used to commit fraud or identity theft.
- Check the default settings on your software that reads customers' credit card numbers and processes the transactions. Sometimes it's preset to keep information

permanently. Change the default setting to make sure you're not inadvertently keeping information you don't need.

- If you must keep information for business reasons or to comply with the law, develop a written records retention policy to identify what information must be kept, how to secure it, how long to keep it, and how to dispose of it securely when you no longer need it.

3. Lock It: Protect the Information That You Keep

What's the best way to protect the sensitive personally identifying information you need to keep? It depends on the kind of information and how it's stored. The most effective data security plans deal with four key elements: physical security, electronic security, employee training, and the security practices of contractors and service providers.

Physical Security

Many data compromises happen the old-fashioned way—through lost or stolen paper documents. Often, the best defense is a locked door or an alert employee.

- Store paper documents or files, as well as CDs, floppy disks, zip drives, tapes, and backups containing personally identifiable information in a locked room or in a locked file cabinet. Limit access to employees with a legitimate business need. Control who has a key, and the number of keys.
- Require that files containing personally identifiable information be kept in locked file cabinets except when an employee is working on the file. Remind employees not to leave sensitive papers out on their desks when they are away from their workstations.
- Require employees to put files away, log off their computers, and lock their file cabinets and office doors at the end of the day.
- Implement appropriate access controls for your building. Tell employees what to do and whom to call if they see an unfamiliar person on the premises.
- If you maintain offsite storage facilities, limit employee access to those with a legitimate business need. Know if and when someone accesses the storage site.
- If you ship sensitive information using outside carriers or contractors, encrypt the information and keep an inventory of the information being shipped. Also use an overnight shipping service that will allow you to track the delivery of your information.

ELECTRONIC SECURITY

Computer security isn't just the realm of your IT staff. Make it your business to understand the vulnerabilities of your computer system, and follow the advice of experts in the field.

General Network Security

- Identify the computers or servers where sensitive personal information is stored.
- Identify all connections to the computers where you store sensitive information. These may include the Internet, electronic cash registers, computers at your branch offices, computers used by service providers to support your network, and wireless devices like inventory scanners or cell phones.
- Assess the vulnerability of each connection to commonly known or reasonably foreseeable attacks. Depending on your circumstances, appropriate assessments may range from having a knowledgeable employee run off-the-shelf security software to having an independent professional conduct a full-scale security audit.
- Don't store sensitive consumer data on any computer with an Internet connection unless it's essential for conducting your business.
- Encrypt sensitive information that you send to third parties over public networks (like the Internet), and consider encrypting sensitive information that is stored on your computer network or on disks or portable storage devices used by your employees. Consider also encrypting email transmissions within your business if they contain personally identifying information.
- Regularly run up-to-date anti-virus and anti-spyware programs on individual computers and on servers on your network.
- Check expert websites (such as www.sans.org) and your software vendors' websites regularly for alerts about new vulnerabilities, and implement policies for installing vendor-approved patches to correct problems.
- Scan computers on your network to identify and profile the operating system and open network services. If you find services that you don't need, disable them to prevent hacks or other potential security problems. For example, if email service or an Internet connection is not necessary on a certain computer, consider closing the ports to those services on that computer to prevent unauthorized access to that machine.
- When you receive or transmit credit card information or other sensitive financial data, use Secure Sockets Layer (SSL) or another secure connection that protects the information in transit.

SECURITY CHECK

Question:
We encrypt financial data customers submit on our website.

But once we receive it, we decrypt it and email it over the Internet to our branch offices in regular text. Is there a safer practice?

Answer:

yes. Regular email is not a secure method for sending sensitive data. The better practice is to encrypt any transmission that contains information that could be used by fraudsters or ID thieves.

- Pay particular attention to the security of your web applications—the software used to give information to visitors to your website and to retrieve information from them. Web applications may be particularly vulnerable to a variety of hack attacks. In one variation called an "injection attack," a hacker inserts malicious commands into what looks like a legitimate request for information. Once in your system, hackers transfer sensitive information from your network to their computers. Relatively simple defenses against these attacks are available from a variety of sources.

Password Management

- Control access to sensitive information by requiring that employees use "strong" passwords. Tech security experts say the longer the password, the better. Because simple passwords like common dictionary words can be guessed easily, insist that employees choose passwords with a mix of letters, numbers, and characters. Require an employee's user name and password to be different, and require frequent changes in passwords.
- Explain to employees why it's against company policy to share their passwords or post them near their workstations.
- Use password-activated screen savers to lock employee computers after a period of inactivity.
- Lock out users who don't enter the correct password within a designated number of log-on attempts.

SECURITY CHECK

Question:

Our account staff needs access to our database of customer financial information. To make it easier to remember, we just use our company name as the password. Could that create a security problem?

Answer:

yes. Hackers will first try words like "password," your company name, the software's default password, and other easy-to-guess choices. They'll also use programs that run through common English words and dates. To make it harder for them to crack your system, select strong passwords the longer, the better—that use a combination of letters, symbols, and numbers. And change passwords often.

- Warn employees about possible calls from identity thieves attempting to deceive them into giving out their passwords by impersonating members of your IT staff. Let employees know that calls like this are always fraudulent, and that no one should be asking them to reveal their passwords.
- When installing new software, immediately change vendor-supplied default passwords to a more secure strong password.
- Caution employees against transmitting sensitive personally identifying data—Social Security numbers, passwords, account information—via email. Unencrypted email is not a secure way to transmit any information.

Laptop Security

- Restrict the use of laptops to those employees who need them to perform their jobs.
- Assess whether sensitive information really needs to be stored on a laptop. If not, delete it with a "wiping" program that overwrites data on the laptop. Deleting files using standard keyboard commands isn't sufficient because data may remain on the laptop's hard drive. Wiping programs are available at most office supply stores.
- Require employees to store laptops in a secure place. Even when laptops are in use, consider using cords and locks to secure laptops to employees' desks.
- Consider allowing laptop users only to access sensitive information, but not to store the information on their laptops. Under this approach, the information is stored on a secure central computer and the laptops function as terminals that display information from the central computer, but do not store it. The information could be further protected by requiring the use of a token, "smart card," thumb print, or other biometric—as well as a password—to access the central computer.
- If a laptop contains sensitive data, encrypt it and configure it so users can't download any software or change the security settings without approval from your IT specialists. Consider adding an "auto-destroy" function so that data on a computer that is reported stolen will be destroyed when the thief uses it to try to get on the Internet.
- Train employees to be mindful of security when they're on the road. They should never leave a laptop visible in a car, at a hotel luggage stand, or packed in checked luggage unless directed to by airport security. If someone must leave a laptop in a car, it should be locked in a trunk. Everyone who goes through airport security should keep an eye on their laptop as it goes on the belt.

Firewalls

- Use a firewall to protect your computer from hacker attacks while it is connected to the Internet. A firewall is software or hardware designed to block hackers from accessing your computer. A properly configured firewall makes it tougher for hackers to locate your computer and get into your programs and files.

- Determine whether you should install a "border" firewall where your network connects to the Internet. A border firewall separates your network from the Internet and may prevent an attacker from gaining access to a computer on the network where you store sensitive information. Set "access controls"—settings that determine who gets through the firewall and what they will be allowed to see—to allow only trusted employees with a legitimate business need to access the network. Since the protection a firewall provides is only as effective as its access controls, review them periodically.
- If some computers on your network store sensitive information while others do not, consider using additional firewalls to protect the computers with sensitive information.

Wireless and Remote Access

- Determine if you use wireless devices like inventory scanners or cell phones to connect to your computer network or to transmit sensitive information.
- If you do, consider limiting who can use a wireless connection to access your computer network. You can make it harder for an intruder to access the network by limiting the wireless devices that can connect to your network.
- Better still, consider encryption to make it more difficult for an intruder to read the content. Encrypting transmissions from wireless devices to your computer network may prevent an intruder from gaining access through a process called "spoofing"—impersonating one of your computers to get access to your network.
- Consider using encryption if you allow remote access to your computer network by employees or by service providers, such as companies that troubleshoot and update software you use to process credit card purchases.

Detecting Breaches

- To detect network breaches when they occur, consider using an intrusion detection system. To be effective, it must be updated frequently to address new types of hacking.
- Maintain central log files of security-related information to monitor activity on your network so that you can spot and respond to attacks.
- If there is an attack on your network, the log will provide information that can identify the computers that have been compromised.
- Monitor incoming traffic for signs that someone is trying to hack in. Keep an eye out for activity from new users, multiple log-in attempts from unknown users or computers, and higher-than-average traffic at unusual times of the day.
- Monitor outgoing traffic for signs of a data breach. Watch for unexpectedly large amounts of data being transmitted from your system to an unknown user. If large amounts of information are being transmitted from your network, investigate to make sure the transmission is authorized.

- Have in place and implement a breach response plan. See pages 22–23 for more information.

Employee Training

Your data security plan may look great on paper, but it's only as strong as the employees who implement it. Take time to explain the rules to your staff, and train them to spot security vulnerabilities. Periodic training emphasizes the importance you place on meaningful data security practices. A well-trained workforce is the best defense against identity theft and data breaches.

- Check references or do background checks before hiring employees who will have access to sensitive data.
- Ask every new employee to sign an agreement to follow your company's confidentiality and security standards for handling sensitive data. Make sure they understand that abiding by your company's data security plan is an essential part of their duties. Regularly remind employees of your company's policy—and any legal requirement—to keep customer information secure and confidential.
- Know which employees have access to consumers' sensitive personally identifying information. Pay particular attention to data like Social Security numbers and account numbers. Limit access to personal information to employees with a "need to know."
- Have a procedure in place for making sure that workers who leave your employ or transfer to another part of the company no longer have access to sensitive information. Terminate their passwords, and collect keys and identification cards as part of the check-out routine.

SECURITY CHECK

Question:

I'm not really a "tech" type. Are there steps our computer people can take to protect our system from common hack attacks?

Answer:

Yes. There are relatively simple fixes to protect your computers from some of the most common vulnerabilities. For example, a threat called an "SQL injection attack" can give fraudsters access to sensitive data on your system, but can be thwarted with a simple change to your computer. Bookmark the websites of groups like the Open Web Application Security Project, www.owasp.org, or SANS (SysAdmin, Audit, Network, Security) Institute's Twenty Most Critical Internet Security Vulnerabilities, www.sans.org/top20, for up-to-date information on the latest threats—and fixes. And check with your software vendors for patches that address new vulnerabilities.

- Create a "culture of security" by implementing a regular schedule of employee training. Update employees as you find out about new risks and vulnerabilities. Make sure training includes employees at satellite offices, temporary help, and seasonal workers. If employees don't attend, consider blocking their access to the network.
- Train employees to recognize security threats. Tell them how to report suspicious activity and publicly reward employees who alert you to vulnerabilities.
- Tell employees about your company policies regarding keeping information secure and confidential. Post reminders in areas where sensitive information is used or stored, as well as where employees congregate. Make sure your policies cover employees who telecommute or access sensitive data from home or an offsite location.
- Warn employees about phone phishing. Train them to be suspicious of unknown callers claiming to need account numbers to process an order or asking for customer or employee contact information. Make it office policy to double-check by contacting the company using a phone number you know is genuine.
- Require employees to notify you immediately if there is a potential security breach, such as a lost or stolen laptop.
- Impose disciplinary measures for security policy violations.
- For computer security tips, tutorials, and quizzes for everyone on your staff, visit www.OnGuardOnline.gov.

Security Practices of Contractors and Service Providers

Your company's security practices depend on the people who implement them, including contractors and service providers.

- Before you outsource any of your business functions— payroll, web hosting, customer call center operations, data processing, or the like—investigate the company's data security practices and compare their standards to yours. If possible, visit their facilities.
- Address security issues for the type of data your service providers handle in your contract with them.
- Insist that your service providers notify you of any security incidents they experience, even if the incidents may not have led to an actual compromise of your data.

4. Pitch It: Properly Dispose of What You No Longer Need

What looks like a sack of trash to you can be a gold mine for an identity thief. Leaving credit card receipts or papers or CDs with personally identifying information in a dumpster facilitates fraud and exposes consumers to the risk of identity theft. By properly disposing of sensitive information, you ensure that it cannot be read or reconstructed.

- Implement information disposal practices that are reasonable and appropriate to prevent unauthorized access to—or use of—personally identifying information. Reasonable measures for your operation are based on the sensitivity of the information, the costs and benefits of different disposal methods, and changes in technology.

My company collects credit applications from customers. The form requires them to give us lots of financial information. Once we're finished with the applications, we're careful to throw them away.

Is that sufficient?

Answer:

No. Have a policy in place to ensure that sensitive paperwork is unreadable before you throw it away. Burn it, shred it, or pulverize it to make sure identity thieves can't steal it from your trash.

- Effectively dispose of paper records by shredding, burning, or pulverizing them before discarding. Make shredders available throughout the workplace, including next to the photocopier.
- When disposing of old computers and portable storage devices, use wipe utility programs. They're inexpensive and can provide better results by overwriting the entire hard drive so that the files are no longer recoverable.

- Deleting files using the keyboard or mouse commands usually isn't sufficient because the files may continue to exist on the computer's hard drive and could be retrieved easily.
- Make sure employees who work from home follow the same procedures for disposing of sensitive documents and old computers and portable storage devices.
- If you use consumer credit reports for a business purpose, you may be subject to the FTC's Disposal Rule. For more information, see Disposing of Consumer Report Information? New Rule Tells How at www.ftc.gov/privacy (click on Credit Reporting, Business Guidance).

5. Plan Ahead: Create a Plan for Responding to Security Incidents

Taking steps to protect data in your possession can go a long way toward preventing a security breach. Nevertheless, breaches can happen. Here's how you can reduce the impact on your business, your employees, and your customers:

- Have a plan in place to respond to security incidents. Designate a senior member of your staff to coordinate and implement the response plan.
- If a computer is compromised, disconnect it immediately from the Internet

I own a small business. Aren't these precautions going to cost me a mint to implement?

Answer:

No. There's no one-size-fits-all approach to data security, and what's right for you depends on the nature of your business and the kind of information you collect from your customers. Some of the most effective security measures—using strong passwords, locking up sensitive paperwork, training your staff, etc.—will cost you next to nothing and you'll find free or low-cost security tools at non-profit websites dedicated to data security. Furthermore, it's cheaper in the long run to invest in better data security than to lose the goodwill of your customers, defend yourself in legal actions, and face other possible consequences of a data breach.

- Investigate security incidents immediately and take steps to close off existing vulnerabilities or threats to personal information.
- Consider whom to notify in the event of an incident, both inside and outside your organization. You may need to notify consumers, law enforcement, customers, credit bureaus, and other businesses that may be affected by the breach. In addition, many states and the federal bank regulatory agencies have laws or guidelines addressing data breaches. Consult your attorney.

Additional Resources

These websites and publications have more information on securing sensitive data:

National Institute of Standards and Technology (NIST)'s Computer Security Resource Center
www.csrc.nist.gov

NIST's Risk Management Guide for Information Technology Systems
www.csrc.nist. gov/publications/nistpubs/800-30/sp800-30.pdf

Department of Homeland Security's National Strategy to Secure Cyberspace
www .dhs.gov/xlibrary/assets/ National_Cyberspace_Strategy.pdf

SANS (SysAdmin, Audit, Network, Security) Institute's Twenty Most Critical Internet Security Vulnerabilities
www.sans.org/top20

United States Computer Emergency Readiness Team (US-CERT)
www.us-cert.gov

Carnegie Mellon Software Engineering Institute's CERT Coordination Center
www. cert.org/other_sources

Center for Internet Security (CIS)
www.cisecurity.org

The Open Web Application Security Project
www.owasp.org

Institute for Security Technology Studies
www.ists.dartmouth.edu

OnGuard Online
www.OnGuardOnline.gov

In: Identity Theft Breaches
Editor: Cary S. Logweller

ISBN 978-1-60692-227-9

Chapter 5

DATA BREACHES ARE FREQUENT, BUT EVIDENCE OF RESULTING IDENTITY THEFT IS LIMITED; HOWEVER, THE FULL EXTENT IS UNKNOWN*

WHAT GAO FOUND

While comprehensive data do not exist, available evidence suggests that breaches of sensitive personal information have occurred frequently and under widely varying circumstances. For example, more than 570 data breaches were reported in the news media from January 2005 through December 2006, according to lists maintained by private groups that track reports of breaches. These incidents varied significantly in size and occurred across a wide range of entities, including federal, state, and local government agencies; retailers; financial institutions; colleges and universities; and medical facilities.

The extent to which data breaches have resulted in identity theft is not well known, largely because of the difficulty of determining the source of the data used to commit identity theft. However, available data and interviews with researchers, law enforcement officials, and industry representatives indicated that most breaches have not resulted in detected incidents of identity theft, particularly the unauthorized creation of new accounts. For example, in reviewing the 24 largest breaches reported in the media from January 2000 through June 2005, GAO found that 3 included evidence of resulting fraud on existing accounts and 1 included evidence of unauthorized creation of new accounts. For 18 of the breaches, no clear evidence had been uncovered linking them to identity theft; and for the remaining 2, there was not sufficient information to make a determination.

Requiring affected consumers to be notified of a data breach may encourage better security practices and help mitigate potential harm, but it also presents certain costs and challenges. Notification requirements can create incentives for entities to improve data security practices to minimize legal liability or avoid public relations risks that may result from a publicized breach. Also, consumers alerted to a breach can take measures to prevent or mitigate identity theft, such as monitoring their credit card statements and credit reports. At

*Excerpted from GAO Report GAO-07-737, dated June 2007.

the same time, breach notification requirements have associated costs, such as expenses to develop incident response plans and identify and notify affected individuals. Further, an expansive requirement could result in notification of breaches that present little or no risk, perhaps leading consumers to disregard notices altogether. Federal banking regulators and the President's Identity Theft Task Force have advocated a notification standard— the conditions requiring notification—that is risk based, allowing individuals to take appropriate measures where the risk of harm exists, while ensuring they are only notified in cases where the level of risk warrants such action. Should Congress choose to enact a federal notification requirement, use of such a risk-based standard could avoid undue burden on organizations and unnecessary and counterproductive notifications of breaches that present little risk.

WHY GAO DID THIS STUDY

In recent years, many entities in the private, public, and government sectors have reported the loss or theft of sensitive personal information. These breaches have raised concerns in part because they can result in identity theft— either account fraud (such as misuse of credit card numbers) or unauthorized creation of new accounts (such as opening a credit card in someone else's name). Many states have enacted laws requiring entities that experience breaches to notify affected individuals, and Congress is considering legislation that would establish a national breach notification requirement.

GAO was asked to examine (1) the incidence and circumstances of breaches of sensitive personal information; (2) the extent to which such breaches have resulted in identity theft; and (3) the potential benefits, costs, and challenges associated with breach notification requirements. To address these objectives, GAO reviewed available reports on data breaches, analyzed 24 large data breaches, and gathered information from federal and state government agencies, researchers, consumer advocates, and others.

ABBREVIATIONS

DHS	Department of Homeland Security
FBI	Federal Bureau of Investigation
FDIC	Federal Deposit Insurance Corporation
FTC	Federal Trade Commission
SSN	Social Security number
USPIS	United States Postal Inspection Service
VA	Department of Veterans Affairs

June 4, 2007
The Honorable Spencer Bachus Ranking Member
Committee on Financial Services House of Representatives
The Honorable Michael N. Castle House of Representatives
The Honorable Darlene Hooley House of Representatives

The Honorable Steven C. LaTourette House of Representatives
The Honorable Dennis Moore House of Representatives

As a result of advances in computer technology and electronic storage, many different sectors and entities now maintain electronic records containing vast amounts of personal information on virtually all American consumers. In recent years, a number of entities—including financial service firms, retailers, universities, and government agencies have collectively reported the loss or theft of large amounts of sensitive personal information. Some of these data breaches such as those involving TJX Companies and the Department of Veterans Affairs (VA) have received considerable publicity and have highlighted concerns about the protections afforded sensitive personal information.[1] Policymakers, consumer advocates, and others have raised concerns that data breaches can contribute to identity theft, in which an individual's sensitive personal information is used fraudulently. The Federal Trade Commission (FTC), which is responsible for taking complaints from victims and sharing them with law enforcement agencies, has noted that identity theft is a serious problem—millions of Americans are affected each year, and victims may face substantial costs and time to repair the damage to their good name and credit record.

Although there is no commonly agreed-upon definition, the term "data breach" generally refers to an organization's unauthorized or unintentional exposure, disclosure, or loss of sensitive personal information, which can include personally identifiable information such as Social Security numbers (SSN) or financial information such as credit card numbers.[2]Data breaches can take many forms and do not necessarily lead to identity theft. The term "identity theft" is broad and encompasses many types of criminal activities, including fraud on existing accounts such as unauthorized use of a stolen credit card number or fraudulent creation of new accounts such as using stolen data to open a credit card account in someone else's name. Depending on the type of information compromised and how it is misused, identity theft victims can face a range of potential harm, from the inconvenience of having a credit card reissued to substantial financial losses and damaged credit ratings.

Beginning with California in 2002, at least 36 states have enacted breach notification laws that is, laws that require certain entities that experience a data breach to notify individuals whose personal information was lost or stolen. There is no federal statute that requires most companies or other entities to notify affected individuals of data breaches, although federal banking regulatory agencies have issued guidance on breach notification to the banks, thrifts, and credit unions they supervise.[3]In addition, the Office of Management and Budget has issued guidance—developed by the President's Identity Theft Task Force—on responding to data breaches at federal agencies.[4]Because a number of bills have been introduced in Congress that would establish a national breach notification requirement, you asked us to review the costs and benefits of such a requirement and the link between data breaches and identity theft.[5] As agreed with your offices, this report examines (1) what is known about the incidence and circumstances of breaches of sensitive personal information; (2) what information exists on the extent to which breaches of sensitive personal information have resulted in identity theft; and (3) the potential benefits, costs, and challenges associated with breach notification requirements.

This report focuses on breaches of sensitive personal data that can be used to commit identity theft, and not on breaches of other sensitive data, such as medical records or proprietary business information. To address the first two objectives, we obtained and analyzed information on data breaches that have been reported in the media and aggregated by three private research and advocacy organizations, as well as information on breaches collected by state agencies in New York and North Carolina, federal banking regulators, and federal law enforcement agencies.[6]We also collected information on breaches experienced by federal agencies compiled by the House Government Reform Committee in 2006 and by the Department of Homeland Security (DHS).[7]In addition, we conducted a literature search of relevant articles, reports, and studies. We also conducted interviews with, and obtained documents from, representatives of federal agencies, including the FTC, the Department of Justice, DHS, and the federal banking regulatory agencies; selected state government agencies and the National Association of Attorneys General; private and nonprofit research organizations; and consumer protection and privacy advocacy groups. Further, we obtained information from industry and trade associations representing key sectors—including financial services, retail sales, higher education, health care, and information services—that have experienced data breaches. In addition, for the second objective, we examined the 24 largest (in terms of number of records breached) data breaches reported by the news media from January 2000 through June 2005 and tracked by private groups. For each of these breaches, we reviewed media reports and other publicly available information, and conducted interviews, where possible, with representatives of the entities that experienced the breaches, in an attempt to identify any known instances of identity theft that resulted from the breaches. We also examined five breaches that involved federal agencies, which were selected because they represented a variety of different circumstances. For the third objective, we reviewed the federal banking regulatory agencies' proposed and final guidance related to breach notification, and interviewed representatives of each agency regarding their consideration of potential costs, benefits, and challenges during development of the guidance. Further, we reviewed the strategic plan and other documents issued by the President's Identity Theft Task Force. In addition, we conducted a review of the effects of California's breach notification law, which included interviewing and gathering information from California state officials and selected California companies, educational institutions, and other entities subject to the law's notification requirements.

We conducted our review from August 2006 through April 2007 in accordance with generally accepted government auditing standards. A more extensive discussion of our scope and methodology appears in appendix I

Results in Brief

While comprehensive data do not exist, available evidence suggests that breaches of sensitive personal information have occurred frequently and under widely varying circumstances. For example, more than 570 data breaches have been reported in the news media from January 2005 through December 2006, according to our analysis of lists maintained by three private organizations that track such breaches. Further, a House Government Reform Committee survey of federal agencies identified more than 788 data breaches at 17 agencies from January 2003 through July 2006. Of the roughly 17,000 federally supervised banks, thrifts, and credit unions, several hundred have reported data breaches to their federal regulators over the past 2 years. In addition, officials in New York

State— which requires public and private entities to report data breaches to a centralized source—reported receiving notice of 225 breaches from December 7, 2005, through October 5, 2006. Data breaches have occurred across a wide range of entities, including federal, state, and local government agencies; retailers; financial institutions; colleges and universities; and medical facilities. Some studies indicate that most publicly reported breaches resulted from intentional actions, such as a stolen laptop computer, rather than accidental occurrences, such as a lost laptop computer, but this may be because breaches related to criminal activity are perhaps more likely to be reported. Media-reported breaches have varied significantly in size, ranging from 10 records to tens of millions of records. Most of these breaches have compromised data that included personally identifiable information, while others have involved only account information such as credit card numbers.

The extent to which data breaches result in identity theft is not well known, in large part because it can be difficult to determine the source of the data used to commit identity theft. Although we identified several cases where breaches reportedly have resulted in identity theft—that is, account fraud or unauthorized creation of new accounts—available data and interviews with researchers, law enforcement officials, and industry representatives indicated that most breaches have not resulted in detected incidents of identity theft. For example, our review of the 24 largestbreaches that appeared in the news media from January 2000 through June 2005 found that 3 breaches appeared to have resulted in fraud on existing accounts, and 1 breach appeared to have resulted in the unauthorized creation of new accounts. For 18 of the breaches, no clear evidence had been uncovered linking them to identity theft; and for the remaining 2, we did not have sufficient information to make a determination. Determining the link between data breaches and identity theft is challenging, primarily because identity theft victims often do not know how their personal information was obtained, and it may be up to a year or more before stolen data are used to commit a crime. Some studies by private researchers have found little linkage between data breaches and identity theft, although our review found these studies had methodological limitations. Finally, the circumstances of a breach can greatly affect the potential harm that can result. For example, unauthorized creation of new accounts generally can occur only when a breach includes personally identifiable information. Further, breaches that are the result of intentional acts generally are considered to pose more risk than accidental breaches, according to federal officials.

Requiring consumer notification of data breaches may encourage better data security practices and help deter or mitigate harm from identity theft, but it also involves monetary costs and challenges such as determining an appropriate notification standard. Representatives of federal banking regulators, other government agencies, industry associations, and other affected parties told us that breach notification requirements have encouraged companies and other entities to improve their data security practices to minimize legal liability or avoid public relations risks that may result from a publicized breach of customer data. Further, notifying affected consumers of a breach gives them the opportunity to mitigate potential risk—for example, by reviewing their credit card statements and credit reports, or placing a fraud alert on their credit files. Some privacy advocates and others have noted that even when the risk of actual financial harm is low, breach notification is still important because individuals have a basic right to know how their personal information is being handled and when it has been compromised. At the same time, affected entities incur monetary costs to comply with notification requirements. For example, 31 companies that responded to a 2006 survey said they incurred an average of $1.4 million per breach, for costs such as mailing notification letters, call center expenses, courtesy discounts or services, and legal fees. In addition, organizations subject to notification requirements told us they face several challenges, including the lack of clarity in some state statutes about when a notification is required, difficulty identifying and locating affected individuals, and difficulty complying with varying state requirements. Notification standards—that is, the circumstances surrounding a data breach that "trigger" the required notification—vary among the states. Some parties, such as the National Association of Attorneys General, have advocated that a breach notification requirement should apply broadly in order to give consumers a greater level of protection and because the risk of harm is not always known. The guidance provided by federal banking regulators lays out a more risk-based approach, aimed at ensuring that affected individuals receive notices only when they are at risk of identity theft or other related harm. Such an approach was also adopted by the President's Identity Theft Task Force, which recommended a risk-based standard for breach notification applicable to both government agencies and private entities. As we have noted in the past, care is needed in defining appropriate criteria for incidents that merit notification. Should Congress choose to enact a federal breach notification requirement, use of such a risk-based standard could avoid undue burden on organizations and unnecessary and counterproductive notifications of breaches that present little risk.

This report contains no recommendations. We provided a draft of this report to FTC and provided selected portions of the draft to federal banking regulatory agencies and relevant federal law enforcement agencies. These agencies provided technical comments, which we have incorporated in this report as appropriate.

Background

Breaches of sensitive personal data in recent years at companies, universities, government agencies, and other organizations have heightened public awareness about data security and the risks of identity theft, and have led to the introduction of breach notification requirements in many state legislatures. As of April 2007, at least 36 states had enacted some form of law requiring that affected individuals be notified in the event of a data breach; California's law, enacted in 2002, was the first such state requirement.[8] States' notification requirements vary, particularly with regard to the applicable notification standard—the event or circumstance that triggers a required notification. Requirements also vary in terms of the data to which they apply—for example, some apply to paper documents as well as electronic records.

There is currently no federal statute that requires most companies and other entities that experience a data breach to notify individuals whose personal information was lost or stolen. However, the Gramm-Leach-Bliley Act established requirements for federally supervised financial institutions to safeguard customer information.[9] To clarify these requirements, the federal banking regulators issued interagency guidance in 2005 to the banks, thrifts, and credit unions they supervise related to their handling of data breaches. Under this guidance, these institutions are expected to develop and implement a response program to address unauthorized access to customer information maintained by the institution or its service providers; and if they experience a breach, they are to notify their primary federal regulator as soon as possible and—depending on the circumstances of the incident—notify their affected customers. In addition, in September 2006 the President's Identity Theft Task Force developed guidance for federal agencies on responding to breaches involving agency data, including the factors to consider in determining whether to notify affected individuals. The task force released a strategic plan for combating identity theft in April 2007, which contained among its recommendations a proposal for establishing a national breach notification requirement.[10] Further, in December 2006, the Department of Veterans Affairs Information Security Enhancement Act of 2006 became law, which, among other things, requires VA to prescribe regulations providing for the notification of data breaches occurring at the department.[11] A number of bills have been introduced in Congress that would more broadly require companies and other entities to notify individuals when such breaches occur, and Congress has held several hearings related to data breaches.[12]

Identity theft occurs when individuals' identifying information is used without authorization in an attempt to commit fraud or other crimes.[13] There are two primary forms of identity theft. First, identity thieves can use financial account identifiers, such as credit card or bank account numbers, to take over an individual's existing accounts to make unauthorized charges or withdraw money. Second, thieves can use identifying data, which can include such things as SSNs and driver's license numbers, to open new financial accounts and incur charges and credit in an individual's name, without that person's knowledge. This second form of identity theft is potentially the most damaging because, among other things, it can take some time before a victim becomes aware of the problem, and it can cause substantial harm to the victim's credit rating. While some identity theft victims can resolve their problems quickly, others face substantial costs and inconvenience repairing damage to their credit records. According to FTC, millions of Americans have their identities stolen each year. Roughly 85 percent of these cases involve the misuse of existing accounts and 35 percent involve new account creation or other fraud. (Twenty percent of the total involve both.) Identity thieves obtain sensitive personal information using a variety of methods. One potential source is a breach at an organization that maintains large amounts of sensitive personal information. However, identity theft can also occur as a result of the loss or theft of data maintained by an individual, such as a lost or stolen wallet or a thief digging through household trash.

The Identity Theft and Assumption Deterrence Act of 1998 made identity theft a federal crime and charged FTC with taking complaints from identity theft victims; sharing these complaints with federal, state, and local law enforcement agencies; and providing the victims with informational materials to assist them[14]. Because identity theft is typically not a stand-alone crime but rather a component of one or more crimes such as bank fraud, credit card fraud, and mail fraud, a number of federal law enforcement agencies can have a role in investigating identity theft crimes, including the Federal Bureau of Investigation (FBI), U.S. Postal Inspection Service (USPIS), U.S. Secret Service (Secret Service), the Office of the Inspector General of the Social Security Administration, and Immigration and Customs Enforcement.

Available Evidence Indicates That Data Breaches Occur Frequently and under Varying Circumstances

Available evidence from media reports, federal and state agencies, and private institutions, collectively, suggests that data breaches occur with some frequency. For example, our analysis of the lists of data breaches compiled by three private research and advocacy organizations shows more than 570 breaches reported by the news media from January 2005 through December 2006. Data breaches have occurred across a range of entities, including federal, state, and local government agencies; retailers; financial institutions; colleges and universities; and medical facilities. Breaches have varied in size and have resulted from both criminal actions and accidental incidents. Most of the breaches reported in the news media have involved data that included personal identifiers such as SSNs, while others have involved only account information such as credit card numbers.

Several Sources Indicate That Breaches of Sensitive Personal Information Are Frequent

No federal agency or other organization tracks all data breaches, and definitions of what constitutes a data breach may vary. Although there are no comprehensive data on the extent of data breaches nationwide, government officials, trade association representatives, researchers, and consumer and privacy advocates we interviewed agreed that breaches of sensitive personal information occur frequently. For example, representatives of a variety of organizations—including the Department of Justice, California's Office of Privacy Protection, the Consumer Data

Industry Association (a trade group representing many information resellers), and the Ponemon Institute (a private research organization)—characterized data breaches in the United States as being "prevalent" or "common." Although we did not identify comprehensive data on the extent of data breaches, available information from several sources does corroborate the anecdotal evidence that such breaches occur frequently.[15]

Media Reports

Over the past few years, several hundred data breaches have been reported each year by newspapers and other news media. Three private organizations that focus on information privacy and security issues.

Privacy Rights Clearinghouse, Identity Theft Resource Center, and Attrition—track data breaches reported in newspapers, magazines, and other publicly available sources of news and information.[16] Our analysis of the three lists of data breaches maintained by these organizations indicated that at least 572 breaches were reported in the news media from January 2005 through December 2006.[17] These breaches were reported to have affected more than 80 million records.18 However, for several reasons, these lists likely understate the true extent of data breaches in the United States. First, organizations might not voluntarily disclose data breaches that they experience. Second, some breaches that organizations do disclose may not appear in the news media, particularly if the breach was limited in scope. Finally, the three organizations compiling these lists may not have identified all of the breaches reported in the news media—for example, many breaches did not appear on all three lists, suggesting that none represents an exhaustive list of all breaches that have appeared in the news

Federal Law Enforcement Agencies

Officials at federal law enforcement agencies told us that each year they conduct a significant number of criminal investigations that involve alleged breaches of sensitive personal information. For example, officials of the FBI's Cyber Division told us that presently it has more than 1,300 pending cases of computer or network intrusions where data breaches resulted from unauthorized electronic access to computer systems, such as hackings, at public and private organizations.[19] Officials at the Secret Service, which investigates certain cases where financial information has been lost or stolen, told us that in 2006, the service opened 327 cases involving network intrusions or other breaches at retailers, banks, credit card processors, telephone companies, educational institutions, and other organizations. Officials noted that they have seen a steady increase in the number of data breaches since 1986, when they began tracking computer fraud violations. Investigators at USPIS, the division of the U.S. Postal Service that investigates mail fraud, external mail theft, fraudulent changes of addresses, and other postal-related crimes, told us that the agency does not specifically track the number of data breaches in the private sector. However, despite limited data, investigators said their impression is that such data breaches likely occur frequently.

To obtain information on the prevalence of data breaches at federal agencies, in July 2006 the House Government Reform Committee asked federal agencies to provide details about incidents involving the loss or compromise of any sensitive personal information held by an agency or contractor from January 1, 2003, through July 10, 2006. Our analysis of the committee's report found that 17 agencies reported that they experienced at least one breach and, collectively, the agencies reported to the committee more than 788 separate incidents.[20]

The Federal Information Security Management Act of 2002 requires all federal agencies to report computer security incidents to a federal incident response center.[21] The U.S. Computer Emergency Readiness Team—a component of DHS that monitors computer security incidents at federal agencies—serves as this response center. As such, data breaches at federal agencies involving certain sensitive information must be reported to the team within 1 hour of discovery of the incident.[22] DHS staff told us that they receive information about breaches at federal agencies on a daily basis. In fiscal year 2006, the center tracked 477 incidents at 59 federal agencies or at federal contractors with access to government-owned data, according to information available as of January 29, 2007. In addition, a March 2007 audit investigation found that at least 490 laptop computers owned by the Internal Revenue Service and containing taxpayer information had been lost or stolen since 2003.[23]

Federal Banking Regulators

The 2005 guidance issued by the five federal banking regulators provided that a depository institution should notify its primary federal regulator when it becomes aware of an incident involving unauthorized access to or use of sensitive customer information.[24] The guidance applies to breaches that have occurred at the financial institutions themselves, as well as third- party entities such as data processors that act as service providers and maintain customer information.[25] The five regulators differ in their methods and criteria for tracking breaches, but collectively they have tracked several hundred breaches over the past few years at roughly 17,000 institutions they supervise and at third-party entities.[26] For example, the Federal Deposit Insurance Corporation (FDIC)—the primary federal supervisor for more than 5,000 state-chartered banks that are not members of the Federal Reserve System—received reports of 194 breaches at its regulated institutions from May 2005 through December 2006, as well as reports of 14 breaches at third-party companies that also affected these institutions' customers. Similarly, officials at the Office of Thrift Supervision—which supervises more than 860 savings associations—told us that from April 2005 through December 2006, 56 of its institutions reported breaches at the institution itself and approximately 72 reported breaches at third-party entities that maintained their customer information.

State Agencies

Some states require entities experiencing data breaches to report them to designated state agencies.[27] For example, the New York State Information Security Breach and Notification Act requires entities that experience security breaches to notify the state Attorney General's Office, Consumer Protection Board, and the state Office of Cyber Security and Critical Infrastructure Coordination in cases when New York residents must be notified.[28] Such data breaches include the unauthorized acquisition of computerized data that compromises the security, confidentiality, or integrity of unencrypted private information. Officials of the Office of New York State Attorney General told us that from December 7, 2005, through October 5, 2006, their office received notice of 225 breaches. Similarly, a North Carolina law requires that breaches of personal information (maintained in computerized, paper, or other media) affecting at least 1,000 persons be reported to the Consumer Protection Division of the state Office of the Attorney General.[29] An official in that office told us that from December 2005 through December 2006, it had received reports of 91 breach incidents.

Other Sources

Information that we obtained from several other sources suggests that breaches of sensitive personal information occur with some frequency across a variety of sectors. For example,

- EDUCAUSE, a nonprofit association that addresses technology issues in higher education, conducted a survey in 2005 on data security at higher education institutions in the United States and Canada. Twenty- six percent of the 490 institutions that responded said they had experienced a security incident in the past year that resulted in the compromise of confidential information.[30]

- The American Hospital Association collected information, at our request, in October 2006 from a nonrepresentative group of 46 large hospitals on breaches of sensitive personal information (excluding medical records) that they had experienced since January 2003. Collectively, 13 of the 46 hospitals reported a total of 17 data breach incidents.[31]
- The Ponemon Institute, a private company that researches privacy and security practices, conducted a survey of 51,433 U.S. adults and received responses from 9,154 (a response rate of about 18 percent). About 12 percent of the survey respondents said they recalled receiving notification of a data security breach involving their personal information.[32]
- The CMO Council, an organization serving marketing executives, reported that 16 percent of consumers who responded to a Web-based panel reported that a company had lost or compromised their personal, financial, or medical information. An additional 32 percent of respondents said they were not sure.[33]
- Several other studies, while not focusing specifically on breaches of sensitive personal information, have found more generally that information security vulnerabilities are widespread among U.S. and global companies.[34]

Information from multiple sources indicates that data breaches at companies, government agencies, retailers, and other entities have occurred frequently in recent years, involving millions of records of sensitive personal information. We have reported in the past that no federal law explicitly requires most companies and other entities to safeguard all of the sensitive personal information they may hold. We also have suggested that to ensure that sensitive personal information is protected on a more consistent basis, Congress should consider expanding requirements to safeguard such information.[35] The frequency of data breaches identified in this report underscores the need for entities in the public and private sectors to improve the security of sensitive personal information and further corroborates that additional federal action may be needed in this area.

Source, Cause, Size, and Content of Breaches Have Varied Widely

Type of Entity

According to government officials, researchers, and media reports, data breaches have occurred among a wide variety of entities and as a result of both intentional actions and accidental losses. These breaches also have varied in size and in the types of data compromised. Data breaches have been reported at a wide range of public and private institutions, including federal, state, and local government agencies; publicand private colleges and universities; hospitals and other medical facilities; retailers; banks and other financial institutions; information resellers; and others. For example, in the weeks leading up to the highly publicized 2005 CardSystems breach, the media also had reported breaches at, among other entities, a large hospital, a university, a global financial institution, a federal regulatory agency, and a major technology company.

According to Attrition, of the breaches it tracked as reported in the news media in 2005 and 2006, 33 percent of the breaches occurred at educational institutions, 32 percent at financial services institutions, 25 percent at government agencies, and 10 percent at medical facilities, although breaches reported in the news media may not be representative of all breaches.[36] Similarly, the data security firm ID Analytics examined 70 data breaches that were reported by the news media from February through September 2005. According to company officials, 46 percent of these breaches occurred at educational institutions, 16 percent at financial institutions, 14 percent at retailers, 11 percent at government agencies, 7 percent at medical facilities, and 6 percent at information resellers.[37]

Another way to analyze where data breaches have occurred is to look at the number of records breached (as opposed to the number of breaches themselves). Our analysis of the list maintained by Attrition found that 54 percent of breached records involved financial institutions, 34 percent involved government agencies, 4 percent involved educational institutions, and 3 percent involved medical facilities. ID Analytics' report found that 57 percent of breached records involved financial institutions, 22 percent involved retailers, 13 percent involved educational institutions, 4 percent involved information resellers, 2 percent involved government agencies, and 2 percent involved medical facilities.

Cause of Breach

According to government officials, researchers, and media reports, data breaches of sensitive personal information have occurred as a result of both intentional actions as well as negligence or accidental losses. In some cases, individuals intentionally steal information for the purpose of committing fraud or identity theft. Breaches involving intentional actions have included:

- Hacking, or accessing computer systems without authorization. For example, in 2007 the retailer TJX Companies reported unauthorized intrusions into its computer systems that may have breached millions of customers' credit card and driver's license information.
- Employee theft. For example, in 2006, a former employee of the American Red Cross pled guilty to stealing personally identifiable information from a blood donor database.
- Theft of physical equipment. In 2005, for instance, a laptop containing the names and SSNs of more than 98,000 students, alumni, and others was stolen from the University of California at Berkeley.
- Deception or misrepresentation to obtain unauthorized data. In 2005, the information reseller ChoicePoint acknowledged that the personal records it held on approximately 162,000 consumers had been compromised by individuals who posed as legitimate subscribers to the company's information services.

Breaches involving negligence or accidental losses of data have included the following:

- Loss of laptop computers or other hardware. For example, in 2006, the Department of Labor reported that an employee lost a laptop containing personal information on 1,137 individuals.
- Loss of data tapes. For example, in 2004, Bank of America lost backup tapes containing personal information of 1.2 million government charge card holders while the tapes were being transported to a data center.
- Unintentional exposure on the Internet. In 2006, according to media reports, the U.S. Department of Education left unprotected on a Web site the personally identifiable information, including SSNs, of up to 21,000 recipients of federal student loans.
- Improper disposal of data, such as leaving sensitive personal data on unshredded documents in a publicly accessible dumpster.

We did not identify comprehensive data that reliably provide overall statistics on the causes of known data breaches. However, our review of the 24 largest data breaches reported in the news media (discussed in more detail later in this report) found that 12 breaches apparently involved intentional acts by hackers or employees illegally accessing or using data, 5 involved stolen laptops or other computer equipment, 4 involved lost computer backup tapes, 2 involved the use of deception to gain access to data, and 1 involved the possible unauthorized disclosure of data. In addition, some studies indicate that most breaches reported in the news media resulted from intentional acts rather than accidental occurrences such as a lost laptop computer. For example, in its study of 70 breaches, ID Analytics determined that 48 involved thefts committed with the apparent intention of accessing sensitive data. Eleven of the breaches involved thefts where sensitive consumer information was apparently stolen inadvertently as part of another crime (such as the theft of a laptop computer for its resale value), and another 11 breaches involved accidental loss (such as misplacement of a laptop computer). However, these data may overrepresent the proportion of all breaches that involve criminal activity, as such breaches are probably more likely than accidental losses to be reported to authorities and by the news media.

Number of Records Breached

Our analysis of the list maintained by Attrition of breaches reported by the news media found the median number of records breached to be 8,650. However, these data breaches varied considerably in size—ranging, for example, from a breach involving 10 records at a law firm to a breach involving as many as tens of millions of records at a credit card processing company. The breaches involving federal agencies that were reported to the House Government Reform Committee also varied in size—for example, several affected fewer than five records, while a breach at VA affected 26.5 million records.

Types of Data Breached

Our analysis of the list maintained by Attrition of breaches reported by the news media found the median number of records breached to be 8,650. However, these data breaches varied considerably in size—ranging, for example, from a breach involving 10 records at a law firm to a breach involving as many as tens of millions of records at a credit card processing company. The breaches involving federal agencies that were reported to the House Government Reform Committee also varied in size—for example, several affected fewer than five records, while a breach at VA affected 26.5 million records.

Comprehensive information does not exist on the types of data involved in all known data breaches. Among the list maintained by Attrition of breaches reported by the news media in 2005 and 2006—which may not be representative of all breaches—more than half involved SSNs and 11 percent involved credit card numbers (and 3 percent of the total involved both). In the remaining breaches, other types of account or personal information were involved, or the type of data breached was not reported. Logically, there may be an association between the type of data compromised and the type of entity experiencing the breach. For example, several educational institutions have experienced breaches of SSNs, which they may maintain as student identifiers, and several retail stores have experienced breaches of credit card numbers, which they often maintain on their customers.

Consequences of Data Breaches Are Not Fully Known, but Clear Evidence of Identity Theft Has Been Found in Relatively Few Breaches

Comprehensive information on the outcomes of data breaches is not available. Several cases have been identified in which a data breach appears to have resulted in identity theft, but available data and information from law enforcement and industry association representatives indicated that most breaches have not resulted in detected incidents of identity theft. For example, of 24 very large breaches we reviewed, 3 appeared to have resulted in fraud on existing accounts and 1 in the unauthorized creation of new accounts. Determining the link between data breaches and identity theft is challenging because, among other things, identity theft victims often do not know how their personal information was obtained. However, the circumstances of a breach, including the type of information compromised and how the breach occurred, can greatly affect the potential risk of identity theft.

Federal Law Enforcement Agencies and Industry Associations Identified Limited Instances of Breaches Leading to Identity Theft

In general, representatives of law enforcement agencies, industry and trade associations, and consumer and privacy advocacy organizations told us that no comprehensive data are available on the consequences of data breaches. Several cases have been identified where there is evidence that a data breach resulted in identity theft, including account fraud or unauthorized creation of new accounts. At the same time, available data and information from the officials we contacted indicated that most breaches have not resulted in detected incidents of identity theft.

We asked representatives of the FBI, Secret Service, USPIS, and Immigration and Customs Enforcement—a component of DHS that has investigated cases where stolen identities were used to secure jobs—the extent to which data breaches they investigated resulted in some form of identity theft. Representatives of all of these agencies told us that their investigations of data breaches do not typically allow them to fully ascertain how stolen data are used. Similarly, they noted that investigations of identity theft do not always reveal the source of the data used to commit the crime.

However, the representatives were able to provide us with a limited number of examples in which data breaches they investigated had allegedly resulted in some form of identity theft. For example, in a 2006 investigation by USPIS, an employee of a credit card call center allegedly compromised at least 35 customers' accounts and used some of the information to purchase approximately $65,000 in gift cards. The representatives of federal law enforcement agencies noted that cases in which data breaches have been linked to identity theft often have involved instances of unauthorized access by employees. For example, an official at Immigration and Customs Enforcement stated that her agency, in cooperation with other agencies, has investigated cases in which government employees allegedly had improperly accessed and sold sensitive personal information that was then used by illegal immigrants to secure employment.

In addition, in 2005 FTC settled charges with BJ's Wholesale Club in which alleged security breaches resulted in several million dollars in fraudulent purchases using customers' credit and debit card data.[38] As discussed later in this report, FTC has also taken enforcement actions related to data breaches at several other companies, including ChoicePoint, CardSystems, and DSW, in which it uncovered evidence that the breaches resulted in identity theft.

Many of the law enforcement officials said that, based on their experience, data breaches that result in harm have usually involved fraud on existing accounts (such as credit card fraud) rather than the unauthorized creation of new accounts. Secret Service representatives noted that using illicit credit and debit card numbers and bank account information is much easier and less labor intensive than using personally identifiable information to fraudulently open new accounts. Officials at Secret Service, FBI, and USPIS all said that identity theft involving the creation of new accounts often results not from data breaches, but from other sources, such as retrieving personal information by sifting through a family's household trash.

In examining a selection of five breaches that occurred from 2003 through 2005 that were reported as having involved five federal agencies— Department of Justice, FDIC, Internal Revenue Service, National Park Service, and the Navy—we found that the circumstances behind these breaches varied widely. At least two of the breaches occurred at vendors or contractors that held sensitive data on agency employees, rather than at the agency itself. In addition, we found that a breach reported in the news media as having involved the National Park Service actually involved a not-for-profit organization that manages eParks, according to a representative of that organization. Four of the five breaches reported as having involved federal agencies were not believed to have resulted in identity theft, according to officials of the entities involved. The breach atFDIC resulted in an estimated 27 cases of identity theft when data inappropriately accessed by a former FDIC intern were used to take out more than $425,000 in fraudulent loans in the names of FDIC employees, according to agency officials.[39]

Industry and trade associations representing entities that maintain large amounts of information—banks, retailers, colleges, information resellers, and hospitals—told us that they had limited knowledge about the harm caused by data breaches that occur in their industries. However, in some cases, they provided information or anecdotal evidence on the extent to which such breaches may have led to some form of identity theft. For example, the 46 hospitals that the American Hospital Association surveyed at our request reported that of 17 breaches that had occurred since 2003, three had resulted in fraudulent activity on existing accounts and another three resulted in other forms of identity theft, including one case where the information was used to file false income tax refunds. The identity theft in these cases involved small numbers of victims—usually just one.

Representatives of the American Council on Education and two other higher education associations stated that while data breaches at colleges and universities were not uncommon, they were aware of little to no identity theft that had resulted from such breaches. Representatives of the American Bankers Association, the National Retail Federation, and the Consumer Data Industry Association told us they were unable to determine how prevalent data breaches are among their institutions or how often such breaches lead to consumer harm. Representatives at the National Retail Federation noted that breaches at retailers may be more likely to result in fraud on existing accounts than in new account creation, since most retailers do not maintain the personally identifiable information needed to steal someone's identity.

Of 24 Large Publicly Reported Breaches, Four Apparently Resulted in Known Cases of Identity Theft

Using lists of data breaches compiled by the Identity Theft Resource Center, Privacy Rights Clearinghouse, and Congressional Research Service, we identified the 24 largest breaches (measured by number of records) that were reported in the news media from January 2000 through June 2005.[40] To gather information on these incidents, we interviewed or collected written responses from representatives of the entity experiencing the breach and reviewed publicly available information, such as media reports, news releases, testimonies, and court documents. In some cases, when feasible, we also spoke with law enforcement investigators. We identified those cases where this information collectively indicated that the breach appeared to have resulted in some form of identity theft. Ultimately, the determination of whether particular conduct violated a law prohibiting identity theft would be a matter of law for the courts.

Although these lists characterized each of these 24 incidents as data breaches, the circumstances of the incidents varied. While 19 of the incidents clearly met our definition of data breach (i.e. unauthorized or unintentional exposure, disclosure, or loss of sensitive personal information), four cases involved hackers who may or may not have actually accessed sensitive information. In one other incident, a university employee with access to sensitive personal data was indicted on unrelated fraud charges. A university official told us he did not believe this incident should necessarily be characterized as a data breach since there was no evidence the employee actually misused university data.

The available evidence that we reviewed indicated that 18 of these 24 breaches were not known to have resulted in any identity theft. As shown in table 1, three breaches were believed to have resulted in account fraud and one resulted in the unauthorized creation of new accounts. In two other cases, we were not able to gather sufficient information on whether harm appeared to have resulted from the breach. Further, because of the challenges in linking data breaches with identity theft, in some cases our review may not have uncovered instances of harm potentially resulting from these breaches. In some instances, investigators or company representatives reported that they were able to determine with a high degree of certainty—through forensic investigation or other means—that unauthorized parties had not accessed the data. In other instances, these representatives said that they were not aware of any account fraud that resulted, but they acknowledged that there was no way to know for sure. Moreover, determining potential harm may be particularly challenging with very large breaches because the volume of records involved can make it difficult to link individual victims to the breach.

Table 1. Twenty-Four Large Publicly Reported Data Breaches and Evidence of Resulting Identity Theft, January 2000–June 2005

The fact that we did not identify evidence of identity theft from a breach does not necessarily mean that no such harm has occurred or will occur in the future.

Year[a]	Type of organization	Nature of breach	Available evidence of identity theft?b
2000	Retail	Hacking	Account fraud
2000	Retail	Hacking	None identified
2002	Healthcare	Stolen computer equipment	None identified
2003	Higher education	Stolen computer equipment	None identified
2004	Financial services	Stolen computer equipment	None identified
2004	Higher education	Hacking	None identified
2004	Higher education	Hacking	None identified
2004	Higher education	Hacking	None identified
2004	Financial services	Lost data tapes	None identified
2005	Financial services	Hacking	Account fraud
2005	State government	Hacking	None identified
2005	Information services	Deception/Misrepresentation	Unauthorized new accounts
2005	Higher education	Hacking	None identified
2005	Higher education	Stolen computer equipment	None identified
2005	Retail	Hacking	Account fraud
2005	Information services	Deception/Misrepresentation	Unknown
2005	Healthcare	Stolen computer equipment	None identified
2005	Retail	Hacking	Unknown
2005	Financial services	Lost data tapes	None identified
2005	Financial services	Employee crime	None identified
2005	State government	Hacking	None identified
2005	Media	Lost data tapes	None identified
2005	Financial services	Lost data tapes	None identified

Table 1. (Continued)

The fact that we did not identify evidence of identity theft from a breach does not necessarily mean that no such harm has occurred or will occur in the future.			
Year[a]	Type of organization	Nature of breach	Available evidence of identity theft?[b]
2005	Higher education	Other[c]	None identified

Source: GAO.

Note: To identify the 24 largest data breaches reported in the news media from January 2000 through June 2005, GAO analyzed lists of such breaches maintained by Identity Theft Resource Center, Privacy Rights Clearinghouse, and Congressional Research Service. [a]Year breach occurred or was publicized. [b]The presence or lack of evidence of identity theft resulting from a breach was based on our review of news reports and other publicly available information, as well as interviews, as feasible, with representatives of entities experiencing the breach and law enforcement officials investigating the breach. The fact that we were unable to identify evidence at this time of identity theft resulting from a breach does not mean that no such harm has occurred or that none will occur in the future. Further, factual determinations of the existence and cause of identity theft in any particular case are matters for the courts to decide. In this case, a former university employee with access to sensitive personal information had been indicted on bank fraud charges unrelated to the university. Some press reports characterized this as a breach, but according to a representative of the university, there is no evidence that the employee misused university data.

The one large breach we identified that apparently resulted in the unauthorized creation of new accounts involved ChoicePoint, an information reseller. In 2005, the company acknowledged that the personal records it held on approximately 162,000 consumers had been compromised by individuals who posed as legitimate subscribers to the company's information services. FTC reached a civil settlement in 2006 with the company that established a fund for consumer redress to reimburse potential victims of identity theft, and the agency has worked with law enforcement officials to identify such victims.[41] The three large breaches we identified that appeared to result in fraud on existing accounts included the following:

- CardSystems, a credit card payment processor, reported a May 2005 breach in which a hacker accessed data such as names, card account numbers, and expiration dates. The total number of compromised accounts is unclear. FTC staff alleged in a 2006 civil complaint that the breach had compromised data associated with tens of millions of credit and debit cards, but a CardSystems official stated in congressional testimony that only 239,000 accounts were compromised. Officials of the Office of the Comptroller of the Currency—who surveyed the national banks they supervise in order to determine the amount of fraudulent charges that resulted from the breach—said that customers of 110 banks were affected by this incident and losses of more than $13
- million in fraudulent charges on customers' cards were reported by 24 of these institutions.
- DSW, a shoe retailer, said in an April 2005 news release that it had experienced a data breach in which a hacker accessed the names and card numbers associated with

1.4 million credit and debit card transactions at 108 of its stores, as well as checking account numbers and driver's license numbers from 96,000 check transactions. According to a complaint filed by FTC in March of 2006, there allegedly have been fraudulent transactions on some of these accounts.

- CD Universe, an Internet-based music store, reportedly experienced a breach in December 1999 in which a hacker accessed as many as 300,000 names, addresses, and credit card numbers from the company Web site, according to media reports and a company official. The hacker allegedly used some of the stolen credit card numbers to obtain money for himself.[42]

Challenges Exist in Determining the Link between Data Breaches and Identity Theft

Determining the link between data breaches and identity theft is challenging for several reasons. First, identity theft victims often do not know how their personal information was obtained. According to FTC, in approximately 65 percent of the identity theft complaints it received from October 1, 2005, through August 31, 2006, the victim did not know or report how the information was compromised. Second, victims may misattribute how their data were obtained. For example, federal officials and representatives of a private group that assists victims said that consumers who are notified of a breach often assume that any perceived mistakes on their credit card statements or credit report were a result of the breach. As a result, no government agency maintains comprehensive data on the underlying cause of identity theft. FTC told us that its Identity Theft Data Clearinghouse is limited to self-reported complaints and therefore does not contain statistically reliable information that would allow the agency to determine a link between data breaches and identity theft. Similarly, according to FBI, data maintained by the Internet Crime Complaint Center does not include information sufficient to determine the link between data breaches and identity theft.

Third, law enforcement officials told us that in some cases, stolen data may be held for up to a year or more before being used to commit identity theft. Further, once stolen data have been sold or posted on the Web, fraudulent use of that information may continue for years. As a result, studies that attempt to measure the harm resulting from data breaches cannot necessarily rule out all future harm. Finally, conducting comprehensive studies of data breaches and identity theft can be hindered by issues of privacy and confidentiality. For example, companies that have experienced breaches may be unable or unwilling to provide information about affected individuals to researchers.

Some studies conducted by private researchers have sought to determine the extent to which data breaches result in identity theft, but our review found them to contain methodological limitations.[43] One research firm conducted a study of four data breaches, analyzing credit and other application data for suspicious relationships that indicated fraud.[44] The study estimated that no more than 0.10 percent of individuals whose data had been breached experienced resulting identity theft in the form of unauthorized new account creation. However, because the study reviewed only four data breaches, it cannot be considered representative of other breaches. Moreover, two of these breaches did not involve personally identifiable information and thus would not be expected to create a risk of fraud involving new account creation.

Another private research firm surveyed approximately 9,000 individuals about whether they had ever received a notification from an organization about the loss or theft of their personal information.[45] Of the approximately 12 percent of individuals who reported they had received such a notification, 3 percent—or 33 people—said they believed they had suffered identity theft as a result. However, these data are subject to limitations; among other things, individuals are often unaware of whether any fraud they have suffered was, in fact, due to a data breach. A third firm projected in a study that 0.8 percent of consumers whose information a data breach compromised would experience fraud as a result.[46] However, we question the reliability of this estimate, in part because of assumptions made about the number of consumers affected by data breaches

Type of Data Compromised and Other Factors Influence Potential for Resulting Consumer Harm

The type of data compromised in a breach can effectively determine the potential harm that can result. For example, credit or debit card information such as card numbers and expiration dates generally cannot be used alone to open unauthorized new accounts. Some of the largest and most highly publicized data breaches in recent years largely involved credit or debit card data rather than personally identifiable information. As a result, these breaches put affected consumers at risk of account fraud but not necessarily at risk of fraud involving unauthorized creation of new accounts—the type of identity theft generally considered to have a more harmful direct effect on consumers. While credit and debit card fraud is a significant problem—the FTC estimates it results in billions of dollars in losses annually—existing laws limit consumer liability for such fraud and, as a matter of policy, some credit and debit card issuers may voluntarily cover all fraudulent charges.47 In contrast, the unauthorized creation of new accounts—such as using someone else's identity to open credit card or bank accounts, originate home mortgages, file tax returns, or apply for government benefits—can result in substantial financial costs and other hardships.

In addition to the type of data compromised in a breach, several additional factors can influence the extent to which a breach presents the risk of identity theft. These include the following:

- Intent. Breaches that are the result of intentional acts—such as hacking into a server to obtain sensitive data—generally are considered to pose more risk than accidental breaches such as a lost laptop or the unintentional exposure of sensitive data on the Internet, according to federal agency officials. However, in some cases, such as the theft of a laptop containing personal information, it may be unknown whether the laptop was stolen for the hardware, the personal data, or both.
- Encryption. Encryption—encoding data so that it can only be read by authorized individuals—can in some cases prevent unauthorized access. However, some forms of encryption are more effective than others, and encryption does not necessarily

preclude fraudulent use of data—for example, if the key used to unencrypt the data is also compromised.

- Hardware requirements. Data that only can be accessed using specialized equipment and software may be less likely to be misused in the case of a breach. For example, some entities that have lost data tapes have stated that criminals would require specific data reading equipment and expertise in how to use it to access the information.
- Number of records. Larger breaches may pose a greater overall risk that at least one individual would become a victim of identity theft. At the same time, given the resources needed to commit identity theft, breaches of very large numbers of records may pose less risk to any one individual whose data were compromised.

Breach Notification Requirements Can Serve to Encourage Better Data Security Practices and Alert Consumers, but They Also Present Costs and Challenges

Breach notification requirements have several potential benefits, including creating incentives for entities to improve their data security practices (and thus prevent potential breaches from occurring), allowing affected consumers to take measures to prevent or mitigate identity theft, and serving to respect individuals' basic right to know when their personal information is compromised. At the same time, breach notification requirements present costs, both for developing compliance strategies and for actual notifications in the event of a breach. Further, there is the risk of overnotification, or inundating consumers with frequent notifications of breaches that may present little or no risk of identity theft or other harm. Thus, policymakers face the challenge of setting a notification standard that allows individuals to take steps to protect themselves where the risk of harm exists, while ensuring they are only notified in cases where the level of risk warrants such action.

Notification Requirements may Create Incentives for Improved Data Security and Allow Consumers the Opportunity to Mitigate Risks

According to our review of studies and interviews with representatives in government, academia, and private industry, breach notification requirements have several potential benefits, as follows:

- Incentives for Improved Data Security. Breach notification requirements can provide an incentive for companies and other entities to increase their data security measures to avoid the possible financial and reputational risks that can be associated with a publicly reported data breach.[48] Representatives we contacted in the private, nonprofit, and government sectors told us that they believe that existing breach notification requirements in state laws, or the breach notification provisions in federal banking regulatory guidance, have provided entities with incentives to improve data security practices. For example, some representatives of companies and other organizations noted that passage of state notification laws led to companies reexamining data security procedures and making improvements, such as encrypting sensitive data and restricting consumer data that can be accessed online. Similarly, federal banking regulators told us that they believe their notification guidance has motivated regulated institutions to enhance data security. For example, according to officials at the Office of Thrift Supervision, its institutions have taken steps such as improving electronic firewalls and implementing formal incident response reporting systems.

- Prevention of Identity Theft. Breach notification can provide consumers with the opportunity to take steps to protect themselves from possible identity theft. For example, consumers whose account information has been breached can monitor their bank or credit card statements for suspicious activity or close the affected accounts. Consumers whose personally identifiable information, such as SSN, has been breached can review their credit reports for suspicious activity or may choose to purchase a credit monitoring product that alerts them to changes that could indicate identity theft. In addition, affected consumers can place a fraud alert on their credit reports, which requires businesses to take certain identity verification steps before issuing credit.[49]In some states, consumers can implement credit freezes, which block unauthorized third parties from obtaining the consumer's credit report or score.[50] Limited information exists on the steps individuals actually take when notified of a breach. In the 2005 Ponemon Institute survey of individuals that received notification letters, 50 percent said they did nothing, while the rest indicated they took actions such as monitoring their credit reports, canceling credit or debit cards, or closing bank accounts.[51] Respecting Consumers' Right to Know. Some consumer advocates and others have argued that consumers have a right to know how their information is being handled. According to this view, basic rights of privacy dictate that consumers should be informed when their personal information has been compromised, even if the risk of harm is minimal. The principle that individuals should have ready means of learning about the use of their personal information is embedded in the Fair Information Practices, a set of internationally recognized privacy protection principles.[52]
- Improving Public Awareness. Public reporting of data breaches may raise general awareness among consumers about the risks of identity theft and ways they can mitigate these risks, such as periodically reviewing their credit reports. In addition, publicity surrounding a data breach resulting from notification can serve to deter the use of stolen information because presumably the thief knows that the breach is likely being investigated and the stolen data are being carefully monitored.

Breach Notification Requirements Present a Variety of Potential Costs

According to company representatives, researchers, regulators, and others, there are several different types of costs that may be associated with breach notification requirements. To begin with, entities subject to breach notification requirements may incur certain costs, regardless of whether they actually suffer a breach, or—if they do—regardless of whether they have to notify consumers. For example, entities may incur costs for developing and formalizing incident response plans.

There are also the costs associated with actual notifications—potentially including printing, postage, legal, investigative, and public relations expenses.[53] Although comprehensive data on these costs do not exist, a 2006 Ponemon Institute survey of companies experiencing a data breach found that 31 companies that responded incurred an average of $1.4 million per breach, or $54 per record breached, for costs related to mailing notification letters, call center expenses, courtesy discounts or services, and legal fees.[54] Similarly, a study by Gartner Research found that ChoicePoint spent $79 per affected account following its 2005 breach for professional fees, legal expenses, and communications to affected customers.[55] A representative of the San Jose Medical Group told us it spent $100,000 to send notification letters to 187,000 patients following a data breach that occurred in 2005. Entities also may incur costs related to staffing call centers to field inquiries from consumers about the breach. For example, representatives of the University of California at Berkeley told us that following a 2005 breach of 98,000 records, the university spent $75,000 in staffing, telecommunications, and other call center costs.

Finally, banks whose customers' account information is breached also may incur costs for remedial steps such as canceling existing accounts or replacing affected customers' credit or debit cards—although such steps may not be required by the applicable breach notification requirements.

Entities experiencing a breach also often provide affected individuals with free credit monitoring services. For example, a representative of a large financial management company noted that offering free credit monitoring services after a breach has become standard industry practice, and costs, on average, between $20 and $40 per customer.

Challenges Exist in Complying with and Developing Breach Notification Requirements

Officials of companies and other entities we interviewed identified challenges such as interpreting ambiguous statutory language, identifying and locating affected consumers, and developing effective notification letters. In addition, policymakers face challenges in developing breach notification requirements, particularly in setting the appropriate standard to establish the circumstances under which consumers should be notified.

Complying with Notification Requirements

Companies and other entities we interviewed said they can face a number of challenges related to complying with the breach notification requirements in state laws or federal banking guidance. These include the following:

- Interpreting ambiguous provisions. Entities subject to breach notification requirements sometimes face challenges interpreting certain terms or provisions of notification laws. For example, an information security expert told us that some laws do not adequately define encryption, which could refer to anything from simple password protection to complex coding. Similarly, federal banking regulators acknowledged that their institutions sometimes face difficulty determining whether misuse of breached information is "reasonably possible," such as when little information exists about the location of the data, the intent of a criminal who stole data, or the effectiveness of security features designed to render data inaccessible.
- Addressing who is responsible. Notification requirements do not always fully address who should bear the cost of and responsibility for notification, particularly in cases where a third party is responsible for the breach. For example, representatives of some federal banking regulators and industry associations cited particular challenges associated with breaches of credit and debit card information by retailers. Banks that issue credit and debit cards compromised by a merchant that is not the bank's service provider are generally not required by the banking regulators' guidance to notify their customers, but nevertheless in some cases, they feel obliged to do so. Bank representatives with whom we spoke expressed concern that breaches of credit card information by third parties can adversely affect a bank's reputation and result in costs related to notifying customers and reissuing cards.
- Identifying affected consumers. Some entities we interviewed said that it can be difficult to identify which consumers may have been affected by a breach and obtain their contact information. For example, one representative at a state agency involved in a breach told us officials were unsure what data had been downloaded among records that may have been accessed on 600,000 people. Obtaining accurate and current mailing addresses for affected parties also can be difficult and costly, many entities told us. This can be a particular problem for entities, such as merchants, that have breached credit card numbers but do not themselves possess the mailing addresses associated with those numbers.
- Developing clear and effective notification letters. We have noted in the past that public notices should be useful and easy to understand if they are to be effective.[56] However, the 2005 study conducted by the Ponemon Institute found that 52 percent of survey respondents who received a notification letter said the letter was not easy to understand.[57] In addition, consumers might be confused by other mail solicitations that may resemble notification letters. For example, officials at one large national bank noted that marketing solicitations for credit monitoring services often are made to resemble breach notification letters, potentially desensitizing or confusing consumers when a true notification letter arrives.

- Complying with multiple state laws. Officials of companies with customers in multiple states and their trade associations noted that they face the challenge of complying with breach notification requirements that vary among the states, including who must be notified, the level of risk that triggers a notice, the nature of the notification, and exceptions to the requirement. Officials of companies we contacted noted that it is challenging to comply with these multiple requirements since most breaches involve customers in many states.

Setting an Appropriate Notification Standard

Existing state laws vary in terms of the notification standard—that is, the event or circumstance that triggers a required notification. For example, California has an expansive standard that requires notification in nearly all cases where unencrypted sensitive personal data "is reasonably believed to have been acquired by an unauthorized individual." Other states employ a risk-based approach that incorporates into the standard the extent to which the data are likely to be misused. The standards vary in terms of what is required in cases where the risk of harm is unknown. For example:

Vermont requires notification unless an entity can demonstrate that misuse of the breached data "is not reasonably possible." In contrast, North Carolina requires notification only when it has been determined that the breach has resulted, or is reasonably likely to result, in illegal use of the data or creates a material risk of harm to a consumer. As shown in figure 1, whether or not a breach is subject to notification can depend on.

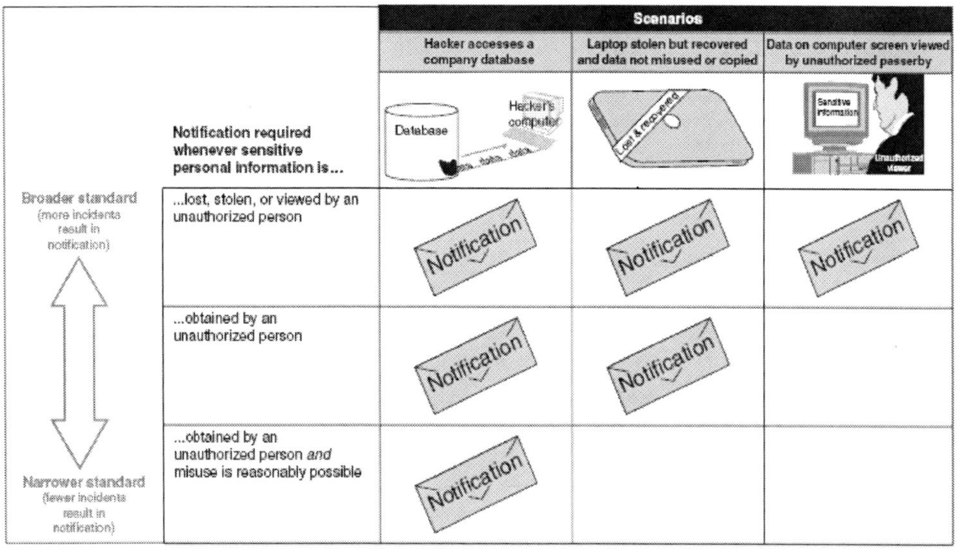

Source: GAO (analysis); Art Explosion (images).

Note: Figure presents hypothetical scenarios and notification standards and is shown for illustrative purposes only.

Figure 1. Application of Notification Standards under Different Breach Scenarios.

Because of the difficulty of complying with multiple state requirements, many companies and industry representatives have argued for a consistent federal standard for breach notification that would preempt state notification laws. However, the National Association of Attorneys General, as well as some consumer and privacy groups, have expressed concern that a federal breach notification law could weaken consumer protections if it were to preempt stronger state laws. These groups have advocated a strong notification standard because, they say, the link between breaches and identity theft is not always clear and entities are not well equipped to assess the risk of harm resulting from a given breach. As a result, too narrow a notification standard may prevent consumers from taking action in cases that do in fact present some risk. Also, as noted earlier, some privacy groups and others believe that consumers have basic rights to be notified when their personal information has been breached, no matter what the circumstances. Moreover, they say that fears of "overnotification"—where consumers are inundated by frequent notifications—are unfounded, given that they are aware of no evidence of this occurring in states that currently have strict notification requirements.

By contrast, some representatives of the federal banking regulatory agencies, FTC, private companies, and other experts have expressed concern about overly expansive breach notification standards. They say that such standards may require businesses to notify consumers about minor and insignificant breaches. This in turn could eventually lead to overnotification and cause consumers to spend time and money taking proactive steps that are not necessary or, alternatively, to ignore notices when action is warranted. In addition, businesses and federal banking regulators have expressed concern about the financial burden that overnotification could cause. Overly broad notification standards could also have the effect of limiting entities' reputational incentives for improving data security, if nearly all entities regularly issue notifications as a result of minor breaches. Representatives of the federal banking regulatory agencies have noted that they sought to strike an appropriate balance with their notification standard. Their guidance provides that, when a financial institution becomes aware of an incident of unauthorized access to sensitive customer information, the institution should conduct a reasonable investigation to promptly determine the likelihood that the information has been or will be misused.[58] If the institution determines thatmisuse of the information has occurred or is reasonably possible, it should notify affected customers as soon as possible. The guidance is intended to provide notice to customers only when there is a reasonable expectation of misuse.[59]

Similarly, the guidance for federal agencies developed by the President's Identity Theft Task Force recommended that if an agency experiences a breach, it should analyze the risk of identity theft and tailor its response— which may include notifying individuals—to the nature and scope of the risk presented. The guidance noted that such a risk assessment can minimize the potentially significant costs of notification where little risk exists. The task force's April 2007 strategic plan recommended the development of a national standard requiring all entities that maintain sensitive consumer information, in both the public and private sectors, to provide notice to consumers and law enforcement in the event of a breach. As with its guidance to federal agencies, the task force recommended that the standard be risk based to provide notice when consumers face a significant risk of identity theft but to avoid excessive notification.

As we have noted in the past, care is needed in defining appropriate criteria for data breaches that merit notification.[60] The frequency of data breaches identified in this report suggests that a national breach notification requirement may be beneficial, in large part because of its role in further encouraging entities to improve their data security practices. However, because breaches vary in the risk they present, and because most breaches have not resulted in detected incidents of identity theft, a notification that is risk based appears appropriate. Should Congress choose to enact a federal breach notification requirement, use of the risk- based approaches that the federal banking regulators and the President's Identity Theft Task Force advocate could avoid undue burden on organizations and unnecessary and counterproductive notifications to consumers.

AGENCY COMMENTS

We provided a draft of this report to FTC, which provided technical comments that were incorporated in this report as appropriate. In addition, we provided selected portions of the draft to the Board of Governors of the Federal Reserve System, the Department of Justice, DHS, FDIC, the National Credit Union Administration, the Office of the Comptroller of the Currency, the Office of Thrift Supervision, the Social Security Administration, and USPIS, and also incorporated their technical comments as appropriate.

As agreed with your offices, unless you publicly announce the contents of this report earlier, we plan no further distribution of it until 30 days from the date of this letter. We will then send copies of this report to the Chairman, House Committee on Financial Services; the Chairman and Ranking Member, Senate Committee on Banking, Housing, and Urban Affairs; the Chairman and Ranking Member, Senate Committee on the Judiciary; the Chairman and Ranking Member, House Committee on the Judiciary; the Chairman and Vice Chairman, Senate Committee on Commerce, Science, and Transportation; and the Chairman and Ranking Member, House Committee on Energy and Commerce. We will also send copies to the Chairman of the Board of Governors of the Federal Reserve System, the Attorney General, the Secretary of the Department of Homeland Security, the Chairman of the Federal Deposit Insurance Corporation, the Chairman of the Federal Trade Commission, the Chairman of the National Credit Union Administration, the Comptroller of the Currency, the Director of the Office of Thrift Supervision, the Commissioner of the Social Security Administration, and the Postmaster General and Chief Executive Officer of the U.S. Postal Service. We will also make copies available to others upon request. In addition, the report will be available at no charge on GAO's Web site at http://www.gao.gov.

APPENDIX: SCOPE AND METHODOLOGY

Our report objectives were to examine (1) what is known about the incidence and circumstances of breaches of sensitive personal information; (2) what information exists on the extent to which breaches of sensitive personal information have resulted in identity theft; and (3) the potential benefits, costs, and challenges associated with breach notification requirements. We use the term "data breach" to refer to the unauthorized or unintentional exposure, disclosure, or loss of sensitive personal information by a company, government agency, university, or other public or private entity. Our scope was limited to breaches involving personal data, including financial data, that could be used to commit identity theft or other related harm, and we excluded breaches involving other types of sensitive data, such as medical records or proprietary business information. For the purposes of this report, the term "identity theft" is used broadly to refer to both fraud on existing accounts and the unauthorized creation of new accounts.

To address all three objectives, we conducted a literature search of relevant articles, reports, and studies. We also collected and analyzed documents from, and interviewed, officials of government agencies that investigate and track data breaches, including the Federal Trade Commission, the Department of Homeland Security, the Department of Justice, the U.S. Postal Inspection Service, and the Social Security Administration. We also interviewed staff at the five federal banking regulators—the Board of Governors of the Federal Reserve System, the Federal Deposit Insurance Corporation, the Office of the Comptroller of the Currency, the Office of Thrift Supervision, and the National Credit Union Administration. In addition, we spoke with representatives of the National Association of Attorneys General and organizations that address consumer protection and privacy issues, including Consumers Union, Electronic Privacy Information Center, Privacy Rights Clearinghouse, Attrition, and the Identity Theft Resource Center. We also spoke with three academic researchers who study issues related to data breaches and notification and an attorney who helps companies address data privacy and security issues. In addition, we reviewed studies on data breaches conducted by private and nonprofit research organizations, including the Ponemon Institute, ID Analytics, and Javelin Strategy and Research. We interviewed the studies' authors and took other steps to ensure that the data and methodologies were sufficiently reliable for our purposes. We also spoke with representatives of the California Office of Privacy Protection and its advisory group and reviewed the office's recommended practices for notification.

To address the first objective on the incidence and circumstances of data breaches, we reviewed lists of news media-reported data breaches that are compiled and maintained by three private research and advocacy organizations—Privacy Rights Clearinghouse, Attrition, and the Identity Theft Resource Center. We analyzed the three independent lists to create a single, nonduplicative list of data breaches that had been reported in the news media from January 2005 through December 2006. We took measures to ensure the lists were of sufficient quality for our purposes, including spot checking selected data and interviewing representatives of the three organizations on their methodologies. The Privacy Rights Clearinghouse, Attrition, and Identity Theft Resource Center lists contained 436, 453, and 462 breaches, respectively, for the time period we analyzed. Of the 572 breaches they collectively compiled, 59 percent appeared on all three lists, 19 percent appeared on two, and 22 percent appeared on one. Our analysis was based on the lists as they stood on February 15, 2007; these data may have changed because the lists are occasionally updated when the compilers learn of new breaches that may have occurred in the past.

We also collected available data from federal law enforcement agencies on the breaches they have investigated in recent years. In addition, the five federal banking regulators provided, at our request, data on the breaches of which they have been notified by the institutions they supervise. These data varied in usefulness and comprehensiveness because of the regulators' differing methods of counting and tracking breaches and maintaining data on them. We also gathered data from two states, New York and North Carolina, which were selected because they were two large states that maintain centralized information on breaches.

Further, we obtained available data from industry and trade associations representing key sectors—such as financial services, retail sales, higher education, hospitals, and information services—that have experienced data breaches. We also collected information on breaches experienced by federal agencies compiled by the House Government Reform Committee and the U.S. Computer Emergency Readiness Team, a component of the Department of Homeland Security.

To address the second objective, we selected for more detailed examination the 24 largest (in terms of number of records breached) data breaches reported in the news media from January 2000 through June 2005. We selected these breaches in August 2006 using the lists maintained by Privacy Rights Clearinghouse and Identity Theft Resource Center, as well as a similar compilation of breaches collected by the Congressional Research Service. We were not aware of the Attrition list at the time we made our selection. For each of these breaches, we reviewed news reports as well as publicly available documents such as testimonies and criminal indictments. We also conducted interviews, where possible, with representatives of the entities that experienced the breach and law enforcement agencies that investigated the breach. We identified those cases where this information collectively indicated that the breach appeared to have resulted in some form of identity theft. Ultimately, the determination of whether particular conduct violated a law prohibiting identity theft would be a matter of law for the courts. We did not directly contact individuals whose data had been affected by the breaches because of privacy concerns and because we did not have a systematic means of identifying them. We also reviewed five breaches that reportedly involved federal agencies—the Navy; the Internal Revenue Service; the Federal Deposit Insurance Corporation; the National Park Service; and the Department of Justice. These were selected to represent breaches that included different causes, types of data, and involvement by third-party vendors.

To examine the potential benefits, costs, and challenges associated with breach notification requirements, we reviewed the federal banking regulators' proposed and final guidance related to breach notification, and interviewed representatives of each agency regarding their consideration of potential costs, benefits, and challenges during development of the guidance. Further, we reviewed the strategic plan and other documents issued by the President's Identity Theft Task Force. In addition, we conducted a review of the effects of California's breach notification law. We interviewed representatives of, and gathered information from, seven organizations to learn about their experiences complying with California's breach notification law. These organizations were selected to represent a range of organization sizes and industry sectors. We also interviewed representatives of the California State Information Security Office, California State Assembly, California Office of Privacy Protection, and California Bankers Association.

We conducted our review from August 2006 through April 2007 in accordance with generally accepted government auditing standards.

REFERENCES

[1] In January 2007, The TJX Companies, Inc., publicly disclosed a data breach that compromised sensitive personal information, including credit and debit card data,

associated with more than 45 million customer accounts. In May 2006, VA reported that computer equipment containing sensitive personal information on approximately 26.5 million veterans and active duty members of the military was stolen from the home of a VA employee. The equipment was eventually recovered, and forensic analysts concluded that it was unlikely that the personal information contained therein was compromised. See GAO, Privacy: Lessons Learned About Data Breach Notification, GAO-07-657 (Washington, D.C.: Apr. 30, 2007).

[2] In this report we use "personally identifiable information" to refer to any information that can be used to distinguish or trace an individual's identity—such as name, Social Security number, driver's license number, and mother's maiden name—because such information generally may be used to establish new accounts, but not to refer to other "means of identification," as defined in 18 U.S.C. § 1028(7), including account information such as credit or debit card numbers.

[3] See Interagency Guidance on Response Programs for Unauthorized Access to Customer Information and Customer Notice, 70 Fed. Reg. 15736 (Mar. 29, 2005). The five federal banking regulatory agencies are the Office of the Comptroller of the Currency, the Office of Thrift Supervision, the Board of Governors of the Federal Reserve System, the Federal Deposit Insurance Corporation, and the National Credit Union Administration. The National Credit Union Administration issued its guidance (which was substantially identical) separately from the other four regulators (see Security Program and Appendix B—Guidance on Response Programs for Unauthorized Access to Member Information and Member Notice, 70 Fed. Reg. 22764 (May 2, 2005)).

[4] The President's Identity Theft Task Force—chaired by the Attorney General and cochaired by the Chairman of the Federal Trade Commission and comprising 17 federal agencies and departments—was charged with developing a comprehensive national strategy to combat identity theft. Exec. Order No. 13,402, Strengthening Federal Efforts to Protect Against Identity Theft, 71 Fed. Reg. 27945 (May 10, 2006). The task force's guidance was distributed in a memorandum from the Office of Management and Budget to the heads of federal agencies and departments. See Office of Management and Budget Memorandum for the Heads of Departments and Agencies, Recommendations for Identity Theft Related Data Breach Notification, Sept. 20, 2006. In May 2007, the Office of Management and Budget issued a memorandum that updated the September 2006 guidance and, among other things, required agencies to develop and implement breach notification policies within 120 days. See Office of Management and Budget Memorandum for the Heads of Executive Departments and Agencies, Safeguarding Against and Responding to the Breach of Personally Identifiable Information, M-07-16 (May 22, 2007).

[5] See, for example, Data Security Act of 2007, H.R. 1685, 110th Cong. (2007); Notification of Risk to Personal Data Act of 2007, S. 239, 110th Cong. (2007); Personal Data Privacy and Security Act of 2007, S. 495, 110th Cong. (2007); Data Accountability and Trust Act, H.R. 958, 110th Cong. (2007); and Identity Theft Prevention Act, S. 1178, 110th Cong. (2007).

[6] The three private organizations are Attrition, Identity Theft Resource Center, and Privacy Rights Clearinghouse. We reviewed data on breaches in New York and North Carolina because they represent two large states that maintain centralized information on data breaches.

[7] The House Government Reform Committee was renamed the House Oversight and Government Reform Committee in the 110th Congress
[8] Cal. Civ. Code § 1798.82.
[9] Pub. L. No. 106-102, tit. V, subtit. A, 113 Stat. 1338 (Nov. 12, 1999) (codified at 15 U.S.C. § 6801-6809).
[10] President's Identity Theft Task Force, Combating Identity Theft: A Strategic Plan (Washington, D.C.: Apr. 11, 2007).
[11] Pub. L. No. 109-461, tit. IX, 120 Stat. 3450 (Dec. 22, 2006), codified at 38 U.S.C. § 572 1- 5728, 7901-7907.
[12] For example, Identity Theft: Recent Developments Involving the Security of Sensitive Consumer Information: Hearing Before the Senate Comm. on Banking, Housing, and Urban Affairs, 109th Cong., 1st Sess. (2005); Securing Electronic Personal Data: Striking a Balance Between Privacy and Commercial and Governmental Use: Hearing Before the Senate Comm. on the Judiciary, 109th Cong., 1st Sess. (2005); Assessing Data Security: Preventing Breaches and Protecting Sensitive Information: Hearing Before the House Comm. on Financial Services, 109th Cong., 1st Sess. (2005); Securing Consumers' Data: Options Following Security Breaches: Hearing Before the Subcomm. on Commerce, Trade, and Consumer Protection of the House Comm. on Energy and Commerce, 109th Cong., 1st Sess. (2005).
[13] For additional information on identity theft, see GAO, Identity Theft: Some Outreach Efforts to Promote Awareness of New Consumer Rights Are Under Way, GAO-05-710 (Washington, D.C.: Jun. 30, 2005) and Identity Theft: Prevalence and Cost Appear to be Growing, GAO-02-363 (Washington, D.C.: Mar. 1, 2002)
[14] Pub. L. No. 105-318, 112 Stat. 3007 (Oct. 30, 1998). In addition to FTC, other federal agencies maintain data on identity theft. For example, the Internet Crime Complaint Center, a joint venture of the FBI and the National White Collar Crime Center, receives Internet-related identity theft complaints, which it shares with law enforcement agencies throughout the country.
[15] 15Because the breaches cited in this section of the report derive from different sources, there may be some overlap among the numbers cited by these sources.
[16] Privacy Rights Clearinghouse is a nonprofit consumer education and advocacy project whose purpose is to advocate for consumers' privacy rights in public policy proceedings. Identity Theft Resource Center is a nonprofit organization that provides consumer and victim support and advises governmental agencies, legislators, and companies on the issue of identity theft. Attrition is an information security-related Web site maintained by volunteers.
[17] Representatives of these three organizations indicated that their definition of a data breach was consistent with the definition used in this report. However, we did not independently confirm whether the individual breaches reported by the media and tracked by these groups met the criteria for this definition, and it is possible that some of them do not. We reviewed these lists as they appeared as of February 15, 2007; additional breaches that occurred during the 2-year period we reviewed may have been subsequently added as they were discovered. Our analysis eliminated overlap among the three lists; the 572 breaches we cite represent unique breaches that appeared on at least one list.

[18] There were 83 million records collectively reported to have been affected by the 572 breaches. However, in some cases, the number of records affected was unknown or unreported, and the total does not reflect those breaches. Also, the number of breached records containing personal information may not be the same as the number of individuals affected by breaches because some individuals may be victims of more than one breach or may have multiple records compromised in a single breach. Finally, in addition to the 83 million records, as many as 40 million additional records may have been affected by a single breach involving the credit card processor CardSystems, although the exact number of affected records is unclear. In a complaint following the breach, FTC alleged that a hacker obtained unauthorized access to magnetic stripe data for tens of millions of credit and debit cards. However, according to testimony by a CardSystems official, only 263,000 of these records (containing 239,000 discrete account numbers) included sensitive personal information.

[19] According to these officials, not all 1,300 pending computer intrusion cases necessarily involved breaches that compromised sensitive personal information, although the vast majority have. The term hacking is commonly used to refer to accessing a computer system without authorization, with the intention of destroying, disrupting, or carrying out illegal activities on the network or computer system.

[20] Government Reform Committee, U.S. House of Representatives, Staff Report: Agency Data Breaches Since January 1, 2003 (Washington, D.C.: Oct. 13, 2006). The federal agencies covered in the report were the Departments of Agriculture, Commerce, Defense, Education, Energy, Health and Human Services, Homeland Security, Housing and Urban Development, Interior, Justice, Labor, State, Transportation, Treasury, and Veterans Affairs, as well as the Office of Personnel Management and the Social Security Administration. In addition to 788 incidents reported by 16 federal agencies, the Committee received information on data breaches from the Department of Veterans Affairs, which the report characterized only as "hundreds" of incidents.

[21] Pub. L. No. 107-347, tit. III, 116 Stat. 2946 (Dec. 17, 2002), codified at 44 U.S.C. § 3541- 3549; 40 U.S.C. § 11331.

[22] Office of Management and Budget Memorandum for Chief Information Officers, Reporting Incidents Involving Personally Identifiable Information and Incorporating the Cost for Security in Agency Information Technology Investments, M-06-19 (July 12, 2006). The U.S. Computer Emergency Readiness Team defines a computer security incident as "a violation or imminent threat of violation of computer security policies, acceptable use policies, or standard computer security practice" and the Office of Management and Budget requires reporting if the incident includes personally identifiable information, which under its definition refers to "any information about an individual maintained by an agency, including, but not limited to, education, financial transactions, medical history, and criminal or employment history and information which can be used to distinguish or trace an individual's identity, such as their name, Social Security number, date and place of birth, mother's maiden name, biometric records, etc., including any other personal information which is linked or linkable to an individual."

[23] Treasury Inspector General for Tax Administration, The Internal Revenue Service Is Not Adequately Protecting Taxpayer Data on Laptop Computers and Other Portable Electronic Media Devices, Ref. No. 2007-20-048 (Washington, D.C.: Mar. 23, 2007).

[24] 70 Fed. Reg. 15736 (Mar. 29, 2005) and 70 Fed. Reg. 22764 (May 2, 2005).

[25] Only data breaches at the financial institutions and at third-party entities that are their service providers and maintain their customer information are subject to the guidance; this requirement is codified at 12 C.F.R. Pt. 30, App. B, Supp. A § II(A)(2); 12 C.F.R. Pt. 208, App. D-2, Supp. A § II(A)(2); 12 C.F.R. Pt. 225, App. F, Supp. A § II(A)(2); 12 C.F.R. Pt. 364, App. B, Supp. A § II(A)(2); 12 C.F.R. Pt. 570, App. B, Supp. A § II(A)(2); and 12 C.F.R. Pt. 748, App. B § II(A)(2). However, data collected by the regulators may also include some breaches that affected their institutions but were not covered by the guidance.

[26] Regulators note that while they track breaches occurring at third-party service providers involving customer information of regulated financial institutions, these breaches are typically due to lapses in data security by the third-party entity and not the financial institution itself.

[27] We did not determine the precise number of states with centralized reporting requirements. For illustrative purposes, we obtained information on data breaches from New York and North Carolina because they are two large states known to require that data breaches be reported to state agencies.

[28] N.Y. Gen. Bus. Law § 899-aa.

[29] N.C. Gen. Stat § 75-65.

[30] EDUCAUSE Center for Applied Research, Safeguarding the Tower: IT Security in Higher Education 2006, Volume 6, 2006.

[31] The association received information from 46 of the 78 hospitals it surveyed, a response rate of 59 percent. As agreed in advance, to preserve confidentiality the association provided us with a summary of their findings but did not identify the hospitals, and we did not independently verify the data.

[32] Ponemon Institute, LLC, National Survey on Data Security Breach Notification (Sept. 26, 2005). The reliability of this study's findings may be limited by a low survey response rate.

[33] CMO Council, Securing the Trust of Your Brand: How Security and IT Integrity Influence Corporate Reputation, September 2006. The reliability of this study's findings may be limited because they are based on a self-selected group of respondents to a Web- based panel. Also, we were unable to determine a response rate because, according to a CMO Council representative, the total number of survey respondents was not available.

[34] For example, see Deloitte, 2006 Global Security Survey (2006); Small Business Technology Institute, Small Business Information Security Readiness (San Jose, California: July 2005); Ponemon Institute, LLC, U.S. Survey: Confidential Data at Risk (Aug. 15, 2006); and Ponemon Institute, LLC, Benchmark Study of European and U.S. Corporate Privacy Practices (Apr. 26, 2006).

[35] GAO, Personal Information: Key Federal Privacy Laws Do Not Require Information Resellers to Safeguard All Sensitive Data, GAO-06-674 (Washington, D.C.: Jun. 26, 2006).

[36] For our analysis, we used the categories provided by Attrition for the industry sector where the breach occurred. We did not independently verify the accuracy of these categorizations.

[37] ID Analytics, Inc., National Data Breach Analysis (San Diego, California: January 2006). The data we cite reflect a combination of data presented in the report and additional data provided to us by ID Analytics.

[38] In the Matter of BJ's Wholesale Club, Inc., F.T.C. No. 0423160 (2005). A consent agreement does not constitute an admission of a violation of law.

[39] According to an FDIC representative, the agency took several steps to address the possible misuse of employee information, including promptly notifying affected employees and offering them 2 years of credit monitoring services.

[40] These three organizations periodically update their lists by adding breaches they learn about that occurred in the past, including some that occurred between January 2000 and June 2005. Our list of the 24 largest media-reported breaches was based on information provided by these lists as of August 2006. We were not aware of the Attrition list at the time we made our selection. See Congressional Research Service, Personal Data Security Breaches: Context and Incident Summaries, Order Code RL33 199 (Washington, D.C.: Dec. 16, 2005). Because our time frame covered only breaches that occurred on or before June 30, 2005, our list does not include highly publicized breaches that occurred subsequently, such as those involving the Department of Veterans Affairs and the TJX Companies. Several banks have reported fraudulent transactions on existing accounts resulting from the TJX breach, according to a January 24, 2007, press release by the Massachusetts Bankers Association.

[41] United States v. ChoicePoint, Inc., No. 1:06-cv-00198-JTC (N.D. Ga., Feb. 15, 2006). As part of the settlement, ChoicePoint admitted no violations of the law. According to ChoicePoint, the company has subsequently taken steps to enhance its customer screening process and to assist affected consumers. FTC staff told us that law enforcement officials have determined that as many as 2,900 people have experienced the fraudulent creation of new accounts as a result of the breach. According to a ChoicePoint official, the criminal indictments indicated that 46 people may have been defrauded, but the accused individuals may not have used data acquired from ChoicePoint in all the crimes cited in the indictments.

[42] This breach occurred in December 1999 but was included in the 24 breaches we reviewed because it was reported in the media in January 2000

[43] Although we found limitations in how these studies linked data breaches and identity theft, we determined other aspects of these studies to be sufficiently reliable, and we refer to them elsewhere in this report.

[44] ID Analytics, Inc., National Data Breach Analysis (2006).

[45] Ponemon Institute, National Survey (2005). As noted earlier, this study may also be limited by a low survey response rate.

[46] Javelin Strategy & Research, Data Breaches and Identity Fraud: Misunderstanding Could Fail Consumers and Burden Businesses (Pleasanton, California, August 2006).

[47] For unauthorized credit card charges, consumer liability is limited to a maximum of $50 per account, 15 U.S.C. § 1643. For unauthorized ATM or debit card transactions, the Electronic Fund Transfer Act limits consumer liability, depending on how quickly the consumer reports the loss or theft of the card. Pub. L. No. 90-321, tit. IX, as added Pub. L. No. 95-630, tit. XX, § 2001, 92 Stat. 3728 (Nov. 10, 1978); 15 U.S.C. § 1693g. Consumers may incur additional costs if they inadvertently pay charges they did not incur. In addition, account fraud can cause inconvenience or temporary hardship—such

as losing temporary access to account funds or requiring the cancellation and reactivation of cards and the redirecting of automatic payments and deposits.

[48] Such costs can be significant. For example, according to a 2006 survey, 31 companies that responded to the survey incurred an average of $98 per record, or $2.6 million per company, in costs associated with the loss of existing customers, recruitment of new customers, and damage to the reputation of their brand name. Ponemon Institute, LLC, 2006 Annual Study: Cost of a Data Breach, 2006. Due to sampling limitations, these findings are not necessarily representative of the costs incurred by all companies that experience breaches

[49] See 15 U.S.C. § 168 1c-1.

[50] Congressional Research Service, Identity Theft Laws: State Penalties and Remedies and Pending Federal Bills (Washington, D.C.: Jan. 11, 2007).

[51] Ponemon Institute, National Survey (2005). As noted earlier, this study may be limited by a low survey response rate.

[52] The Fair Information Practices were first proposed in 1973 by a U.S. government advisory committee. A revised version was developed in 1980 by the Organization for Economic Cooperation and Development, a group of 30 member countries that are market democracies. For more information, see GAO, Personal Information: Agency and Reseller Adherence to Key Privacy Principles, GAO-06-421 (Washington, D.C.: Apr. 4, 2006)

[53] The distinction between the costs associated with a notification requirement versus a breach itself can be ambiguous. For example, the cost of postage can clearly be attributed to notification, whereas legal costs can be attributed to notification, the breach itself, or both, depending on the circumstances.

[54] Ponemon Institute, Annual Study (2006). As noted earlier, due to sampling limitations, these findings are not necessarily representative of the costs incurred by all companies that experience breaches.

[55] Gartner Research, Data Protection Is Less Costly Than Data Breaches (Stamford, Connecticut: September 16, 2005). The report, issued in 2005, based its findings on the breach having affected 145,000 records, but company officials later reported that 162,000 records were affected.

[56] See GAO-06-833T, Privacy: Preventing and Responding to Improper Disclosures of Personal Information (Washington, D.C.: Jun. 8, 2006), pp. 15-18, which discusses specific elements that should be incorporated in a breach notification.

[57] Ponemon Institute, National Survey (2005). As noted earlier, this study may be limited by a low survey response rate.

[58] 12 C.F.R. Pt. 30, App. B, Supp. A § III(A); 12 C.F.R. Pt. 208, App. D-2, Supp. A § III(A); 12 C.F.R. Pt. 225, App. F, Supp. A § III(A); 12 C.F.R. Pt. 364, App. B, Supp. A § III(A); 12 C.F.R. Pt. 570, App. B, Supp. A § III(A); and 12 C.F.R. Pt. 748, App. B § III(A

[59] The guidance states that institutions should notify their primary federal regulator as soon as possible when the institution becomes aware of an incident involving unauthorized access to or use of sensitive customer information, even for incidents that may not warrant customer notification. Banking regulators told us they review institutions' response programs as part of their supervisory procedures and, in many cases, work with institutions as they respond to specific incidents to ensure their actions

are in accordance with the guidance. See 12 C.F.R. Pt. 30, App. B, Supp. A § II(A)(1)(b); 12 C.F.R. Pt. 208, App. D-2, Supp. A § II(A)(1)(b); 12 C.F.R. Pt. 225, App. F, Supp. A § II(A)(1)(b); 12 C.F.R. Pt. 364, App. B, Supp. A § II(A)(1)(b); 12 C.F.R. Pt. 570, App. B, Supp. A § II(A)(1)(b); and 12 C.F.R. Pt. 748, App. B § II(A)(1)(b).

[60] GAO, Personal Information: Key Federal Privacy Laws Do Not Require Information Resellers to Safeguard All Sensitive Data, GAO-06-674 (Washington, D.C.: Jun. 26, 2006) and GAO-06-833T.

In: Identity Theft Breaches
Editor: Cary S. Logweller

ISBN 978-1-60692-227-9

Chapter 6

IDENTITY THEFT LAWS: STATE PENALTIES AND REMEDIES AND PENDING FEDERAL BILLS*

Tara Alexandra Rainson
Law Librarian, Knowledge Services Group

ABSTRACT

This report provides an overview of state laws on identity theft. It discusses state laws that penalize identity theft, as well as state laws that assist identity theft victims, including those that permit consumers to block unauthorized persons from obtaining their credit information, known as "security freezes." The report also includes a survey of state "credit freeze" statutes. The report concludes with summaries of federal identity theft legislation pending in the 1 10th Congress.

INTRODUCTION

This report provides an overview of state laws on identity theft.[1] Forty-eight states and the District of Columbia have criminal identity theft statutes.[2] Many of these include both monetary penalties and imprisonment. For example, in California imposters are subject to a fine and confinement in jail for up to one year.[3] In Louisiana, imposters are subject to a fine of up to $10,000 and confinement in jail for up to 10 years[4] Several state statutes include restitution provisions. In Texas, Virginia, and Maryland, the court may order the imposter to reimburse the victim for expenses incurred because of the theft, such as lost income or expenses associated with correcting an inaccurate credit report.[5] Other states impose civil penalties for identity theft activities and provide victims with judicial recourse for damages incurred as a result of the theft. In Washington, imposters are liable for civil damages of $1,000 or actual damages, whichever is greater.[6] The definition of identity theft varies

* Excerpted from CRS Report RL34028, dated June 1, 2007.

across state codes. Idaho, for example, simply criminalizes the use of "identifying information."[7] In Oregon and Maine, criminal identity theft includes fraudulent use of credit cards.[8] Massachusetts and Illinois criminalize fraudulent credit card use, but also specifically address the fraudulent use of a credit card number or other identifying number.[9]

STATE "CREDIT FREEZE" LAWS[10]

Thirty-five states and the District of Columbia currently have "security freeze" laws (also "credit freeze" laws) as a form of identity theft victim assistance.[11] A security freeze law allows a consumer to block unauthorized third parties from obtaining his or her credit report or score. A consumer who places a security freeze on his or her credit report or score receives a personal identification number to gain access to credit information or to authorize the dissemination of credit information. A survey of these laws is provided in Table 1.

Benefits of security freeze laws include increased consumer control over access to personal information and corresponding decreased opportunities for imposters to obtain access to credit information. Critics of security freeze laws argue that security freezes may cause consumers unwanted delays when they must provide third party institutions access to credit histories for such purposes as qualifying for loans, applying for rental property leases, and obtaining mortgage rate approval.[12] In an effort to balance these interests of security and accessibility, seven states permit consumers to initiate security freezes only if they have been victims of identity theft or attempted identity theft.[13]

State laws also differ regarding what fees, if any, a credit reporting agency (CRA) may charge consumers for requesting a security freeze. Twenty-three states and the District of Columbia prohibit CRAs from charging fees to an identity theft victim who requests a freeze.[14] For example, the Wisconsin identity theft statute provides that there shall be no fee imposed on an individual who submits "evidence satisfactory to the consumer reporting agencies" that he or she has filed an identity theft report with a law enforcement agency.[15] In Vermont, CRAs may impose a fee when the requester is not an identity theft victim.[16] Under the Kansas identity theft statute, CRAs may not charge a security freeze fee to seniors 65 years of age or older.[17] Most state laws specify the maximum fee a CRA may charge per security freeze request.[18] The relevant Utah statute states only that security freeze fees must be "reasonable."[19]

In addition to security freeze statutes, five states have enacted "credit information blocking" laws.[20] Alabama, Colorado, Idaho, and Washington require consumer credit reporting agencies to block false information resulting from identity theft from victims' credit reports.[21] California requires a debt collector to stop collection when the alleged debtor provides evidence of his status as an identity theft victim.[22]

Table 1. Survey of State "Security Freeze" Laws

State Security Freeze Statute	Applies to All Consumers?	Credit Reporting Agency Fees for Freeze Requests?	Effective Date
Arkansas, 2007 Ark. Act 391	No. Applies to identity theft victims.	Yes.	Jan. 1, 2008
California, Cal. Civ. Code §§ 1785.11.2- 1785.11.6	Yes	Yes. No fee for identity theft victims.	Jan. 1, 2003
Colorado, Colo. Rev. Stat. § 12-14.3-102, *et seq.*	Yes	No fee for first request. No fee for identity theft victims.	July 1, 2006
Connecticut, Conn. Gen. Stat. § 36a-701a	Yes	Yes	Jan. 1, 2006
Delaware, Del. Code Ann. tit. 6, § 2201, *et seq.*	Yes	Yes	Sept. 29, 2006
District of Columbia, D.C. Code §§ 28-3861- 28-3864	Yes	Yes. No fee for identity theft victims.	July 1, 2007
Florida, Fla. Stat. § 501.005	Yes	Yes. No fee for identity theft victims.	July 1, 2006
Hawaii, Haw. Rev. Stat. Ann. §§ 489P-3 - 489P-5	No. Applies only to identity theft victims.	No	Jan. 1, 2007
Illinois, 815 Ill. Comp. Stat. 505/2MM	Yes	Yes. No fee for identity theft victims or seniors 65+ years old.	Jan. 1, 2007
Indiana, 2007 Ind. Legis. Serv. P.L. 104-2007 (S.E.A. 403) (West)	Yes	No	Sept. 1, 2007
Kansas, 2006 Kan. Sess. Laws ch. 149	No. Applies only to identity theft victims.	No	Jan. 1, 2007
Kentucky, Ky. Rev. Stat. §§ 367.363 - 367.370	Yes	Yes. No fee for identity theft victims.	July 11, 2006

Table 1. (Continued)

State Security Freeze Statute	Applies to All Consumers?	Credit Reporting Agency Fees for Freeze Requests?	Effective Date
Louisiana, La. Rev. Stat. §§ 9:357 1.1 (H) to (Y)	Yes	Yes. No fee for identity theft victims or for seniors 62+ years old.	July 1, 2005
Maine, Me. Rev. Stat. Ann. tit. 10 § 1313-C	Yes	Yes. No fee for identity theft victims.	Feb. 1, 2006
Maryland, 2007 Md. Laws Ch. 307	Yes	Yes. No fee for identity theft victims.	Jan. 1, 2008
Minnesota, Minn. Stat. § 13C.016	Yes	Yes. No fee for identity theft victims.	Aug. 1, 2006
Mississippi, S.B. 3034, 2007 Leg., Reg. Sess	No. Applies only to identity theft victims.	Yes	July 1, 2007
Montana, 2007 Mont. Laws ch. 138	Yes	Yes. No fee for identity theft victims.	July 1, 2007
Nevada, Nev. Rev. Stat. § 598C.010, et seq.	Yes	Yes. No fee for identity theft victims.	Oct. 1, 2005

State Security Freeze Statute	Applies to All Consumers?	Credit Reporting Agency Fees for Freeze Requests?	Effective Date
New Hampshire, Rev. Stat. N.H. §§ 359-B:22-B:29	Yes	Yes. No fee for identity theft victims.	Jan. 1, 2007
New Jersey, N.J. Stat. Ann. §§ 56:11-44 - 56:11-50	Yes	Yes. No fee for first request.	Jan. 1, 2006
New Mexico, 2007 N.M. Laws ch. 106	Yes.	Yes. No fee for identity theft victims or seniors 65+ years old.	July 1, 2007
New York, N.Y. Gen. Bus. Law §§ 380-a - 380-u	Yes	Yes. No fee for identity theft victims.	Nov. 1, 2006
North Carolina, N.C. Gen. Stat. § 75-60, et seq.	Yes	Yes. No fee for identity theft victims.	Dec. 1, 2005
North Dakota, H.B. 1417, 60th Leg. Assem. (2007) (to be codified, N.D. Cent. Code ch. 5 1-33)	Yes	Yes. No fee for identity theft victims.	July 1, 2007
Oklahoma, Okla. Stat. tit. 24, § 149, et seq.	Yes	Yes. No fee for identity theft victims or seniors 65+ years old.	Jan. 1, 2007
Pennsylvania, 2006 Pa. Laws ch. 163	Yes	Yes. No fee for identity theft victims or seniors 65+ years old.	Jan. 1, 2007

Table 1. (Continued)

State Security Freeze Statute	Applies to All Consumers?	Credit Reporting Agency Fees for Freeze Requests?	Effective Date
Rhode Island, R.I. Gen. Laws §§ 6-48-1 - 6-48-9	Yes	Yes. No fee for identity theft victims or seniors 65+ years old.	Jan. 1, 2007
South Dakota, S.D. Codified Laws §§ 54-15-1, *et seq.*	No. Applies to identity theft victims only.	No	July 1, 2006
Texas, Tex. Bus. & Com. Code §§ 20.03 1-20.04	No. Applies to identity theft victims only.	Yes. No charge on expiration of 45- day security alert.	Sept. 1, 2003
Utah, Utah Code Ann. § 13-42-102 and §§ 13-45-201 - 13-45-205	Yes	Yes. Allows for "reasonable fees."	Sept. 1, 2008
Vermont, Vt. Stat. Ann. tit. 9, §§ 2480a- 2480j	Yes	No	July 1, 2005
Washington, Wash. Rev. Code §§ 19.182.170 - 19.182-200	No. Applies to identity theft victims.	No	July 24, 2005
West Virginia, 2007 W. Va. Acts ch. 45	Yes	Yes. No fee for identity theft victims.	June 8, 2007
Wisconsin, Wis. Stat. § 100.54	Yes	Yes. No fee for identity theft victims.	Jan. 1, 2007
Wyoming, 2007 Wyo. Sess. Laws Act 76	Yes	Yes. No fee for identity theft victims.	July 1, 2007

Source: Lexis.com and state government websites.

SOCIAL SECURITY NUMBERS

Several state laws are intended to protect consumers' Social Security numbers (SSNs) from identity theft.23 Michigan's Social Security Number Privacy Act, the first state law of its kind, requires employers to adopt a policy to insure the confidentiality of employee SSNs.24 The employer policy must include document destruction protocols and impose penalties on persons who violate the policy. The statute requires employers to publish the policy in an employee handbook or through other means. California also has enacted a statute intended to protect the integrity of employees' SSNs.25 The statute prohibits employers from publicly displaying SSNs or printing the numbers on employee identification cards or badges. Other states have restricted the collection of SSNs for use in consumer transactions. In Rhode Island, for example, it is a misdemeanor to require a consumer to disclose his or her SSN, "incident to the sale of consumer goods or services."26 The law includes exceptions for insurance and healthcare services and applications for consumer credit.

PROPOSED FEDERAL IDENTITY THEFT LEGISLATION

Several bills have been introduced in the 1 10th Congress to combat identity theft, address security breaches, and protect personal information. Summaries of the bills provided below are from the Legislative Information System [http://www.congress.gov].

H.R. 136 (Gallegly)

Identity Theft Notification Act of 2007. This bill would amend title II (Old Age, Survivors and Disability Insurance) of the Social Security Act to require the Commissioner of Social Security to notify individuals and appropriate authorities of evidence of a certain misuse of individual Social Security account numbers. The bill also requires the Commissioner to determine, in certain instances of wage reports involving multiple addresses for the same employee name, whether there is evidence that the wages were not paid to the individual to whom the Social Security account number was assigned.

H.R. 138 (Gallegly)

Employment Eligibility Verification and Anti-Identity Theft Act. This bill would direct the Commissioner of the Social Security Administration to notify a person or entity each time that the combination of name and Social Security account number it has submitted for an individual does not match Social Security Administration records. The bill also directs the Secretary of the Department Homeland Security (DHS) to notify a person or entity each time that (1) an immigration status or employment authorization document presented or referenced by an individual during the employment eligibility verification process was assigned to another person; or (2) there is no agency record that the document was assigned to any person. Additionally, the bill directs the DHS Secretary to establish a system, meeting specified requirements, for verifying an individual's identity and employment eligibility. Requires any person or entity that has received a discrepancy notice under this act to verify the individual's employment authorization and identity through such system. The bill places the burden of resolving errors in the verification mechanism on the individual whose employment eligibility and identity have not been verified and requires the individual to terminate any employment in the United States if a final nonverification is received. The bill also requires the Commissioner of Social Security to provide the last known name, address, and location of a nonverified individual to the Secretary of DHS and provides for sanctions against employers who continue to employ an individual after receiving a final nonverification. The bill also amends the Illegal Immigration Reform and Immigrant Responsibility Act of 1996 to require any person or entity that receives written notice about more than 20 individuals in one calendar year to (1) participate in a basic pilot project for employment eligibility confirmation; and (2) comply with specified terms and conditions. The bill also provides for (1) a remedy under the Federal Tort Claims Act for job dismissals occasioned by verification mechanism errors; and (2) protection from civil and criminal liability for persons or entities that take action in good faith on the basis of verification mechanism information.

H.R. 220 (Paul)

Identity Theft Protection Act of 2007. This bill would amend title II (Old Age, Survivors and Disability Insurance) of the Social Security Act and the Internal Revenue Code to prohibit using a Social Security account number except for specified Social Security and tax purposes. The bill also prohibits the Social Security Administration from divulging the Social Security account number of an individual to any federal, state, or local government agency or instrumentality, or to any other individual. Additionally, the bill amends the Privacy Act of 1974 to prohibit any federal, state, or local government agency or instrumentality from requesting an individual to disclose his Social Security account number on either a mandatory or a voluntary basis and prohibits any two federal agencies or instrumentalities from implementing the same identifying number with respect to any individual (except as authorized by the Social Security Act). The bill also prohibits any federal agency from (1) establishing or mandating a uniform standard for identification of an individual that is required to be used by any other federal or state agency, or by a private person, for any purpose other than that of conducting the authorized activities of the standard-establishing or -mandating federal agency; or (2) conditioning receipt of any federal grant, contract, or other federal funding on the adoption, by a state or local government, or by a state agency, of such a uniform standard.

H.R. 246 (Reichert)

Methamphetamine and Identity Theft Study Act of 2007. This bill would direct the Attorney General to conduct a study evaluating whether there is a connection between the commission of crimes involving methamphetamine and the commission of identity theft crimes. The bill also requires such study to include a statistical analysis of any correlation and to evaluate (1) imposing a sentencing enhancement if a person commits both; (2) establishing a password-protected electronic clearinghouse within the Department of Justice for federal, state, and local law enforcement agencies to share information on crimes involving both; and (3) whether individuals who use methamphetamine are more likely to commit certain kinds of identity theft crimes, such as through the use of mail, than are others who commit identity theft crimes.

H.R. 336 (S. Davis)

Identity Theft Protection and Timely Reporting Act of 2007. This bill would direct the National Technical Information Service of the Department of Commerce to provide monthly updates of the Death Master List prepared by the Social Security Administration to each consumer reporting agency described in the Fair Credit Reporting Act. The bill also amends the Fair Credit Reporting Act to require each such consumer reporting agency to include a fraud alert in the consumer file of each consumer whose name appears on the Death Master List prepared by the Social Security Administration so long as the agency continues to maintain such file.

H.R. 531 (Lynch)

Retirement Security Education Act of 2007. This bill would authorize the Secretary of Health and Human Services to award grants to eligible entities to provide financial education programs to mid-life and older individuals who reside in local communities in order to (1) enhance their financial and retirement knowledge; and (2) reduce financial abuse and fraud, including telemarketing, mortgage, and pension fraud, among them. The bill also authorizes the Secretary to award a grant to one or more eligible entities to (1) create and make available instructional materials and information that promote financial education; and (2) provide training and other related assistance regarding the establishment of financial education programs. Additionally, the bill expresses the sense of Congress that organizations with demonstrated experience in providing financial education to older women should receive high priority for assistance under this act.

H.R. 605 (Hayes)

Seniors Taking on Phony Marketers Act of 2007. This bill would amend the federal criminal code to increase from 10 to 15 years the additional term of imprisonment for telemarketing fraud aimed at individuals over the age of 55. The bill also authorizes appropriations for FY2008 for (1) 50 new postal inspectors to investigate telemarketing fraud; (2) 30 new assistant U.S. attorneys to prosecute telemarketing fraud cases; and (3) public awareness and prevention initiatives to educate senior citizens about telemarketing fraud.

H.R. 836 (L. Smith)

Cyber-Security Enhancement and Consumer Data Protection Act of 2007. This bill would amend the federal criminal code to (1) prohibit accessing or remotely controlling a protected computer to obtain identification information; (2) revise the definition of "protected computer" to include computers affecting interstate or foreign commerce or communication; (3) expand the definition of racketeering to include computer fraud; (4) redefine the crime of computer-related extortion to include threats to access without authorization (or to exceed authorized access of) a protected computer; (5) impose criminal penalties for conspiracy to commit computer fraud; (6) impose a fine and/or five year prison term for failure to notify the U.S. Secret Service or Federal Bureau of Investigation (FBI) of a major security breach (involving a significant risk of identity theft) in a computer system, with the intent to thwart an investigation of such breach; (7) increase to 30 years the maximum term of imprisonment for computer fraud and require forfeiture of property used to commit computer fraud; and (8) impose criminal penalties for damaging 10 or more protected computers during any one-year period. The bill also directs the U.S. Sentencing Commission to review and amend its guidelines and policy statements to reflect congressional intent to increase criminal penalties for computer fraud and authorizes additional appropriations in FY2007-FY201 1 to the U.S. Secret Service, the Department of Justice, and the FBI to investigate and prosecute criminal activity involving computers.

H.R. 948 (Markey)

Social Security Number Protection Act of 2007. This bill would amend title II (Old Age, Survivors and Disability Insurance) of the Social Security Act (SSA) to make it unlawful for any person to sell or purchase a Social Security number in a manner that violates a regulation promulgated by the Federal Trade Commission (FTC), except in certain circumstances.

H.R. 958 (Rush)

Data Accountability and Trust Act. This bill would require the Federal Trade Commission (FTC) to promulgate regulations requiring each person engaged in interstate commerce that owns or possesses electronic data containing personal information to establish security policies and procedures. The bill also authorizes the FTC to require a standard method or methods for destroying obsolete nonelectronic data. The bill also requires information brokers to submit their security policies to the FTC in conjunction with a security breach notification or on FTC request, requires the FTC to conduct or require an audit of security practices when information brokers are required to provide notification of such a breach, and authorizes additional audits after a breach. Additionally, the bill requires information brokers to (1) establish procedures to verify the accuracy of information that identifies individuals; (2) provide to individuals whose personal information it maintains a means to review it; (3) place notice on the Internet instructing individuals how to request access to such information; and (4) correct inaccurate information. Furthermore, the bill directs the FTC to require information brokers to establish measures which facilitate the auditing or retracing of access to, or transmissions of, electronic data containing personal information and prohibits information brokers from obtaining or disclosing personal information by false pretenses (pretexting). Additionally, the bill prescribes procedures for notification to the FTC and affected individuals of information security breaches. The bill also sets forth special notification requirements for breaches (1) by contractors who maintain or process electronic data containing personal information; (2) involving telecommunications and computer services; and (3) of health information. H.R. 958 preempts state information security laws.

H.R. 1008 (Bean)

Safeguarding America's Families by Enhancing and Reorganizing New and Efficient Technologies (SAFER NET) Act of 2007. This bill would require the Federal Trade Commission (FTC) to establish an Office of Internet Safety and Public Awareness to be headed by a Director. The bill requires the FTC, acting through the Office, to carry out a nationwide program to increase public awareness and education regarding Internet safety, that utilizes existing resources and efforts of all levels of government and other appropriate entities and that includes (1) evaluating and improving the efficiency of Internet safety efforts provided by such entities; (2) identifying and promoting best practices; (3) establishing and carrying out a national outreach and education campaign; (4) serving as the primary contact in the federal government and as a national clearinghouse for Internet safety information; (5) facilitating access to, and the exchange of, such information; (6) providing expert advice to the FTC; and (7) providing technical, financial, and other appropriate assistance to such entities.

H.R. 1307 (H. Wilson)

Veterans Identity Protection Act. This bill would establish as an independent office in the executive branch, the Office of Veterans Identity Protection Claims, headed by a Director, to receive, process, and pay claims for injuries suffered as a result of the unauthorized use, disclosure, or dissemination of identifying information stolen from the Department of Veterans Affairs (VA) or otherwise compromised as a result of a security breach. The bill also authorizes judicial review of claim determinations.

H.R. 1525 (Lofgren)

Internet Spyware (I-SPY) Prevention Act. This bill would amend the federal criminal code to prohibit intentionally accessing a protected computer without authorization, or exceeding authorized access, by causing a computer program or code to be copied onto the protected computer, and intentionally using that program or code (1) in furtherance of another federal criminal offense; (2) to obtain or transmit personal information (including a Social Security number or other government-issued identification number, a bank or credit card number, or an associated password or access code) with intent to defraud or injure a person or cause damage to a protected computer; or (3) to impair the security protection of that computer. The bill also prohibits any person from bringing a civil action under state law premised upon the defendant's violating this act. Additionally, the bill provides that this act does not prohibit any lawfully authorized investigative, protective, or intelligence activity of a law enforcement agency or a U.S. intelligence agency. The bill also authorizes appropriations to the Attorney General for prosecutions needed to discourage the use of spyware and the practices called phishing and pharming and expresses the sense of Congress that the Department of Justice should vigorously prosecute those who use spyware to commit crimes and those that conduct phishing and pharming scams.

H.R. 1860 (McCarthy)

Identity Theft Relief Act of 2007. This bill would amend the Internal Revenue Code of 1986 by adding Section 224, Expenses Related to Identity Theft. Section 224 allows an individual to deduct all ordinary and necessary expenses paid or incurred during the taxable year, not compensated for by insurance or otherwise, in connection with a qualified identity theft

S. 238 (Feinstein)

Social Security Number Misuse Prevention Act. This bill would amend the federal criminal code to prohibit the display, sale, or purchase of Social Security numbers without the affirmatively expressed consent of the individual, except in specified circumstances. It also directs the Attorney General to study and report to Congress on all the uses of Social Security numbers permitted, required, authorized, or excepted under any federal law, including the impact of such uses on privacy and data security. Additionally, the bill establishes a public records exception to the prohibition and directs the Comptroller General to study and report to Congress on Social Security numbers in public records. The bill also grants the Attorney General rulemaking authority to enforce this act's prohibition and to implement and clarify the permitted uses occurring as a result of an interaction between businesses, governments, or business and government. The bill also amends title II (Old Age, Survivors, and Disability Insurance) of the Social Security Act (SSA) to prohibit (1) the use of Social Security numbers on checks issued for payment by governmental agencies; and (2) inmate access to Social Security account numbers. The bill prohibits a commercial entity from requiring an individual to provide a Social Security number when purchasing a commercial good or service or denying an individual the good or service for refusing to provide that number, with exceptions. The bill both establishes civil and criminal penalties and extends civil monetary penalties for misuse of a Social Security number and provides for (1) criminal penalties under SSA title II for the misuse of a Social Security number; (2) civil actions and civil penalties against persons who violate this act; and (3) federal injunctive authority with respect to any violation by a public entity.

S. 239 (Feinstein)

Notification of Risk to Personal Data Act of 2007. This bill would require any federal agency or business entity engaged in interstate commerce that uses, accesses, transmits, stores, disposes of, or collects sensitive, personally identifiable information, following the discovery of a security breach, to notify (as specified): (1) any U.S. resident whose information may have been accessed or acquired; and (2) the owner or licensee of any such information the agency or business does not own or license. Additionally, the bill exempts (1) agencies from notification requirements for national security and law enforcement purposes and for security breaches that do not have a significant risk of resulting in harm, provided specified certification or notice is given to the U.S. Secret Service; and (2) business entities from notification requirements if the entity utilizes a security program that blocks unauthorized financial transactions and provides notice of a breach to affected individuals. The bill also requires notifications regarding security breaches under specified circumstances to the Secret Service, the Federal Bureau of Investigation, the United States Postal Inspection Service, and state attorneys general. Furthermore, the bill sets forth enforcement provisions and authorizes appropriations for costs incurred by the Secret Service to investigate and conduct risk assessments of security breaches.

S. 495 (Leahy)

Personal Data Privacy and Security Act of 2007. This bill would amend the federal criminal code to (1) make fraud in connection with the unauthorized access of sensitive personally identifiable information (in electronic or digital form) a predicate for racketeering charges; and (2) prohibit concealment of security breaches involving such information. The bill also directs the U.S. Sentencing Commission to review and amend its guidelines relating to fraudulent access to, or misuse of, digitized or electronic personally identifiable information (including identify theft). Additionally, the bill requires a data broker to (1) disclose to an individual, upon request, personal electronic records pertaining to such individual maintained for disclosure to third parties; and (2) maintain procedures for correcting the accuracy of such records. The bill also establishes standards for developing and implementing safeguards to protect the security of sensitive personally identifiable information. Additionally, the bill imposes upon business entities civil penalties for violations of such standards and requires such business entities to notify (1) any individual whose information has been accessed or acquired; and (2) the U.S. Secret Service if the number of individuals involved exceeds 10,000. Furthermore, the bill authorizes the Attorney General and state attorneys general to bring civil actions against business entities for violations of this act. The bill requires the Administrator of the General Services Administration in considering contract awards totaling more than $500,000, to evaluate (1) the data privacy and security program of a data broker; (2) program compliance; (3) the extent to which databases and systems have been compromised by security breaches; and (4) data broker responses to such breaches. The bill also requires federal agencies to conduct a privacy impact assessment before purchasing personally identifiable information from a data broker.

S. 699 (Allard)

Social Security Number Fraud and Identity Theft Prevention Act. This bill would amend the Immigration and Nationality Act to authorize the Secretary of the Department of Homeland Security (DHS), the Secretary of Labor, and the Attorney General to require an individual to provide the individual's Social Security account number for inclusion in any (1) record of the individual maintained by either such Secretary or the Attorney General; or (2) any application, document, or form provided under or required by the immigration laws. (Currently, the Attorney General is authorized to require any alien to provide a Social Security account number for inclusion in any record maintained by the Attorney General or the Bureau of Citizenship and Immigration Services.) The bill also requires the Commissioner of Social Security to provide the DHS Secretary with information regarding the name, date of birth, and address of each individual who used the same Social Security account number, and the name and address of the person reporting the earnings for each such individual. Additionally, the bill requires the Commissioner to provide such information to the DHS Secretary, in an electronic form, if more than one person reports earnings for an individual during a single tax year. The bill directs the Commissioner, at the DHS Secretary's request and expense, to perform and report on a search or manipulation of Social Security Commission records if the Secretary certifies that the purpose is to obtain information likely to assist in identifying individuals (and their employers) who are (1) using false names or Social Security account numbers; (2) sharing a single valid name and Social Security account number among multiple individuals; (3) using the Social Security account number of a person who is deceased, too young to work, or not authorized to work; or (4) otherwise engaged in a violation of the immigration laws. Furthermore, the bill declares inadmissible to receive visas and to be admitted to the United States any alien who falsely represents himself or herself to be a U.S. national for any purpose or benefit under immigration and nationality or any other federal or state law.

S. 806 (Pryor)

Consumer ID Protection and Security Act. This bill would authorize a consumer to place a security freeze on his or her credit report by making a request to a consumer credit reporting agency in writing, by telephone, or through a secure electronic connection if such a connection is made available by the agency, subject to specified requirements.

S. 1178 (Inouye)

Identity Theft Prevention Act. This bill would require any commercial entity or charitable, educational, or nonprofit organization that acquires, maintains, or uses sensitive personal information (covered entity) to develop, implement, maintain, and enforce a written program, containing administrative, technical, and physical safeguards, for the security of sensitive personal information it collects, maintains, sells, transfers, or disposes of. The bill defines "sensitive personal information" as an individual's name, address, or telephone number combined with at least one of the following relating to that individual: (1) the social security number or numbers derived from that number; (2) financial account or credit or debit card numbers combined with codes or passwords that permit account access, subject to exception; or (3) a state driver's license or resident identification number. The proposed act requires a covered entity (1) to report a security breach to the Federal Trade Commission (FTC); (2) if the entity determines that the breach creates a reasonable risk of identity theft, to notify each affected individual; and (3) if the breach involves at least 1,000 individuals, to notify all consumer reporting agencies specified in the Fair Credit Reporting Act. The bill also authorizes a consumer to place a security freeze on his or her credit report by making a request to a consumer credit reporting agency, and prohibits a reporting agency, when a freeze is in effect, from releasing the consumer's report for credit review purposes without the consumer's prior express authorization. Additionally, this legislation requires (1) the establishment of the Information Security and Consumer Privacy Advisory Committee; (2) a related crime study, including the correlation between methamphetamine use and identity theft crimes. Also, this bill treats any violation of this act as an unfair or deceptive act or practice under the Federal Trade Commission Act, requires enforcement under other specified laws, allows enforcement by state attorneys general, and preempts state laws requiring notification of affected individuals of security breaches.

S. 1202 (Sessions)

Personal Data Protection Act of 2007. This bill would require agencies and individuals who possess computerized data containing sensitive personal information to disclose security breaches that pose a significant risk of identity theft.

REFERENCES

[1] For further information, see New Data Security Laws Take Effect in Several States, 75 U.S.L.W. 25 (2007); Emily Farr, Identity Theft: Liability for Furnishers of Credit Information, 17 S.C. Law. 42 (2006); Sean C. Honeywill, Data Security and Data Breach Notification for Financial Institutions, 10 N.C. Banking Inst. 269 (2006); Kasim Razvi, To What Extent Should State Legislatures Regulate Business Practices as a Means of Preventing Identity Theft?, 15 Alb. L.J. Sci. & Tech. 639 (2005); Lilia Rode, Database Security Breach Notification Statutes: Does Placing the Responsibility on the True Victim Increase Data Security?, 43 Hous. L. Rev. 1597 (2007); Paul M. Schwartz and Edward J. Janger, Notification of Database Security Breaches, 105 Mich. L. Rev. 913 (2007); Kenneth M. Siegel, Protecting the Most Valuable Corporate Asset: Electronic Data, Identity Theft, Personal Information, and the Role of Data Security in the Information Age, 111 Penn St. L. Rev. 779 (2007); Gary M. Victor, Identity Theft, Its Environment and Proposals for Change, 18 Loy. Consumer L. Rev. 273 (2006); Kamaal Zaidi, Identity Theft and Consumer Protection: Finding Sensible Approaches to Safeguard Personal Data in the United States and Canada, 19 Loy. Consumer L. Rev. 99 (2007).

[2] To date, Colorado and Vermont have not enacted criminal identity theft statutes. For a complete list of state criminal identity theft statutes, see [http://www.consumer.gov/ idtheft /law_laws_state_criminal.htm].

[3] Cal. Penal Code §§ 530.5-530.7.

[4] La. Rev. Stat. Ann. § 14:67.16.

[5] Tex. Penal Code § 32.51; Va. Code Ann. §§ 18.2-186.3, et seq.; Md. Crim. Law Code Ann. § 8-301.

[6] Rev. Code Wash. § 9.35.020(3).

[7] Idaho Code Ann. § 18-3 126.

[8] Ore. Rev. Stat. § 165.055; Me. Rev. Stat. Ann. tit. 17-A, § 905-A.

[9] Mass. Gen. Laws ch. 266, § 37E; 720 Ill. Comp. Stat. 5/16G-10.

[10] Pursuant to recent Fair and Accurate Credit Transactions Act (FACT) amendments to the Fair Credit Reporting Act (FCRA), federal law may preempt some state provisions

relating to identity theft. P.L. 108-159, 117 Stat. 1952. For effective dates, see 68 Fed. Reg. 74,467 and 68 Fed. Reg.74,529 (December 24, 2003). The preemption of these provisions in state law does not apply to any state law in effect on the date of enactment of the Consumer Credit Reporting Reform Act of 1996. 15 U.S.C. 168 1t(b)(1)(E). The FCRA, as amended, includes several provisions aimed at preventing identity theft or assisting victims. These new provisions preempt similar state laws relating to the blocking of information in a consumer's credit report resulting from identity theft,with some exceptions. For more information see CRS Report RS21449, Fair Credit Reporting Act: Preemption of State Law, by Margaret Mikyung Lee.

[11] The states with enacted security freeze laws are: Arkansas, California, Colorado, Connecticut, Delaware, District of Columbia, Florida, Hawaii, Illinois, Indiana, Kansas, Kentucky, Louisiana, Maine, Maryland, Minnesota, Mississippi, Montana, Nevada, New Hampshire, New Jersey, New Mexico, New York, North Carolina, North Dakota, Oklahoma, Pennsylvania, Rhode Island, South Dakota, Texas, Utah, Vermont, Washington, West Virginia, Wisconsin, and Wyoming. See State Security Freeze Laws [http://www.consumersunion.org/campaigns/learnmore/003484indiv.html].

[12] Statement of Stuart K. Pratt, President and Chief Executive Officer, Consumer Data Industry Association, in Congress, Senate, Hearing Before the Senate Committee on Banking, Housing, and Urban Affairs, Examining The Financial Services Industry'Responsibilities and Role in Preventing Identity Theft and Protecting the Sensitive Financial Information of Their Customers, hearings, 109th Cong., 1st sess., September 22, 2005, available at [http://banking.senate.gov/_files/pratt.pdf]. Hearing available online at [http://banking.senate.gov/index.cfm? Fuseaction= Hearings. Detail&HearingID= 170].

[13] 2007 Ark. Act 391; Haw. Rev. Stat. Ann. §§ 489P-3 - 489P-5; 2006 Kan. Sess. Laws ch. 149; S.B. 3034, 2007 Leg., Reg. Sess (Miss. 2007) (approved by Governor, April 21, 2007); S.D. Codified Laws § 54-15-1, et seq.; Tex. Bus. & Com. Code §§ 20.03 1-20.04; Wash. Rev. Code §§ 19.182.170 - 19.182-200.

[14] Cal. Civ. Code §§ 1785.11.2-1785.11.6; Colo. Rev. Stat. § 12-14.3-102, et seq.; D.C. Code §§ 3861-3864; Fla. Stat. § 501.005; 815 Ill. Comp. Stat. 505/2MM; Ky. Rev. Stat. §§ 367.363 - 367.370; La. Rev. Stat. § 9:3571.1 (H) to (Y); Me. Rev. Stat. Ann. tit. 10 § 1313- C; Minn. Stat. § 13C.016; 2007 Mont. Laws ch. 138; Nev. Rev. Stat. § 598C.010, et seq.; Rev. Stat. N.H. §§ 359-B:22 et seq.; 2007 N.M. Laws ch. 106; N.Y. Gen. Bus. Law 380-a, et seq; N.C. Gen. Stat. § 75-60, et seq.; H.B. 1417, 60th Leg. Assem. (N.D. 2007) (to be codified at N.D. Cent. Code ch. 5 1-33); Okla. Stat. tit. 24, § 149, et seq.; 2006 Pa. Laws ch. 163; R.I. Gen. Laws § 6-48-1 et seq.; Tex. Bus. & Com. Code §§ 20.03 1-20.04; Utah Code Ann. § 13-42-102 and §§ 13-45-201 - 13-45-205; 2007 W. Va. Acts ch. 45; Wis. Stat. § 100.54; 2007 Wyo. Sess. Laws Act 76.

[15] Wis. Stat. § 100.54.

[16] Vt. Stat. Ann. tit. 9, § 2480h.

[17] 2006 Kan. Sess. Laws ch. 149.

[18] See, e.g., Cal. Civ. Code § 1785.11.2; Conn. Gen. Stat. § 36a-701a; and D.C. Code § 28- 3862, specifying a maximum ten dollar charge.

[19] Utah Code Ann. § 13-45-204

[20] For further information, see [http://www.ftc.gov/bcp/edu/microsites/idtheft/ law-enforcement/credit-info-blocking.html].

[21] Ala. Code § 13A-8-200; Colo. Rev. Stat. §§ 12-14.3-106.5 to 12-14.3-109; Idaho Code § 28-51-102; Rev. Code Wash. § 19.182.160.

[22] Cal. Civ. Code § 1788.18.

[23] . For further information, see CRS Report RL303 18, The Social Security Number: Legal Developments Affecting Its Collection, Disclosure, and Confidentiality, by Kathleen S. Swendiman.

[24] Mich. Comp. Laws. § 445.84.

[25] Cal. Civ. Code §§ 1798.85-1798.97.

[26] R.I. Gen. Laws § 6-13-17

In: Identity Theft Breaches
Editor: Cary S. Logweller

ISBN 978-1-60692-227-9

Chapter 7

REMEDIES AVAILABLE TO VICTIMS OF IDENTITY THEFT*

Gina Marie Stevens
Legislative Attorney, American Law Division

ABSTRACT

According to the Federal Trade Commission, identity theft is the most common complaint from consumers in all fifty states, and complaints regarding identity theft have grown for four consecutive years. Victims of identity theft may incur damaged credit records, unauthorized charges on credit cards, and unauthorized withdrawals from bank accounts. Sometimes, victims must change their telephone numbers or even their social security numbers. Victims may also need to change addresses that were falsified by the impostor. With media reports of information security breaches increasing, concerns about new cases of widespread identity theft have received significant attention in Congress.

This report provides an overview of the federal laws that could assist victims of identity theft with purging inaccurate information from their credit records and removing unauthorized charges from credit accounts, as well as federal laws that impose criminal penalties on those who assume another person's identity through the use of fraudulent identification documents. This report will be updated as events warrant.

INTRODUCTION[1]

According to the Federal Trade Commission, identity theft is the most common complaint from consumers in all 50 states, and complaints regarding identity theft have grown for 4 consecutive years.[2] Victims of identity theft may incur damaged credit records, unauthorized charges on credit cards, and unauthorized withdrawals from bank accounts. Sometimes, victims must change their telephone numbers or even their social security numbers. Victims may also need to change addresses that were falsified by the impostor.

* Excerpted from CRS Report RL31 919, dated January 23, 2007.

With media reports of information security breaches increasing, concerns about new cases of potentially widespread identity theft have received significant attention in Congress.[3]

This report provides an overview of the federal laws that could assist victims of identity theft with purging inaccurate information from their credit records and removing unauthorized charges from credit accounts, as well as federal laws that impose criminal penalties on those who assume another person's identity through the use of fraudulent identification documents. This report will be updated as warranted.

FEDERAL LAWS RELATED TO IDENTITY THEFT

Identity Theft Assumption and Deterrence Act. While not exclusively aimed at consumer identity theft, the Identity Theft Assumption Deterrence Act prohibits fraud in connection with identification documents under a variety of circumstances.[4] Certain offenses under the statute relate directly to consumer identity theft, and impostors could be prosecuted under the statute. For example, the statute makes it a federal crime, under certain circumstances,[5] to knowingly and without lawful authority produce an identification document[6] or false identification document; or to knowingly possess an identification document that is or appears to be an identification document of the United States which is stolen or produced without lawful authority knowing that such document was stolen or produced without such authority.[7] It is also a federal crime to knowingly transfer or use, without lawful authority, a means of identification of another person with the intent to commit, or aid or abet, any unlawful activity that constitutes a violation of federal law, or that constitutes a felony under any applicable state or local law.[8]

The punishment for offenses involving fraud related to identification documents varies depending on the specific offense and the type of document involved.[9] For example, a fine or imprisonment of up to 15 years may be imposed for using the identification of another person with the intent to commit any unlawful activity under state law, if, as a result of the offense, the person committing the offense obtains anything of value totaling $1,000 or more during any one-year period.[10] Other offenses carry terms of imprisonment up to three years.[11] However, if the offense is committed to facilitate a drug trafficking crime or in connection with a crime of violence, the term of imprisonment could be up to twenty years.[12] Offenses committed to facilitate an action of international terrorism are punishable by terms of imprisonment up to twenty-five years.[13]

Identity Theft Penalty Enhancement Act

The Identity Theft Penalty Enhancement Act was signed on July 15, 2004, (P.L. 108-275). The act amends Title 18 of the United States Code to define and establish penalties for aggravated identity theft and makes changes to the existing identity theft provisions of Title 18. Under the new law, aggravated identity theft occurs when a person "knowingly transfers, possess, or uses, without lawful authority, a means of identification of another person" during and in relation to the commission of certain enumerated felonies.[14] The penalty for aggravated identity theft is a term of imprisonment of two years in addition to the punishment provided for the original felony committed. Offenses committed in conjunction with certain terrorism offenses are subject to an additional term of imprisonment of five years. The act also directs the United States Sentencing Commission to "review and amend its guidelines and its policy statements to ensure that the guideline offense levels and enhancements appropriately punish identity theft offenses involving an abuse of position" adhering to certain requirements outlined in the legislation.[15]

In addition to increasing penalties for identity theft, the act authorized appropriations to the Justice Department "for the investigation and prosecution of identity theft and related credit card and other fraud cases constituting felony violations of law, $2,000,000 for FY2005 and $2,000,000 for each of the 4 succeeding fiscal years."[16]

Fair Credit Reporting Act

While the Fair Credit Reporting Act (FCRA) does not directly address identity theft, it could offer victims assistance in having negative information resulting from unauthorized charges or accounts removed from their credit files.[17] The purpose of the FCRA is "to require that consumer reporting agencies adopt reasonable procedures for meeting the needs of commerce for consumer credit, personnel, insurance, and other information in a manner which is fair and equitable to the consumer, with regard to the confidentiality, accuracy, relevancy, and proper utilization of such information."[18] The FCRA outlines a consumer's rights in relation to his or her credit report, as well as permissible uses for credit reports and disclosure requirements. In addition, the FCRA imposes a duty on consumer reporting agencies to ensure that the information they report is accurate, and requires persons who furnish information to ensure that the information they furnish is accurate.

The FCRA allows consumers to file suit for violations of the act, which could include the disclosure of inaccurate information about a consumer by a credit reporting agency.[19] A consumer who is a victim of identity theft could file suit against a credit reporting agency for the agency's failure to verify the accuracy of information contained in the report and the agency's disclosure of inaccurate information as a result of the consumer's stolen identity. Under the FCRA, as recently amended, a consumer may file suit not later than the earlier of two years after the date of discovery by the plaintiff of the violation that is the basis for such liability, or five years after the date on which the violation occurred.[20]

Fair and Accurate Credit Transactions (FACT) Act of 2003

The FACT Act, signed on December 4, 2003, includes, inter alia, a number of amendments to the Fair Credit Reporting Act aimed at preventing identity theft and assisting victims.[21] Generally, these new provisions mirror laws passed by state legislatures and create a national standard for addressing consumer concerns with regard to identity theft and other types of fraud.[22]

Credit card issuers, who operate as users of consumer credit reports, are required, under a new provision of the FCRA, to follow certain procedures when the issuer receives a request for an additional or replacement card within a short period of time following notification of a change of address for the same account.[23] In a further effort to prevent identity theft, other new provisions require the truncation of credit card account numbers on electronically printed receipts,[24] and, upon request, the truncation of social security numbers on credit reports provided to a consumer.[25]

Consumers who have been victims of identity theft, or expect that they may become victims, are now able to have fraud alerts placed in their files.[26] Pursuant to the new provisions, a consumer may request a fraud alert from one consumer reporting agency and that agency is required to notify the other nationwide consumer reporting agencies of the existence of the alert. In general, fraud alerts are to be maintained in the file for 90 days, but a consumer may request an extended alert which is maintained for up to seven years. The fraud alert becomes a part of the consumer's credit file and is thus passed along to all users of the report. The alert must also be included with any credit score generated using the consumer's file, and must be referred to other consumer reporting agencies.[27]

In addition to the fraud alert, victims of identity theft may also have information resulting from the crime blocked from their credit reports.[28] After the receipt of appropriate proof of the identity of the consumer, a copy of an identity theft report, the identification of the alleged fraudulent information, and a statement by the consumer that the information is not information relating to any transaction conducted by the consumer, a consumer reporting agency must block all such information from being reported and must notify the furnisher of the information in question that it may be the result of identity theft. Requests for the blocking of information must also be referred to other consumer reporting agencies.[29]

Victims of identity theft are also allowed to request information about the alleged crime. A business entity is required, upon request and subject to verification of the victim's identity, to provide copies of application and business transaction records evidencing any transaction alleged to be a result of identity theft to the victim or to any law enforcement agency investigating the theft and authorized by the victim to take receipt of the records in question.[30]

Fair Credit Billing Act

The Fair Credit Billing Act (FCBA) is not an identity theft statute per se, but it does provide consumers with an opportunity to receive an explanation and proof of charges that may have been made by an impostor and to have unauthorized charges removed from their accounts. The purpose of the FCBA is "to protect the consumer against inaccurate and unfair credit billing and credit card practices."[31] The law defines and establishes a procedure for resolving billing errors in consumer credit transactions. For purposes of the FCBA, a "billing error" includes unauthorized charges, charges for goods or services not accepted by the consumer or delivered to the consumer, and charges for which the consumer has asked for an explanation or written proof of purchase.[32]

Under the FCBA, consumers are able to file a claim with the creditor to have billing errors resolved. Until the alleged billing error is resolved, the consumer is not required to pay the disputed amount, and the creditor may not attempt to collect, any part of the disputed amount, including related finance charges or other charges.[33] The act sets forth dispute resolution procedures and requires an investigation into the consumer's claims. If the creditor determines that the alleged billing error did occur, the creditor is obligated to correct the billing error and credit the consumer's account with the disputed amount and any applicable finance charges.[34]

Electronic Fund Transfer Act

Similar to the Fair Credit Billing Act, the Electronic Fund Transfer Act is not an identity theft statute per se, but it does provide consumers with a mechanism for challenging unauthorized transactions and having their accounts recredited in the event of an error. The purpose of the Electronic Fund Transfer Act (EFTA) is to "provide a basic framework establishing the rights, liabilities, and responsibilities of participants in electronic fund transfer systems."[35] Among other things, the EFTA limits a consumer's liability for unauthorized electronic fund transfers. If the consumer notifies the financial institution within two business days after learning of the loss or theft of a debt card or other device used to make electronic transfers, the consumer's liability is limited to the lesser of $50 or the amount of the unauthorized transfers that occurred before notice was given to the financial institution.[36]

Additionally, financial institutions are required to provide a consumer with documentation of all electronic fund transfers initiated by the consumer from an electronic terminal. If a financial institution receives, within 60 days after providing such documentation, an oral or written notice from the consumer indicating the consumer's belief that the documentation provided contains an error, the financial institution must investigate the alleged error, determine whether an error has occurred, and report or mail the results of the investigation and determination to the consumer within 10 business days.[37] The notice from the consumer to the financial institution must identify the name and account number of the consumer; indicate the consumer's belief that the documentation contains an error and the amount of the error; and set forth the reasons for the consumer's belief that an error has occurred.[38]

In the event that the financial institution determines that an error has occurred, the financial institution must correct the error within one day of the determination in accordance with the provisions relating to the consumer's liability for unauthorized charges.[39] The financial institution may provisionally recredit the consumer's account for the amount alleged to be in error pending the conclusion of its investigation and its determination of whether an error has occurred, if it is unable to complete the investigation within 10 business days.[40]

References

[1] This report was originally prepared by Angie A. Welborn, Legislative Attorney.

[2] Federal Trade Commission, ID Theft Clearinghouse Data, January 25, 2006, [http://www.consumer.gov/idtheft/pdf/clearinghouse_2005.pdf]. CY 2005 is the last year for which data are currently available.

[3] Legislation that has been introduced in response to the increase in information security breaches is discussed in CRS Report RL33273, Data Security: Federal Legislative Approaches, by Gina Marie Stevens. For more information on security breaches, see

CRS Report RL33 199, Personal Data Security Breaches: Context and Incident Summaries, by Rita Tehan.

[4] 18 U.S.C. 1028. The statute lists several actions that constitute fraud in connection with identification documents. However, for the purposes of this report, they do not all relate to consumer-related identity theft, i.e. situations where a consumer's Social Security number or driver's license number may be stolen and used to establish credit accounts by an impostor.

[5] According to the statute, the prohibitions listed apply when "the identification document or false identification document is or appears to be issued by or under the authority of the United States or the document-making implement is designed or suited for making such an identification document or false identification document;" the document is presented with the intent to defraud the United States; or "either the production, transfer, possession, or use prohibited by this section is in or affects interstate or foreign commerce, including the transfer of a document by electronic means, or the means of identification, identification document, false identification document, or document-making implement is transported in the mail in the course of the production, transfer, possession, or use prohibited by this section." 18 U.S.C. 1028(c).

[6] Identification document is defined as "a document made or issued by or under the authority of the United States Government, a State, political subdivision of a State, a foreign government, political subdivision of a foreign government, an international governmental or an internal quasi-governmental organization which, when completed with information concerning a particular individual, is of a type intended or commonly accepted for the purpose of identification of individuals." 18 U.S.C. 1028(d)(2). Identification documents include Social Security cards, birth certificates, driver's licenses, and personal identification cards.

[7] 18 U.S.C. 1028(a)(1) and (2).

[8] 18 U.S.C. 1028(a)(7).

[9] 18 U.S.C. 1028(b).

[10] 18 U.S.C. 1028(b)(1)(D).

[11] 18 U.S.C. 1028(b)(2).

[12] 18 U.S.C. 1028(b)(3).

[13] 18 U.S.C. 1028(b)(4).

[14] P.L. 108-275, Sec. 2, to be codified at 18 U.S.C. 1028A. Offenses that could give rise to aggravated identity theft are enumerated in this section, and include offenses relating to theft of public money, property, or rewards; theft, embezzlement, or misapplication by a bank officer or employee; theft from employee benefit plans; false personation of citizenship; false statements in connection with the acquisition of a firearm; mail, bank, and wire fraud; obtaining consumer information by false pretenses; and certain immigration violations. The list of enumerated offenses will be codified at 18 U.S.C. 1028A(c).

[15] P.L. 108-275, Sec. 5.

[16] P.L. 108-275, Sec. 6.

[17] For more information on a consumer's rights under the FCRA, see CRS Report RL3 1666, Fair Credit Reporting Act: Rights and Responsibilities, by Angie A. Welborn.

[18] 15 U.S.C. 168 1(b).

[19] 15 U.S.C. 1681n; 15 U.S.C. 1681o.
[20] P.L. 108-159, Section 156.
[21] P.L. 108-159. For effective dates, see 68 FR 74467 and 68 FR 74529 (December 24, 2003).
[22] Generally, many of these new federal provisions preempt similar state laws. For more information on the preemptive effects of the Fair Credit Reporting Act, see CRS Report RS21449, Fair Credit Reporting Act: Preemption of State Law, by Angie A. Welborn.
[23] P.L. 108-159, Section 114.
[24] P.L. 108-159, Section 113.
[25] P.L. 108-159, Section 115.
[26] P.L. 108-159, Section 112.
[27] P.L. 108-159, Section 153.
[28] P.L. 108-159, Section 152.
[29] P.L. 108-159, Section 153.
[30] P.L. 108-159, Section 151.
[31] 15 U.S.C. 160 1(a).
[32] 15 U.S.C. 1666(b); 12 C.F.R. 226.13(a).
[33] 15 U.S.C. 1666(c); 12 C.F.R. 226.13(d)(1).
[34] 15 U.S.C. 1666(a); 12 C.F.R. 226.13(e).
[35] 15 U.S.C. 1693(b).
[36] 15 U.S.C. 1693g(a), 12 C.F.R. 205.6(b)(1).
[37] 15 U.S.C. 1693f(a), 12 C.F.R. 205.11(b) and (c).
[38] Id.
[39] 15 U.S.C. 1693f(b).
[40] 15 U.S.C. 1693f(c), 12 C.F.R. 205.11(c).

In: Identity Theft Breaches
Editor: Cary S. Logweller

ISBN 978-1-60692-227-9

Chapter 8

To Buy or Not to Buy: Identity Theft Spawns New Products and Services to Help Minimize Risk

Recent headlines about data breaches and losses of personal information have prompted many companies to advertise products or services to help consumers prevent or minimize their risk of identity theft.

The Federal Trade Commission (FTC), the nation's consumer protection agency, says before you pay for an identity theft prevention product or service, make sure you understand exactly what you're paying for. Many people find value and convenience in paying an outside party to help them exercise their rights and protect their information. At the same time, some rights and protections you have under federal or state laws can help you protect your identity and recover from identity theft at no cost. Knowing and understanding your rights can help you determine whether — or which — commercial products or services may be appropriate for you.

Fraud Alerts

A *fraud alert* is a signal placed in your credit report or credit file to warn potential creditors that they must use what the law calls "reasonable policies and procedures" to verify your identity before they issue credit in your name. Fraud alerts may be effective at stopping someone from unts in your name, but they may not prevent the misuse of your existing accounts.

Under the federal Fair Credit Reporting Act (FCRA), you may be entitled to two kinds of free fraud alerts: *initial* and *extended*.

You may ask a consumer reporting company to place an *initial* fraud alert on your credit report if you suspect you have been, or are about to be, a victim of identity theft. This may be appropriate after your wallet or another source of personal information is lost or stolen. An *initial* fraud alert is good for 90 days, and can be renewed when appropriate. To place an *initial* fraud alert, call the toll-free fraud number of any one of the three national consumer reporting companies. The company you call is required to contact the other two; they, in turn, will place an alert on their versions of your report. Expect to receive a confirmation from each of the companies.

Equifax: 1 -800-525-6285
Experian: 1 -888-EXPERIAN (397-3742)
TransUnion: 1 -800-680-7289

When you place an initial fraud alert on your credit report, you're entitled to order one free credit report from each of the consumer reporting companies; if you ask, only the last four digits of your Social Security number will appear on your reports.

If you have been a victim of identity theft, you may ask for an extended alert, which stays on your credit report for seven years. To get an extended fraud alert placed on your report, you will need to contact one of the credit bureaus, and provide an Identity Theft Report, such as a police report or other report to a law enforcement agency, including a report to the FTC. If your credit report has an extended alert, potential creditors must contact you in person, or by phone or some other method you have provided before they can issue credit in your name. When you place an extended alert on your credit report, you're entitled to two free credit reports from each of the consumer reporting companies within 12 months. In addition, the consumer reporting companies must remove your name from marketing lists for pre-screened offers of credit for five years — unless you ask them to put your name back on the list.

Credit Freezes

A credit freeze allows you to restrict access to your credit report. If you place a freeze on your report, potential creditors and certain other people or businesses can't get access to it unless you lift the freeze temporarily or permanently. For more information about credit freezes, check with your state attorney general's office or visit www.naag.org.

Limiting access to your credit report makes it more difficult for identity thieves to open new accounts in your name. That's because most creditors will need to view a credit file before opening a new account; if they can't see the file, they may not extend the credit. Still, a credit freeze may not prevent the misuse of your existing accounts or certain other types of identity theft.

A credit freeze is different from a fraud alert in a number of ways. A freeze generally stops all access to your credit report, while a fraud alert permits creditors to get your report as long as they take steps to verify your identity. The availability of a credit freeze depends on state law or a consumer reporting company's policies; fraud alerts are federal rights intended for consumers who believe they may have been, or actually have been, victims of identity theft. And some states charge a fee for placing or removing a freeze, although it is free to place or remove a fraud alert.

Most states have laws that allow consumers to place a credit freeze with consumer reporting companies. In many of these states, any consumer can freeze their credit file; in others, only identity theft victims can freeze their files. The cost of placing a credit freeze and the lead times vary.

In many states, credit freezes are free for identity theft victims; other consumers typically are charged about $10 per credit reporting company. Contact your state attorney general for the particulars of your state's freeze laws. To place a freeze, contact each of the nationwide consumer reporting companies because a credit freeze placed at one company is not referred to the other companies. And be aware that the three major credit reporting companies have begun offering credit freezes directly to consumers — for a fee — regardless of whether their state has a freeze law.

Placing a credit freeze does not affect your credit score, keep you from getting your free annual credit report, or keep you from buying your credit report or score. It doesn't prevent you from opening a new account yourself, applying for a job, renting an apartment, or buying insurance, either. In these situations, the business usually needs to review your credit report. You can ask the consumer reporting company to lift your credit freeze temporarily, or remove it altogether. But the cost and lead times to lift or remove a freeze vary, so it's wise to check with your state authorities or with a consumer reporting company in advance if possible.

Free Credit Reports

Federal law gives every consumer the right to one free credit report from each nationwide consumer reporting company every 12 months. Staggering these reports — that is, getting a report from a different company every few months — can help you monitor activity on your credit reports. For more information, or to request your free credit reports, visit www.annualcreditreport.com..

Identity Theft Protection Products and Services for Sale

Identity theft protection companies offer a range of products and services for sale. Some allow you to "lock," "flag," or "freeze" your credit reports. Often, the companies advertising these services simply are offering to place a fraud alert or credit freeze on your report. These services also may renew or update your alerts or freezes utomatically, as long as you continue to pay. Under the law, initial fraud alerts and renewals are available for free if you have reason to believe you have been — or are about to be — a victim of identity theft.

Some companies, including consumer reporting companies, offer subscriptions to credit monitoring services. These services track your credit report, and generally send you an email alert reflecting recent activity, such as an inquiry or new account. Typically, the more frequent or more detailed the report, the more expensive the service.

Some companies offer services to help you rebuild your identity in the event of identity theft. Typically, these services operate by obtaining a limited power of attorney from you, which enables the company to act on your behalf when dealing with consumer reporting companies, creditors, or other information sources.

Many companies may offer additional services, including removing your name from mailing lists or pre-screened offers of credit or insurance, representing your legal interests, "guaranteeing" reimbursement in the event you experience a loss due to identity theft, or helping you track down whether your personal information has been exposed online. Before you agree to pay for any of these services, read the fine print. You can get some of them yourself at no cost: for example, if you decide you don't want to receive pre-screened offers of credit and insurance, you can opt out for five years or permanently by calling toll-free 1 - 888-5-OPTOUT (1-888-567-8688) or visiting www.optoutprescreen.com.

The FTC has a library of resources to help victims of identity theft report the crime and take steps to recover their identity. Visit www.ftc.gov/idtheft.

The FTC works for the consumer to prevent fraudulent, deceptive, and unfair business practices in the marketplace and to provide information to help consumers spot, stop, and avoid them. To file a complaint or to get free information on consumer issues, visit www.ftc.gov or call toll-free, 1-877-FTCHELP (1-877-382-4357); TTY: 1-866-653-4261. The FTC enters Internet, telemarketing, identity theft, and other fraud-related complaints into Consumer Sentinel, a secure online database available to hundreds of civil and criminal law enforcement agencies in the U.S. and abroad.

In: Identity Theft Breaches
Editor: Cary S. Logweller
ISBN 978-1-60692-227-9

Chapter 9

FTC Facts for Consumers

Your Access to Free Credit Reports

The Fair Credit Reporting Act (FCRA) requires each of the nationwide consumer reporting companies — Equifax, Experian, and TransUnion — to provide you with a free copy of your credit report, at your request, once every 12 months.

The FCRA promotes the accuracy and privacy of information in the files of the nation's consumer reporting companies. The Federal Trade Commission (FTC), the nation's consumer protection agency, enforces the FCRA with respect to consumer reporting companies.

A credit report includes information on where you live, how you pay your bills, and whether you've been sued or arrested, or have filed for bankruptcy. Nationwide consumer reporting companies sell the information in your report to creditors, insurers, employers, and other businesses that use it to evaluate your applications for credit, insurance, employment, or renting a home.

Here are the details about your rights under the FCRA and the Fair and Accurate Credit Transactions (FACT) Act, which established the free annual credit report program.

Q: How Do I Order My Free Report?

A: The three nationwide consumer reporting companies have set up a central website, a toll-free telephone number, and a mailing address through which you can order your free annual report.

To order, visit annualcreditreport.com, call 1-877-322-8228, or complete the Annual Credit Report Request Form and mail it to: Annual Credit Report Request Service, P.O. Box 105281, Atlanta, GA 30348-528 1. The form is on the back of this brochure; or you can print it from ftc.gov/credit. Do not contact the three nationwide consumer reporting companies individually. They are providing free annual credit reports only through annualcreditreport.com, 1-877-322-8228, and Annual Credit Report Request Service, P.O. Box 105281, Atlanta, GA 30348-5281.

You may order your reports from each of the three nationwide consumer reporting companies at the same time, or you can order your report from each of the companies one at a time. The law allows you to order one free copy of your report from each of the nationwide consumer reporting companies every 12 months.

A WARNING ABOUT "IMPOSTER" WEBSITES

Only one website is authorized to fill orders for the free annual credit report you are entitled to under law — annualcreditreport.com. Other websitesthat claim to offer "free credit reports," "free credit scores," or "free credit monitoring" are not part of the legally mandated free annual credit report program. In some cases, the "free" product comes with strings attached. For example, some sites sign you up for a supposedly "free" service that converts to one you have to pay for after a trial period. If you don't cancel during the trial period, you may be unwittingly agreeing to let the company start charging fees to your credit card.

Some "imposter" sites use terms like "free report" in their names; others have URLs that purposely misspell annualcreditreport.com in the hope that you will mistype the name of the official site. Some of these "imposter" sites direct you to other sites that try to sell you something or collect your personal information.

> Only one Website is authorized to fill orders for the free annual credit report you are entitled to under law — annualcreditreport.com

Annualcreditreport.com and the nationwide consumer reporting companies will not send you an email asking for your of your file, eachpersonal information. If you get an email, see a pop-up ad, or get a phone call from someone claiming to be from annualcreditreport. com or any of the three nationwide consumer reporting companies, do not reply or click on any link in the message. It's probably a scam. Forward any such email to the FTC at spam@uce.gov.

Q: What information do I need to provide to get my free report?

A: You need to provide your name, address, Social Security number, and date of birth. If you have moved in the last two years, you may have to provide your previous address. To maintain the security credit report. Inaccurate information like that ationwide consumer reporting company may ask you for some information that only you would know, like the amount of your monthly mortgage payment. Each company may ask you for different information because the information each has in your file may come from different sources.

Q: Why do I want a copy of my credit report? A: Your credit report has information that affects whether you can get a loan — and how much you will have to pay to borrow money. You want a copy of your credit report to:

- make sure the information is accurate, complete, and up-to-date before you apply for a loan for a major purchase like a house or car, buy insurance, or apply for a job
- help guard against identity theft. That's when someone uses your personal information — like your name, your ocial Security number, or your credit card number — to commit fraud. Identity thieves may use your information to open a new credit card account in your name. Then, when they don't pay the bills, the delinquent

account is reported on your could affect your ability to get credit, insurance, or even a job.

Q: How long does it take to get my report after I order it?

A: If you request your report online at annualcreditreport.com, you should be able to access it immediately. If you order your report bycalling toll-free 1-877-322-8228, your report will be processed and mailed to you within 15 days. If you order your report by mail using the Annual Credit Report Request Form, your request will be processed and mailed to you within 15 days of receipt.

Whether you order your report online, by phone, or by mail, it may take longer to receive your report if the nationwide consumer reporting company needs more information to verify your identity.

There also may be times when the nationwide consumer reporting companies receive a high volume of requests for credit reports. If that happens, you may be asked to re-submit your request. Or, you may be told that your report will be mailed to you sometime after 15 days from your request. If either of these events occurs, the nationwide consumer reporting companies will let you know.

Q: Are there any other situations where I might be eligible for a free report?

A: Under federal law, you're entitled to a free report if a company takes adverse action against you, such as denying your application for credit, insurance, or employment, and you ask for your report within 60 days of receiving notice of the action. The notice will give you the name, address, and phone number of the consumer reporting company. You're also entitled to one free report a year if you're unemployed and plan to look for a job within 60 days; if you're on welfare; or if your report is inaccurate because of fraud, including identity theft. Otherwise, a consumer reporting company may charge you up to$10.50 for another copy of your report within a 12-month period.

> If you request your report online at annualcreditreport. com, you should be able to access it immediately.

To buy a copy of your report, contact:

Equifax:1-800-685-1 111; equifax.com
Experian: 1-888-397-3742; experian.com
TransUnion: 1-800-916-8800; transunion.com

Under state law, consumers in Colorado, Georgia, Maine, Maryland, Massachusetts, New Jersey, and Vermont already have free access to their credit reports.

Q: Should I order a report from each of the three nationwide consumer reporting companies?

A: It's up to you. Because nationwide consumer reporting companies get their information from different sources, the information in your report from one company may not reflect all, or the same, information in your reports from the other two companies. That's not to say that the information in any of your reports is necessarily inaccurate; it just may be different.

Q: Should I order my reports from all three of the nationwide consumer reporting companies at the same time?

A: You may order one, two, or all three reports at the same time, or you may stagger your requests. It's your choice. Some financial advisors say staggering your requests during a 12-month period may be a good way to keep an eye on the accuracy and completeness of the information in your reports.

Q: What if I find errors — either inaccuracies or incomplete information — in my credit report?

A: Under the FCRA, both the consumer reporting company and the information provider (that is, the person, company, or organization that provides information about you to a consumer reporting company) are responsible for correcting inaccurate or incomplete information in your report. To take full advantage of your rights under this law, contact the consumer reporting company count as your annual free report under the FACT Act.) If an item is changed or deleted, the consumer reporting company cannot put the disputed information back in your file unless the information provider verifies that it is accurate and complete. The consumer reporting company also must send you written notice that includes the name, address, and phone number of the information provider.

Tell the consumer reporting company, in writing, what information you think is inaccurate.

Tell the creditor or other information provider in writing that you dispute an item. Many providers specify an address for disputes.and the information provider.

Consumer reporting companies must investigate the items in question — usually within 30 days unless they consider your dispute frivolous. They also must forward all the relevant data you provide about the inaccuracy to the organization that provided the information. After the information provider receives notice of a dispute from the consumer reporting company, it must investigate, review the relevant information, and report the results back to the consumer reporting company. If the information provider finds the disputed information is inaccurate, it must notify all three nationwide consumer reporting companies so they can correct the information in your file.

When the investigation is complete, the consumer reporting company must give you the written results and a free copy of your report if the dispute results in a change. (This free report does not If the provider reports the item to a consumer report under the FACT Act.) If an item is changed or deleted, the consumer reporting company cannot put the disputed information back in your file unless the information provider verifies that it is accurate and complete. The consumer reporting company also must send you written notice that includes the name, address, and phone number of the information provider.

Tell the creditor or other information provider in writing that you dispute an item. Many providers specify an address for disputes. reporting company, it must include a notice of your dispute. And if you are correct — that is, if the information is found to be inaccurate — the information provider may not report it again.

Q: What can I do if the consumer reporting company or information provider won't correct the information I dispute?

A: If an investigation doesn't resolve your dispute with the consumer reporting company, you can ask that a statement of the dispute be included in your file and in future reports. You also can ask the consumer reporting company to provide your statement to anyone who received a copy of your report in the recent past. You can expect to pay a fee for this service.

If you tell the information provider that you dispute an item, a notice of your dispute must be included any time the information provider reports the item to a consumer reporting company.

> Tell the consumer reporting company, in writing, what information you think is inaccurate.

Q: How long can a consumer reporting company report negative information?

A: A consumer reporting company can report most accurate negative information for seven years and bankruptcy information for 10 years. There is no time limit on reporting information about criminal convictions; information reported in response to your application for a job that pays more than $75,000 a year; and information reported because you've applied for more than $150,000 worth of credit or life insurance. Information about a lawsuit or an unpaid judgment against you can be reported for seven years or until the statute of limitations runs out, whichever is longer.

Q: Can anyone else can get a copy of my credit report?

A: The FCRA specifies who can access your credit report. Creditors, insurers, employers, and other businesses that use the information in your report to evaluate your applications for credit, insurance, employment, or renting a home are among those that have a legal right to access your report.:

Q:Can my employer get my credit report? A: Your employer can get a copy of your credit report only if you agree. A consumer reporting company may not provide information about you to your employer, or to a prospective employer, without your written consent.

For More Information

The FTC works for the consumer to prevent fraudulent, deceptive, and unfair business practices in the marketplace and to provide information to help consumers spot, stop, and avoid them. To learn more about credit issues and protecting your personal information, visit ftc.gov/credit.

To file a complaint or to get free information on other consumer issues, visit ftc.gov or call toll-free, 1-877-FTC-HELP (1-877-382-4357); TTY: 1-866-653-4261. The FTC enters Internet, telemarketing, identity theft, and other fraud-related complaints into Consumer Sentinel, a secure online database available to hundreds of civil and criminal law enforcement agencies in the U.S. and abroad.

EQUIFAX experian TransUnion

Annual Credit Report Request Form

You have the right to get a free copy of your credit file disclosure, commonly called a credit report, once every 12 months, from each of the nationwide consumer credit reporting companies - Equifax, Experian and TransUnion.

For instant access to your free credit report, visit www.annualcreditreport.com.

For more information on obtaining your free credit report, visit www.annualcreditreport.com or call 1-877-322-8228.

Use this form if you prefer to write to request your credit report from any, or all, of the nationwide consumer credit reporting companies. The following information is required to process your request. Omission of any information may delay your request.

Once complete, fold (do not staple or tape), place into a #10 envelope, affix required postage and mail to:

Annual Credit Report Request Service P.O. Box 105281 Atlanta, GA 30348-5281.

Please use a Black or Blue Pen and write your responses in PRINTED CAPITAL LETTERS without touching the sides of the boxes like the examples listed below:

A B C D E F G H I J K L M N O P Q R S T U V W X Y Z 0 1 2 3 4 5 6 7 8 9

Social Security Number: ___ - __ - ____

Date of Birth: Month / Day / Year

Fold Here — Fold Here

First Name M.I.

Last Name JR, SR, III, etc.

Current Mailing Address:

House Number Street Name

Apartment Number / Private Mailbox For Puerto Rico Only: Print Urbanization Name

City State ZipCode

Previous Mailing Address (complete only if at current mailing address for less than two years):

House Number Street Name

Fold Here — Fold Here

Apartment Number / Private Mailbox For Puerto Rico Only: Print Urbanization Name

City State ZipCode

Shade Circle Like This → ●

Not Like This → ⊗ ✓

I want a credit report from (shade each that you would like to receive):

- ○ Equifax
- ○ Experian
- ○ TransUnion

○ Shade here if, for security reasons, you want your credit report to include no more than the last four digits of your Social Security Number.

31238

If additional information is needed to process your request, the consumer credit reporting company will contact you by mail.

Your request will be processed within 15 days of receipt and then mailed to you.

In: Identity Theft Breaches
Editor: Cary S. Logweller

ISBN 978-1-60692-227-9

Chapter 10

FTC CONSUMER ALERT: HOW NOT TO GET HOOKED BY A "PHISHING" SCAM

"We suspect an unauthorized transaction on your account.
To ensure that your account is not compromised,
please click the link below and confirm your identity."
"During our regular verification of accounts, we couldn't verify your information.
Please click here to update and verify your information."

Have you received email with a similar message? It's a scam called "phishing" — and it involves Internet fraudsters who send spam or pop-up messages to lure personal information (credit card numbers, bank account information, Social Security number, passwords, or other sensitive information) from unsuspecting victims.

According to the Federal Trade Commission (FTC), the nation's consumer protection agency, phishers send an email or pop-up message that claims to be from a business or organization that you may deal with — for example, an Internet service provider (ISP), bank, online payment service, or even a government agency. The message may ask you to "update," "validate," or "confirm" your account information. Some phishing emails threaten a dire consequence if you don't respond. The messages direct you to a website that looks just like a legitimate organization's site. But it isn't. It's a bogus site whose sole purpose is to trick you into divulging your personal information so the operators can steal your identity and run up bills or commit crimes in your name.

The FTC suggests these tips to help you avoid getting hooked by a phishing scam:

- If you get an email or pop-up message that asks for personal or financial information, do not reply. And don't click on the link in the message, either. Legitimate companies don't ask for this information via email. If you are concerned about your account, contact the organization mentioned in the email using a telephone number you know to be genuine, or open a new Internet browser session and type in the company's correct Web address yourself. In any case, don't cut and paste the link from the message into your Internet browser — phishers can make links look like they go to one place, but that actually send you to a different site.
- Area codes can mislead. Some scammers send an email that appears to be from a legitimate business and ask you to call a phone number to update your account or access a "refund." Because they use Voice Over Internet Protocol technology, the

area code you call does not reflect where the scammers really are. If you need to reach an organization you do business with, call the number on your financial statements or on the back of your credit card. In any case, delete random emails that ask you to confirm or divulge your financial information.

- Use anti-virus and anti-spyware software, as well as a firewall, and update them all regularly. Some phishing emails contain software that can harm your computer or track your activities on the Internet without your knowledge.
- Anti-virus software and a firewall can protect you from inadvertently accepting such unwanted files. Anti-virus software scans incoming communications for troublesome files. Look for antivirus software that recognizes current viruses as well as older ones; that can effectively reverse the damage; and that updates automatically.
- A firewall helps make you invisible on the Internet and blocks all communications from unauthorized sources. It's especially important to run a firewall if you have a broadband connection. Operating systems (like Windows or Linux) or browsers (like Internet Explorer or Netscape) also may offer free software "patches" to close holes in the system that hackers or phishers could exploit.
- Don't email personal or financial information. Email is not a secure method of transmitting personal information. If you initiate a transaction and want to provide your personal or financial information through an organization's website, look for indicators that the site is secure, like a lock icon on the browser's status bar or a URL for a website that begins "https:" (the "s" stands for "secure"). Unfortunately, no indicator is foolproof; some phishers have forged security icons.
- Review credit card and bank account statements as soon as you receive them to check for unauthorized charges. If your statement is late by more than a couple of days, call your credit card company or bank to confirm your billing address and account balances.
- Be cautious about opening any attachment or downloading any files from emails you receive, regardless of who sent them. These files can contain viruses or other software that can weaken your computer's security.
- Forward spam that is phishing for information to spam@uce.gov and to the company, bank, or organization impersonated in the phishing email. Most organizations have information on their websites about where to report problems.
- If you believe you've been scammed, file your complaint at ftc.gov, and then visit the FTC's Identity Theft website at www.consumer.gov/idtheft. Victims of phishing can become victims of identity theft. While you can't entirely control whether you will become a victim of identity theft, you can take some steps to minimize your risk. If an identity thief is opening credit accounts in your name, these new accounts are likely to show up on your credit report. You may catch an incident early if you order a free copy of your credit report periodically from any of the three major credit bureaus. See www.annualcreditreport.com for details on ordering a free annual credit report.

You can learn other ways to avoid email scams and deal with deceptive spam at ftc.gov/spam.

The FTC works for the consumer to prevent fraudulent, deceptive, and unfair business practices in the marketplace and to provide information to help consumers spot, stop, and avoid them.

To file a complaint or to get free information on consumer issues, visit ftc.gov or call toll-free, 1-877-FTC-HELP (1-877-382-4357); TTY: 1-866-653-4261. The FTC enters Internet, telemarketing, identity theft, and other fraud-related complaints into Consumer Sentinel, a secure, online database available to hundreds of civil and criminal law enforcement agencies in the U.S. and abroad.

INDEX

A

B

C

D

E

F

G

H

I

J

K

L

M

N

O

P

Q

T

U

V